Florentine Essays

Florentine Essays

Selected Writings
of Marvin B. Becker

MARVIN B. BECKER

———

COLLECTED BY
James Banker and Carol Lansing

Ann Arbor
THE UNIVERSITY OF MICHIGAN PRESS

2005   2004   2003   2002   4   3   2   1

A CIP catalog record for this book is available from the British Library.

Library of Congress Cataloging-in-Publication Data

Becker, Marvin B.
    Florentine essays : selected writings of Marvin B. Becker / Marvin B.
Becker ; collected by James Banker and Carol Lansing.
        p.   cm.
    Includes index.
    ISBN 0-472-11225-2 (alk. paper)
        1. Florence (Italy)—Politics and government—To 1421.   2. Florence
(Italy)—Church history.   3. Republicanism—Italy—Florence—History.
4. Church and state—Italy—Florence—History.   5. Catholic Church—
Italy—Florence—Political activity.   6. Renaissance—Italy—Florence.
I. Banker, James R.   II. Lansing, Carol, 1951–   III. Title.

DG736.B43   2002
945′.5105—dc21
                                                        2002020290

This collection is dedicated to my students,
graduate and undergraduate,
whom I have taught Medieval and Renaissance history.

Preface

The students of Marvin Becker have chosen to present this selection of his essays on fourteenth-century Florence and Tuscany as a tribute to his teaching and scholarship. Becker's essays have a conceptual unity and an enduring value. Many were published two to four decades ago, but it is only in recent years that scholarship is catching up with Becker's historical thinking. This is especially true of his interest in the formation of the territorial state. Becker explored the sources of loyalty to the state, arguing that it was constructed of attitudes shaped by the economic interests of particular social groups, the impact of the growth of the public debt, and the benefits of rule by impersonal laws. At the same time and as these essays show, he is no sentimental idealizer of the modern state. Instead, Becker explored the social and cultural costs of state formation, as older ways of life were destroyed.

The essays are a pleasure to read, yielding a real sense of the constructive nature of the historical enterprise and the complexity of historical experience. Becker's innovative reconstruction of fourteenth-century Florence in his two-volume *Florence in Transition* remains a compelling vision of the city as it changed from a medieval town to a Renaissance state. The essays also demonstrate his hard-nosed archival research. Whereas the turn-of-the-century German historian Robert Davidsohn read all the Florentine records deriving from Dante's lifetime, Becker examined the less-charted territory between the better-known periods of the medieval commune and the fifteenth-century Renaissance. Among Anglo-American scholars he began the project of examining the vast collection of notarial contracts in the State Archive of Florence for the middle of the fourteenth century. At the same time, his work is genuinely interdisciplinary and his wide reading in literary criticism, philosophy, and classical literature is integral to his historical scholarship.

These essays convey the play of the mind that sets Becker apart from other historians of his generation. Yes, the hard-won documentary

evidence from notarial and governmental sources was always prominent and engaged him, but it is Becker's brilliant insights that remain
with the reader years after. Becker taught his students to examine historical evidence as if the documents were diamonds emanating discrete
rays, undifferentiated data that then had to be filtered through the
knowledge and imagination of the historian. While not ideological
about avoiding the pitfalls of positivism, Becker has encouraged his
students to accept multivalent readings of the historical record.

As Marvin Becker's students, we freely admit that these articles are
best complemented by the excitement of conversation with him. Personal discussions are always an intellectual challenge as he relates his
wide reading of historical and nonhistorical literature with his and your
research interests. Becker's interpretations are forcefully expressed but
understood to be tentative. He always seeks and respects, by either acceptance or reasoned rejection, his students' judgments. Our expectation is that the essays nevertheless offer readers a chance to engage with
Becker's challenging readings of the late medieval Florentine evidence,
readings that remain innovative and compelling even decades after
their first publication.

James Banker,
Professor of History,
North Carolina State University,
Raleigh

Carol Lansing,
Professor of History,
University of California,
Santa Barbara

Acknowledgments

My thanks to Richard Goldthwaite, whose companionship and generosity I have enjoyed for more than forty years. It was at his suggestion that there be a collection of my articles after my former graduate students James Banker and Carol Lansing, whose valuable friendship have been my pleasurable lot, originally conceived the idea for a festschrift. They then undertook the formidable task of organizing the articles. Carol also arranged a conference, assembling a group of historians to meet at the University of California in Santa Barbara in November of 2000 to discuss my work. Daniel Lesnick, another former graduate student and dear friend, volunteered to translate the first article in this volume from the Italian. Donald Weinstein, friend over fifty years, wrote the Introduction, and I'm most appreciative of his kind words. His favorable view of my "liberalism" and "exuberant intellectual energy" might be balanced by noting my more prosaic and empirical cast of mind. Gene Brucker and I shared a passion for archival research, as well as the happiest days of a golden time in Florence. It is one of my great satisfactions that recently we "knitted up the raveled sleeve of care." Philip and Carla Jones are always with us in thought, as are the lively times spent in Florence during 1956–57: never have I learned so much medieval Italian history than from my conversations with Philip. At the University of Michigan Press, Collin Ganio and Erin Snoddy have been the two whose consideration and assistance were of maximum benefit in this endeavor. My gratitude to Betty, with whom I've had a lifetime of friendship and love, for the penitential task of typing and proofreading over a half-century.

Contents

Introduction

Donald Weinstein

I

When Marvin Becker arrived in Florence as a Fulbright scholar in 1953, Italy was still struggling in the turbulent wake of World War II, just eight years past. Two decades of fascism had led to the ruin and trauma of foreign invasion and civil war, a devastated economy, and a corrosive cynicism about politics and government. Unemployment and poverty were widespread, and strikes and demonstrations were daily events. The Savoy monarchy, discredited by its complicity with the Fascists, had been ousted by a plebiscite, but the young Republic was polarized by extremist parties of both the Right and Left. Whether the Italians could marshal their resources for economic recovery and muster enough will and political capital to make the new democratic constitution work remained to be seen. Becker followed the situation intently, with a sense of a personal stake in the outcome. He had come to Italy in search of a usable past. Like many other Americans of his generation, he had formed his liberal values in the experiences of the Great Depression, the New Deal, and the war against fascism. If the Cold War, with its loyalty oaths and McCarthyite witch-hunts, seemed to endanger those values at home, Italy's trials suggested a more general crisis of democracy spanning both sides of the Atlantic. In studying Florence's republican history, Becker was interweaving personal, intellectual, and professional goals. Here, in the capital of civic humanism, he initiated what was to be a lifelong examination of the Western civil tradition. In Florence he could study the interplay of ideas and action in what he was to call the "public world," which had so much resonance for him. The rise of this world out of the private, feudal, and corporate structures of the medieval commune, its functioning and its eventual subversion by the authoritarian structures of the early modern state, he thought, provided valuable information for modern political cultures.

In 1953 Florentine historiography was not yet the thriving industry it was to become. Comprehensive histories of the city were few and dated, a choice between Gino Capponi's campanilist *Storia della Repubblica di Firenze* (1877), Pasquale Villari's ethnocentric *I primi due secoli della storia di Firenze* (1893), F. Perrens's largely narrative *Histoire de Florence* (1877–83), and Romolo Caggese's sweeping *Firenze della decadenza di Roma al Risorgimento d'Italia* (1912–21). English-only readers made do with Ferdinand Schevill's highly readable but derivative *History of Florence* (1936). With a few notable exceptions, the important specialized studies of the pre-Medicean period had been initiated before the turn of the century. Robert Davidsohn's *Forschungen* (1896–1908) and *Geschichte von Florenz* (1896–1927) were still indispensable but barely reached the fourteenth century. Gaetano Salvemini's *Magnati e popolani in Firenze dal 1280 al 1290* (1899) was a ground-breaking work. His Marxian, class-based, interpretation had been countered by Nicola Ottokar, who, in *Il comune di Firenze alla fine del dugento* (1926), showed that by the late thirteenth century *il ceto dirigente* was already an amalgam of old-line nobles and rich major guildsmen.[1] Ottokar concluded his book by observing that, despite the Republic's appearance of democracy, the oligarchy continued to rule Florence down to the time of the Medici. This extension of his thesis was largely impressionistic, but it was (and continues to be) enormously influential. In the 1930s and 1940s Ottokar's pupil Nicolai Rubinstein had published important articles, including "La lotta contro i magnati a Firenze"[2] and "The Beginnings of Political Thought in Florence,"[3] but the bulk of Rubinstein's great contribution to Florentine studies was still to come. Except for Gino Scaramella's *Firenze allo Scoppio del Tumulto dei Ciompi* (1914) and Niccolò Rodolico's *Il popolo minuto* (1899) and *La democrazia fiorentino nel suo tramonto* (1905) on the Ciompi period, the century between the Ordinances of Justice and the onset of Medici rule had barely been explored. The outlines of Hans Baron's thesis on the Visconti threat and the coming of civic humanism

---

1. On the ideological significance of the introduction of Gaetano Mosca's term *political class,* or *governing class,* in the debate over late medieval Florentine government, see Renzo Pecchioli, *Dal "mito" di Venezia all'ideologica americana: Itinerari e modelli della storiografia sul republicanesimo dell'etá moderna* (Venice, 1983), 192–93.

2. Pt. 1, *Archivio storico italiano* 93 (1935): 161–72; pt. 2, *La lotta contro i magnati a Firenze* (Florence, 1939).

3. *Journal of the Warburg Institute* 5 (1942): 198–227.

was known through some articles,[4] but its major impact came only after the publication of *The Crisis of the Early Italian Renaissance* in 1955.[5]

Working alongside Becker in the Archivio di Stato in its old quarters at the Uffizi were such up-and-coming historians of republican Florence as Gene Brucker, Charles de la Roncière, Elio Conti, David Herlihy, and Louis Marks. The discomforts of the dingy, cramped, alternately freezing and sweltering reading room and the frustrations of its labyrinthine catalogues and antiquated procedures only sharpened the sense of excitement and discovery with which this small, self-consciously pioneering group set about exploring the *mare magnum* of Florence's archival sources. They talked over morning coffee and socialized after hours, exchanging ideas and information, although the stock of their shared assumptions was limited. All agreed that Florentine history should be reestablished on a solid documentary basis, and for the most part they were more interested in social analysis than in intellectual or religious history, but, while most Italian and some of the younger English scholars were inclined to follow Salvemini's Marxist lead, emphasizing the bourgeoisification of the Florentine elite, its financial stake in the Republic and persistent fear of revolution from an exploited and unfranchised working class, the Americans tended to accept Ottokar's concept of a socially composite *ceto dirigente* and agreed with Rubinstein that consensus was at least as operative as conflict in Florentine governance. Most of the Americans shared Becker's liberal views, although they may have approached their subjects with greater detachment.[6] Except for some tentative collaboration between Brucker and Becker, each followed his own bent. At that time Brucker's specialty was politics and society; Conti and de la Roncière were mainly interested in the socio-economic history of the Florentine *contado;* Herlihy's main Florentine

4. For example, "Cicero and the Roman Civic Spirit in the Middle Ages and Early Renaissance," *Bulletin of the John Rylands Library* 22 (1938): 72–97; "A Struggle for Liberty in the Renaissance: Florence, Venice, and Milan in the Early Quattrocento," *American Historical Review* 58 (1952–53): 265–89, 544–70.

5. Eugenio Garin's comparably influential *L'umanesimo italiano* appeared in Italian (Bari, 1952). It was probably little known in the United States in its original German edition, *Die italienische Humanismus* (Bern, 1947).

6. Pecchioli's analysis of the influence of liberal ideology on the American and British historians of Florence (see n. 1) is valuable but, I think, overstated and excessively generalized as well as polemical. For further discussion of Pecchioli's critique, see my review in *Journal of Modern History* 57 (1985): 153–56.

work was in demography. With his predilection for synthesis and his exuberant intellectual energy, Becker cast his net widely. He was looking for ways to relate material conditions, experience, and ideas, not in the manner of Marxist historians, who regarded consciousness as mere superstructure, nor in the manner of the increasingly influential anthropologists, by the construction of static cultural models, but by tracing the dynamic interplay of politics, economic activity, social identities, warfare, religion, and ideology in effecting structural change.

In 1967 Becker published the first volume of *Florence in Transition*, following with the second in 1968.[7] In it he charted the city's transformation from local commune to territorial state and from a loosely organized, largely amateur, association of powerful private interests to a more bureaucratic, efficient, and centralized administration. A funded public debt replaced the ad hoc fiscal devices of the medieval commune, while public business, including foreign affairs, was increasingly administered by a paid cadre of professionals. As Becker saw it, the "new men" who entered political life in the 1340s weakened the exclusive hold of the old elites—members of feudal clans and families, high-born clerics, rich guildsmen—on the levers of power. The *nuova gente* adopted policies including more rigorous and objective law enforcement, the recovery of alienated communal property, restrictions of ecclesiastical privilege, and disenfranchisement of those nobles thought to be dangerous to the *res publica*. This newly sovereign state produced its own ethos. Not Florentine resistance to Milanese aggression in the fifteenth century, as Hans Baron declared, but the Florentine republican experience of the fourteenth, in Becker's view, was the matrix of civic humanism.

Florence in Transition was the fruit of assiduous archival work, deep and extensive reading in the historical literature, and a working familiarity with social science theory and method. It is an ambitious book, bringing together a wide variety of aspects of fourteenth-century life and out of them fashioning a comprehensive, original synthesis of politics, economics, religion, and art. It is a bold book, venturesome in its inferences, unexpected linkages, and broad conclusions. Not surprisingly, it drew fire. Some reviewers complained that Becker posited too sharp a break between the medieval commune and the Renaissance re-

---

7. Vol. 1: *The Decline of the Commune* (Baltimore, 1967); vol. 2: *Studies in the Rise of the Territorial State* (Baltimore, 1968).

public. Some held that he anticipated the development of the territorial state by at least a century. Some were put off by his idiosyncratic terminology, for example, his use of *gentle paideia* and *stern paideia* to distinguish between the modus operandi of the pre- and post-1343 Florentine republic and his persistent use of the term *polis* to describe the commune. One reviewer doggedly scrutinized Becker's sources and, finding lapses in citation and errors of transcription, dismissed the work as a "mere essay."[8] Other scholars, however, recognized that *Florence in Transition* was a signal contribution not only to the continuing debate over the Florentine commune but to Italian history generally. Philip Jones, while critical of certain aspects, described it as "the most sustained attempt yet to get to the bottom of fourteenth-century politics. And not only Florentine politics. The questions raised have implications for all Italian history."[9]

Florence in Transition appeared just as the great international boom in Italian Renaissance history was getting into full swing. A younger generation of historians trained in archival research by Rubinstein, Myron Gilmore, Eugenio Garin, and Paul Oskar Kristeller, as well as, increasingly, Becker, Brucker, and the others of their cohort, were crowding into archives and libraries, tackling new subjects, and amassing great amounts of new information. Research became even more specialized and standards of documentary verification more exacting, with the further result that generalization became an endangered species and received ideas fair game for revisionists. On one hand, the younger scholars of the 1970s and 1980s continued the rigorous empiricism of their teachers; on the other, they were critical of the older generation's positivism, liberal assumptions, and presentist orientation. Launching out in directions of their own, they looked to philosophy and semiotics for theory and to the social sciences, particularly anthropology, for new methods of analysis and even subject matter. Among other targets of the revisionists was the idea of the Renaissance state, particularly of its modernity, a mainstay of Renaissance political history since the late

---

8. Lauro Martines, review of *Florence in Transition*, vol. 1, *Speculum* 43 (1968): 689–92.

9. Philip Jones, review of *Florence in Transition*, vol. 1, *English Historical Review* 85 (1970): 563–67. See also John M. Najemy's references to the joint work of Becker and Brucker and to the separate work of each in *Corporatism and Consensus in Florentine Electoral Politics, 1280–1400* (Chapel Hill, 1982), 118, 142–44.

nineteenth century. In 1969 Daniel Waley had pointed out that the men who, according to Jakob Burckhardt, had created "the state as a work of art" in their efforts to legitimate their usurpation of power were really the blood descendants of medieval landed elites who had never relinquished their primacy or their feudal ways.[10] Sergio Bertelli, Philip Jones, and others emphasized the oligarchy's manipulation of power for their common interests.[11] In place of Federico Chabod's Weberian conception of Renaissance states as centralized public entities impartially administered by cadres of trained professionals, it was now widely held that the Renaissance state was "a vacuous entity occupied by political parties dedicated to patronage—namely, the control of administration for the purpose of allocating public resources to special interests."[12] If any currency was still given to the phrase "the discovery of the world and of man," the rediscovery of the medieval roots of classicism, humanism, science, law, and political thought dispelled it, while the popular notion of the Renaissance as the great turning point from medieval to modern times was countered by a new awareness of continuity and *longue durée.*

The new orthodoxy was neither intellectually congenial to Becker or receptive to the thesis of his book, nor did it encourage the kind of scholarly discussion on which he thrives. All of this may help explain why, instead of publishing a third volume of *Florence in Transition,* as he had intended, he turned his attention elsewhere, although a more compelling reason may have been the unavailability for the fifteenth century of the runs of documentary sources on which he had based his fourteenth-century work. This was a change of timing, however, not of direction; the Renaissance was only a part of the story Becker wanted to tell, and sooner or later he was bound to move on to other chapters of it. First he went back in time, to identify the material and spiritual changes that he thought made possible the communal, commercial society of pre-Renaissance Italy.[13] He then enlarged his scope to early

---

10. *The Italian City-Republics,* 3d ed. (London, 1988), esp. chap. 7.

11. Sergio Bertelli, *Il potere oligarchico nello stato-città medievale* (Florence, 1978); Philip Jones, "Economia e società nell'Italia medievale: la leggenda della borghesia," in *Storia d'Italia Annali* (Turin, 1978), 1:185–372.

12. Julius Kirshner, "The State Is 'Back In,'" in *Journal of Modern History* 67 suppl. (December 1995): S1–S10.

13. *Medieval Italy: Constraints and Creativity* (Bloomington, 1981).

modern Europe as a whole to study the emergence of new modes of social behavior and new definitions of self vis-à-vis community—what he called "the tilt toward civility."[14] Next came a study of the formation of civil society in the eighteenth century, a development he saw as more competitive than compatible with the public world of the Renaissance.[15] Although the works are self-contained, there is a remarkable continuity of theme and approach. Becker continues to study forms of identity, community, and the cultural imperatives and constraints that have characterized and shaped Western culture in its various stages, and he deals with a diverse range of topics including business, religion, language, philosophy, popular culture, the arts, and literature. Overall, he has come to concentrate more on literature and formal thought than he did in the early work, which was more sociological and more dependent on political and fiscal archival sources, but his approach remains global. Currently he is writing a book on modernism, which he regards as a central development of European and American culture, from its roots in the late eighteenth century to its decline by the mid–twentieth century. With this, and perhaps in other books to follow, he will bring his story down to the present. Ironically, what was once said dismissively of his first book—that it was a mere essay—may be said more accurately and appreciatively of his life's work. Becker *is* an essayist, both in the original sense, a thoughtful risk taker, and in the conventional sense, an interpretive thinker. For him the study of the past is both scholarly pursuit and personal reflection. His need to understand his own place in modern culture is both starting point and goal of his effort to illuminate the course of that culture. For, as he has shown, the need itself defines intellectuals in the modern world.

II

"The origin of the modern state in Europe has once again become a central topic of contemporary historical research, no doubt in part because of current debate over the future of the state as a viable entity for collective action and over the future of the political organization of Eu-

---

14. *Civility and Society in Western Europe, 1300–1600* (Bloomington, 1988).

15. *The Emergence of Civil Society in the Eighteenth Century: A Privileged Moment in the History of England, Scotland, and France* (Bloomington, 1994).

rope."[16] Thus Julius Kirshner in introducing the papers of a recent conference, one of several, on the subject of state formation. Current debates over the future of the state aside, historians of the last two decades have come around to admitting that the state does indeed have a premodern past, Revisionist skepticism about Renaissance statism reached its high point in the 1970s and 1980s. Since then a more nuanced, historicist view has taken hold, based on the rethinking of assumptions and detailed research by such outstanding scholars as Giorgio Chittolini and his associates, Elena Fasano Guarini, David Herlihy, Anthony Molho, and others.[17] Rejecting the single, anachronistic paradigm of the state, they adopted a pluralistic approach, showing that, in ways of organizing and exercising power, late medieval and early modern Europeans were richly innovative, that sovereignty claims were neither absolute nor nugatory, and that old forms such as lordship, patronage, honor, and clerical privilege were shaped into new patterns of relation between central governments and peripheries and between rulers and their subjects.[18] Moreover, they have taught a new generation of Florentinists "the necessity of abandoning the confines of the city's walls with its internal conflicts to concentrate their attention on the process of territorialization, the focal element of Tuscan political life between the fourteenth and fifteenth centuries."[19] Becker himself could not have put it better.

---

16. See n. 11.

17. See the assessment by Elena Fasano Guarini, "Centro e periferia, accentramento e particolarismi: dicotomia o sostanza degli stati in età moderna?" in G. Chittolini, A. Molho, and P. Schiera, eds., *Origini dello Stato. Processi di formazione statale in Italia fra medioevo ed età moderna* (Bologna, 1994), 147; and, specifically on Florence, the acute essay by John M. Najemy, "The Dialogue of Power in Florentine Politics," in A. Molho, K. Raaflaub, and J. Emden, eds., *City States in Classical Antiquity and Medieval Italy* (Ann Arbor, 1991), 269–88.

18. See Philip Jones, *The Italian City-State, 500–1300* (Oxford, 1997) for the latest, most balanced, and most authoritative overview of late medieval state formation in Italy.

19. "L'incontro ha confermato infatti l'esistenza di una generazione di specialisti che ha compiutamente assorbito la lezione di quegli studiosi come Elena Fasano, David Herlihy o Giorgio Chittolini, che per primi segnalarono la necessità di uscire dal chiuso della mura urbane e dei loro conflitti interni per concentrare invece l'attenzione sul processo di territorializzazione quale elemento focale della vita politica toscana fra tre e quattrocento." Luca Mannori, "Lo stato di Firenze e i suoi storici," *Società e Storia* 76 (1997): 402. The "incontro" to which Mannori refers are the meetings at San Miniato al Tedesco, 7–8 June 1996, or-

The new revisionism has duly fostered a reconsideration of some of the prime targets of 1950s and 1960s skepticism. Most notably, the Baron thesis on civic humanism, criticized as an anachronistic mix of German historical idealism and Anglo-American liberalism, has received a more favorable reappraisal by Ricardo Fubini, William Connell, Ronald Witt, and others. Rejecting the reductive logic that demoted the writings of Salutati, Bruni, Poggio, and other humanist-chancellors to supple exercises in propaganda by hired publicists,[20] they have reconciled rhetoric and politics and situated civic humanism in the larger context of the history of republicanism.[21] Similarly, second sight and broader perspectives have also renewed attention to Becker's early writings on Florence. This is not to say that his thesis on the rise of the Florentine territorial state has suddenly gained universal acceptance but that it still stands as the best available paradigm for further research and one with which historians must come to terms. Besides, this is a synthesis in which the individual parts are important in themselves. In the 1950s and 1960s Becker produced about twenty essays dealing with a wide variety of themes. Some of these themes he incorporated in *Florence in Transition;* others remained outside its boundaries. Although the master narrative that links them is the formation of the state, each is interesting in its own right, both methodologically and topically. In these essays Becker deals with issues raised by the work of Davidsohn, Salvemini, Ottokar, Panella, Rodolico, Barbadoro, Baron, and others, so that they constitute a review of the first and second great periods of Florentine historiography. He also introduces his own formulations on a range of subjects including the political role of Florence's minor guilds (with Brucker), usury, taxation, public debt, popular heresy, church-state relations, the city's chroniclers, the influence of "new men" upon

---

ganized by William Connell and Andrea Zorzi and entitled "Lo Stato territoriale fiorentino (secoli xiv–xv): Ricerche, linguaggi e confronto," *Società e Storia* 76 (1997): 402.

20. For example, Jerrold E. Seigel, "'Civic Humanism' or Ciceronian Rhetoric? The Culture of Petrarch and Bruni," *Past and Present* 34 (1966): 3–48; and Hans Baron's reply, "Leonardo Bruni: 'Professional Rhetorician' or 'Civic Humanist'?" ibid. 36 (1967): 21–37.

21. See William Connell's discussion and references, "The Republican Tradition, in and out of Florence," in D. Weinstein and V. Hotchkiss, eds. *Girolamo Savonarola: Piety, Prophecy, and Politics in Renaissance Florence* (Dallas, 1994), 95–105.

Florentine government, and changing *mentalités,* which made such a powerful contribution to the third great period of Florentine historiography, to which Becker himself belongs. For the next great period, the one that has just begun, these essays, in their originality, their richness of documentation, and their suggestiveness, have yet a contribution to make. The editors of this volume have made an important selection of them available for the convenience of readers who may know Becker only through his books or from the myriad footnotes of other scholars who have drawn so much from his work.

1

The Execution of the Legislation against Monopolistic Practices of the Florentine Guilds in the Middle of the Fourteenth Century

Translated by Daniel R. Lesnick

The question of monopolies has been a fundamental problem ever since Pohlmann's 1870 research.[1] Doren demonstrated the significance of this legislation in the juridical and social context of Florentine civic life,[2] while Salvemini brought to light the political meaning of the Ordinances of Justice in relation to monopolistic practices.[3] The broad implementation of this legislation has not, however, received the consideration it merits. Quite often statutes had been approved by the councils of the Republic and then, immediately following their approval, fell into disuse;[4] this was the case even though it may appear from a reading of the commune's statutes that the lawmakers were reluctant to abrogate laws approved by their predecessors.[5] Laws could be put into effect against

From *Archivio Storico Italiano* 117 (1959): 8–28. Reprinted with permission.

1. *Die Wirtschaftspolitik der florentiner Renaissance. Das Princip der Verkehrsfreiheit* (Leipzig, 1878), 65. All the documents cited in the present article are conserved in the Archivio di Stato di Firenze.

2. A. Doren, *Das florentiner Zunftwesen vom vierzehten bis zum sechzehnten Jahrhundert* (Stuttgart and Berlin, 1908), 574–76.

3. G. Salvemini, *Magnati e popolani in Firenze dal 1280 al 1295* (Florence, 1899), 388. For a consideration of the theoretical aspects of this problem, see the informative study by A. Sapori, *Studi di storia economica medioevale* (Florence, 1948), 188–227.

4. This is what happened with the anti-Ghibelline legislation of 1347, which was vacated until 1354. The successive continuance appears in *Camera del Comune 25*, c. 78r. It is probable that the law of 1354 was never implemented; cf. *Consulte e Pratiche, I*, cc. 97–100.

5. *Statuto del Capitano (1355)*, col. 2, bk. 1, rub. 177. The statute refers to the seven minor guilds long after their number had reached fourteen.

particular classes or groups and at the same time neglected for others. This can be explained by the changed political position of the group against which the laws were originally directed. The statutes were often directed against the Church because of its usurpation of functions jealously held to be the exclusive prerogative of the commune itself.[6] Laws dealing with the nobility had a similar destiny (though it must be warned that it is impossible to generalize about the status of these *grandi* without specifying the precise moment under consideration).[7] The commune was subject to a variety of political pressures and frequently would modify its policies by choosing not to observe the statutes (despite not wanting to admit that its actions might be dictated by extralegal considerations). This pragmatic stance was perhaps reinforced by the political flexibility of the legislators themselves.[8] Such practices are no more clearly illustrated than in the application of legislation against monopolies.

The very oldest documents of the government of the Republic reveal that the priorate and the councils were vitally interested in maintaining competition among the members of the guilds; the government included in the Ordinances of Justice an entire rubric prohibiting guildsmen from any practice that might raise the price to the consumer of any goods or services.[9] This disposition, vague and common to all the statutes of the medieval period, does not shed much light on the specific policies regarding implementation of laws that the commune was fol-

---

6. Legislation against ecclesiastical liberties was periodically renewed, but it seems that it was enforced only sporadically, and that was only when relations between Florence and Avignon were strained. A. Panella, "Politica ecclesiastica del comune fiorentino," *Archivio storico italiano* (1913): 321ff.

7. See the discussions in the *consulte* of 1349. The speakers were divided on the extent to which antimagnate legislation should be enforced (*Consulte e Pratiche,* 1, c. 6).

8. For manifestations of this attitude in foreign affairs, see N. Rubinstein, "Florence and the Despots: Some Aspects of Florentine Diplomacy in the Fourteenth Century," *Transactions of the Royal Historical Society* 2 (1952): 21–45. For a consideration of the flexibility of Florentine politics toward the nobility, cf. N. Ottokar, *Il comune di Firenze* (Florence, 1926), 123–74.

9. F. Bonaini, *Ordinamenta iustitiae comunis et populi Florentiae 1293* (Florence, 1855), 12; *Statuto del Podestà del 1325,* ed. R. Caggese (Florence, 1921), bk. 3, rub. 97; *Statuto del Capitano 1322–1325,* ed. R. Caggese (Florence, 1910), bk. 5, rub. 30. Cf. A. Lattes, *Il diritto commerciale nella legislazione statutaria delle città italiane* (Milan, 1884), 140ff., for similar norms in the statutes of other Italian cities.

lowing at the moment. Fortunately, however, we have extant two volumes of documents of the Treasury of the Commune (*Camera del Comune*) from the period prior to 1343. The first is from 1334 and covers the months of July and August, that is, the time in which a certain notary Ser Gaiano was head of the office created to remove customs and monopolies.[10] No other evidence survives until that of October 1342, when the Florentine government ordered that all sentences of the city's courts and communal officials be revised. Here again the question of monopolies is tied to the documents of the *Camera*.[11]

The decade of 1330–40 began under good auspices for the minor guildsmen; there had been a temporary reaction in favor of popular government after the death of Charles, duke of Calabria.[12] Periodically during the first half of the Trecento, there had been democratic movements following the cessation of military dictatorship.[13] In this case, however, the reaction was of short duration, and once again the minor guildsmen would fall under the domination of the old oligarchy.[14] At the end of De-

---

10. *Camera del Comune*, 1, c. 1 (1 July 1334). (From here forward this source will be abbreviated as "Cam.")

11. Ibid., 1, bis. For a general appraisal of this source, see M. Becker, "Gualtiero di Brienne e l'uso delle dispense giudiziarie," *Archivio storico italiano* (1955): 245–51.

12. A wide representation in the councils of the Captain and of the Podestà was allotted the minor guildsmen, but this involved those who previously had been supporters of the oligarchy. Andrea Benni, a butcher, had favored the proposals of the *signoria* since 1321. Cf. *Capitoli, Protocolli*, 12, c. 25; *Libri Fabarum*, 13, pt. 1, c. 58; ibid., pt. 2, cc. 5–38; *Provvisioni*, reg. 23, c. 89; ibid., reg. 24, cc. 38, 60, and 76. For other examples, see *Libri Fabarum*, 13, pt. 2, c. 83; and *Provv.*, reg. 216, c. 125.

13. See the treaty between Florence and Pisa of 1329, containing the clause according to which neither of the signatories may elect a dictator, edited in F. Dal Borgo, *Diplomi pisani* (Pisa, 1765), 3: 363. For the reactions to the dictatorship of Charles of Calabria, see F. Davidsohn, *Geschichte von Florenz* (Berlin, 1912), 3: 531; G. Villani, *Cronica* (Florence, 1845), 10: 108–10; *Cronica fiorentina di Marchionne di Coppo Stefani*, in *Rerum Italicarum Scriptores* (Città di Castello, 1903–13), vol. 30, r. 446.
For the documents relating to the electoral reform of November 1328, see *Provv.*, reg. 25, c. 25.

14. *Provvisioni, Protocolli*, 6, c. 254. The representation of the minor guilds and of the new men (*gente nuova*) was reduced under the pretext that foreigners and inhabitants of the countryside (*contado*) were infiltrating the government. The same stance was taken by the oligarchs in 1347 to break the foundations of the

cember 1330 a law authorizing the nomination of a foreign notary was approved; he was to serve as the official responsible for executing the statutes against monopolistic practices.[15]

In May of the following year the office was renewed, and on the occasion it was explicitly established that a notary should be entrusted with the regulation of guild monopolies and citizen artisans;[16] he should have at his disposal knights, police, and scribes, to whom he should pay every year the sum of 1,320 lire in small florins (*fiorini piccoli*). This considerable expense of public monies indicates clearly the seriousness with which the priors regarded the problem of monopolies. The first condemnation pronounced by this official and recorded in the documents of the *Camera* occurred on 1 July 1334,[17] but it is highly probable that in the interval between promulgation of the legislation and this first extant condemnation many citations were handed out for violations of the ordinances against monopolies, since the documents that have come down to us today bear witness that the law was rigorously administered during the decade in question.[18] The first six persons to be condemned, still according to the evidence of documents conserved in the *Camera del Comune*, were butchers fined for having sold meat above the already extremely elevated prices established by the communal authorities.[19] Two other people were found guilty of the same offense, but they were innkeepers. In the two following months minor guildsmen of varying occupations were subject to penalties that reached a grand total of twelve lire in small florins: bakers, general vendors of food and fowl, tailors, and fishmongers all fell victims to the rigors of the laws against monopolistic practices. The sentences and fines exacted during the preceding period for such transgressions were all directed

---

popular government. Cf. *Provv.*, reg. 34, cc. 93r–94r. In both cases those *minori* and tradesmen who remained in the government were supporters of the oligarchy. For the careers of two of these extremely faithful followers of the oligarchy, Perus Durantiis and Chele Dini, see *Libri Fabarum*, 13–21.

15. *Libri Fabarum*, 14, c. 95.

16. *Strozzi*, Diplomatico, at the date 6 May 1331.

17. *Cam.*, 1, c. 1. Some of the convictions involved some of the most important *minori* families: the Falchi, the Dolcibene, the Fantini, and the Lori. Cf. the list published in S. Peruzzi, *Storia del commercio e dei banchieri di Firenze* (Florence, 1868), 221.

18. *Cam.*, 1 bis, cc. 212ff.

19. Ibid., 1, cc. 1–6.

against the petty merchants[20] and more particularly against the vendors of general foodstuffs.[21] Considering the problem of insuring adequate provisioning for the city's population, the conduct of the communal rectors was completely rational and justified. From later laws we know that the commune kept a book that recorded the maximum allowable prices for the goods and services rendered by the petty merchants and artisans.[22] It remains for us to reexamine the historical setting in which antimonopolistic legislation was applied.

The members of the major guilds in fact held an irrefutable hegemony from the end of the *Dugento* until the affirmation of the dictatorship of Walter of Brienne in 1343.[23] During this period in which control of the state belonged to the members of the major guilds, antimonopolistic legislation was applied exclusively against the small artisans; nor is there, as far as we know, a single example of application of these measures against any member of the major guilds. It would seem, therefore, that the actual implementation of legislation against monopolies implied something quite different from the intention of the law as it is expressed in the Ordinances of Justice. In fact, in the second rubric of the Ordinances the requirement is clearly established to punish severely the monopolistic practices of all guildsmen, while the application of this article was directed exclusively against that part of the population deprived of political influence.[24] The major guildsmen continued to remain under the jurisdiction of their own consuls, and there is no evidence indicating that these consuls ever sought to enforce the communal antimonopoly laws.[25] On the other hand, it appears clear from

20. The oldest monopoly conviction is recorded in the *Camera del Comune* in April 1323. The convicted was a butcher of the countryside, sentenced to a fine of twenty-five *fiorini piccoli* (*Cam.*, 1 bis, c. 120).

21. The execution of the legislation against monopolies indicates that 90 percent of those convicted were retail merchants and sellers of foodstuffs who sold their merchandise above the maximum prices established by the communal authorities. There are examples of fines against weavers and tanners of skins for similar violations (ibid., 1, cc. 1–80).

22. *Provv.*, reg. 36, cc. 25–25v. (13 November 1348).

23. For a discussion of the situation of the priors from the power classes up until 1342, see N. Rodolico, *I Ciompi* (Florence, 1945), 1–33. Eighty percent of the members of the *signoria* from 1328 until 1342 belonged to the five major guilds: *Cambio, Lana, Giudici e notai, Calimala,* and *Seta.*

24. Salvemini, *Magnati e popolani,* 388.

25. The registers that contain the records of the cases discussed before the

later communal history that the governing classes of the state attempted
on many occasions to weaken and to eliminate totally the authority of
the consuls of the minor guilds;[26] nor does it seem that the members of
the oligarchy trusted the leaders of the minor guilds to execute the law.
The major guildsmen tried to follow a hands-off policy when their own
interests were secure. In 1342, however, this stance was radically altered,
and it became possible for the consuls of the minor guilds to assert their
authority.[27] The change was the result of the minor guildsmen having
now acquired political influence in affairs of state.

      During the summer of 1342 the exponents of commerce, who for at
least a half-century also had dominated Florentine political life, suffered
a series of reversals on the field of battle and in commercial affairs,[28] and
they decided that the only effective means to save their fortunes and
their political preeminence would be to institute a dictatorship.[29] This
line of conduct seems to have been well received by the minor artisans
and the *popolo minuto,* who had become increasingly displeased under
the hegemony of the oligarchy.[30] Therefore, from September 1342 until
July 1343 the lordship of the city was placed in the hands of Walter of
Brienne, who sought to create a popular base for his dictatorship by con-

---

rectors of the Wool Guild indicate that there were no efforts on the part of the
consuls to enforce antimonopolistic legislation against the wool manufacturers.
See *Arte della Lana, Partiti, atti e sentenze.*

      26. Cf. A. Doren, *Entwicklung und Organisation der florentiner Zünfte im XIII. und
XIV. Jahrhundert* (Leipzig, 1897), 30–33; *Statuto del Capitano del 1355,* bk. 1, rub. 177.

      27. In the period of Brienne's dictatorship the dyers were conceded the priv-
ilege of electing their own consuls, and they were at the same time freed from
the control of the Wool Guild. (Cf. C. Paoli, *Della signoria di Gualtieri duca d'Atene
in Firenze* [Florence, 1862], 82–83, doc. 83.)

      28. This defeat led to the loss of the city of Lucca, which only recently had
been acquired from the della Scala, lords of Verona. For a consideration of the
economic repercussions of these events on the families that were guiding Florentine foreign policy, see A. Sapori, *La crisi delle compagnie mercantili dei Bardi e
dei Peruzzi* (Florence, 1926); see also G. Villani, *Cronica* (Trieste, 1857), bk. 11, 138.

      29. Among the families recorded in the documents to have assisted in the
affirmation of the dictatorship, we find the Gherardi, the Buonsostegni, the
Baroncelli, the Rossi, the Guicciardini, the Ricci, the Dell'Antella, the Alberti, the
Pazzi, the Gianfigliazzi, the Altoviti, the Del Bello, the Adimari, the Bardi, the
Velluti, the Scali, and others. In this regard, see *Provv.,* reg. 3, cc. 17r–22r; *Libri
Fabarum,* 21, cc. 95–109r; *Cam.,* 1 bis, cc. 130r, 137r–38, 161, 206r.

      30. Cf. G. Brucker and M. Becker, "Una lettera in difesa della dittatura nella
Firenze del Trecento," *Archivio storico italiano* (1955): 251–52.

ceding favors to the petty artisans and salaried workers.[31] In fact, during his brief period of dictatorship the lower classes obtained notably substantial economic and political advantages.[32] One of the most important benefits that they obtained was in the area of monopolistic practices, for Walter did not enforce the second rubric of Ordinances of Justice against the minor guildsmen and the *minuti*.[33] But this was not enough; the dictator went a step further and absolved those members of the lower classes who had suffered convictions and punishments because of these laws in the period before his installation.[34]

After the expulsion of Brienne, Florence entered its first long period of popular government,[35] and for the first time in its history minor guildsmen were admitted to the government of the Republic in rather notable numbers.[36] The influence of the humbler classes on communal politics now reached the highest level, and this resulted in the cancelation of the legislation against monopolies. As had been the case in the preceding period of major guild political dominance, the democratic interlude, too, was characterized by nonenforcement of the statutes against monopolies.[37] Such a state of affairs was inevitably anything but

---

31. Other classes greatly benefited as well from the politics of dictatorship. For a consideration of the ambiguities connected to the efforts to ensure popular favor, see B. Barbadoro, *Le finanze della repubblica fiorentina* (Florence, 1929), 618.

32. Among the concessions made to the minor guildsmen were the reduction of tolls on foodstuffs, greater representation on the priorate, and limitation of the authority of the consuls of the major guilds (*Balìe*, 2, c. 5; *Cam.*, 1 bis, cc. 25r and 263). For further considerations regarding this question, see N. Rodolico, *Il popolo minuto (1343–1378)* (Bologna, 1899), 34–44.

33. Cf. *Cam.*, 1 bis, cc. 212ff.

34. Ibid., c. 212. On 26 January 1336 Cenne Dati Carli was fined one hundred lire in *fiorini piccoli* for having sold meat above the maximum price established by the officials entrusted with enforcement of the legislation against monopolies. This *tavernarius* of the countryside—who did not pay the fine—was pardoned by Brienne in 1343. This, and many other cases, indicate clearly that the laws were enforced less vigorously in the countryside.

35. Approximately half of the 270 priors were *minori*, or men who had not previously served on the priorate.

36. The minor guildsmen who served on the priorate during the period 1343–48 were among the most important members of the minor guilds. The median of their holdings in the *Monte* was around fifty-seven florins, which equaled the rental income from a shop or a house for at least ten years.

37. Treasury documents as well as judicial documents indicate that the laws were not enforced against the *minori*.

satisfactory for certain strata of the Florentine citizenry, who leveled numerous accusations against the guilds.[38] In this situation, however, accusations were directed as much against the consuls of the major guilds as against those of the minor guilds. Individual guildsmen were not directly involved; rather, all twenty-one guilds were summoned to appear before the seat of justice. This was not an isolated phenomenon; indeed, there are as many as five such summonses in the judicial records of the time. An example of this development appears in the resistance to a more democratic composition of the Florentine government in this period.[39] What we see is that *minori* and *minuti* were not treated differently than others; rather, everyone was treated the same in respect to monopolies. All monopoly accusations against the twenty-one guilds, without exception, were dropped, and there is no evidence of declarations by any legally constituted body of guilt resulting from accusations of this type.

In 1348, when the city struggled with the disaster of the Plague, the greater guildsmen took advantage of the situation to crush the *minori* and render them impotent in affairs of state.[40] In the preceding five years resentment had grown steadily against the lower classes, and the disorganization accompanying the Plague offered the *maggiori* an excellent opportunity to retake undisputed control in the affairs of the commune;[41] once again, antimonopolistic legislation was enforced selectively against the lower classes.[42] In November 1348 the commune

---

38. *Atti dell'Esecutore*, 6, cc. 5ff.; idem, 17, cc. 25ff.; idem, 79 cc. 11r and ff. These accusations were anonymous and said that the guilds and their consuls had made "monopolium, conspirationem" concerning "certo modo et forma seu pretio" of goods and services.

39. N. Rodolico, *La democrazia fiorentina nel suo tramonto (1378–1382)* (Bologna, 1905), 121ff.

40. The number of minor guilds was reduced from fourteen to seven. Cf. Doren, *Entwicklung*, 30–31.

41. Representation of the lower classes in the government was substantially reduced in 1348 (cf. *Manoscritti vari*, 269, cc. 1–15). On the intricacy of Florentine electoral procedures, see D. Marzi, *La cancelleria della repubblica fiorentina* (Rocca S. Casciano, 1910), 557–65.

42. The condemnations began in September 1348 and continued into the following decade; from 1354 until 1382, however, they occurred only sporadically. With the late-Trecento oligarchic reaction, legislation restricting the economic activities of the *minori* in every area, including the area of monopolistic practices, was applied with renewed vigor. The political decline of the lower classes,

authorized its officials to set prices for goods and services furnished by merchants and the minor guildsmen.[43] The pertinent *provvisione* (record of legislative council proceedings) is significant not only because it throws a bright light on the events of 1348 but also because it provides a notable contribution to a greater comprehension of the preceding period. The officials "super platee Orti S. Michaelis" and their foreign notary were authorized to put into execution the statutes of the commune, especially those written in an old codex regarding monopolies.[44] These rectors, charged with regulating the sale of foodstuffs in the main Florentine market, were ordered to examine this codex. Here they discovered that many of the norms relating to maximum prices had been canceled. It is very probable that the abrogation took place during the period of popular government, when butchers, bakers, vendors of grain and of fish, and second-hand clothing dealers had reached the apogee of their influence. When the priorate gave authority to these officials, it established that they should exercise their duties notwithstanding the contrary dispositions of the statutes and the *provvisioni;* this means that the acts had been passed during the democratic interlude to stop the regulatory officials from acting.[45] In the following year the authority of the said officials was extended until March 1349,[46] and violators were sentenced by the foreign notary against monopolistic practices.[47] As in

---

coming hard on the failure of the *Ciompi,* appears to have been the decisive factor in encouraging the major guilds in the successful attempts to extend their hegemony over the *minori.* Cf. *Cam.,* 29, 30, 34, 54; *Provv.,* reg. 76, c. 246; idem, 112, c. 6; *Statuto (1408),* 12, rub. 114; *Statuto (1415),* vol. 2, rub. 109.

43. *Provv.,* reg. 36, cc. 25–25v.

44. For the first references to the political activity of these officials, see A. Gherardi, *Consulte della repubblica fiorentina* (Florence, 1896), 1: 69 and 273. They had criminal jurisdiction over individuals who violated the grain laws. Cf. Davidsohn, *Forschungen zur Geschichte von Florenz* (Berlin, 1908), 4:307.

45. *Provv.,* reg. 36, c. 47. The first record of putting the antimonopolistic legislation into operation coincides with the decline in the political influence of the *minori.* An official "super reprimandis doganis, monopolis" was instituted in June 1347 (*Provv.,* reg. 34, c. 159); his jurisdiction was in large part limited to the small vendors of foodstuffs who were not matriculated in any guild.

46. *Provv.,* reg. 36, c. 47. For the statutes regarding these officials, see G. Masi, ed., *Statutum bladi reipublicae florentinae (1348)* (Milan, 1934), 133: "quod offitiales possint procedere contra facientes monopolia." Appeals to the decisions of these officials were not allowed.

47. On 1 December 1348 Ser Matteo Giovanni di Reggio, official "super do-

the period before 1343, those struck by these measures were minor guildsmen and individuals belonging to the *popolo minuto* found to be selling at prices above the legal maximum.

The events of 1348 notably increased the resentment of the minor guildsmen, who in the two following years were fully occupied in an effort, in large part achieved, to recoup their lost political positions.[48] In August 1349 the consuls of the minor guilds presented a petition to the priors,[49] declaring that they were at the moment suffering the damages of a rubric of the ordinances dealing with monopolies and approved the previous November (1348) in a different situation. They asked, therefore, that the priors and their colleges review the statutes against monopolies. In this attempt they were supported by some of the major guildsmen—probably from among those belonging to the faction opposed to the one in power who hoped to secure the political support of the lower classes.[50] The petition was approved and led to the formation of a commission of eight citizens, two of whom were minor guildsmen. In October 1349 these officials, who in the meantime had been given the authority to do so, published their revision of the ordinances concerning monopolies.[51] The effect of their actions was the cancelation of the work of the commission that had been constituted in November 1348, which had denied authority to the consuls of the minor guilds in matters vital to the *minori*. From November 1349 until October of the next year, the butchers, hosiers, bakers, tanners, knitters, tailors, tavern keepers, innkeepers, cloth sellers, rope sellers, and grain vendors were all subject to the jurisdiction of the foreign notary and the official over monopolistic practices;[52] the consuls of the minor guilds had no authority

---

ganis et monopolis tollendis," was paid a salary of six hundred lire in small florins (*Cam.*, 49, c. 308r).

48. In October 1348 the number of guilds was restored to fourteen (*Provv.*, reg. 39, c. 83). For demonstration of the increased participation of the minor guild representation in the government, see *Libri Fabarum*, 29, cc. 63ff. (1350).

49. *Provv.*, reg. 36, c. 151.

50. The motion was approved by a wide majority in both of the councils: 95–25 and 90–15. It was supported by Francesco Vigorosi, one of the most influential members of the Wool Guild (cf. ibid., c. 152r). Cf. also D. Velluti, *Cronica*, ed. I. Del Lungo and G. Volpi (Florence, 1914), 221–22, for a description of the relations among the two contending factions and the *minori*.

51. *Balìe* 5, 20 October 1349.

52. Ibid., cc. 1r–2.

over issues regarding monopolies during this period. In November 1349 the consuls of the guilds were again authorized to assume jurisdiction in this area.[53] Once again there had been a change in the application of the legislation against monopolies owing to the increased political influence of the minor guildsmen. The victory achieved by this group was confirmed by the communal statutes of 1355,[54] in which the authority of the consuls was reaffirmed, and in the Statute of the Captain of the People *(Capitano del Popolo)* it was actually established that any contrary laws were to be canceled.

Despite the fact that this statute put power in the hands of the minor guild consuls, the situation remained fluid until the period of the Ciompi, and in that brief time of lower-class predominance antimonopolistic legislation was administered by the consuls of the guilds. This was significant, for, to put it simply, during this time the laws were not put into force against members of the minor guilds. It is therefore clear that during this interval the laws were executed in inverse proportion to the degree of political influence that the *minori* were capable of exercising.[55] Indeed, nothing illustrates this better than the history of the Guild of Butchers during this time.

The intransigence of this guild is seen throughout the history of Florence of the thirteenth and fourteenth centuries.[56] Always in the vanguard of popular insurrections against communal authority, the guild's members were always a political force in the public life of the time, such that the holders of public authority were forced to come to agreement with them.[57] Even when plutocratic control of the affairs of state was most accentuated, the butchers were among the most influential citizens of the state.[58] Not only did some members of this guild unite with the

---

53. Ibid., cc. 5ff.

54. The pertinent rubric is published in Rodolico, *Il popolo minuto,* 181–82, doc. 24.

55. E. Fiumi, "Sui rapporti tra città e contado nell'età comunale," *Archivio storico italiano* (1956): 46–57.

56. D. Compagni, *Cronica,* ed. I. Del Lungo (Florence, 1889), 1: 13, 18.

57. For a consideration of the political support given by the butchers to Walter of Brienne, see G. Villani, *Cronica,* 12:17.

58. For the career of the most famous of the Florentine butchers, Dino Pecora, see N. Ottokar, *Il comune di Firenze alla fine del Dugento* (Florence, 1926), 107. For the *Monte* shares held by his descendants, see *Campione d'impianto del quartiere di S. Giovanni,* cc. 273r and 414. Sciatta di Ricco, a hog butcher, was one

upper classes through marriage and accumulate vast patrimonies, but the guild itself was among the richest of the minor guilds,[59] and its most prominent members always exercised considerable influence in the councils of the commune. A study of their political behavior indicates that they supported the politics of the oligarchy only when their own interests were not at stake;[60] like the major guildsmen, they sought to impede the communal authorities from interfering with their prerogatives.[61] The butchers were especially anxious to prevent foreigners and immigrants from the countryside from dedicating themselves to the sale of meat within the confines of the city.[62] Desirous of protecting their monopoly of the sale of meat, their consuls harassed individuals who sold their merchandise without officially being matriculated in the guild,[63] while the members of the oligarchy wished to open the sale of meat to all, and they accused the butchers of attempting to create a monopoly. It is probable that the priorate was seeking to win the support of the immigrants as a means, by increasing competition, of pursuing their political goals.[64] The irony of this plan could not have escaped the notice of the meat merchants. The members of the major guilds, in fact, were trying to eliminate competition among themselves, while they repeatedly attempted to promote competition within the ranks of the minor guilds.[65] By 1354 there was a pause in the conflict between the major guildsmen and the minor guildsmen. The problem had become so seri-

---

of the officials, along with Andrea de' Bardi, overseeing the conduct of the war against Pisa (cf. *Provv.*, reg. 51, c. 1: 1 August 1363; also, *Consulte e Pratiche*, 8, c. 67r). He also headed a company that involved him in foreign commerce (cf. S. Peruzzi, op. cit., 221).

59. The loans they made to the commune in 1329 placed them in the front rank of the commune's minor creditors (cf. *Provv.*, reg. 17, cc. 61r and ff; and *Archivio notarile antecosimiano, Matteo Biliotti*, 2, cc. 28–29r).

60. *Libri Fabarum*, 13, c. 86r; idem, 16, cc. 2r and 44; *Capitoli Protocolli*, 12, c. 41; *Provv.*, reg. 44, c. 114; *Libri Fabarum*, 32, c. 58r.

61. The rectors of the major guilds had the duty of revising the statutes of all the guilds (cf. *Provv.*, reg. 8, c. 70r). Appeals to the decisions of the consuls of the major guilds were not allowed, while appeals to the decisions of the consuls of the minor guilds were permitted (cf. idem, 6, cc. 24, 90r, and 140).

62. *Statuto de' Beccai, 1346,* 61. This statute was in direct contrast with the statute of 1344 (cf. N. Rodolico, *I Ciompi*, 41).

63. They were warned by the *signoria* in 1352 to abstain from this practice (cf. *Provv.*, reg. 40, c. 1).

64. Rodolico, *Il popolo minuto*, 67, docs. 12, 16, 17, and 23.

65. For restrictions on admissions, see *Arte della Lana*, 41, cc. 65 and 67.

ous that the council records (*consulte*) devoted an entire session to consideration of the monopolistic practices of the guild of butchers.[66] On this occasion the representatives of the government neglected all other issues of ordinary administration in order to discuss what measures the authorities should take against the butchers. From the discussion reported in the records we can see immediately that the butchers refused to submit themselves to the laws of the commune relative to the sale of meat. At this moment the councilors were in disagreement in the judgments regarding this problem. Some insisted that the government punish the offenders for their illegal conduct, while others favored a politics of indulgence, even though the butchers had made themselves culpable of monopolistic practices.[67] The majority advised the priors (the members of the *signoria*), however, not to proceed against the accused or, alternatively, to punish them mildly. The consequences of this discussion were entirely negligible, and they left matters in the same state as before. In October of that same year some penalties were imposed on butchers and other sellers of foodstuffs by the officials responsible for restraining monopolies; those found guilty were prohibited from buying or selling in the public markets for the rest of their lives.[68] This condemnation was annulled by the councils of the Republic, and the individuals found guilty were pardoned.[69]

The dispute between the guild of butchers and the communal authorities continued to disturb the tranquillity of the Florentine citizenry. The controversy finally reached its culmination when the *signoria* took the drastic measure of abolishing the consulate of the butchers' guild. The bill that was approved to these ends is of considerable interest for its attempt to justify the severe measure adopted.[70] It was established

---

66. *Consulte e Pratiche*, 1, cc. 76r and 94r–v.

67. On 14 May 1354 the government was advised that the butchers needed to be punished for violation of the ordinances relating to the sale of meat (cf. *Consulte e Pratiche*, 1, c. 76r). In the discussion held on 17 July of the same year the councilors were profoundly divided. The division, however, was not determined by membership in this or that social class. Matteo Federighi Soldi, an innkeeper, advised the *signoria* to punish the butchers, while Piero Canigiani, an oligarch and captain of the Guelf Party, proposed that they should be treated "misericorditer" (cf. idem, 1, cc. 94r–v).

68. For the condemnation of twenty-eight butchers who sold meat above the price fixed by the communal authorities, see *Cam.*, 54, c. 153r.

69. *Provv.*, reg. 41, c. 86.

70. Ibid., reg. 42, c. 117. This extremely important law was approved by votes of 99–46 and 85–17.

that, because of their monopolistic practices, the butchers had to be placed under the jurisdiction of the guild of the sellers of oil and salt, there to be punished for violation of the communal law. It is evident that previously the butchers, even when they had been found guilty of monopolistic practices, had not been punished by their consuls. Now, instead, the communal authorities wanted to enforce the legislation against monopolies, placing the appropriate enforcement in the hands of an impartial body. The priorate recognized the revolutionary nature of this step. The fundamental laws of the commune had accorded to the butchers a corporative organization. By taking this new action, therefore, the priorate was making little account of the Florentine constitution.[71] The *signoria* declared, in fact, that they should be absolved of any punishment that might arise from the approval of the bill, and they thereby recognized that the action they had undertaken was contrary to the law, if not indeed against the constitution.[72]

Fortunately, allowing us to comprehend clearly the political repercussions that followed the approval of this bill, the testimony of the contemporary chronicler Donato Velluti, who was himself a member of the priorate in the autumn of 1356, has come down to us. He describes for us the actions of the government in his *Domestic Chronicle:* "In consequence of the bad practices of the butchers," he writes, "and at the instigation of the colleges, it was approved. The butchers, ignoring the true duties of the consuls of the guild of butchers, was abolished."[73] In this laconic narration the writer insists on the fact that he and a certain number of the priors were opposed to this drastic action, but because they were in the minority the foolish measure passed and, according to the chronicler, his colleagues regarded him with great enmity.[74] Velluti, a doctor of law, had served in various regimes that had been in power in Florence since the first decade of the fourteenth century. He had a great amount of experience in statecraft and was an individual who was most able in political maneuvering. Not the least of his triumphs had been the subtle manner of ending the dictatorship of Walter of Brienne. When the tyrant came to Florence, Velluti had been among the most

---

71. This was a patent violation of the Ordinances of Justice, which fixed the number of guilds at twenty-one.

72. See n. 70.

73. *Cronica,* 222.

74. Ibid. For Villani's early career, see *S. Maria Novella, Diplomatico* at the date 15 December 1332; *Libri Fabarum,* 17, 162.

loyal of his followers, but when he saw that Walter was rapidly losing his popularity, he quickly withdrew from this sinking ship. Velluti's withdrawal from Brienne's camp was so well timed that he was put into the government that replaced Brienne after the tyrant's flight.[75]

Donato was a shrewd politician and sensitive to the city's internal pressures.[76] This lawyer was not a member of either of the two factions struggling for power at the middle of the fourteenth century.[77] Since he was a political independent, it is logical to think that he should not have wanted to risk the enmity of the most influential members of the guild of butchers, and, unlike the members of the political factions who showed themselves to be either hostile or favorable to the interests of the minor guilds, Velluti sought to remain neutral.[78] The possibility that he might earn a reputation of showing himself against the butchers could have had serious repercussions for him because the minor guilds had a wide representation in the nominating process and in the electoral organs of the commune.[79] It is evident that Velluti was disturbed by the fact of his incurring the enmity of the butchers. This incident is significant, not just because it indicates the political influence that the butchers had managed to achieve but also because it reflects the personal character of the political men of the time. Toward the middle of the Trecento, Florence had about fifty thousand inhabitants;[80] of this number only about 6 percent took an effective part in the political life of the

---

75. *Cronica*, 163: "io veggendo ciò e che venia in disgrazia a' cittadini dolcemente mi cominciai a scostare da lui, ne andandovi se non in dì di festa a udire la messa, e anche in rade feste, rendendogli riverenza e partendome." Cf. also A. Mercati, "Tentativo del Duca d'Atene di ottenere l'investitura della Romagna," *Rivista storica degli archivi toscani* (1932): 159–60. Cf. also *Cam.*, 3, c. 29r; idem, 11, c. 1; idem, 22, c. 61r; idem, 24, c. 48; and idem, 29, c. 665r. In 1364 Velluti paid a huge *prestanza* (forced loan) of sixty-four florins (*Prestanze*, 116, c. 53r).

76. See his judgment of the political situation of 1350–51 in *Cronica*, 241. The facts he describes are recorded by no other chronicler of the period.

77. He condemns the factions being able to destroy the political careers of "quei cari e antichi cittadini," who were thus denied the honors due them (ibid., 242).

78. In 1366 Velluti remained silent on the issue of the butchers when it was brought up among the councilors, of which he was one. He preferred instead to speak on the neutral subject of the construction of the city walls (cf. *Consulte e Pratiche*, 8, c. 1r). On the Velluti's prudent counsel regarding Ghibellinism, see ibid., 1, c. 99.

79. See n. 41; and Rodolico, *Il popolo minuto*, 170.

80. Cf. G. Pardi, "Disegno della storia demografica di Firenze," *Archivio storico italiano* (1916): 58; E. Fiumi, "La demografia fiorentina nelle pagine di Gio-

commune,[81] while less than 10 percent of that group held posts of a certain prominence in the government of the Republic.[82] The reputations of the more important figures—members of factions as well as independents—were apparently well known by the masses, and it very often seems that these men, such as Velluti, had done very little to earn the love or the enmity of the lower classes. Silvestro dei Medici became a hero of the minor guilds even though there is nothing to prove that during this time he favored their interests. In a highly personal and closed society, as was that of Florence in the Trecento, many citizens were reluctant to put their own political careers in danger by being marked as enemies of the influential and politically experienced minor guilds.[83]

At the very beginning of 1357 some consuls of the minor guilds addressed a petition to the *signoria* asking for a restoration of the consulate of the guild of butchers; the petition was approved by a crushing majority in both councils.[84] By acting thus, the major guildsmen were acknowledging having gone too far when, the previous year, they had approved the law abolishing the consulate; now they were trying to remedy the situation.

---

vanni Villani," *Archivio storico italiano* (1950): 106ff.; N. Rodolico, *La democrazia fiorentina nel suo tramonto*, 33.

81. This statistic is based on the fact that in the second half of the Trecento about three thousand men were matriculated in the guilds and thus qualified to be entered in the Chancellory lists of those eligible for office. Other individuals whose names are included in this total appear in the records of the *Camera del Comune*. Cf. Ottokar, *Il comune di Firenze*, 26–27.

82. This statistic is based not only on the number of men who sat on the *signoria* during the period 1350–60 but also includes those who spoke in the councils and the names of those mentioned in the *Consulte e Pratiche* and in the *Libri Fabarum*.

83. According to Stefani, there was also a practical reason for favoring the minor guildsmen: "s' io arò per compagnia un artefice, egli mi sarà suggetto, o reverente, e farà quello vorrò" (*Cronica*, rub. 588). According to Velluti, in 1350–51 both the factions of the Albizzi and the Ricci voted in favor of the *minori* (*Cronica*, 242). The Ricci achieved their objectives: they helped the *minori*, even helping them gain positions as captains of the Guelf Party (cf. *Consulte e Pratiche*, 8, c. 1r–17). Ricco Taldi, a prominent *calderarius*, thanked the oligarchy "de honore facto artificibus" (idem, c. 7, 7 December 1366). On Ricco's political career, see *Libri Fabarum*, 39, cc. 133, 137, and 145; and *Consulte e Pratiche*, 8, c. 17.

84. *Provv.*, reg. 44, c. 55. The relevant votes were 145–17 and 87–14. The petition was made by Francesco Bonaiuti, a tailor, and by Paolo Tondi, as baker—

In the following months, however, some members of the oligarchy attempted to win approval for punitive measures against the newly re-constituted guild, but their efforts to restrict the guild's authority failed completely.[85] A compromise was finally reached, according to which the foreign notary was to have jurisdiction over the monopolistic practices of the butchers and there was to be elected a four-member commission to establish maximum prices for meat, while the butchers were given jurisdiction over all the individuals selling meat within the jurisdiction of the commune.[86] The authority of the butchers was confirmed in every area, save that pertaining to the execution of the laws against monopolies. This was an important victory because it reaffirmed the authority of the consuls over everyone who sold meat, even those not matriculated in the guild.[87] The problem of monopolies, however, continued to distress the rulers of the commune until the explosion of the tumult of the Ciompi. Apparently, the members of the group in power did not want to bring on themselves the enmity of the minor guilds by too rigorously enforcing this legislation, nor did they want to oppose these *minori* with arbitrary and violent methods.[88] The discussions taking place in the *consulte* reveal that the members of those advisory bodies were divided between the desire to placate the *minori* and a profound solicitude

---

both influential council members of the day (cf. *Libri Fabarum*, 34, cc. 108, 116, 118, and 121; idem, 35, c. 68; idem, 39, c. 171). These two *minori* were always faithful followers of the *popolani grassi*.

85. *Libri Fabarum*, 34, cc. 141–45 (28 March and 17 April 1357). Two defenders of this measure were Francesco Vigorosi, consul of the Wool Guild, and the magnate Valore Buondelmonte. A third, Pela Nuccii, may have been a member of the minor guilds (cf. *Monte, campione, dell'impianto del 1345, Santo Spirito*, c. 557).

86. *Provv.*, reg. 44, c. 114 (27 April 1357). Bartolomeus Loris, one of the consuls of the Butchers' Guild, spoke in favor of this law. The votes of the two councils were 133–39 and 93–37.

87. Ibid., 44, c. 114. During the next decade the speakers made serious objections to this line of politics, suggesting that the sale of meat should be open to all (cf. *Consulte e Pratiche*, 8, cc. 62ff., esp. Paolo Vettori's declaration of 26 June 1367).

88. The *signoria* proposed the law according to which the consuls of the butchers should have the duty of enforcing the antimonopoly legislation. They should have a notary and two police officals at their disposition and service from the executor of the Ordinances of Justice. This law was supported by Benedetto Giani, consul of the butchers, and passed with votes of 145–29 and 100–26 (*Provv.*, reg. 55, c. 10: 28 June 1367). It was also favored by Matteo Piero Sofferoni, a member of the *gente nuova*, who was also a strong defender of proposals put forward by the *signoria* (idem, cc. 1 and 15; *Libri Fabarum*, 37, cc. 159, 160, and 163).

for the public well-being.[89] In the decade from 1360 to 1370 the enforcement of antimonopolistic legislation had become virtually synonymous with the maintenance of maximum price limits for foodstuffs.
The councilors of the government faced a dilemma: placate the minor
guildsmen or prevent an inflationary spiral of prices.[90]

The dominating oligarchy in this period was divided into two contending factions, and each tried to procure the support of the minor
guildsmen and artisans. In the end, however, only the Ricci faction was
able to achieve this objective, if the testimony of an anonymous contemporary is true.[91] Having come this far, we can better understand
what took place in the years 1361–62, when once again the Republic
found itself facing the problem of monopolies. An eight-member commission was elected with the job of revising the statutes dealing with
maximum prices for foodstuffs; this group was formed exclusively of
members of the oligarchy.[92] Two months later these men were replaced
by other men, from both the major and minor guilds.[93] The concession
to the *minori* was sponsored by Rosso di Riccardo de' Ricci, the head of
the faction bearing his name.[94]

It seems that the minor guildsmen in the years immediately following obtained notable advantages, profiting from the divisions within
the upper bourgeoisie. This conclusion is confirmed, without exception,
by the judgments of every contemporary chronicler. Obtaining representation on the commission to revise the statutory norms relating to
monopolies was not their final victory.[95]

---

89. From this point of view, the affirmation of Simone dell'Antella is typical:
"super facto beccariorum domini videant modum per quem honor civitatis et
bonum singulorum civium conserventur" (cf. *Consulte e Pratiche*, 8, c. 78r: 24
May 1367).

90. See the discussion of 5 November 1366, in ibid., 8, c. 5r.

91. *Manoscritti*, 222, c. 182.

92. *Libri Fabarum*, 36, c. 92 (11 December 1361); *Provv.*, reg. 49, c. 72.

93. Ibid., c. 117 (26 February 1362). To the *signoria* was reserved the power to
elect eight "cives florentinos populares et guelfos, mercatores seu artifices quos
volent ex quibus aliqui sint de alique seu aliquibus quattordecim minorum artium."

94. *Libri Fabarum*, 36, c. 104. Stefano Altoviti also supported the proposal,
which passed in the councils by votes of 141–52 and 98–35. For an analysis of
the political situation during this period, see Stefani, *Cronica*, rub. 775 and 788.

95. On the profits attained by the butchers regarding the issues relating to
the enforcement of antimonopolistic legislation, see n. 88.

The events that led to the revolution of the lower classes in 1378 and the brief period in which the *popolo minuto* held power, besides confirming the import of the legislation against monopolies, can be understood only within their political context.[96] The legislation regarding monopolies was put in force at the moment in which the lesser classes found themselves without adequate political representation, while in the contrary case the tendency was reversed. It seems that the pressure exercised by the lower guilds did not bring about changes in the laws but, rather, resulted in modifications in their enforcement. During democratic interludes the *minori* were able to gain for themselves important concessions, but when they lost their political vigor the situation returned to the previous selective enforcement.[97]

For contemporary judgments of advantages the *minori* guaranteed themselves in this period, see the *Anonimo,* published by G. Capponi in *Storia della repubblica di Firenze* (Florence, 1930), 1:592; and Stefani, *Cronica,* rub. 734. The *minori* also were able to secure for themselves representation among the captains of the Guelf Party and on the *Mercanzia* (Court Merchant). Regarding these successes, it would nonetheless be a great error to claim that the minor guildsmen had a high degree of class consciousness or class unity in all areas of their interests. Even regarding the enforcement of antimonopolistic legislation entrusted to the butchers' consuls, other guildsmen feared that the authority of their own leaders might be damaged by the actions of the butchers. Niccolò di Brunetto Venturi, a vendor of oil and salt, supported the butchers in their requests for jurisdiction over "pretio carnium" but added also that "pro hoc non intelligatur ars pizzicaglorum in aliquo supponi consulibus becchariorum seu ipsi arti" (cf. *Libri Fabarum,* 39, c. 10: 28 June 1367; *Provv.,* reg. 55, c. 30).

96. In 1378 the *minuti* presented to the priors a petition asking for the abolition of the office entrusted with setting the prices of foodstuffs (cf. E. Fiumi, "Sui rapporti tra città e contado," 75; Rodolico, *La democrazia fiorentina nel suo tramonto,* 150–58.

97. Rodolico, *I Ciompi,* 179–237. For references to the butchers' regulating their activities after the fall of the Ciompi, see *Statutum bladi,* 55ff. For the material relating to the accusation of monopolistic practices pressed against the dyers before the fall of the Ciompi, see Rodolico, *Il popolo minuto,* 179–80. It is of interest to recall the fact that during this period the dyers and the butchers could win more concessions from the *signoria* than any other group—the first, perhaps, because of their intransigence, the second probably because of their wealth (cf. *Monte, campione dell'impianto del 1345,* S. Giovanni, cc. 734r–735; idem, S. Croce, cc. 92r, 177r, 222r and ff.

2

Florentine Politics and the Diffusion of Heresy in the Trecento: A Socioeconomic Inquiry

There are numerous studies on the nature and influence of the teachings of the Spiritual Franciscans. Florence, in the second half of the Trecento, has been an area of special interest for those researchers who have concerned themselves with the implications of this problem.[1] Art historians, as well as those who are interested in communal politics, have demonstrated that the rise of the Fraticelli and the attendant spread of their doctrines played a decisive role in bringing about significant historical changes.[2] The purpose of the present inquiry is to examine the

---

From *Speculum* 34 (1959): 60–75.

The research for this article was done in Florence while the author was a recipient of a Guggenheim Fellowship.

1. For a general bibliography on the subject of the Fraticelli, see D. Douie, *The Nature and Effect of the Heresy of the Fraticelli* (Manchester, 1932), xiii–xviii. For their activities in Florence during the latter part of the Trecento, see L. Oliger, "Beitrage zur Geschichte der Spiritualen Fratizellen und Clarerer," *Zeitschrift für Kirchengeschichte* 45 (1926): 215ff.; N. Rodolico, *I Ciompi* (Florence, 1945), 53ff.; F. Tocco, *Studii francescani* (Naples, 1909), 406ff.

I do not purport to deal with the orthodox or heretical ideological matrix in which the events described took place. At the outset, however, it might be suggested that the sources cited here agree that there was a fundamental ambiguity in the institutional norms of the Trecento. Feudalistic tradition sanctified a caste society, while the Christian ideal encouraged the concept of a universalistic equality. The latter tended to set limits upon the injustices of worldly existence. The Fraticelli, like other heterodoxical movements, responded to this norm, and, under the pressure of social and economic problems that resulted from the rise of the cities, they extended their basic concept of the inherent evil of private property to include the notion of the sinfulness of the rich and the desirability of taking from them to ameliorate the lot of the poor.

2. See especially Millard Meiss's judicious treatment of the influence of the Fraticelli upon Florentine cultural life in *Painting in Florence and Siena after the*

underlying political situation that enabled this sect to increase its influence during the decade of the 1340s and to sustain it throughout the third quarter of the fourteenth century. This will also involve an attempt to explain the reasons for its suppression at the end of the Trecento and to elaborate upon the important general discussions of these questions to be found in the works of Tocco and Rodolico.[3]

The problem pertaining to the spread of heretical ideas is intimately connected with the policies of the Florentine government during this era.[4] The survival of heresy is predicated upon the degree of cooperation that existed between communal authorities and the office of the inquisitor.[5] From the beginning of the fourteenth century until the establishment of popular government in 1343, the Signoria was solicitous in its attitude toward the inquisition and appointed communal syndics to aid the inquisitor in the performance of his function.[6] Davidsohn has demonstrated that this office was more active than earlier scholars had suspected.[7] The inquisitorial and other ecclesiastical courts had not only

---

Black Death (Princeton, 1951), 80–93; F. Antal, *Florentine Painting and Its Social Background* (London, 1947), 71–72; N. Sapegno, *Storia letteraria d'Italia: il Trecento* (Milan, 1934), 528–40; A. T. Sheedy, *Bartolus on Social Conditions in the Fourteenth Century* (New York, 1942), 193.

3. The former suggested that, while the source of the ideas of the Fraticelli was purely religious, the movement drew sustenance from contemporary political and social developments. Cf. F. Tocco, op. cit., 408. The latter is interested in the part that this heresy played in stimulating class consciousness among *il popolo minuto*. Cf. N. Rodolico, *Democrazia fiorentina nel suo tramonto* (Bologna, 1905), 47–86.

4. For a consideration of this question as it pertained to the preceding century, see R. Manselli, "Per la storia dell'eresia catara nella Firenze. Il processo contro Saraceno Paganelli," *Bullettino dell'Istituto Storico Italiano* 62 (1950): 123–38.

5. For the juridical aspects, see U. Dorini, *Il diritto penale e la delinquenza in Firenze nel sec. XIV* (Lucca, 1916), 130ff.

6. For this regular feature of communal life during this era, see *Provvisioni*, 16, f. 20r. (The documents cited in this article are to be found in the Archivio di Stato in Florence unless otherwise designated.) Henceforth the *Provvisioni* will be abbreviated as *P.* Cf. also *P.*, 28, f. 8r; *Libri Fabarum*, 16, I, f. 102. Henceforth this source will be abbreviated as *L.F.*

7. "Un libro del inquisitore fiorentino," *Archivio Storico Italiano* 27 (1901): 346–55. It is important to note that members of leading patrician families were among those condemned by the inquisition and that the upper classes may well have had their personal reasons for desiring to curtail the authority of this

occupied themselves with the suppression of heresy, but they had also been concerned with the punishment of the sin of usury.[8] Existing evidence suggests that this era marked the apogee of effective clerical opposition to usurious practices.[9]

With the formation of the popular government in 1343, there was an important change in the attitude of communal authorities toward the church courts and the office of the inquisitor that was destined to permit a wider diffusion of the teachings of the Fraticelli. This new Signoria no longer cooperated with the inquisitor; in fact, it sought to prevent him from performing his duties.[10] This might lead one to suspect that the men who held communal office at this time were themselves in sympathy with the Spiritual Franciscans. In order to determine the motives of those who opposed the policies pursued by the inquisition, it will be necessary to view their actions within the context of the general history of the commune at this time.

---

office. For example, two members of the Peruzzi family were among the victims, and the company itself was condemned to pay two hundred lire for having extracted usury. Cf. *Diplomatico*, S. Maria Novella (15 October 1337). In contracts involving the sale of property, promises were made by the parties to defend the real estate in any litigation stemming from the charge of heresy by the inquisitor. Cf. *Diplomatico*, Spedale degli Innocenti (15 March 1287); *Diplomatico*, Bigallo (31 August 1302).

8. Cf. *Diplomatico*, S. Maria Novelle (3 May 1338); Badia (22 October 1338); S. Annunziata (29 July 1333).

9. The number of convictions stemming from this charge appears to have declined appreciably during the second half of the Trecento. Evidence from the notarial archives suggests that there was also a decline in the practice of the restitution of usury. Compare the token payments that were designated for this purpose by various members of the Medici family, in the second half of the fourteenth century, with those of the Strozzi in the earlier period. Cf. G. Brucker, "The Medici in the Fourteenth Century," *Speculum* 32 (1957): 11–12; P. Jones, "Florentine Families and Florentine Diaries in the Fourteenth Century," *Papers of the British School at Rome* 24 (1956): 191–92. Examples of restitution that are cited by A. Sapori, occurred, for the most part, prior to the advent of the second half of the Trecento. Cf. *Compagnie e mercanti di Firenze antica* (Florence, 1955), xcvi ff.

10. On 27 January 1344, only three months after the establishment of the new regime, the Council of Captain rejected a provision entitled "prime super provvisione sindicorum pro facto inquisitoria." Cf. *L.F.*, 24, f. 25r. On 14 February 1344 a similar fate befell a petition presented to the councils by the inquisitor. Cf. *L.F.*, 24, f. 29.

Representation in the Signoria was evenly divided between the old oligarchical families and the *novi cives*.[11] The former were characterized by their great wealth and social status. They were, for the most part, international traders and bankers who had maintained a close liaison with Avignon in matters pertaining to finance and foreign policy.[12] During the first four decades of the Trecento, these urban patricians had derived extensive benefits from this close relationship. While there had been minor disagreements at times on such questions as the right of the commune to tax the clergy or to try ecclesiastics in secular courts, the government was mindful of the prerogatives of the church.[13] By 1343, however, this once symbiotic partnership had altered materially. The great banking houses that were the nucleus of patrician power found themselves in the precarious position of being unable to make restitution to their creditors. Their disastrous financial plight had been accelerated, in their own opinion, by the hostile and uncooperative attitude of Avignon. Clement VI had jettisoned the companies in their hour of need and compounded this injury by demanding that the ecclesiastical creditors of these companies be granted preferential treatment in the matter of the repayment of their claims.[14] When Avignon sought to uti-

---

11. Cf. G. Brucker and M. Becker, "The *Arti Minori* in Florentine Politics, 1342–1378," *Medieval Studies* 18 (1956): 96–97; *La cronica domestica di Messer Donato Velluti, scritta fra il 1367 e il 1370,* ed. I. del Lungo and G. Volpe (Florence, 1914), 167, 192–93.

12. On the subject of the relationship between the Florentine patricians and the papacy, see Y. Renouard, *Les relations des Papes d'Avignon et des compagnies commerciales et bancaires de 1316 a 1378* (Paris, 1941).

13. Until 1343 the cornerstone of Florentine foreign policy was the Guelf system of alliances. With the death of King Robert of Naples, in that year, Florence assumed a much more independent position in international affairs. This involuntary step involved a fundamental estrangement of relationships between Florence and the Holy See. By the 1360s certain advisors to the Signoria expressed sentiments that indicated that they were more apprehensive about the papal attempt to reconquer the Patrimony than they were concerning the Visconti threat from the north. See especially the discussions in which the counselors advised the regime to keep peace with Milan and cooperate with Bernabò: *Consulte et Pratiche,* 2, fols. 173ff. (Henceforth this source will be abbreviated as *C.P.*) For a detailed analysis of possible motives behind the split between Florence and the papacy, see A. Sapori, *La crisi delle compagnie mercantile dei Bardi e dei Peruzzi* (Florence, 1926), 117ff.

14. A. Panella, "Politica ecclesiastica del comune fiorentine," *Archivio Storico Italiano* 2 pt. 4 (1913): 281–83; A. Sapori, op. cit., 197ff.; Y. Renouard, op. cit., 198–99.

lize the church courts and the inquisition to press these claims, the patricians denied that these ecclesiastical agencies had any authority in matters such as these.[15] Without the active support of the *gente nuova,* however, this disclaimer could not have been implemented into law.[16]

The question of why the *novi cives* supported the oligarchs in their conflict can best be approached within the context of the objectives of the most "democratic" Florentine Signoria up to this date. Traditionally, regimes composed of representatives who were new to the scene of Florentine politics tended to disregard the immunities and privileges that the feudal ethic ascribed to the first two estates.[17] The *gente nuova,* unlike their social superiors, the *haute bourgeoisie,* did not have representation within the ranks of the upper clergy. Nor were they related by marriage to the Florentine nobility.[18] They tended, therefore, to regard the traditional privileges of these classes with an indifference that was shocking to certain of their contemporaries.[19] Their tenure in office was characterized by enactments that had the effect of strengthening the im-

---

15. The pertinent documents are published by A. Panella, op. cit., 327–65.

16. The legislation in question was passed in 1345–46. At that time the *gente nuova* occupied approximately half of all communal offices. Since the Florentine constitution required a two-thirds majority for the passage of legislation, it is clear that there was close collaboration between the *novi cives* and the patricians on the subject of the curtailment of ecclesiastical liberties. The socioeconomic status of the newcomers was close to that of their social superiors; they held credits in the funded communal debt, which averaged fifty-seven florins. Cf. G. Brucker and M. Becker, op. cit., 101.

17. The only two earlier popular regimes in communal history (1293–95 and 1328–29) also took strong measures to curtail certain traditional prerogatives of the church. Cf. *P.,* 3, f. 143 (3 February 1293); *Provisioni Protocoli,* 6, fols. 252–53 (8 December 1328). For a consideration of this problem as it affected Florence at the end of the thirteenth century, see N. Ottokar, *Il comune di Firenze alla fine del dugento* (Florence, 1926), 278ff.

18. Bishops and other members of the ecclesiastical hierarchy were selected, almost exclusively, from the upper reaches of Florentine and Tuscan society. Cf. Luca Guiseppe Cerrachini, *Cronologia sacra de'vescovi e archivescovi* (Florence, 1716), 102ff. On the question of intermarriage, see N. Ottokar, op. cit., 135.

19. For the opinions of the most obdurate of the *arciguelfi,* the famous canon lawyer, Lapo Castiglionchio, see P. Jones, op. cit., 191–92. The more moderate Giovanni Villani, blamed the newcomers to Florentine politics for the enactment of legislation compelling certain nobles to restore lands with which previous governments had rewarded them for their meritorious services to the republic. Cf. Villani, *Cronica,* ed. F. Dragomani (Florence, 1844), bk. 12, chap. 44.

personal and impartial rule of communal law.[20] This objective was in accord with the interests of the urban patriciate, who were anxious to pass legislation that would curtail ecclesiastical authority in cases that involved their own bankruptcies.[21]

Contemporary chroniclers contended that there was yet another motive that animated communal policy toward the office of the inquisitor and the clerical tribunals. Piero dell'Aquila, the inquisitor at this time, had exacted heavy fines from those citizens who either loaned money usuriously or sought to justify this reprehensible practice.[22] Between 1345 and 1346 the Republic passed legislation that was calculated to curb this form of inquisitorial activity.[23] Communal opposition toward the inquisitor was intensified as a result of his actions in another sphere. He had also been acting as procurator for Cardinal Sabina and, in this capacity, he was seeking to compel the Acciaiuoli Company to restore the deposit of his client.[24] When the Signoria blocked this attempt,

---

20. An analysis of the *Camera del Comune* suggests that, during intervals when the *gente nuova* had extensive representation in the Signoria, communal policy was directed toward the equalization of the tax burden, the regularization of administration in the contado, and the restitution of state property by wealthy and influential oligarchs.

21. A notary, and Pepo Frescobaldi, a scion of the famous magnate and banking family, were the two spokesmen for the law in question. Cf. *Provvisioni Duplicati*, 5, f. 54.

22. Villani, bk. 12, chap. 58.

23. One of the principal motives behind passage of these measures was the desire of certain segments of the citizenry to prevent victims of contracts, alleged to be usurious, from appealing to ecclesiastical courts. Since this type of case was *de foro misto*, it could be tried in either lay or ecclesiastical tribunal. From 1345 until the fall of the popular government in 1348, jurisdiction over these cases was reserved for communal authorities. The last appeal to a church court occurred in January 1345. Cf. *Camera del Comune*, 10, f. 85. This motive runs counter to A. Panella's thesis that the anticlericalism of the lower classes was the chief factor in precipitating this legislation, since it can hardly be suggested that the protection of usurers was in the interest of the Florentine masses. Cf. "Politica ecclesiastica del comune fiorentino," op. cit., 281–83. It is possible that the *gente nuova*, in their quest for social and economic mobility, were not averse to usurious practices and, therefore, antagonistic toward the inquisitor when he sought to oppose them.

24. G. Villani, loc. cit. One of the most intransigent foes of the inquisitor was Bishop Angelo Acciaiuoli, who, according to the testimony of the chronicler Stefani, was vigorous in his support of the Signoria and its efforts to protect the

Piero dell'Aquila ordered the *podestà* to seize Salvestro Baroncelli, a partner in the Acciaiuoli Company. The regime was outraged by this action
and the priorate responded by releasing Baroncelli and severely repri-
manding the *podestà* for obeying the request of an ecclesiastical official.
At this juncture communal authorities took measures to prevent the inquisitor from usurping the prerogatives of secular authority. Future intervention in communal affairs was not to be countenanced, nor were
Florentine citizens required to pay fines to this office. The inquisitor was
no longer permitted to use a section of the communal prison for hous-
ing heretics.[25] The zeal of this official in prosecuting alleged usurers and
his persistence in advancing the claims of his fellow ecclesiastics were
prime factors in the decline of the prestige and power of his office.[26] The
waning of his authority is further explicable in terms of the political and
economic exigencies that came to the fore in the years immediately preceding the Black Death. The nouveau riche and the urban aristocracy
had joined forces against the inquisitor for reasons that were essentially
practical. Aside from the obvious motive of endeavoring to protect the
Florentine companies from the precipitate demands of their ecclesiasti-

---

patrimony of his kinsmen. Cf. *Cronica Fiorentina di Coppo Stefani,* ed. N. Rodolico,
Rerum Italicarum Scriptores, new ed., 3, pt. 1 (Città di Castello, 1903–55), rub. 588.
See A. Panella, op. cit., 304–5, on the bishop's refusal to comply with the terms
of the interdict placed on Florence and his defense of communal interests before
the Curia.

25. Villani contended that Piero had acted under the pretense that there were
heretics in Florence, when in reality, there was "quasi niuno" (Cf. loc. cit.). On
the question of the decline of heresy in the second half of the thirteenth century,
see G. Volpe, *Movimenti religiosi e sette ireticali nella società medievale italiana (secoli XI–XIV),* 2d ed. (Florence: 1926), 214. Condemnations on charges of heresy
dating from the decade of the 1320s, suggest that the Holy Office convicted Florentines on this count. While this does not prove that heresy was widely diffused,
it does tend to support the conclusions of Davidsohn, previously cited, and to
suggest that Villani's view may need modification. For convictions on a charge
of heresy during this era, see Biblioteca Marucelliana, Firenze, BI, 14, 6, cc. 193–
93r, 199–200.

26. It was not until 1382 that the Signoria resumed its policy of cooperation
with the inquisition. The motives for this change will be considered in a subsequent section of this essay. For an expression of literary opinion about the inquisitor, see tale number eleven in Sacchetti, trans. M. Steegman (London, 1908),
16–17. According to a manuscript in the Biblioteca Marucelliana, Firenze (BI, 14,
6, c. 197), Piero dell'Aquila was the model for the figure of the inquisitor in the
Decameron.

cal creditors, there was the additional factor, that has previously been mentioned, of the antipathy that was harbored by the *novi cives* against the bestowal of extralegal status on the church.[27] Even Giovanni Villani, a virulent and intransigent foe of the popular government and a staunch supporter of the "liberties" of the church, bitterly castigated the inquisitor for precipitating the arrest of Salvestro Baroncelli, on the grounds that this action constituted a clear violation of the sovereignty of the state.[28]

If the behavior of the upper classes toward the inquisition and the ecclesiastical tribunals can be explained in terms of their economic interests without resorting to the possible influence of heretical teachings as a motive force for their actions, then what can be discerned about the status of this question as it pertains to the lower classes? No class in Trecento society is more difficult to define with precision than the *minuti* of Florence. Official documents that might serve to chronicle the history of *il popolo minuto* are rare, because this class did not have those political and economic privileges that would have permitted it to keep extensive records. Denied direct representation in the government and prohibited by law from organizing worker's associations, either for their economic betterment or spiritual welfare, the history of this class must be deduced

---

27. It is of interest to note that the same invective was launched against the feudal nobility by *il popolo* at the end of the preceding century. This group, like the clergy, were accused of using their power to oppress the weak and of being able to escape the rigors of communal law. Cf. G. Salvemini, *Magnati e popolani in Firenze dal 1280 al 1295* (Florence, 1899), 60. When the commune took action against the church, it sought to justify its position by claiming that certain members of the nobility who held high church office were guilty of these offenses. Cf. A. Panella, "La guerra degli Otto Santi e le vicende della legge contro i vescovi," *Archivio Storico Italiano* 1 (1941): 36–45.

The support that segments of the clergy had given to the short-lived dictatorship of Walter of Brienne and the aristocratic government that followed may have caused supporters of the popular regime to become apprehensive about the role of the clergy in Florentine politics. Cf. *Camera del Comune*, 1 bis, f. 297r; ibid., 2, f. 4r; L. Bruni, *Dell'historia fiorentina*, trans. D. Acciaiuoli (Venice, 1561), 133. The Irish Franciscan chronicler Luke Wadding states that Piero dell'Aquila was accused of having incited the *ottimati* against the popular regime. Cf. *Annales Minorum* (Rome, 1733) 7:329. Villani's statement that Piero had given permission to 250 Florentines to bear arms (bk. 7, 58), suggests that there may have been some truth to this allegation. For a contrary interpretation, see A. Panella, "Politica ecclesiastica del comune fiorentino," op. cit., 312.

28. The chronicler contends that similar action was taken by the king of Spain "e di più altri signori e comuni" (bk. 7, 58); cf. also Stefani, rub. 628.

from the sporadic evidence contained in the judicial records that chronicle only the activities of those who refuse to conform to the dictates of their economic and social superiors—the masters of the guilds.[29] Therefore, we know very little about those who docilely served their employers or those who reluctantly submitted to the hegemony of the *popolani grassi*. Nor is it possible to presume that this heterogeneous order achieved a strong feeling of class-consciousness.[30] Rather, it would appear that *il popolo minuto* lacked cohesion within their ranks and were, therefore, ineffectual as a political force unless members of the upper classes would provide them with the necessary dynamic leadership. The revolution of 1293–95 offers a striking example of this phenomenon. Aristocrats, such as the renowned Giano della Bella, were able to forge *il popolo minuto* into a unified political force and use them to undermine the traditional privileges and immunities of those classes which, by virtue of their status, tended to live outside of the realm of communal law.[31] In 1345–46 this situation was duplicated; the urban patriciate and

---

29. Since those records that have been utilized by modern scholars date only from 1343, the impression has been created that discontent among these segments of *il popolo minuto* also began in that year. The *Archivio del Giudice degli Appelli,* however, contains cases involving subversive behavior by *minuti* dating from 1326. (See esp. vol. 122, pt. 3, f. 25.) It appears that disaffection among the *minuti* was a continuous phenomenon throughout the early Trecento. Cf. *Camera del Comune,* 1 bis.

30. In 1343 many *minuti* joined the patricians and overthrew the rule of Walter of Brienne, self-appointed benefactor of the lower orders. Cf. G. Brucker and M. Becker, "Una lettera in difesa della dittatura," *Archivio Storico Italiano* 113 (1955): 251–57.

Il popolo minuto was composed of various strata of Florentine society. The tax records suggest that the dyers, fullers, and finishers were among the most affluent of the members of the artisan world. They were, however, classified as *minuti,* since they were not permitted to form their own guilds and were compelled to remain under the domination of the consulate of the *arti maggiori.* But in economic status they were much closer to the greater guildsmen than to the Florentine proletariat, whom they themselves frequently employed as day laborers. Existing evidence suggests that the Fraticelli made many converts among this class. A possible explanation may be that affluent *minuti* were without social status and juridical position in Florentine society and, therefore, sought compensation in the egalitarianism of the Fraticelli. Cf. F. Tocco, *Studii francescani,* 412ff.; "I Fraticelli," *Archivio Storico Italiano* 25 (1905): 345ff.

31. See the account of the contemporary chronicler, Paolino Pieri, in *Cronica delle cose d'Italia,* ed. A. Adami (Rome, 1755), 56–58. Other sources agree that af-

the *gente nuova,* with the support of the *minuti* were able to curtail certain of the liberties of the church. Contemporary chroniclers maintained that the fury of the mob was directed principally against the upper clergy, who were the scions of aristocratic families and had, by virtue of their high office and power, exploited "the poor and the weak."[32] Utilizing this animus to their own advantage, the government achieved its objectives. Precious time was gained for the bankers by effectuating the postponement of restitution to their ecclesiastical creditors; clerical opposition to usurious contracts was frustrated and clergymen were brought under the purview of communal law.[33] These advantages were gained, however, at the cost of the diffusion of heresy among the lower classes.[34] Subsequent events suggest that the ruling patricians believed that they could control the economic, social, and political manifestations of these heretical tendencies among *il popolo minuto.* The rebellion of the *Ciompi* in 1378 was to prove that this assessment of their own capacity was some distance from the truth.[35]

The lower orders, heterogeneous in composition and divided upon fundamental issues, had expressed discontent with the economic status quo at various intervals before 1343.[36] These sporadic outbursts revealed the important fissures within the ranks of *il popolo minuto* and indicated the absence of a class ideology. The dyers and other members of the highly skilled crafts that were under the hegemony of the Lana guild were able to secure important concessions from the great wool manufacturers.[37] In their own right, however, these beneficiaries were them-

---

ter the banishment of their leader, "il popolo minuto, perde ogni rigoglio e vigore." For a detailed discussion of this problem, see N. Ottokar, op. cit., 288–89.

32. Cf. Stefani, op. cit., rub. 616; also *Priorista,* quoted by N. Rodoloco in *I Ciompi* (Florence, 1945), 42.

33. M. Becker, "Three Cases Concerning the Restitution of Usury in Florence," *Journal of Economic History* (1957): 446–47.

34. F. Tocco, *Studii francescani,* 412–13. The Fraticelli wrote in the vernacular "Quidam tractatus de vita christiana pro simplicibus vulgariter compilatus," which enjoined all men to practice apostolic poverty and blessed those who had been condemned to do so as a result of the exigencies of this life.

35. The major chroniclers maintain that both factions contending for political power during this period vied for the support of the lower orders. Cf. Stefani, rub. 734; Velluti, 242.

36. Cf. n. 30; M. Becker, "Gualtieri di Brienne e l'uso delle dispense guidiziarie," *Archivio Storico Italiano* 113 (1955): 246–51.

37. C. Paoli, *Della signoria di Gualtieri duca d'Atene* (Florence, 1862), 82–83.

selves employers of labor and among the most affluent members of the artisan world.[38] They do not appear to have been prone to champion the cause of their more unfortunate brethren. Another example of a possible source of friction within these ranks involved the question of the authority of the consuls of the minor guilds over *i minuti*. The wealthiest segment of *minori* leadership sought to compel all individuals who plied any given trade to enroll in one of the fourteen lesser guilds.[39] Since this would entail the payment of a matriculation fee, and what was even more significant, submission to the authority of the consulate of these minor guilds, it can not be expected that this step would be embraced with enthusiasm by *il popolo minuto*.[40] As a matter of fact, the lower echelons of Florentine society were characterized by sharp economic antipathies.[41] In an age when each socioeconomic class sought to justify its existence at the bar of religion, *il popolo minuto* appear to have inaugurated its search for an identity by rejecting religious rationalizations of the upper classes. It might be fair to paraphrase Calmette and suggest that religion was a type of Kantian category in terms of which the men of the Trecento perceived the social world.[42] This fact operated with greater intensity among the membership of *i minuti*. The urban patriciate could look toward a modification of Saint Thomas's Aristotelian political philosophy that would buttress their own republican sentiments. *Il popolo minuto*, on the other hand, had no secularized ideology with which to sanctify their socioeconomic aspirations and, therefore, sought for confirmation at the fount of Christianity.[43] This would not

---

38. On the distinction between *membra minora* of the *arti* and day laborers, see G. Scaramella *Firenze allo scoppio del tumulto dei Ciompi* (Pisa, 1914), 27–29.

39. The lower guilds followed a policy of attempting to extend their jurisdiction over all individuals who practiced a métier similar to their own. They were not motivated by democratic proclivities, as Rodolico contends, but, rather, they sought to compel all men who plied a given trade to assume fiscal responsibility for communal fines and assessments. Cf. *Atti Esecutore*, 29, fols. 196r–197 (9 April 1345); ibid., 40, 112 (30 July 1345). For a contrasting interpretation, see N. Rodolico, *I Ciompi* (Florence, 1945), 42.

40. Similar legislation was passed in the year 1380. Cf. *P.*, 69, f. 97.

41. See especially A. Doren, *Studien aus der florentiner Wirthschaftsgeschichte* (Stuttgart, 1901), 1:233.

42. Quoted from W. Ferguson, "The Church in a Changing World: A Contribution to the Interpretation of the Renaissance," *American Historical Review* 59 (1953): 4.

43. The *minuti*, denied representation in the Signoria, could not be expected

only provide them with an element of cohesion, but it would also furnish a weapon with which to humble their social superiors.

The teachings of the Spiritual Franciscans, which cast doubt upon the sanctity of private property and contended that wealth was a consequence of original sin, acted as a catalytic agent to further agitate the already disturbed state of popular conscience.[44] Important concessions granted by Walter of Brienne, dictator of the city of Florence in 1342–43, to *il popolo minuto* had stimulated the revolutionary ardor of this class.[45] The workers now demanded rights and privileges that formerly had been the exclusive prerogative of the upper classes. Ultimately, they sought to justify these claims in terms of the prevailing "heretical" ethic.[46] Their newly acquired sense of importance was heightened when they discerned that the oligarchs were dependent upon their assistance to effectuate the overthrow of the tyranny of Brienne.[47] The doctrine of the Fraticelli further reinforced the confidence of *il popolo minuto* by ascribing the highest virtues to the poor.[48]

---

to find solace for their depressed socioeconomic position by identifying themselves with a regime composed of "cari e antichi cittandini" (D. Velluti, 242). This situation was intensified by the fact that the *lanifices* utilized communal power to sustain their hegemony over the *minuti*. As early as 1326, speeches were being made to the populace by certain discontented Florentines who advised the workers that they lived as "servitores artium." Cf. *Camera del Comune,* 1 bis, f. 187r.

For a consideration of the identification of heretical teachings with the aspirations of a particular social class during the thirteenth century, see E. Dupré Theseider's review of Arno Borst's, *Die Katharer* (Stuttgart, 1953), in *Rivista Storica Italiana* 67 (1955): 579–80.

44. It should be noted that the defense of poverty and the censure of ecclesiastical wealth was not confined to the Fraticelli and other heretical sects but was also pervasive in nonsectarian circles during the Trecento. Cf. H. Baron, "Franciscan Poverty and Civic Wealth as Factors in the Rise of Humanistic Thought," *Speculum* 13 (1938); 4–5.

45. C. Paoli, op. cit., 37ff.; N. Rodolico, op. cit., 34–36.

46. See the prophecy of a Minorite recorded in a Florentine diary of the second half of the fourteenth century in which it is predicted that the *gente minuta* will force the *popolani* and the clergy to give up their possessions. *Diario di Anonimo,* ed. A. Gherardi in *Documenti di Storia Italiana* (Florence, 1876), 6: 286–87.

47. In a document dated 4 January 1344 reference is made to the revolution of the preceding September as having been fought "pro tuenda libertate plebis." Cf. *L.F.,* 22, unnumbered folio.

48. It is important to note, in this context, that the *minuti* referred to them-

At this juncture the Augustinian hermit, Simone da Cascia, arrived in Florence and began to preach in favor of the doctrine of evangelical poverty; this he did in defiance of a papal bull prohibiting such pronouncements.[49] The Dominicans threatened him with excommunication for disseminating ideas alleged to be heretical. The Signoria, however, thwarted this attempt by openly and efficaciously protecting him from prosecution on this charge. A factor that may have played a part in encouraging affluent members of the regime to take this stand was the attitude of the Dominicans toward an important piece of communal legislation. From 1343 to 1345 the Signoria was concerned with the establishment of a funded communal debt.[50] Negotiable shares were issued that were interest bearing. This latter step was vigorously opposed by the Dominicans on the grounds that it was a violation of the canonical prohibition against usury.[51] It would appear that the Signoria was willing to countenance the spread of heretical ideas among the lower orders since they did not constitute as great a threat to their interests as did certain segments of the Florentine clergy.[52]

The years that followed the Black Death were marked by an oligarchical reaction leading to the amelioration of relations between

---

selves as "il popolo di Dio" when they seized power in 1378. The populace also spoke of the "Eight Saints" as being the directors of the war against the papacy in 1375.

49. Tocco, in his last work, dated the delivery of these sermons shortly before Simone's death in 1348. Cf. *Studii francescani*, 412; U. Dorini, op. cit., 132–33. For a consideration of treatises written for the layman by Angelo da Clareno at the request of Simone, see Ciro da Pesaro, *Il beato Angelo Clareno* (Macerata, 1920), 401ff. These writings deal with the sanctity of poverty and the sinfulness of wealth.

50. B. Barbadoro, *Le finanze della repubblica fiorentina* (Florence, 1929), 629–64.

51. For the details of this controversy, see G. Brucker, "Un documento fiorentino sulla guerra, sulla finanza e sulla amministrazione pubblica (1375)," *Archivio Storico Italiano* 115 (1957): 167. R. De Roover, "Il trattato di fra Santi Rucellai sul Cambio, il monte comune e il monte delle doti," ibid. (1953), 3–23; M. Villani, *Cronica*, bk. 3, chap. 106. Piero Strozzi and Iacopo Passavanti, the two most influential Dominicans in Florence at this time, were both intransigent foes of the *Monte* on the grounds that it constituted a violation of the canonical prohibitions against usury.

52. The councils voted a subsidy for the Franciscans in 1364 because they had "always defended Florence from her enemies." Cf. *P.*, 52, f. 29; ibid., 59, f. 124. Eight years later the only petition to be presented by the Dominicans during this era was rejected. Cf. *L.F.*, 40, f. 38.

church and state. The personnel of the new government were less hostile toward the church than their immediate predecessors. Fewer *gente nuova* and minor guildsmen sat in the council halls during this regime.[53] One would expect, therefore, that the trend toward impersonal government was in the process of being reversed. If the criteria of the communal attitude concerning the traditional privileges and immunities of the church and the nobility is utilized, then it might be fair to suggest that this government was more mindful of the ancient "liberties" of these classes than was the preceding regime.[54] Other factors accelerated this trend; the Florentine banking houses had made restitution to their ecclesiastical creditors and, therefore, there was no longer conflict on this score. When these settlements had been made, the interdict laid on the city was lifted and once again the papacy began to avail itself of the resources and services that the Florentine bankers were so admirably equipped to offer.[55] It would naturally follow that these members of the *Cambio*, well represented in the new government, were, therefore, not anxious to antagonize Avignon. The Curia, bent upon the reconquest of the Patrimony, was well aware of the advantages to be gained from a closer liaison with Florence. Impetus was given to this newly established accord when Clement VI accepted a petition from the Florentine Signoria asking that the papal inquisitor in Tuscany, Pietro dell'Aquila, be removed from office and Michele di Lapo Arnolfi, a member of an important Florentine patrician family, be appointed in his stead. The pontiff accepted this suggestion and another source of friction was eradicated.

The new inquisitor took an unusual step, upon assuming office, when he reversed a condemnation for heresy pronounced by his predecessor.[56] In this revocation it is stated that a confession had been ex-

---

53. Representation of these classes was cut by approximately 25 percent. Cf. D. Marzi, *La cancelleria della repubblica fiorentina* (Rocca S. Casciano, 1910), 557–65.

54. The Signoria, after 1348, did modify certain enactments against the feudal nobility and the clergy. There were, however, important areas of disagreement between church and state that generated severe tensions. Cf. F. Baldasseroni, "Una controversia tra stato e chiesa in Firenze nel 1355," *Archivio Storico Italiano* 50 (1913): 39–54.

55. Y. Renouard, op. cit., 254ff.; A. Panella, op. cit., 292ff.

56. Biblioteca Marucelliana, B I, 14, fols. 205–6. The document is dated 27 March 1350. In the margin is the notation "Revocatio Sententiae Fr. Petro de Aquila."

torted from the alleged heretic "by fear of torture" and that the trial had been conducted "fraudulently." The attitude of the inquisitors appear to have undergone a considerable modification. Andreas Ricchi, who held this office during the decade of the 1370s, sought to win back the errant Fraticelli for the church through persuasion rather than by means of invective and denunciation.[57] Despite the moderation of the inquisitors, the Signoria did not alter its attitude toward this office. The various priorates that ruled the city from the Black Death until the aftermath of the Ciompi (1348–82), permitted that statute against heretics to fall into abeyance and it became "un ricordo storico."[58] The explanation for this laxity on the part of the Signorie can best be discerned within the context of the intricacies of communal politics during this interval. The rapproachement, that was effectuated between the church and state in the years immediately following the Black Death was, at best, an uneasy truce. While the patricians who dominated the priorate were more respectful toward the traditional privileges of the clergy, this attitude was undergoing extensive modification as a result of certain significant changes that were taking place in the field of foreign relations. Chief among these was the influence upon Florentine politics of the papal attempt to reestablish temporal authority in the Papal States. The records of the advisory councils to the Florentine Signoria indicate that the urban patriciate was fearful of the threat that papal power posed to the independence of their beloved city.[59] Zealous of protecting the liberty of the republic, the ruling classes came to regard the inquisition and the ecclesiastical courts with profound suspicion and overt hostility.[60] It

---

57. D. Douie, op. cit., 198.

58. F. Tocco, op. cit., 414.

59. Frequently, counselors admonished the Priorate to follow a course of action that would permit the city to continue "in libertate," and in no case were they to do fealty "to any lord, lay or ecclesiastic." Cf. *Consulte et Pratiche*, I, unnumbered folio (12–14 March 1355). Henceforth this source will be abbreviated as *C.P.* The apprehension of these men increased as a result of Albornoz's successful campaign to recapture the Patrimony. Cf. ibid., II, fols. 17–18, 24, 43; M. Villani, bk. 7, 67.

60. In March 1378, when a treaty of peace was being negotiated between Florence and the Holy See to effectuate the termination of the War of the Eight Saints, governmental advisors were agreed upon all issues except the removal of the ordinances "contra officium inquisitionis." *C.P.*, xv, fols. 93–94.

The commune retained the legislation of 1345 on the statute books throughout this period. These laws curtailed ecclesiastical jurisdiction in cases involv-

would appear that these *popolani grassi* preferred to suffer the spread of heresy rather than to give free rein to these clerical offices.

By 1375 the accumulation of these tensions resulted in the precipitation of a war between the republic and the Holy See.[61] The edifice that housed the inquisition was destroyed and the office of inquisitor was rendered ineffectual within the confines of Florentine territory. The Signoria directing the "War of the Eight Saints" recognized the need for popular support to sustain a war against so formidable an adversary and, therefore, the tenor of their legislative enactments was directed toward this end.[62] Among the chief beneficiaries of these new policies were the Spiritual Franciscans, who were now permitted to spread their doctrine overtly without fear of reprisal; surviving documentation suggests that their efforts were crowned with success. The artisan and shopkeeper class appear to have been most receptive to the teachings of the Fraticelli, who were now able to disseminate their ideas with, at least, the tacit support of the Signoria.[63] Bitterly anti-papal, the Spiritual Franciscans embraced the ideals for which Florence purported to be fighting and justified this role in terms of the prophetic tradition of their order. The influence that they might have exerted upon the masses is difficult to assess, however, public enthusiasm for this war against the papacy suggests that it was not negligible.[64]

The actions of the government for the duration of the war indicate

---

ing a charge of usury. On occasion, however, they were not enforced. Cf. M. Becker, "Nota dei processi reguardanti prestatori di danaro nei tribunali fiorentini dal 1343 al 1379," *Archivio Storico Italiano* 114 (1956): 744.

61. For a consideration of this problem, see A. Gherardi, "La guerra dei fiorentini con papa Gregorio XI detta la guerra degli Otto Santi," *Archivio Storico Italiano* 5 (1867): 34–131.

62. Especially interesting in this light are the numerous purchases of church lands made by members of the lower orders as a result of communal policy that effectuated the confiscation of certain ecclesiastical estates. Cf. *Camera del Comune*, 182–83 (March–May 1378). Important *popolani* and *grandi* were also beneficiaries. Among these families were the Morelli, Strozzi, Tolosini, Bondelmonti, Cambi, Peruzzi, Albizzi, Bardi, Medici, Alberti, Pazzi, and many others. Cf. ibid., 176–81 (January 1377–February 1378).

63. F. Tocco, op. cit., 412. The commune stated that it would protect both citizens and clerics "in their person and property" from accusations of heresy. Cf. *P.*, 65, f. 173. Proceedings against certain individuals charged with heresy were initiated by the papacy in 1374. Cf. ibid., 63, f. 239.

64. See the letter published by G. Brucker, op. cit., 171–76.

that there were motives behind certain communal enactments that were antithetical to the teachings of both the orthodox and heretical clergy. The Signoria seized this opportunity to press for legislative measures removing communal sanctions against usurious practices.[65] They passed a provision in the same vein that endeavored to curtail ecclesiastical jurisdiction over violations of this type.[66] In direct opposition to the Bishop's Constitution, the regime licensed Jewish moneylenders in order that they might be free to ply their trade in the Florentine contado.[67] State officials now assumed the role of executor over the wills of "manifest" usurers.[68] It is clear from these and other legislative enactments that the men who ruled the republic during the Otto Santi war were not unaware of the opportunity presented to them as a result of the elimination of the ecclesiastical courts in general and the inquisitorial tribunals in particular. Their attempts to condone practices hitherto condemned as usurious does not indicate that they were activated by the teachings of the Spiritual Franciscans but, rather, it suggests the converse. The Fraticelli, bitter opponents of usurious practices and fervent advocates of the idea of evangelical poverty, had assuredly failed in their attempts to convert the majority of the ruling class to this ideal. While the Fraticelli may have been utilized by the Signoria to popularize the war among the masses, the upper classes were able to remain immune from the spiritual effects of their economic teachings.

By the year 1378 popular enthusiasm for the war had declined appreciably. This conflict with the Holy See had precipitated certain tensions within the lives of the Florentines. Despite the fact that the papacy placed the city under interdict and, therefore, church services were suspended, there was a strong resurgence of religious emotion. The contemporary chronicler, Stefani, noted that there was greater church at-

---

65. The general effect of these enactments was to make interest recoverable at law. There was, therefore, no need to resort to the subterfuges of an earlier era. Cf. *P.*, 63, f. 85 (8 August 1375). For a description of these practices, see R. de Roover, *The Medici Bank* (New York, 1948), 57.

66. The authority of the church courts was curtailed; any citizen who claimed that he had suffered an injustice at the hands of these tribunals was permitted to appeal to the Signoria. Cf. *P.*, 63, f. 73; *L.F.*, 40, f. 150.

67. *Camera del Comune*, 168, unnumbered folio (30 October 1375); *Capitoli del Comune di Firenze*, ed. C. Guasti (Florence, 1893), 39.

68. Cf. M. Becker, "Three Cases Concerning the Restitution of Usury in Florence," op. cit., 445–50.

tendance at this time than during periods when services were held.[69] Mass religious feeling was also expressed in the form of daily processions attracting thousands of the faithful. The consternation and confusion prevailing among the masses was also reflected within the ranks of other segments of Florentine society. Although Coluccio Salutati, the eminent humanist, acting in his official capacity as Florentine chancellor, had sought to justify this war against the "Chiesa carnale," in terms of the prophetic tradition and in the name of "liberty," certain Florentines harbored serious doubts concerning its morality. In a letter written by Giovanni delle Celle, famous ascetic of Vallombrosa and scion of a noble Tuscan family, to Guido di Neri del Palagio, a member of the urban patriciate, deep concern is expressed over the plight of those who held communal office during the war against the Holy See. The recipient of this letter was torn between his devotion to his beloved native city and his spiritual responsibilities to his church.[70] This same Guido was also in correspondence with the Florentine humanist priest, Luigi Marsili, who held that the Signoria did not have the right to harm those clergy who performed their religious offices but that the regime was not obligated to suffer those who meddled in communal politics.[71] These tensions were further heightened by the intransigent opposition of certain leaders of the *Parte Guelfa*, the most obdurate of which was the renowned canon lawyer, Lapo Castiglionchio, who expressed the conviction that the invincible papacy would humble the City of the Bap-

---

69. *Cronica*, rub. 765.

70. A. Biscioni, *Lettere di Santi e Beati Fiorentini* (Florence, 1736), 13–14. The monk advised Guido that he could serve in the government and pay taxes to support the war against the Holy See, since the excommunication that was launched against the Florentines was unjust and therefore, not binding. While Giovanni was an implacable foe of the Fraticelli, he himself had been profoundly influenced by the Joachimite tradition and had accepted the prediction of the coming of the antichrist and the subsequent advent of the angel popes. The spread of these ideas was at its apogee at this time and, according to the testimony of Giovanni, had made its deepest inroads among the artisan class. Cf. H. Grundmann, "Die papstprophetien des Mittelalters," *Archiv für Kulturgeschichte* 19 (1928): 117–22.

71. This Augustinian was bitterly hostile toward Avignon; during the Otto Santi War he transcribed the antipapal sonnets of Petrarch. The early humanists, especially Bruni and Salutati, were influenced by his teachings. Cf. U. Mariani, *Il Petrarca e gli agostiniani* (Rome, 1946), 66ff.; N. Sapegno, op. cit., 528; N. Valeri, *L'Italia nell' età dei principati, 1343–1516* (Milan, 1949), 206.

tist.[72] Added credence was given to this view by the mercantile class as
a result of the serious decline in trade and the augmentation of taxes for
the purpose of financing the war.[73] By June 1378, however, political
power had passed from the hands of the *popolani grassi*. Factionalism
and extreme partisanship coupled with the divisive effect of the war
with the Holy See had done grave damage to the prestige of the ruling
classes, and they were not to recover absolute hegemony over the state
until the year 1382.[74]

     During the years immediately preceding the outbreak of the *Ciompi*
revolution, the heretics had been left free to think and to teach. Gaspare
di Ricco, *docente* in the *Studio fiorentino*, wore the yellow cross of the
heretic upon his sleeve and was one of the principal leaders of the
Ciompi.[75] It is not surprising to find, therefore, that the government, established by the lower orders, tolerated the Fraticelli and protected
them against the newly established inquisition. In order to secure peace
with the papacy the Florentines had been compelled to recognize the jurisdiction of the inquisitorial court. This acknowledgment was without
practical effect, as far as the Fraticelli were concerned, since the Signoria was unwilling to take action against them.[76] The government, at this
time, was composed mainly of men who belonged to the lower middle
class. According to the chronicler Stefani, these *petits bourgeois* were of
the opinion that the great oligarchs had used the church as a device to
oppress the lower orders.[77] It is possible that these sentiments were
deepened by profound social and economic antipathies. The revolutionaries who sought to sanctify their own aspirations by referring to

------

72. *C.P.*, xv, f. 66 (26 December 1377). Lapo maintained that Florence was in
"magno periculo" because she was waging war "cum hoste invincibili" and,
therefore, should hasten to make peace.

73. Counselors to the Signoria advised that peace should be made with the
Holy See so that the Florentine merchants "possint facere per mundum suas
mercantias et exigere debita, sibi." Cf. ibid., xv, f. 93 (27 March 1378).

74. For a consideration of this problem, see M. Becker, "Un avvenimento
riguardante il cronista Marchionne di Coppo Stefani," *Archivio Storico Italiano*
117 (1959), 137–46.

75. A. Sapori, *Compagnie e mercanti di Firenze antica* (Florence, 1955), lxxxvi.

76. Despite proposals by governmental advisors, the Signoria continued to
follow a laissez-faire policy regarding the Fraticelli. Cf. *C.P.*, xix, f. 167 (8 July
1380).

77. *Cronica*, rub. 616.

themselves as "Il Popolo di Dio" were not unmindful of the debt they owed to the Spiritual Franciscans, who had taught them that they alone were the inheritors of the "true" religion.[78]

At the end of 1382 the urban patriciate regained political control over affairs of state and immediately proposed legislation designed to expel the Fraticelli from Florentine territory.[79] This proposal was the first measure in the annals of communal history that was specifically directed against the Spiritual Franciscans. The Signoria designated certain secular officials to assist the inquisitor in achieving this end. It is of interest to note that there was sufficient opposition to this step among the communal counselors to bring about its defeat.[80] On the following day the same measure was introduced again and was barely able to muster enough votes to insure its passage.[81] The hostility toward this law can be explained on two possible grounds: antipathy against the inquisitor and sympathy for the Fraticelli. That the opposition was so extensive suggests the possibility that both of these sentiments were pervasive among the more affluent members of the *arti minori*. This element of Florentine society was well represented in the communal councils at this time.[82] Within the next few years, however, they were to become a negligible factor in republican politics and hegemony was to fall into the hands of the most restricted oligarchy in communal history.[83] From its inception this Signoria demonstrated a willingness to cooperate with the inquisitor in matters pertaining to the suppression of heresy. Speakers in the council halls were unanimous in the opinion that the government should assist the clerical tribunals in driving the Fraticelli from the city.[84] This policy culminated with the burning of Michele da Calci. This itinerant preacher

---

78. Cf. n. 48; A. Doren, *Le arti fiorentine* (Florence, 1940), 2:231–33.

79. *L.F.*, 41, f. 77 (12 December 1382).

80. The subject of rejected legislation has not been studied systematically by scholars, since the *Libri Fabarum* have, hitherto, not been utilized.

81. *P.*, 77, fols. 175r–76r; *L.F.*, 41, fols. 78–80 (13 December 1382).

82. The members of the lesser guilds held approximately one-fourth of all important communal offices. On their representation in the councils, see *P.*, 71, f. 185; *L.F.*, 41, f. 80 (16 December 1382).

83. On the politics of this era, see A. Rado, *Maso degli Albizzi e il parte oligarchie, 1382–1393* (Florence, 1926); G. Brucker, "The Medici in the Fourteenth Century," op. cit., 22.

84. *C.P.*, xxiii, f. 71r (17 July 1383); ibid., f. 108r (22 October 1383).

was convicted on a charge of embracing the heretical teachings of the Spirituals and disseminating their doctrine among the people.[85]

The revolution of 1378 was not soon forgotten by the oligarchs and it is clear from their subsequent policies that they had come to regard the Fraticelli as one of the principal factors in its precipitation. The regime after 1382 was willing to cooperate with the inquisition in order to prevent another uprising like that of the *Ciompi*. This does not imply, however, that there were no important divisive issues to separate church and state.[86] Despite these areas of conflict, this government did not encourage anticlericalism among the populace—either tacitly or overtly—in order to achieve its own ends. Apparently, history had taught the patricians that the risks involved far outweighed the advantages to be gained.

By the end of the Trecento the problem of heresy had become peripheral and the Signoria was no longer obliged to take cognizance of its existence.[87] The oligarchical regime in power at this time had been able to eradicate its overt manifestations among *il popolo minuto* and in this effort they were aided by the fact that this particular class had become politically apathetic. Contemporary intellectual developments, with their emphasis upon philology and history and their tendency to ignore this controversial question in favor of secular studies, also contributed to the waning of the influence of the teachings of the Fraticelli.[88]

---

85. F. S. Zambrini, "Storia di Fra Michele minorita, come fu arso in Firenze nel 1389," *Scelta di Curiosità* (Bologna, 1864), 1–57.

86. Some of these involved the jurisdiction of church courts, the authority of the commune to tax the clergy, and the restitution of ecclesiastical property. Cf. *P.*, 83, fols. 212r–13; *L.F.*, 42, f. 26; ibid., 58, f. 89r.

87. The last time that the question of the Fraticelli was discussed by the advisory council in the Trecento, the speakers proposed that the bishop and the inquisitor receive the aid of the secular arm in order to suppress the Fraticelli. *C.P.*, xxvi, fols. 182–82r (18 March 1388).

88. It should be noted that the Florentine chancellor, Coluccio Salutati, composed his ascetic treatise, *De Saeculo et Religione*, at the height of the activity of the Fraticelli in 1381. His thesis is that the two "civitates," the Church and the *Imperium*, were both established by the poor, only to be corrupted and later destroyed by the rich. See Hans Baron's important article, "Franciscan Poverty and Civic Wealth as Factors in the Rise of Humanistic Thought," op. cit., 16. With the decline of the influence of the teachings of the Fraticelli after 1382, Salutati showed little interest in this theme and in his later work tends to extol "la vita attiva." Cf. E. Garin, *L'umanesimo italiano* (Bari, 1952), 41. There was also a pro-

No longer were anonymous chronicles in evidence that exhibited Franciscan overtones of sympathy for the plight of the lower classes. Finally, the fact that the humanist historical tradition was intensely hostile to the participation of the lower orders in communal life and opposed any force that might tend to agitate the conscience of *il popolo minuto* was a further deterrent to the diffusion of this heresy.[89]

The absence of a satisfactory synthetic history on the subject of religious life in Trecento Italy and the fact that only three volumes of the records of the inquisition (dating from the sixteenth century) are to be found in the state archives of Florence tends to make the establishment of general conclusions extremely tenuous.[90] It might be fair to suggest, however, based upon Florentine historical experience, that the diffusion of heresy was intimately related to political considerations—just as its suppression ultimately stemmed from the same source.[91]

---

found change in the attitudes of other Florentine humanists, such as Leonardo Bruni and Poggio Bracciolini, toward the Minorite ideals. These men supported doctrines that justified the active life and the nobility of wealth.

89. See especially Poggio Bracciolini's polemic against those hypocritical parasites who, under the guise of religion, preach poverty to others and imbue in them a disrespect for private property. Quotations from this anti-Franciscan dialogue "De Avaritia" are to be found in E. Garin, op. cit., 60. Cf. Leonardo Bruni Aretino, *Historiarum Florentii Populi*, ed. E. Santini, *Rerum Italicarum Scriptores*, new ed., vol. 30 pt. 3 (Città di Castello, 1914), 169ff.; F. Guicciardini, *Le cose fiorentine*, ed. R. Ridolfi (Florence, 1945), 72.

90. G. Volpe's *Movimenti religiosi e sette ireticali nella società medievale italiana (secoli XI–XIV)*, 2d ed. (Florence, 1926), contains only chance references to the events of the Trecento, while Charles Dejob's *La foi religieuse en Italie au quatorzième siècle* (Paris, 1906) is a very superficial analysis. For surviving documents, in the Florentine Archives, pertaining to the inquisition, see *Conventi soppressi*, no. 92, 169–71.

91. Nicola Ottokar's article "La condanna postuma di Farinata degli Uberti," published in *Studi Comunali e Fiorentini* (Florence, 1948), 115ff., suggests that similar conclusions can be drawn concerning the events of the preceding century.

3

The Republican City-State in Florence: An Inquiry into Its Origin and Survival (1280–1434)

Despotism, like feudalism, tended to obscure the difference between public and private rights. The origins of the typical North Italian despot can frequently be traced back to a remote feudal lord of the *contado* who, while submitting to the authority of the commune in theory, was, in fact, able to retain certain of his most important signorial prerogatives over men and property. Additions were made to his patrimony through advantageous marriage alliances and grants of land from communes, popes, and emperors. His influence over men and his control over property increased until he was able to capture the leadership of one of the contending urban factions, and within a relatively short period of time he was granted *plenitudo potestatis*.[1] Families such as the Alberti, Pazzi,

---

From *Speculum* 25 (1960): 39–50.

This is a slightly expanded version of a paper read at the seventy-third annual meeting of the American Historical Association on 30 December 1958 at Washington, D.C. I should like to acknowledge my great debt to Dr. Hans Baron of the Newberry Library, Chicago, for his kind help and advice in its preparation. Research for this paper was done while the author was a recipient of a Guggenheim Fellowship. The reason for selection of the date 1280 is that surviving documentation prior to that year is so sporadic that generalizations of any kind would virtually have to be qualified out of existence.

1. I am indebted to Professor Philip Jones of the University of Leeds for permitting me to see his important manuscript on the Malatesta family. For a penetrating analysis of the conflict between communalism and dictatorial trends, see F. Chabod, *Machiavelli and the Renaissance*, trans. D. Moore (London, 1958), 53–61; F. Schneider, *Rom und Romgedanke im Mittelalter* (Munich, 1926). For a discussion of Max Weber's view of the patrimonial endowment of personal rule in feudal society, see L. Krader, "Feudalism and the Tatar Policy of the Middle Ages," *Comparative Studies in Society and History* 1 (1958): 77–78. For recent bibliography, see N. Valeri, *L'Italia nell' età dei principati dal 1343 al 1516* (Milan, 1949), 807–34; F. Catalano, "Rassegna di studi sul comune," *Belfagor* 8 (1953):

Ubaldini, and Uberti were the Florentine equivalents of the Monalde-
schi and Filippeschi of Orvieto and the Malatesta of Rimini,[2] and they
were all willing candidates for rule. While the communal institutions of
many of the other North Italian towns fell into the hands of great feudatories, however, this did not happen in Florence. Surviving documents
suggest that the frustration of the attempt of the Uberti family to establish control toward the end of the twelfth century was related to the
struggle between the firmly entrenched patriciate and the newly arrived
inhabitants of the city.[3] One of the enduring results of this conflict was
the strengthening of the magistracy of the *podestà* for the purpose of
checking similar political aspirations of this and other powerful clans.
Nicola Ottokar, a recent commentator on communal history, maintains
that this office was the indispensable ingredient as far as the foundation
and perpetuation of the Florentine republic was concerned.[4] The addition of other magistracies, such as the "Captain Defender of the Guilds,"
indicates that the most affluent segments of the newcomers were now
organized into *arti* (guilds) and were seeking to advance as well as to
protect their interests through constitutional innovations. Typical of this
group were the Bardi, Cerchi, Frescobaldi, and Mozzi, merchants and
bankers of modest origins who had risen to great wealth and power in
less than a century and were in the vanguard of those who ultimately
succeeded in founding the supreme magistracy of the republic—the Priorate of the Guilds.[5] The vital roles played by both the newcomers and
the guilds in the inauguration of institutions that are to be identified

---

446–65; E. Dupré Theseider, *Roma dal comune di popolo alla signoria pontificia*
(Bologna, 1952), 711–49.

2. Cf. D. Waley, *Mediaeval Orvieto* (Cambridge, 1952), xxiv–xxv; E. Salzer,
Über die Anfänge der Signorie in Oberitalien (Berlin, 1900), 61ff.; P. Jones, "The Vicariate of the Malatesta of Rimini," *English Historical Review* 264 (1952): 321–51.

3. N. Ottokar, *Studi comunali e fiorentini* (Florence, 1948), 73–74; R. Davidsohn, *Geschichte von Florenz* (Florence, 1896), 1:553–59; P. Santini, *Documenti dell'*
antica costituzione del comune di Firenze (Florence, 1895), 28, 47, 49.

4. N. Ottokar, op. cit., 74. For a general treatment of the theme of *il regime*
podestarile, see F. Cognasso, "Le origini della Signoria Lombarda," *Archivio*
Storico Lombardo 83 (1957): 5–19; E. Sestan, "Ricerche intorno ai primi podestà
toscani," *Archivio Storico Italiano* 82 (1924): 177–250.

5. N. Ottokar, *Il comune di Firenze alla fine del dugento* (Florence, 1926),
47–122; R. Davidsohn, op. cit., vol. 2, pt. 2, 474–77; E. Fiumi, "Fioritura e decadenza dell' economia fiorentina," *Archivio Storico Italiano* 115 (1957): 385–439; G.
de Vergottini, *Arti e popolo nella metà del secolo XIII* (Milan, 1943).

with Florentine republicanism suggest that these two groups constituted social forces tending to encourage the triumph of this political
form over that of despotism. This inquiry attempts to describe certain
aspects of this complex process.

The events that occurred between 1280 and 1282 were an out-
growth of a protracted political struggle.[6] The greater guilds had finally
achieved virtual hegemony over the state, and within a decade direct
participation in communal affairs was limited to the membership of the
arti. This victory can be interpreted as the triumph of a particular set of
rights soon to be identified and made synonymous with public law.
Therefore, when we speak of constitutions, statutes, and legislation, it
should be understood that they were principally directed toward the
satisfaction of guild interests and that they tended to evolve in accor-
dance with the socioeconomic demands of these corporate bodies. Private rights, immunities, or prerogatives conflicting with the needs of the
arti tended to be abrogated.[7] By the end of the thirteenth century, therefore, any effort to distinguish between guild interests and communal
policy was foreign to the mentality of those who sat in the council halls
of the republic.[8]

Concomitant with the juridical successes of the guilds were
significant social mutations that resulted in the fusion of the ancient nobility with the new business classes. By the 1280s, it had become extremely difficult to differentiate between the old *magnati* and their more
recent counterparts. Nowhere is this more clearly reflected than in the
matriculae of the guilds; these membership lists reveal that the composition of the *arti* was, in fact, as varied as the upper-reaches of Florentine society. Commerce and industry had acted to merge certain of the

---

6. G. Salvemini, *Magnati e popolani in Firenze dal 1280 al 1295* (Florence,
1899), 1–101; N. Ottokar, "L'istituzione del priorato a Firenze," *Archivio Storico
Italiano* 82 (1924): 5ff.

7. B. Barbadoro, *Le finanze della repubblica fiorentina* (Florence, 1929), 54, 62,
84–86, 140; R. Davidsohn, op. cit., vol. 3, pt. 1, 367–73. On the devaluation of
Florentine coinage, see *Nuovi testi fiorentini del dugento*, ed. A. Castellani (Florence, 1952), 940. For imposts on the clergy, see R. Davidsohn, *Forschungen zur
Geschichte von Florenz* (Berlin, 1908), 4:300.

8. Cf. *Le consulte della repubblica fiorentina dall' anno 1280 al 1298*, ed. A. Gherardi (Florence, 1896–98), 2 vols., which contain the records of the advisory councils that assisted the Signoria in the formulation of legislation. Cf. also *Provvisioni*, vols. 1–5. (Henceforth this source will be abbreviated as *P.*) (All documents
cited in this essay are to be found in the Archivio di Stato of Florence.)

ancient nobility with the new mercantile patriciate, and this fusion minimized the threat of despotism, as there were very few powerful clans
who were not deeply involved in the economic life of the *arti*.[9] When
one considers that the rise of the despot was frequently related to the
bitter struggle between the old aristocracy and the newcomers, the creation of a mercantile nobility in Florence looms as an important socioeconomic fact that helps us to understand the success of republicanism
in the city on the Arno. The guilds may well have acted as a catalytic
agent in the process of leveling the upper classes and creating a pattern
of symbiotic behavior reflected not only in communal politics but also
in the intermarriages and joint business ventures of these two, by now,
almost indistinguishable classes.[10]

The tendency of the *arti* to become more representative of the interests of the upper strata of Florentine society was further intensified
by the diversification of the patrimonies of those who were matriculated
in the guilds. Families such as the Bordoni, Medici, and Strozzi did not
sever their economic and social ties with rural Tuscany when they mi-
grated into the city and achieved eminence in the business world. They
retained their extensive estates in the countryside and their large clien-
tele among the peasantry; they were also immersed in the fiscal life of
the rural communes and *popoli*.[11] Recent studies have disclosed that the
greater guildsmen were not unmindful of the interests of the Florentine

---

9. Cf. A. Sapori, *Studi di storia economica, Secoli XIII–XIV–XV*, 3d ed. (Florence, 1955), 1:585–86. Within the confines of the territory of Florence, the vast
majority of nobility were honorific, that is, they were *magnati* without fiefs. Cf.
E. Fiumi, op. cit., 394ff.

10. Almost half of the noble families cited by the thirteenth-century chroni-
cler Malespini were involved in mercantile pursuits. Cf. P. Jones, "Florentine
Families and Florentine Diaries in the Fourteenth Century," *Papers of the British
School at Rome* 24 (1956): 203–5. For a critique of the classical view of Florence as
a tripartite society (*magnati, popolani grassi,* and *il popolo minuto*), see A. Sapori,
La crisi delle compagnie mercantile dei Bardi e dei Peruzzi (Florence, 1926), 118–20;
G. Villani, *Cronica*, ed. F. Dragomanni (Florence, 1845), 4:39.

11. Ottokar, op. cit., 72, 97; Barbadoro, op. cit., 140, 422–23; Jones, op. cit.,
188–89; G. Brucker, "The Medici in the Fourteenth Century," *Speculum* 32 (1957):
7–8. For the real estate transactions for the Strozzi family in the *contado* during
this period, see *Archivio Notarile*, R. 159, M. 293. On the subject of the followers
and retainers of the great families in the *contado*, see D. Compagni, *Cronica*, ed.
I. del Lungo (Florence, 1889), 2:17; 3:2, 19–20. On the relations between citizens
and *contadini* in the following century, see N. Tamassia, *La famiglia italiana nei
secoli XV e XVI* (Milan, 1910), 39ff.

contado; therefore, classical interpretations that view the relationship between town and country as parasitic can be seriously challenged. With our knowledge of the investment patterns and social contacts of the guildsmen, it is not surprising to find that communal legislation was favorable to agrarian interests as long as the *arti maggiori* dominated the politics of the republic.[12] A similar relationship prevailed between these greater guildsmen and the more affluent members of the minor guilds. Both were large-scale employers of industrial labor and this mutuality of interests reflected itself in communal legislation that governed the economic activities of *il popolo minuto.* During intervals when wealthy *minori* were accorded extensive representation, there was no change in public law on this question.[13] This area of substantial agreement was reinforced by marriage ties, joint business ventures, and monetary obligations.[14]

The Priorate of the republic was equally solicitous concerning the interests of those men of wealth who plied no trade but were matriculated in the guilds by means of a legal fiction. These *scioperati* were permitted to hold office and many played a decisive role in communal politics.[15] Similarly, the nobles who were also permitted to enroll in the guilds were especially well represented in important offices that formulated fiscal policy. In the areas of diplomacy and warfare these *magnati* also performed vital functions on behalf of the republic.[16] The gov-

---

12. It was only during the brief interval that follows the *Ciompi* (1378–82) that this trend was reversed. Cf. N. Rodolico, *I Ciompi* (Florence, 1945), 189–90.

13. In 1344, when the representation of the minor guildsmen was at its height, the Signoria canceled the concessions that Walter of Brienne had made to the workers. Cf. *Atti del Capitano,* 17, f. 72; G. Capponi, *Storia della repubblica di Firenze* (Florence, 1875), 1:245. Minor guildsmen were among the chief proponents of legislation directed against the agricultural workers and laborers hired by the commune. Cf. *P.,* 48, f. 45 (26 September 1360); *Provvisioni Duplicati,* 7, f. 1 (9 February 1347).

14. Ottokar, op. cit., 106–7; M. Becker and G. Brucker, "The *Arti Minori* in Florentine Politics, 1342–1378," *Mediaeval Studies* 18 (1956): 100–101.

15. Cf. N. Ottokar, "Gli scioperati a Firenze nel '300," *Studi storici in onore di Giocchino Volpe* (Florence, 1958), 705–7. For the names of certain of these men who were declared eligible for office, during the decade of the 1360s and 1370s, see *Tratte,* 58, fols. 243ff.

16. The *Camera del Comune,* vols. 2–186 (1342–78), reveal that the *magnati* held approximately one-fourth of the offices that were concerned with these functions. Cf. *Della eccellenza e grandezza della nazione fiorentina* (Florence, 1780), 1ff. Even more significant was the fact that the *magnati* held a similar proportion of

ernment exhibited a like concern toward the Florentine clergy. Affluent members of the greater guilds were committed to the advancement of the ecclesiastical careers of their families and friends and were, therefore, reluctant to risk the alienation of clerical favor.[17] Economic opportunities that stemmed from the close liaison with the Holy See and from the preservation of the Guelf alliance system were other important factors influencing communal policy toward the church.

Since Florentine republicanism came to be closely related to the political hegemony of the guilds, it is essential to recognize that the greater guildsmen who served as Priors of the republic after 1282 represented, in fact, all strata of Florentine society except the working class, which was excluded from participation in the government. The stability and longevity of this political system suggests that the greater guildsmen were extremely mindful of the interests of the diverse segments of communal society. The fact that only the working class can be considered as revolutionary indicates that Florentine republicanism, predicated upon the rule of the *arti,* was able to placate the demands of groups whose constituency lay outside of the corporate structure of the mediaeval guild. This capacity of the Florentine republic to satisfy varied interests was further reinforced by the personal manner in which communal politics was conducted. The Priorate, its councils, and its advisors were composed, for the most part, of influential members of the greater guilds. These men had risen to eminence by winning the adherence of their fellow townsmen in much the same way as the political boss rose to power in the American city of the late nineteenth century. It is, therefore, not surprising to discover that prominent Florentines did not wish to offend or alienate important segments of the public, nor were they likely to forget those who had supported them in their quest for office.[18] This complex of personal relationships was accentuated by the fact that it was difficult to remain anonymous in the mediaeval commune; eco-

---

the offices in the Florentine treasury. On the question of the tax assessment of the nobility, see G. Salvemini, op. cit., 353; *Le consulte della repubblica,* 1:175; *Statuto Capitano (1322–25),* ed. R. Caggese (Florence, 1910), bk. 5, rub. 49.

17. Cf. M. Becker, "Some Economic Implications of the Conflict Between Church and State," *Mediaeval Studies* 21 (1959), 1–16.

18. Cf. the statements of Donato Velluti in *La cronica domestica,* ed. I. del Lungo (Florence, 1914), 163, 222, on the dangers of incurring the enmity of one's fellow citizen as a result of assuming certain political positions on controversial issues. Cf. also M. Becker and G. Brucker, op. cit., 91.

nomic, social, and political affiliations were a matter of public knowledge, and this intimate atmosphere was bound to generate a certain restraint upon the actions of public figures.[19] Typical products of this environment were the chroniclers of fourteenth-century Florence, who
admired most those men who were spokesmen for moderation and
compromise in civic affairs; the records of the advisory councils leave
no doubt that this state of mind was pervasive among those who aided
the governing body (the *Signoria*) in the formulation of communal policy.[20] Those groups and individuals whose political convictions prevented them from searching for compromises on divisive issues were
regarded, by their contemporaries, as intransigent and obdurate foes of
the "good and tranquil state of the commune."[21] That Cicero should
have been selected as a model of political virtue is not inconsistent with
the political ideology of Renaissance Florence.

From this conciliatory environment emerged a fundamental conception of government tending to identify the republican constitution
with satisfaction of the needs of the guilds and their constituency. The
progeny of those guildsmen who had weakened the principal foci of
feudal and ecclesiastical fiscal privilege in the thirteenth century (while
leaving intact certain of the time-honored prerogatives of the first two es-

---

19. Marchionne di Coppo Stefani, *Cronica fiorentina*, ed. N. Rodolico, *Rerum
Italicarum Scriptores*, new ed., 30 (Città di Castello, 1903–55), rub. 685; I. Origo,
The Merchant of Prato (New York, 1957), 48–49, 153; L. Passerini, *Genealogia e sto-
ria della famiglia Ricasoli* (Florence, 1861), 243; Rodolico, op. cit., 95, 188.

20. There was also a strong tendency among the advisors to the Signoria to
avoid all divisive issues, and, therefore, frequent admonitions were made by the
speakers "quod cives reducantur ad unionem et sint uniti." Cf. *Consulte et
Pratiche*, 1, pt. 2, fols. 20–21 (30 July 1351); ibid., 72ff. (9 September 1354). This
moderate point of view was encouraged by the mechanics of the Florentine constitutional system, which required a two-thirds majority for the passage of any
measure. Therefore, this procedure tended to result in the negation of extreme
positions.

21. *Libri Fabarum*, 40, fols. 301ff. (Henceforth this source shall be cited as *L.F.*)
Cf. *P.*, 67, fols. 7r–8r (21 June 1378); Jones, op. cit., 191–92. Compare the opinions
of the advisors to the Signoria on the divisive issue of Ghibellinism with those
of the intemperate leader of the *Parte Guelfa*, Lapo da Castiglionchio. The former urge that the captains proceed "cum temperatione et cum discretione,"
while the latter assumes an antithetical position. Cf. *Consulte et Pratiche*, 2, f. 5r
(12 November 1358); ibid., 15, f. 66 (24 November 1377). For a further analysis
of the political ideology of the eminent decretalist, see R. Davidsohn, "Tre
orazioni di Lapo da Castiglionchio," *Archivio Storico Italiano* 20 (1897): 225–46.

tates) had, in fact, by the beginning of the fourteenth century, created in its stead a more broadly based commercial and economic counterpart.[22] The significance of this development in the area of fiscal policy involved the rejection of the principle that the corporate guilds were liable for taxes, since the republic was authorized only "to maintain and defend the *artifices* and *artes* of the city of Florence."[23] Similarly, the hegemony of the guild system signified the triumph of the principle of indirect over direct taxation; this was particularly beneficial to those who owned extensive real estate within the city. A recent study suggests that two thirds of all communal revenues were acquired through taxes that were regressive and bore more heavily on the poor than on the rich.[24] When additional funds were required by the government, the members of the *arti* tended to favor voluntary loans at high rates of interest.[25] Where monetary policy was concerned, the cloth merchants of the wool guild allowed the *moneta di piccioli* or silver currency to depreciate, with the result that the gold florin rose in value in terms of *piccioli*. This was advantageous to the *lanaiuoli*, since they received payment for their cloth in gold while paying their employees in silver coinage. According to the Statute of the *Podestà*, only the masters of the greater guilds were permitted to use the gold florin as the standard of value in their business transactions and to keep their books in this monetary unit.[26]

The *arti* were also in a position to impose effective controls on ur-

---

22. N. Ottokar, *Studi comunali*, 87; B. Barbadoro, op. cit., 106, 116, 140; R. Davidsohn, *Geschichte von Florenz*, II², 50, 500; *Capitoli*, 25, fols. 143 ff.; ibid., 40, 56ff.; A. Doren, *Le arti fiorentine* (Florence, 1940), 2:229.

23. Fines imposed by the courts on the *arti* were revoked by the *Signoria* on the grounds that the Priorate was obligated "manutenere et defendere artifices et artes civitatis Florentie." Cf. *P.*, 17, f. 111 (25 Sept. 1319). The fact that the Signoria was frequently dependent upon the *arti* for loans, strengthened the political position of the guilds. Cf. *Camera del Comune*, 22, f. 57; *P.*, 11, fols. 41–41r.

24. E. Fiumi, "Sui rapporti tra città e contado," *Archivio Storico Italiano* 114 (1596): 30. There was a strong tendency among the counselors to favor indirect taxation. Cf. *P.*, 7, f. 192 (13 March 1298); *P.*, 36, f. 132r (4 July 1349); *P.*, 45, f. 177 (21 April 1358); Barbadoro, op. cit., 528.

25. *L.F.*, 19. fols. 29–31, 36; *P.*, f. 44, 143 (20 June 1357). Cf. also Stefani, op. cit., rub. 883; N. Rodolico, *La democrazia fiorentina nel suo tramonto, 1378–1382* (Bologna, 1905), 257ff.

26. *Statuti*, 15, bk. 3, f. 16r; M. Becker and G. Brucker, op. cit., 98; R. de Roover, "The Story of the Alberti Company of Florence, 1302–1348, as Revealed in Its Account Books," *Business History Review* 32 (1958): 16.

ban rents and their influence was felt when communal authorities established price ceilings on goods and services.[27] Frequently, they extended the jurisdiction of their own consuls and rectors to encompass
small producers and auxiliary craftsmen. These men were not permitted to make appeals from the decisions of guild officials.[28] In many instances they were also required to post security guaranteeing faithful
execution of their work.[29] Control over the numerous employees of the
wool industry was vested in a "foreign official" elected exclusively by
the masters of the Lana guild. His authority extended over the largest
segment of the city's population, as approximately one-third of the inhabitants depended upon this industry for a livelihood.[30] It is important to note that the actions of this official were not subject to review by
any communal authority and no appeals were permitted from his decisions. Persons convicted in his court were incarcerated in the prison of
the Lana rather than in the jail of the republic.[31] The punishments imposed upon them were much more severe than those dealt out for the
same type of offenses in the communal courts; for example, persons
who were convicted of stealing wool were to be dragged through the
streets of the city and then taken to "the place of justice" to be hanged,
while thefts of meat or grain were simply punished by fines.[32]

The most serious threat to the accrued immunities and privileges
of the guilds during the first half of the fourteenth century was to stem
from the foundation of despotisms. The net effect of this type of regime
was to strengthen the commitment of the greater guildsmen to the principles of republicanism.[33] Charles, duke of Calabria, lord of Florence

27. Doren, op. cit., 2:25–26. For examples of fines against sellers of foodstuffs
who violated communal price ceilings, see *Camera del Comune*, 1 *bis*, f. 120 (April
1323). On the establishment of these ceilings by members of the *arti maggiori*, see
Balìe, 5 (20 October 1349).

28. *P.*, 6, f. 90r (8 August 1296); *Seta*, I, fols. 61, 66–66r (1335).

29. *Statuti originali degli Uffiziali di Grascia*, 2, f. 17 (1375); *Seta*, I, fols. 62–64
(1335).

30. Villani, *Cronica*, 11:94. On the question of the reliability of the statistics
presented in this chronicle, see E. Fiumi, "La demografia fiorentina nelle pagine
di Giovanni Villani," *Archivio Storico Italiano* 108 (1950): 78–158.

31. *Lana*, 5, bk. 1, rub. 16 (1338); *P.*, 22, f. 11r (14 September 1325); *L.F.*, 35, f.
115; *P.*, 48, f. 133 (4 February 1361).

32. Cf. *Archivio del Giudice degli Appelli*, 124, I, f. 88r; IV, f. 16; V, f. 3r.

33. No attempt will be made here to assess the ideological implications of
the failure of Florentine despotisms except to note that in 1329, immediately af-

from 1325 to 1328, reversed the direction of communal fiscal policy when he refused to acknowledge the principle that the guilds were exempt from taxation.[34] He also wrested from the *arti* the fruits of one of their most important legislative victories when the dreaded *estimo* was levied once again upon the lands and capital of the Florentine bankers and merchants. Upon his death in 1328 the *arti maggiori* recaptured control of the Signoria and revoked these enactments.[35] Fourteen years later, with the establishment of the dictatorship of Walter of Brienne, duke of Athens, these alarming measures were again introduced. Communal treasury records covering his brief tenure reveal that this despot, like his predecessor, sought to equalize the tax burden and to recover communal rights and properties from the hands of affluent *popolani grassi* and *magnati*.[36]

Walter of Brienne's policies involved much more than an attempt to achieve a fiscal reformation of the state at the expense of the greater guildsmen. His enactments also had the effect of threatening the delicate social and economic equilibrium that had evolved as a result of

---

ter the republic's bitter experiences with the regime of Charles of Calabria, the councils passed legislation prohibiting the city from ever again submitting to the rule of a despot. Cf. *P.*, 25, f. 51. For a consideration of this problem, see N. Rubinstein, "Florence and the Despots: Some Aspects of Florentine Diplomacy in the Fourteenth Century," *Transactions of the Royal Historical Society*, 5th ser. 2 (1952): 21–45.

34. On 4 February 1326 a tax of 12,000 florins was levied upon the guilds. Cf. *P.*, 23, f. 70r. This tax was repealed shortly after the termination of the despot's tenure. Cf. *P.*, 25, f. 70r (11 October 1329). For a further analysis of the effects of the policies of a *signore* upon the *arti*, see N. Rodolico, *Dal Comune alla Signoria: Saggio sul governo di Taddeo Pepoli in Bologna* (Bologna, 1898), 84ff.

35. Barbadoro, op. cit., 161–64; *P.*, 25, f. 34r (23 January 1329); *L.F.*, 14 f. 28; *P.*, 25, f. 60r (30 August 1329). Revision of the tax system was a commonplace under the rule of the despots. Cf. P. Silva, *Il governo di Pietro Gambacorta in Pisa* (Pisa, 1912), 116–17.

36. On 30 November 1342 Walter of Brienne appointed special officials for the purpose of recovering communal property. They were authorized to keep "unum registrum" in which they were to inscribe all the property and rights ("bona et iura") of the commune. Cf. *Balìe*, 2, fols. 110–12. For condemnation by these officials of individuals who had usurped the property of the state, see ibid., 2, f. 165 (30 March 1343). For fines levied against the powerful Adimari and Rossi families by these officials on the same charge, see *Camera del Comune*, 1 *bis*, fols. 249, 276 (18 April, 14 May 1343). On the establishment of the *estimo* by Walter of Brienne, see Barbadoro, op. cit., 210–11.

three generations of guild hegemony. During those protracted intervals when the Signoria had been the exclusive preserve of the guild masters, the *arti maggiori* had used their political power to reinforce their social and economic primacy over Florentine life. Small masters, such as the dyers, had been consistently denied political representation, and workers had been restrained from forming any *fratellanza* (brotherhood)— even for religious purposes. The greater guildsmen had come to regard these brotherhoods of *sottoposti,* or workers, as conspiracies in restraint of trade, since this type of organization—a combination of labor union and religious fraternity—could be utilized to secure wage increases.[37] Now, under the rule of the despot, certain small masters and highly skilled artisans were, for the first time, permitted to participate in communal affairs and they were also granted autonomy in economic matters. The wool workers were removed from the purview of the Lana guild's "foreign official" and allowed to form their own association; these *minuti* were then organized into military brigades and a coat-of-arms was bestowed upon them by the despot.[38] Long after the fall of Walter of Brienne, the memory of these concessions served as a stimulus for revolutionary ardor, and the discontented *minuti* rallied under this coat-of-arms when they made their bid for power in 1378. Even the name Ciompi, assumed by these revolutionaries, had been given them by the duke's retainers.[39]

Vintners, sellers of oil, small retail food merchants, and venders of fresh meat were also beneficiaries of ducal largesse when they received major tax reductions.[40] Even more significant, from the point of view of these men, was the fact that the duke suspended the price ceilings on the commodities which they handled.[41] By elevating a cask maker and

37. Cf. N. Rodolico, *Il Popolo Minuto, 1343–1378* (Bologna, 1899), 15–22; R. de Roover, "The Concept of the Just Price: Theory and Economic Policy," *Journal of Economic History* 18, 4 (December 1958): 433–34.

38. *Camera del Comune,* 1 *bis,* f. 22r (16 November 1342). This source cites the appointment of "Ser Giovanni Bartholini de Montefalcani offitialis scardesseriorum" by Brienne. Cf. also ibid., f. 57 (21 December 1342). This evidence supports the statements made by the chroniclers G. Villani (12:8) and Stefani (rub. 565) on this question.

39. Rodolico, *I Ciompi,* 142.

40. Cf. *Balìe,* 2, fols. 14–15, 24–25.

41. Cf. M. Becker, "La esecuzione della legislatura contro le pratiche monopolistiche delle arti fiorentine alla metà del secolo quattordicesimo," *Archivio Storico Italiano* 117 (1959): 13–15.

an ironmonger to the highest communal magistracy and by selecting a dealer in used clothing to become *gonfaloniere di giustitia,* the despot conferred unaccustomed status upon this class.[42]

The years immediately following the ouster of Walter of Brienne reveal that certain forces, which the despot had encouraged, tended to gain momentum and to challenge seriously the nexus between Florentine republicanism and the absolute hegemony of the greater guilds. The revolutions of 1343, directed first at the duke and then at a coalition of bourgeois and noble oligarchs, brought to the fore large numbers of new citizens who had played a decisive part in these movements. One of the most important "social facts" concerning communal history is the influence of mass migrations upon the politics of the republic. Demographers agree that the upsurge of Florentine population until the advent of the Black Death was staggering. The "democratic interlude" from 1349 to 1382 witnessed another startling advance. From 1382 until the coming of the Medici in 1434 this influx declined appreciably. Before attempting to assess the effect that these newcomers were to have upon politics. It should be noted that only those *novi cives* from the most affluent strata of communal society were granted representation in 1343.[43] We should, therefore, not expect a sharp reversal of communal economic policy nor should we anticipate any concerted attack upon the interests of the greater guilds by these newcomers. Rather, what is to occur can be described as the emergence of an impersonal political force that is to have a decisive effect upon the republican Signoria.

Despotism had proven to be an ephemeral device in the matter of protecting certain of the greater guildsmen from the claims of their creditors. The Acciaiuoli, Bardi, Baroncelli, Del Bene, Compagni, Peruzzi, and Villani were represented among the three hundred individuals declared bankrupt by the Court Merchant shortly after 1343.[44] This series

---

42. *Tratte,* 92.

43. For recent studies on Florentine demography, see E. Fiumi, op. cit., 78–158; P. Battara, *La popolazione di Firenze alla metà dei '500* (Florence, 1935).

The tax assessments of the *novi cives* who held office at this time stood in a ratio of five to six and a half in comparison to those imposed upon members of the urban patriciate. This ratio is based upon a study of the *estimi* and *prestanze* that survive for the *Trecento.* The holdings of the *novi cives* in the *Monte* of 1345 averaged the considerable sum of fifty-seven florins. Cf. Becker and Brucker, op. cit., 101.

44. *Tratte,* 1155. This source contains the names of all bankrupts from the let-

of events had the effect of accelerating the political mobility of the *novi cives*, and large numbers of these newcomers entered the government, where they remained a vital force in civic affairs until the oligarchical reaction of 1382.

Before 1343 the rule of the *arti maggiori* had been characterized by its attempt to modify certain feudal privileges and immunities of thirteenth-century society and to institutionalize their own socioeconomic prerogatives. Under the aegis of the republican Signoria they strived to make the guild a law unto itself.[45] A half-century of communal history (1293–1342) had witnessed the emergence of a guild plutocracy that had intermarried with the nobility and had obtained a virtual monopoly of high church offices. Their status was solidified as a result of important tax concessions, grants of judicial dispensation, and close ties with prestige-worthy organizations such as the *Parte Guelfa*. Now, for the first time, in 1343 large numbers of *novi cives* entered the Signoria and significant innovations occurred in the character of the republican state. In part these changes stemmed from the social background of these newcomers. As a class, they did not have extensive personal commitments or family connections with the older urban patriciate; they were, therefore, in a position to pursue their objectives with greater freedom, as they were not burdened with traditional ties and obligations. Their activities in the direction of reform were further stimulated by the desperate condition of communal finances. During times of crises there was a strong tendency, evident throughout Florentine history, to strengthen the impersonal machinery of state at the expense of the interests of the urban patriciate. When the electoral base of the republic was broadened, the newly elected representatives directed their efforts toward eradication of the abuses and frauds prevalent under the preceding regime. This entailed systematic collection of taxes and *prestanze*, extension of communal jurisdiction, equalization of the incidence of communal levies, and strict enforcement of the law against the *potentes*.[46] The *novi cives* were also unsympathetic

---

ter *A* through *S* and was to be utilized for the purpose of barring these "falliti" from communal office. The *Atti del Podestà* and the *Camera del Comune* contain additional names.

45. Cf. Becker, op. cit., 8–28.

46. Cf. N. Ottokar, *Il Comune di Firenze*, 278; *P.*, 33, f. 43 (13 May 1345); *P.*, 32, f. 171r (27 May 1344); *P.*, 32, f. 163r (14 May 1344); *Provvisioni Duplicati*, 6, f. 29 (27 March 1346); ibid., 6, f. 43 (11 April 1346). The same type of legislation was passed during intervals when Florence was engaged in warfare. It may well be

to the numerous petitions traditionally presented by those who sought special favor and preferential treatment.[47]

In the fulfillment of their objectives the *novi cives* were aided by the fact that both of the political factions vying for power at this time needed their support.[48] This encouraged the trend toward impersonal government, and the results are reflected in communal policies concerning the church, the nobility, and the *Parte Guelfa*. In each instance the machinery of the government was strengthened at the expense of the time-honored prerogatives of these privileged groups. For the first time in communal history a concerted attack was made upon the "liberties" of the church; this involved an assault upon the fiscal and juridical immunities of the clergy which inadvertently augmented the authority of the republic.[49] Similarly, a sustained effort was made to impose severe limits upon the influence of the nobility; not only were their actions subject to close review by the magistrates of the republic, but the rectors of the city actively sought to recover those communal rights and properties which had fallen into the hands of the *magnati*.[50] The power and the composi-

---

that the exigencies of the republic's military involvements were decisive in preventing the withering away of the state, since the Signoria could not afford to overlook any potential source of revenue. Cf. *Consulte et Pratiche*, vols. 3–4, covering the Pisan War (1362–64).

47. Private petitions received unsympathetic treatment by Signoria from 1343 to 1348. Cf. *P.*, vols. 32–36. With the displacement of many *novi cives* and *minori* from office as a result of the oligarchical reaction, this tendency was reversed. Special requests for dispensation from judicial verdicts were granted to members of the Adimari, Bondelmonti, Ricasoli, Boscoli, Pazzi, Medici, Bordoni, Gherardini, and other important families at this time. Cf. *P.*, vols. 36–42; *Camera del Comune*, 33–34. Quantitatively, however, these remissions do not approach those that were to be granted by the *Signorie* between the end of the *Trecento* and the advent of the Medici.

48. Donato Velluti, 242; Stefani, rub. 734.

49. A. Panella, "Politica ecclesiastica del comune fiorentino," *Archivio Storico Italiano* 2, no. 4 (1913): 281–365. The Signoria was aided in its efforts by the support of certain of the urban patricians, who wanted to avoid making restitution to their ecclesiastical creditors.

50. Condemnations on the charge of occupying the property of the republic (1343–47), were frequently reversed after 1348. Cf. n. 38; *Camera del Comune*, 33, fols. 99ff.; ibid., 34, fols. 150ff. Cf. *Provisioni Duplicati*, 5, f. 64 (13 May 1345), for the measure calculated to recover "bona et iura Comunis Florentie" so that the city might have revenue in order to live "in libertate et iustitia." Cf. also ibid., 6, f. 43 (11 April 1346), for a bill authorizing election of special officials to prevent

tion of the Florentine nobility was also materially altered when the regime granted certain nobles important political concessions in return for substantial payments into the treasury and renunciation of their clan affiliations.[51] Legislation until 1382 was characterized by persistent attempts to buttress the Signoria by discouraging private loyalties and undermining the political influence of the great families—both noble and commoner. A striking instance occurred in 1372, when a special commission with extraordinary powers was founded to preserve the state from the encroachments of the great clans. The bestowal of power upon the *Dieci della Libertà* was justified on the grounds that freedom is of inestimable value.[52] The *novi cives* and their patrician sympathizers (public spirited and opportunistic alike) also sought to curb the influence of the *Parte Guelfa*—that stronghold of the Florentine aristocracy—by reviewing their accounts, judging their officials, and compelling the *Parte* to grant the newcomers representation in their organization.[53] The total effect of these enactments was to encourage the shift of the center of political gravity from the great families into the orbit of the state and thus to negate one of the principal threats to Florentine republicanism.

Until the last decades of the fourteenth century the primary props of the republic had been the great guilds and the *novi cives*. In their different ways they had acted to perpetuate the state and to prevent it from becoming the private preserve of a single family. The organism that they

---

perpetration of frauds in communal affairs. On the syndication of *magnati*, see P., 32, f. 73 (14 November 1343); L.F., 24, fols. 5–6, 7r–8, 10.

51. Cf. G. Villani, 12:23; Stefani, rub. 595. These concessions involved the conferring of *popolano* status upon certain *magnati* and were encouraged by two factors: the need of the republic for revenue and the desire of the Signoria to weaken the power of the great noble families. Cf. P., 33, fols. 1ff.

52. Cf. P., 60, f. 2r (1 April 1372). The creation of this *balìa* was calculated to check the political encroachments of the Ricci and Albizzi families and was regarded as the "pretio libertatis popoli et Comunis Florentie." Filippo di Cionetto Bastari's speech recorded in the chronicle of Stefani (rub. 731), is substantially the same as the one recorded in the *Consulte et Pratiche*, 12, f. 10 (10 March 1372). It is an impassioned plea for liberty and is directed against the great houses that threaten to enslave the citizenry of Florence.

53. For the election of officials authorized to review the accounts and the actions of the *Parte*, see P., 38, f. 226 (10 June 1351); P., 39, f. 15r (28 August 1351). For a discussion of pressures contributing toward admission of *novi cives* into the *Parte*, see U. Dorini, *Notizie storiche sull' università di Parte Guelfa in Firenze* (Florence, 1902), 28–29. For petitions presented to the Signoria requesting admission to the *Parte*, see L.F., 30, f. 13 (21 October 1349); L.F., 31, f. 52 (8 February 1352).

had created had been provided with an effective bureaucracy giving a further tone of impersonality to the life of the state. The authority of the republic had come to extend much further into the recesses of Florentine life than had been the case a century before. The passage of time had witnessed the erosion of many of the ancient prerogatives that the feudal nobility and the church had enjoyed. The fruits of the work of the various Florentine governments of the fourteenth century can, therefore, best be described by the term *territorial state.*

The early fifteenth century saw the decline of the *arti* and the reduction of the influx of the *novi cives.* With the deterioration of the influence of these two forces in Florentine politics, republicanism began to lose its accustomed vigor. Control of the "territorial state" was gradually falling into the hands of the great families. The incidence of a general European economic decline had an adverse effect upon migration and the birthrate. It may also have encouraged the guilds to abandon their quest for autonomy in favor of the paternalistic protection of the emerging Medicean rule.[54]

The decline of Florentine republicanism (1382–1434) was a complex process. Impersonal forces tending to distinguish between public law and private privilege coexisted with government by special favor and private petition.[55] Vying for political hegemony over affairs of state

---

54. For requests to the Signoria by the consuls of the *Arte della Lana* for an increase in the tax upon foreign cloth imports, see *L.F.,* 51, f. 203 (30 May 1418); ibid., f. 206r (9 June 1418). For a discussion of the demands of the *arti maggiori* for protection from foreign competition, see G. Scaramella, *Firenze allo Scoppio del Tumulto dei Ciompi* (Pisa, 1914), 33–34; *Capitoli,* 13, f. 30. On the decline of the *Lana* itself, see R. Davidsohn, "Blüte und Niedergang der Florentiner Tuchindustrie," *Zeitschrift für die gesamte Staatswissenschaft* 85 (1928): 225–55. The decline of the autonomy of the guilds and the loss of certain of their juridical functions under the Signoria of the Medici in the fifteenth century is discussed by A. Doren in his *Die Florentiner Wollentuchindustrie* (Stuttgart, 1901), 412ff.; and in his *Le arti fiorentine* (Florence, 1940), 2:44–45.

I wish to thank Wallace K. Ferguson for permitting me to read his manuscript entitled "Recent Trends in the Economic History of the Renaissance." For a further discussion of this subject, see M. Postan, "Rapport: Histoire economique du moyen âge," *IXe Congres International des Sciences Historiques* (Paris, 1950), 1:225–41; *Relazioni del X Congresso Internazionale de Scienze Storiche* (Florence, 1957), 3:655–811.

55. The *Libri Fabarum* of the late fourteenth and early fifteenth centuries show that there was a marked increase in the number of petitions presented by

were certain of the powerful clans who sought to reconcile, however pragmatically, these two antithetical forces. No longer were the *novi cives* or those autonomous units of power, the guilds, in a position to serve as a rallying point for the dissident. Until the end of the Trecento there had always been a faction within the republic which had stood as a barrier against the rule of any single family. This faction, composed of idealists and political opportunists alike, was dependent upon the existence of a class or a group (the *novi cives* or the *arti*) intent upon using the state as a vehicle for advancing their own social status, economic position, or political power. When these dynamic forces were debilitated, the possibility of a government controlled by a great clan loomed ever larger.

Such Florentine humanists as Salutati, Bruni, and Poggio may be regarded as the intellectual heirs of the *novi cives* and the *arti*. But it is possible to suggest that by the fifteenth century, the defense of republicanism was passing from the plane of internal politics to the realm of foreign policy and the history of ideas.

---

affluent citizens requesting dispensation from the law or preferential treatment in the matter of taxation. Cf. especially vol. 49 (1411–12); also refer to n. 47.

4

Church and State in Florence on the Eve of the Renaissance (1343–1382)

The surviving records of the meetings of the Florentine Signoria from the overthrow of the despotism of Walter of Brienne in 1343 until the oligarchical reaction to the rule of the twenty-one guilds in 1382 reveal that, of all the questions faced by the counselors, the one most certain to provoke bitter and protracted debate was that of the commune's relationship with the church. And yet, except for the studies of Antonio Panella, which treat only a small portion of the interval, this problem remains unexplored.[1] The present inquiry will examine this question for these crucial four decades when communal politics was in the process of being democratized. *Novi cives* were entering public life on an unprecedented scale and the authority of the popular government (*status popularis*) was extended into the farthest recesses of the political community.[2] Ancient liberties, prerogatives, and immunities, rooted in communal life, tended to erode, and we witness the emergence of a new political form—the territorial state. The institution most affected by this transformation was the church, and by the end of the Trecento it had been shorn of many of its

---

From *Speculum* 37 (1962): 509–27.

1. "Politica ecclesiastica del comune fiorentino," *Archivio Storico Italiano* 2, no. 4 (1913): 271–370; "La guerra degli Otto Santi e le vicende della legge contro i vescovi," ibid., XCIX (1941), 36–49; *Storia di Firenze* (Florence, 1949), 107–21.

2. The term *new citizens*, or *novi cives*, is employed in this paper to describe those men who were the first of their clan to hold high communal office. They were drawn from the most affluent strata of Florentine society and their holdings in the *Monte* (funded communal debt) averaged the considerable sum of fifty-seven florins. The tax assessments of the *novi cives* who held office at this particular time stood in a ratio of five to six and a half in comparison to those imposed upon members of the urban patriciate. Cf. M. B. Becker, "The Republican City State in Florence: An Inquiry into Its Origin and Survival (1280–1434)," *Speculum*, XXXV (1960), 46–47.

mediaeval privileges. It was in this secularized milieu that the political consciousness of the early Renaissance humanists was nurtured.

I

At the beginning of the 1340s a series of events, both foreign and domestic, generated severe tensions between the Florentine government and the church. The fiscal plight of the commune was desperate, and, therefore, the Signoria could ill afford to overlook any potential source of revenue. This meant that enmity between church and state was bound to arise over such issues as the right of the Signoria to tax the clergy and the prerogatives of communal courts over ecclesiastical matters.[3] Discord also mounted when the republic advised the papacy that it was no longer possible for Florence to act as the financial fulcrum of the Guelf alliance system against the Ghibelline Roman emperor. In the past the commune had spent "innumerabiles pecunie" in an effort to render service to the church; as a result of this generosity, it was now deeply in debt.[4] A further source of friction arose because Clement VI had given his enthusiastic support to the very unpopular despotism of Walter of Brienne (1342–43). Even after the overthrow of this much despised tyrant by the Florentines, the pope persisted in championing Bri-

---

3. *Missive*, 5, fols. 2–5 (14 October 1340); f. 20 (26 April 1341). (The documents cited in this article are to be found in the *Archivio di Stato* in Florence.) On 11 January 1342 the Signoria was compelled to suspend repayment on certain government loans. Cf. *Libri Fabarum*, 24, f. 46. (Henceforth this source will be abbreviated as *L. F.*) On 17 August 1342 the government was authorized to suspend the assignment of certain revenues to creditors of the commune and the interest rate on the public debt was substantially reduced. Cf. *Provvisioni Duplicati*, 3, f. 15. (Henceforth this source will be abbreviated as *P. D.*)

4. *Missive*, 5, fols. 98–99 (16 October 1340). In another letter dispatched shortly thereafter to the king of Naples, the Signoria informed her old friend that if Florence's Guelf allies of long standing did not come to her defense and assist her in preserving her *libertà*, she would be compelled to seek "other friends" in the camp of the Ghibellines. It was at this juncture that the republic sent ambassadors to the imperial court of Lewis the Bavarian. Cf. A. Sapori, *La crisi delle compagnie mercantili dei Bardi e dei Peruzzi* (Florence, 1926), pp. 141–42; G. Villani, *Cronica*, ed. F. Dragomani (Florence, 1844), XI, 137. See also King Robert's letter to the Florentines in which he reproves them for not consulting with him on their military policies. Cf. C. Paoli, *Della signoria di Gualtieri duca d' Atene in Firenze* (Florence, 1862), p. 63.

enne's hopeless cause.[5] A still more significant factor in precipitating conflict between the city's mercantile patriciate and the Holy See was the pope's desertion of the Florentine banking companies in their hour of financial need; in this way he inadvertently intensified the impending banking crisis. He then compounded this injury when he demanded that the ecclesiastical creditors of these companies be granted preferential treatment. When Avignon sought to use both the church courts and the inquisitorial tribunals to press the claims of clerical depositors, the patriciate denied that these ecclesiastical agencies had any authority in matters such as these. But, without the active support of the new citizens (*novi cives*), this disclaimer could not have been implemented into communal law and the patrician protest would have been ineffectual.

Earlier actions of the *novi cives* indicate that they were very willing to cooperate in enacting programs designed to modify drastically the republic's policies toward the church. This had occurred in 1250–60 and in 1293–95 and now in the fourteenth century history was to repeat itself. The short-lived popular regime of 1328–29 was a precursor of things to come. On 8 December of that year the communal councils passed legislation prohibiting citizens from submitting to the jurisdiction of ecclesiastical courts.[6] At the same session the councils authorized the Signoria to secure money from the clergy for the purpose of furthering the construction of the city walls.[7] Early in the following year communal syndics were selected who were empowered to compel the clergy to make loans to the treasury of the republic.[8] A few months later the Signoria appointed another group of syndics to beseech the bishop of Florence to revoke certain sections of the new episcopal constitution that challenged communal prerogatives. Shortly thereafter a provision was enacted to preserve "libertatem civitatem Florentie" from encroachments of this kind.[9] With the displacement of many of the *novi*

---

5. L. Leoni, "Breve di Clemente VI in favore di Gualtieri di Brienne, duca d' Atene," *Archivio Storico Italiano*, xxii (1875), 181–82.

6. *Provvisioni Protocoli*, 6, fols. 252–53.

7. Ibid., f. 252.

8. *L. F.*, 13, ii, f. 101 (15 March 1329).

9. Ibid., f. 16 (8 July 1329). During the same month further efforts were made by the government to strengthen the jurisdiction of communal courts at the expense of clerical tribunals. Cf. *L. F.*, 14, fols. 18r–20; *Provvisioni*, 25, fols. 51r–52 (27 July 1329). (Henceforth this source will be abbreviated as *P.*) In August relations between the bishop and the Signoria began to improve and while

cives from office, the popular government lost its vigor and the patriciate, who dominated the Signoria during the 1330s, ceased to call for the passage of measures of this type.

An analysis of the political behavior of the *novi cives* during the Dugento and the first part of the Trecento suggests that these men were, in fact, enthusiastic in their support of communal efforts to curb clerical prerogatives. When the patriciate took the same stand after 1343, it is not in the least surprising to discover that the *novi cives* were among their chief allies. Specifically, this involved cooperating in the enactment of two provisions: the first canceled clerical immunity from lay jurisdiction and imposed the penalty of banishment upon clerics who violated this law; the second had the effect of invalidating any verdict of an ecclesiastical tribunal that was favorable to the clerical creditors of the great Florentine banking companies.[10] During the crucial years between 1343 and 1346 the adherence of the *novi cives* was indispensable for the passage of this legislation, since they held approximately one-half of the seats in the Signoria, and by law a two-thirds majority was required for the enactment of any provision. The fact that, for the first time in communal history, two pieces of legislation "pro conservatione libertatis Florentie" were initiated by petitions of the captains of the seven major and fourteen minor guilds indicates that support for these measures was pervasive throughout the city's artisan and shopkeeper class as well as within the ranks of the mercantile patriciate and the *novi cives*. Giovanni Villani, an eyewitness to these events, states categorically in his chronicle that the motive animating the representatives of the lesser guilds to press for the enactment of these laws against the *libertà* of the church stemmed from a realization by the lower orders that "certain wicked clerics from noble

---

there were divisive issues, such as the appropriation of church property by certain great families, neither the *Libri Fabarum* nor the *Provvisioni* contain any record of legislation against ecclesiastical liberties for the decade of the 1330s.

10. A. Panella, op. cit., pp. 327–65. Spokesmen for the enactment of 1345 were Pepo Frescobaldi, a scion of the famous magnate and banking family, and Ser Francesco Vermigli, a notary new to the Florentine political scene. Cf. *P. D.*, 5, f. 54; *L. F.*, 24, f. 39r. The men who favored the measure of 1346 were Buto Guido, a stationer and a *novus homo*, and Lorenzo Sassolini, whose family had been firmly established in the Florentine business community since the decade of the 1280's. Cf. *Archivio Notarile*, C. 102, fols. 4r, 24; *P. D.*, 6, f. 35; *P.*, 34, fols. 24r–25. Lorenzo had been active in communal politics for several years. Cf. *L. F.*, 15, fols. 13r–14; 17, f. 34r.

and powerful *popolani* families, under the guise of ecclesiastical immunity, had done evil things to the weak laymen."[11] Both the Florentine chronicler Stefani and the anonymous author of a *Priorista* concur in this judgment.[12] It would appear, then, that two important factors encouraged the lesser guildsmen and the newcomers to support legislation that adversely affected the juridical prerogatives of the church. First, there was the pervasive suspicion that the ecclesiastical courts were being utilized by the great families to exploit their social inferiors, and, second, there was the resentment of the newer citizens toward a clerical hierarchy exclusively staffed by the scions of these ancient clans. Similar anxieties had been displayed several years before by the urban patriciate when they came to feel that their superiors, the great feudatories of the *contado,* were exercising an inordinate influence over the Tuscan church. A law was passed at that time and incorporated into the Florentine statutes prohibiting the elevation of such *magnati* as the Counts Guidi, the Alberti, the Pazzi of Valdarno, the Ubaldini, and the Ubertini to the bishopric of either Florence or Fiesole.[13] Attempts to limit the authority of the great families over the church were to become a regular feature of Florentine politics during eras when regimes were democratized by the admission of new men into the Signoria.

A serious decline in the city's revenue during 1343, the inability of the commune to meet its immediate financial obligations, and the incidence of rioting among the populace when new taxes were levied were additional factors that caused the Signoria to contest ecclesiastical authority in other areas. Now, between 1343 and 1345, the government enacted legislation of an unprecedented character that went far beyond the traditional remedy of taxing the clergy.[14] With the almost unanimous

---

11. G. Villani, XII, 43.

12. Cf. Marchionne de Coppo Stefani, *Cronica fiorentina,* ed. N. Rodolico, *Rerum Italicarum Scriptores,* new ed., XXX (Città di Castello, 1903–55), rub. 616; and *Priorista* quoted by N. Rodolico in *I Ciompi* (Florence, 1945), p. 42.

13. *Statuti della repubblica fiorentina,* ed. R. Caggese (Florence, 1910–1921), vol. 1, bk. V, p. 78. Legislation was also passed that prohibited any person subject to communal jurisdiction from marrying into the great feudal families of the *contado.* Cf. ibid., V, 98. In the late Trecento it was necessary for those who wished to contract such marriages to petition the Signoria for permission. For examples of this type of request, see P., 77, f. 133 (27 August 1388); P., 80, f. 84 (17 August 1391).

14. For a full treatment of the laws passed during this period, see B. Barbadoro, *Le finanze della repubblica fiorentina* (Florence, 1929), pp. 629–64. Cf. also

support of the Councils of the People and the Captain, the Signoria founded the *Monte* by consolidating the public debt; communal credits were declared unredeemable; however, the creditors were to receive interest, and the shares were made negotiable. Vigorous exception was taken to these enactments by certain segments of the clergy on the grounds that these actions constituted a violation of canon law on the subject of usury.[15] But this deterred the Signoria neither from establishing the *Monte* nor from expanding the scope of its operations. By taking this step the communal treasury was freed from the obligation of repaying over a half-million florins of principal by simply guaranteeing the creditors 5 percent interest each year. This government, unlike its predecessors, did not even take the precaution of making special provision for the spiritual welfare of those to whom it paid interest. Prior to 1343 the commune had appointed officials for the specific purpose of granting remission of the sin of usury to those who had accepted the interest on government loans. This type of pardon or remission was not uncommon in borderline cases that involved the twilight zone between legitimate profit and usury. In the past when the government had borrowed money it had taken cognizance of the existence of this delicate problem.[16] Now with the founding of the *Monte*—a radical step taken in the face of strong ecclesiastical opposition—the Signoria ignored the traditional remedy. Later, when great pressure was exerted upon the commune to cancel a variety of ordinances and statutes that the church considered to be detrimental to the Catholic faith, the Signoria agreed to comply in all instances except that of the revocation of legislation pertaining to the *Monte*.[17]

Fiscal pressures and the broadening of the political base of the republic resulted, as they had in the past, in the strengthening of the

---

P. D., 5, f. 47 (9 March 1345); P. D., 7, f. 52r (20 June 1347); P., 216, f. 163 (7 August 1342).

15. The vote on the founding of the *Monte* in the Council of the Captain was 199 in favor and 9 opposed. In the Council of the Podestà 202 voted for it while 12 were opposed. Cf. L. F., 24, f. 83 (11 October 1345); M. B. Becker, "Some Economic Implications of the Conflict Between Church and State in *Trecento* Florence," *Mediaeval Studies*, XXI (1959), 9–10; R. de Roover, "I. trattato di fra Santi Rucellai sul cambio, il monte comune e il monte delle doti," *Archivio Storico Italiano*, CXI (1953), 3–23; J. T. Noonan, Jr., *The Scholastic Analysis of Usury* (Cambridge, Mass., 1957), 121–28.

16. M. B. Becker, op. cit., 10–11.

17. *Balìe*, 16, f. 7r (1 September 1378).

power of the state at the expense of certain time-honored interests. A note of impartiality was again injected into communal politics that revealed itself in the attempts of the government to recover state property. The Signoria then proceeded to punish members of the former administration who had committed frauds and abuses as well as to systematize the collection of taxes and to tighten the controls over the disbursement of public funds. The most significant manifestation of this impartial trend, as far as the church was concerned, involved the enactment of a law that established severe penalties against any citizen who occupied ecclesiastical property illegally.[18] By taking this step in 1344, the popular Signoria, like its predecessors (1250–60, 1293–95, and 1328–29), demonstrated a concern for the enforcement of what Nicola Ottokar, the Florentine historian, has termed "le norme comuni della vita," as opposed to appeals to force, violence, and extralegal authority on the part of the "magnates" and "potentes." The fact that the Signoria sought to contain the power of the great families over church matters indicates that the ideals of impartial administrative practice had some force and that this regime was motivated by concerns transcending mere anticlericalism.[19]

The major Florentine chroniclers and men of letters were bitter critics of the popular regime. The policies that had been initiated by the Signoria on ecclesiastical questions were judged to be "cruel and harsh" by Giovanni Villani. He contended that the great banking companies and the *novi cives* had been responsible for the passage of legislation that clearly violated the ancient liberties of the church.[20] He was also shocked by the singular lack of regard that the Signoria had shown for other traditionally venerated institutions and individuals. But he reserved his sharpest invective for those Florentines who lacked a com-

---

18. *P.*, 33, fols. 18r–19; *L. F.*, 23, f. 28 (19 June 1344). This measure was counseled by a newcomer, Naldo Nozzi, a swordmaker.

19. M. B. Becker, op. cit., 11–12. Cf. also N. Ottokar, *Studi comunali e fiorentini* (Florence, 1948), 86; *Il comune di Firenze alla fine del dugento* (Florence, 1926), 278. Comparable measures were enacted by *il primo popolo* during the middle years of the thirteenth century. Cf. R. Davidsohn, *Storia di Firenze* (Florence, 1957), II-1, 630–31.

20. G. Villani, XII, 43. For a consideration of the attitude of other chroniclers and men of letters toward the *Signoria* at this time, see G. A. Brucker and M. B. Becker, "The *Arti Minori* in Florentine Politics, 1342–1378," *Mediaeval Studies*, XVIII (1956), 93–94.

mitment to the time-honored Guelf principles of loyalty to the papacy
and its ally, the kingdom of Naples.[21] The actions of the Guelf Party of
Florence during the years 1346–47 reveal that a large segment of the
membership of this powerful organization shared the opinions of the
chronicler. A campaign of vilification was launched against the Signoria
and charges of Ghibellinism were recklessly hurled at its members. Accusations of disloyalty to the church and her Guelf allies were now to
become a regular and unfortunate feature of Florentine politics. By 1347
the Signoria was considerably weakened by attacks of this type and
many of the new men were compelled to relinquish public office.[22]
Meanwhile there was a rapprochement between the urban patriciate
and the papacy; the Florentine banking houses began to pay the claims
of their ecclesiastical creditors, and the interdict that the church had laid
upon the city was lifted. Once again the papacy began to avail itself of
the resources and services the Florentine companies were so admirably
equipped to offer. It would follow that these bankers, well represented
in the new government established in 1347–48, were, therefore, not anxious to antagonize Avignon. The Curia, bent upon the reconquest of the
Patrimony, was also well aware of the advantages to be gained from a
closer liaison with Florence. The issue of papal support for the claims of
Walter of Brienne against the Florentines lost its bitter edge and receded
into the background. Impetus was given to this newly established accord when Clement VI removed the much hated Tuscan inquisitor,

---

21. G. Villani, XII, 116. The new regime concentrated its energies upon recovering the territories Florence had lost as a result of the disasters of 1341–43.
The Signoria also sought security in a series of regional alliances. Cf. N. Rubinstein, "Florence and the Despots: Some Aspects of Florentine Diplomacy in the
Fourteenth Century," *Transactions of the Royal Historical Society*, 5th series, II (1952),
38–46.

22. Some of these men specifically mentioned in the documents were
Lorenzo Bonacursi, a retail cloth merchant; Gallo di Rossi and Jacopo Faloci of
Poggibonsi; Neruccio, a hosier, and Francesco Guerii, a consul of the carpenter's
guild. Cf. *Camera del Comune*, 23, fols. 17r–18 (13 October 1347); 22, f. 61r (21 July
1347); 25, f. 78r (7 February 1348); 25, f. 86 (15 February 1348). (Henceforth this
source will be abbreviated as *Cam.*) In addition to these new men, Uberto In-
fanghati, member of a famous banking family, was condemned as a Ghibelline
and compelled to relinquish public office. However, unlike the *novi cives*, he was
reinstated and two years later was chosen *Gonfaloniere* of the republic and
shortly thereafter he was elected consul of the banker's guild. Cf. *Cam.*, 20, fols.
20–20r (24 April 1347).

Piertro dell' Aquila, and appointed a citizen of Florence who had been highly recommended by the Signoria.[23]

II

The amity that prevailed between church and state in the years immediately following the Black Death was, at best, an uneasy truce. While the patricians who sat in the Signoria were more respectful of the traditional privileges of the clergy, this attitude was to undergo certain basic modifications as a consequence of changes taking place in the area of foreign relations. The effect of these mutations was to cause deep fissures in the ranks of the patriciate itself. The republic's position was being seriously threatened by the reassertion of papal power in central Italy and the extension of Milanese hegemony in the north. At the same time that Cardinal Albornoz was subduing Florence's southern neighbors, the Visconti were pressing their claims in the Romagna. Sharp differences of opinion were expressed by the advisors to the Signoria concerning policies to be pursued by the beleagured republic. The pope called upon Florence to aid him in the reconquest of the Papal States, but eminent citizens such as Simone Peruzzi and Pino Rossi stated that they were reluctant to see the Signoria jeopardize the commune's relations with Milan.[24] And yet, if the papacy was to succeed in reestablishing its primacy over the Patrimony, it required the assistance of her longtime Guelf allies against the Ghibelline *signori* of Milan. If Florence gave the requisite help, however, it ran the risk of being annihilated by the Visconti of Milan. During the decade of the 1350s, even intensely pro-papal Florentines such as Piero degli Albizzi recognized this danger; in 1358 he counseled the Signoria to assist the papal legate on the condition that the peace with Milan was not to be violated.[25] At this time the dominant note in the debates on foreign policy reflected the keen de-

23. M. B. Becker, "Florentine Politics and the Diffusion of Heresy in the Trecento," *Speculum*, XXXIV (1959), 69.

24. *Consulte et Pratiche*, 2, f. 179 (13 March 1360). (Henceforth this source will be abbreviated as *C. P.*) For a discussion of the division among the citizenry on other foreign policy questions, see M. Villani, *Cronica*, ed. F. Dragomani (Florence, 1844), XIII, 13; *C. P.*, 1, part 2, fols. 23–24 (13 January 1354). For a general treatment of Milanese foreign policy at this time, see A. Sorbelli, *La signoria di Giovanni Visconti a Bologna e le sue relazione con la Toscana* (Bologna, 1901).

25. *C. P.*, 2, f. 11 (26 November 1358).

sire of the communal counselors to preserve a strict neutrality in Italian affairs. These men frequently admonished the Signoria to follow a course of action that would permit the city to continue "in libertate," and under no circumstances were the priors to do fealty "to any lord, lay or ecclesiastic."[26] All possible steps were to be taken "pro defensione libertatis comunis Florentie" by the government, and the counselors enjoined the Signoria not to seek an alliance with anyone.[27] There was a strong antipathy among the members of the Signoria against making any fiscal commitments to the republic's old Guelf allies—the papacy and the Kingdom of Naples.[28] These isolationist sentiments continued into the early years of the next decade, and even such staunch supporters of the Holy See as the captains of the Guelf Party counseled against sending aid to the papal legate on the grounds that this might involve Florence in a conflict over the status of its Emilian neighbor, Bologna.[29] By 1365, however, this neutralist position was being seriously challenged by the powerful Albizzi faction, who now advocated an alliance with the church and the Italian Guelf cities against the German emperor, the Visconti, and the marauding companies of mercenaries who were pillaging the Papal States throughout this era.[30] For the next seven years Piero degli Albizzi was relentless in his advocacy of a revivified Guelf alliance. Donato Velluti and Stefani, contemporary commentators on the Florentine political scene, and themselves directly involved in communal affairs, credited Piero with bringing about the liaison between Florence and Urban V in 1366–67.[31] It was this same powerful oligarch, in the opinion of Stefani, who won the Signoria over to the position of supporting the Holy See's projects against the Visconti, and the pope expressed his gratitude to Piero by making his nephew, then bishop of Florence, a cardinal. This pro-papal coup was supported by the captains of the Guelf Party, certain of the *magnati,* and such doctrinaire Guelfs as Lapo da Castiglionchio.[32] Until the early 1370s the Ricci, leaders of the

---

26. C. P., 1, unnumbered folio (12–14 March 1355).

27. C. P., 2, f. 17 (3 December 1358).

28. C. P., 1, part 2, fols. 23–24 (13 January 1854).

29. C. P., 3, f. 15r (4 February 1362).

30. C. P., 6, f. 45 (9 February 1365); 6, f. 80 (24 May 1365).

31. D. Velluti, *La cronica domestica,* ed. I. del Lungo and G. Volpe (Florence, 1914), p. 253; Stefani, rub. 701.

32. Stefani, rub. 720. Lapo had consistently admonished the *Signoria* not to permit Florence to withdraw her obedience from the church; if the pope wants

contending faction, stood in opposition to this alliance on the still sore point that it was bound to involve Florence in a war with Milan and the marauding companies. Uguccione de' Ricci, chief spokesman for his clan, went so far as to propose that Florence make an alliance with Bernabò Visconti, arch enemy of Avignon and principal obstructor of papal ambitions in Italy.[33] When Uguccione became prior of the republic in November 1366, he urged the Signoria to enact legislation designed to weaken the political influence of the pro-papal Albizzi faction and the Guelf Party. Specifically, this involved the admission of lesser guildsmen into the captaincy of the party, and, since these new men from the minor guilds tended to be adherents of the Ricci faction, they could be expected to oppose the policies of the Albizzi.[34] Judging from past experience, these new men of the *arti minori* could be relied upon to reject any proposal that favored giving assistance to the papacy or advocated Florentine participation in a Guelf league with the Holy See. These men, like their predecessors, the *novi cives* of the early Trecento, had little sympathy for the prerogatives of the church or for her ambitious Italian political projects.[35]

The records of the advisory councils from 1366 to 1372 reveal that no issue was more certain to divide the membership of the Signoria than that of the proposed alliance with the papacy.[36] Therefore, when the

---

an alliance, then the city should submit to his will so that the cause of Guelfism not be put in jeopardy. Cf. *C. P.*, 9, fols. 22r–23 (28 December 1367). He also contended that things would go *male* for the commune if the will of the pope were disregarded. Cf. *C. P.*, 9, f. 71 (27 March 1368). At the height of the *Otto Santi* war against the papacy, Lapo maintained that Florence was in "magno periculo" because she was waging war "cum hoste invincibili" and, therefore, she should hasten to make peace. Cf. *C. P.*, 15, f. 66 (26 December 1377).

33. *C. P.*, 8, f. 95 (26 July 1367). Cf. also *C. P.*, 7, f. 131; *C. P.*, 8, fols. 69r–81, 89–92.

34. The reform stated that *minori* were being added to the captaincy of the Party in order to preserve the freedom and tranquillity "maxime mercatorum et artificum." Cf. *P.*, 54, f. 133r (26 March 1367). For a consideration of the ties between the Ricci and the *minori*, see M. B. Becker, "La esecuzione della legislatura contro le pratiche monopolistiche delle arti fiorentine alla metà del secolo quattordicesimo," *Archivio Storico Italiano*, CXVII (1959), 24–26.

35. M. B. Becker, "Florentine Politics and the Diffusion of Heresy in the Trecento," *Speculum* 34 (1959): 63–65.

36. See the statement of Giovanni Mozzi in which he contends that the proposed league with the church has caused great discord among the Florentines. *C. P.*, 6, f. 80 (24 May 1365). Similar sentiments were voiced by Sandro Quaranta

Ricci faction abandoned its former position of opposing a papal alliance
and joined the ranks of the Albizzi in favor of a close liaison with the
Holy See the political reverberations were felt throughout the reaches of
communal government. According to the judicious and well-informed
Stefani, the citizenry were extremely fearful of the consequences of this
move, since now there remained no faction in the city capable of resist-
ing the papacy "per bene di comune."[37] In January 1372 the Guelf Party,
which was becoming increasingly pro-papal, was able to secure enactment of a provision giving this organization virtual autonomy from
communal control, and this further heightened the anxieties of the Florentines.[38] Counselors to the Signoria expressed grave misgivings over
these new developments, and Filippo di Cionetto Bastari, in one of the
most impassioned pleas ever to be recorded in the *Consulte et Pratiche*,
stated that the citizens were now in "magna divisione" because of this
turn of events and called upon the Signoria to restore unity and to conserve the "libertatem Comunis Florentie." He urged the government to
preserve Florentine neutrality at all costs and not to become involved in
any military undertaking on behalf of the papacy that might lead to war
with Milan. The speaker then implored the Signoria to protect the citizenry from the machinations of the powerful Albizzi and Ricci clans,
who were intent upon enslaving the populace, and he pleaded for a
restoration of "libertà." Specifically, he proposed that the Signoria elect
a commission with authority to take reprisals against any Florentine
seeking to involve the republic in a foreign venture that might possibly
culminate in the loss of its communal liberty.[39]

Two weeks after this memorable session of the communal council,
measures were enacted to establish just such a commission consisting of
ten men. This group, the *Dieci della Libertà*, was to act to check the extreme partisanship of the Ricci and Albizzi, thus eradicating factional-

---

at this council session when he maintained that the citizenry were suspicious of
the negotiations that were being conducted between Florence and the papacy.
Ricco Taldi, a leading minor guildsman, opposed this alliance because he believed that it threatened "unitas civium." Cf. C. P., 6, f. 45 (9 February 1365). Various governmental advisors expressed the fear that any alliance with the papacy
might lead to a breach of the peace with Milan, and this, in turn, would arouse
the "passiones" of the citizens. Cf. C. P., 9, fols. 39–40 (31 January 1369).

37. Rub. 726.
38. G. Capponi, *Storia della Repubblica di Firenze* (Florence, 1930), 1:586.
39. C. P., 12, f. 10 (16 March 1372).

ism in the city. A provision was then passed barring members of these two families from holding any public or guild office.[40] Stefani, who was himself a member of the *Dieci,* maintained that the nonfaction men who dominated the Signoria after April 1372 were responsible for this course of action. The Albizzi were suspected of conspiring against the republic with Guillaume Noëllet, cardinal of San Angelo, who was papal legate in Bologna, and with Géraud du Puy, abbot of Marmoutier, who was papal vicar in Perugia. At the same time the Ricci stood accused of accepting ecclesiastical benefices in return for their support of a Florentine papal alliance. Charges were also leveled against other powerful families thought to be exerting undue influence upon the Signoria for their own personal aggrandizement.[41]

The years immediately preceding the outbreak of war between Florence and the Holy See (1372–75) were marked by a resurgence of impartial government at the expense of such clans as the Ricci and Albizzi. The new leadership appearing at this time can best be characterized as being nonfactional. Many of these men were *novi cives* from the greater and lesser guilds that had traditionally opposed a Florentine alliance with the papacy; others were members of patrician families who had broken with their own kinsmen over a variety of political issues. The most affluent of the *novi cives* from the *arti minori*—such as Giovanni Goggio, a used clothing dealer, Ricco Taldi, a coppersmith, Niccolò Delli, a grocer (one of the *Dieci*), Tellino Dini, an ironmonger, Maso di Neri, a seller of rope, and a certain Master Tommaso, all of whom had spoken against an alliance with the church during meetings of the communal council—joined forces with some dissident members of the patriciate.[42] Salvestro de' Medici, guiding spirit of this coalition, had consistently espoused political opinions bound to attract the adherence of the *novi cives.* In 1363 he boldly proposed that the revenues from certain ecclesiastical properties should be assigned to the republic and that the clerics should be compelled to lend money to the *Camera del Comune.*[43]

---

40. Stefani, rub. 733. This ban was to last for five years. On 8 January 1373 the term was increased to ten years "pro conservanda et agenda libertate" of the city. Cf. *P.,* 60, f. 143.

41. *C. P.,* 12, f. 14 (31 March 1372); Stefani, rub. 730.

42. *C. P.,* 2, f. 18 (4 December 1359); *C. P.,* 4, f. 103r (24 September 1363); *C. P.,* 5, f. 131r (10 September 1364); *C. P.,* 6, f. 39 (14 June 1365); *C. P.,* 7, f. 87 (11 February 1366); *C. P.,* 8, fols. 24r, 38r, 50r, 84 (1367).

43. *C. P.,* 4, f. 73 (6 July 1363).

At another session of the communal council, in the following year, he attacked the pro-papal Guelf Party for its attempt to drive Piero Ferrantini from public life for his alleged Ghibelline sympathies, and went on to suggest that the government should conduct an inquiry into this type of nefarious practice. Two years later, in a bitter speech against the captains of the Guelf Party, Salvestro called upon the priors to resist the machinations of the evil *capitani* seeking "to gain control of the city of Florence." He then pleaded for unity between the merchants and artisans in order that they might "avoid being severed by those who desired to seize power."[44] In November 1372 this outspoken member of the Medici family opposed giving aid to the papal legate or becoming involved in any way in the war that then raged between the Holy See and Milan.[45] In 1374 he advised the Signoria not to permit the forces of the papacy to subvert the government of the city of Lucca and to take action to prevent this catastrophe. He also urged that Florentine ambassadors be sent to Milan to discuss the possibility of an alliance.[46] As a spokesman for the college of the *Dodici*, he favored communal taxation of the clergy. When war broke out between Florence and the papacy, Salvestro made an ingenious suggestion calculated to compel the pope to conclude hostilities on terms favorable to the republic. He advocated that "the bishops of Florence and Fiesole and all the prelates of the city of Florence should be sent to the pope in order to procure from him an end to the war and to lead him to peace."[47] If this expedient failed, then the Signoria was to confiscate all ecclesiastical property, sell it, and use the revenues to wage war against the pope. The conclusion of the Otto Santi war between Florence and the papacy (1378) saw Salvestro in the vanguard of those who were leading the assault against the Guelf Party and the great Guelf *magnati*.[48]

The *novi cives* supported those members of the patriciate who had separated themselves politically from their own families and who had challenged the hegemony of the oligarchical factions. With the adherence of these new men, political independents such as Salvestro de'

---

44. G. A. Brucker, "The Medici in the Fourteenth Century," *Speculum* 32 (1957): 17–18.

45. Ibid., 19.

46. C. P., 12, f. 172r (12 November 1374); f. 160r (31 October 1374).

47. C. P., 14, f. 85 (24 September 1376).

48. Cf. G. Scaramella, "La petizione di Salvestro dei Medici e i tumulti di Firenze," *Annuario del R. Liceo Michelangiolo di Firenze* (1927–28), I, 79–86.

Medici, Tommaso Strozzi, Giorgio Scali, Benedetto Alberti, and Filippo di Cionetto Bastari were in a better position to buttress communal prerogatives at the expense of ecclesiastical privileges and immunities. They could now weaken the authority of the great *magnati* clans over public affairs and undermine the prestige of traditional Guelfic principles. Finally, they were to minimize papal influence over the formulation of Florentine foreign policy. This tendency to extol the power of the state to the detriment of time-honored commitments and ideologies gained momentum when both *artifices* and *popolares* demanded that the oligarchs restore communal rights and properties and be compelled to assume their fair share of the tax burden. Similarly, there were requests that the membership of the former governing elite be punished for their repeated violations of public trust.[49] A variety of proposals designed to correct specific abuses were made: appointment of special *rationerii* with extraordinary authority over communal finances; election of foreign judges who were to decide cases involving the claims of the *Camera* against the great families; preparation of a register in which the names of debtors of the commune were to be inscribed; introduction of new procedures for the protection of state property; and reinforcement of the authority of the republic's officials in the *contado*.[50]

This mounting trend toward impartial government was to come into sharp conflict with the inordinate power wielded by the great families over church affairs. Traditionally, the episcopal see had been occupied by scions of the dominant clans; in recent years Angelo Acciaiuoli, Filippo dell' Antella, Pietro Corsini, and Angelo Ricasoli had filled this office. In 1374 the bishop of Fiesole was Neri Corsini who, like his kinsman Pietro, was related to the pro-papal leader of the Albizzi faction. In the following year the communal council took measures to sever the ties between the patriciate and the ecclesiastical hierarchy when it decreed that, if any citizen of the republic accepted either the bishopric of Florence or that of Fiesole, his family were to be declared *magnati* and, therefore, denied admission into public office. If, however, the bishop's family were already of *magnati* status, they were then to be classified as

---

49. C. P., 12, fols. 13, 19r, 55–57 (1375).

50. For the suggestion concerning the *rationerii*, see C. P., 12, f. 56 (22 September 1372); cf. ibid., for the proposal concerning the election of a foreign judge and the register listing the debtors. On the protection of communal property, see ibid., f. 175 (11 December 1374).

supramagnati and proclaimed rebels in perpetuity. The Florentine counselors justified this most grievous violation of ecclesiastical liberty on the grounds that the relatives of the occupants of these episcopal sees were using their power and influence to oppress the *popolares* and the *artifices* of the city and *contado;* they even went so far as to make many extortions "sub colore justiti(a)e."[51]

Concomitant with this frontal assault upon those local dynasts who were taking advantage of their close ties with the church to further their own private interests was the sweeping extension of communal authority into areas that had formerly been under the purview of the church. In 1363, at the height of the Pisan war, when the republic was sorely in need of funds, a law was passed that all bequests made to the numerous Florentine religious brotherhoods since 1345 were to be transferred to the communal treasury and the property of these pious foundations was to be sold to satisfy the claims of the city's creditors. It is interesting to note that the Signoria expressly exempted bequests made to charitable foundations exclusively devoted to ministering to the needs of paupers.[52] The commune reserved the right to examine the accounts of religious confraternities even when they were under the direct jurisdiction of the bishop and were ostensibly using their wealth to aid the poor.[53] One can readily understand the opposition of the church to this and other measures enacted by the republic during this interval.

With the termination of the Pisan war, however, Florence found that she was in desperate need of papal support as a counter to the threat that the Holy Roman Emperor posed to the city's sovereignty. The Signoria, therefore, drew up a provision designed to correct those ordinances that violated ecclesiastical liberty. The council, more responsive to popular anti-papal sentiment than the Signoria, rejected this proposal.[54] In 1367, when the government received word that the pope was prepared to abandon Avignon and restore the papal seat to Rome, one of the principal causes for this antipathy was removed, and the communal counselors found this to be an opportune moment to suggest that a committee be appointed to revise those laws that were said to be

51. *P.,* 63, f. 70r (7 July 1375).
52. *P.,* 51, fols. 7–7r (21 August 1363).
53. *P.,* 52, f. 151 (30 May 1365).
54. *L. F.,* 37, f. 166r (18 August 1365).

"against the liberties of the church so that the pope will be pleased."[55] The Signoria approved of this proposal, and such a revision was immediately undertaken. What emerged was a compromise, with the church gaining a theoretical victory, while certain practical advantages went to the state. All ordinances "contra fidem Catholicam et ecclesiasticam libertatem" were suspended. The government received authority, however, to intrude in precisely that area that the church considered to be its most cherished "liberty"—clerical immunity from communal taxation.[56] In the following year certain monasteries were compelled to pay tribute to the state for all goods that they imported for their own use.[57] Imposts of this type were now to become a regular feature of state policy toward the church, and additional levies were placed upon the real property of the clergy residing within the city.[58] When proposals were later made to enact legislation mitigating the incidence of these revenue measures, the communal council blocked their passage.[59] In the years immediately preceding the outbreak of the Otto Santi war, special commissions, such as the *Dieci*, buttressed the jurisdiction of the state tribunals by denying the traditional liberty of sanctuary.[60] During this interval governmental advisors urged the Signoria to tax the clergy more heavily.[61]

Assaults upon the prerogatives and immunities of the church were intensified and extended into new realms when war broke out between the republic and the Holy See in the summer of 1375. The Florentines had been visited by a terrible famine in 1374 and had asked the papal legate to permit them to purchase grain in the Patrimony. When he refused to allow the precious commodity to be exported from the Papal States, which were in dire need themselves, the Florentine citizens were quick to blame his decision on policies formulated by the pope. In the spring of 1375 Tuscany was ravaged by John Hawkwood's army of freebooters, and, despite the assurances of Gregory XI that he was in no way responsible for this onslaught, many Florentines continued to believe

---

55. C. P., 9, f. 19r (12 December 1367).
56. P., 55, f. 108; L. F., 39, f. 34 (23 December 1367).
57. P., 92, fols. 204r–205r (12 December 1403).
58. P., 61, f. 68 (13 June 1373).
59. L. F., 40, f. 121 (13 October 1374).
60. P., 60, f. 148; L. F., 40, f. 52 (21 January 1374).
61. C. P., 12, f. 38 (5 July 1372).

that the English Company was in the pay of the papacy. By June the city was at war and the Signoria, composed, for the most part, of political independents, *novi cives* and lesser guildsmen, pushed the authority of the state into recesses that had formerly been the exclusive preserve of the clergy: legislation was enacted authorizing the officials of the Florentine *Monte* to act as executors of the wills of all "manifest usurers." These officials were also given the power to review the accounts of all usurers for the purpose of seeing that restitution was made to the victims of usurious contracts. The *Monte* officials were not to be syndicated or condemned for taking these actions by either the magistrates of the commune or the tribunals of the church. The government justified the displacement of the clergy who had previously served in this capacity on the grounds that it was necessary to protect the citizenry from injustice.[62] The officials of the *Monte* were also appointed executors of legacies to minors and empowered to act as guardians with instructions to invest the capital of their wards in the *Monte* "pro utilitate pupillorum." This step was favored by governmental advisors because it would put additional monies "in the hands of the commune."[63] Special rectors were chosen who were given jurisdiction over bequests to clergy and religious establishments; their duties included appropriating these gifts in the name of the republic.[64] The Signoria also seized this opportunity to press for legislation removing certain communal sanctions against usurious practices initiated at the behest of the church.[65] The regime then succeeded in passing a provision designed to curtail ecclesiastical juris-

---

62. The general effect of these enactments was to make interest readily recoverable at law. There was, therefore, no need to resort to the subterfuges that had been designed during an earlier era to permit the lender to escape the rigors of canon law. Cf. *P.*, 63, f. 85 (8 August 1375). For a description of these earlier practices, see R. de Roover, *The Medici Bank* (New York, 1948), p. 57. On the appointment of the *Monte* officials and their actions at this time, see M. B. Becker, "Three Cases Concerning the Restitution of Usury in Florence," *Journal of Economic History*, xvii (September 1957), 445–50. The authority of these officials was increased appreciably during the late fourteenth and early fifteenth century at the expense of traditional ecclesiastical prerogatives over charges of usury. Cf. *Statui Populi Communis Florentiae* (Freiburg, 1778), iii, 325–27, 345–47; *Corpus Juris Canonici, Decretales: c.* Quamquam usurarii, in VI, v, 5, 2.

63. *C. P.*, 15, f. 54r (13 November 1377); *P.*, 65, f. 119 (19 August 1377); f. 280 (23 February 1378).

64. *C. P.*, 15, f. 25 (20 July 1377).

65. *P.*, 63, f. 73; *L. F.*, 40, f. 150 (12 July 1375).

diction over cases involving a charge of usury. These measures, as well as others, were inaugurated by the government in direct opposition to the articles of the Bishop's Constitution.[66]

At the same time that the regime defied customary religious precept with inordinate zeal, it also attacked the patrimonial base of the Tuscan church. From the very outset of the Otto Santi war there was a high degree of unanimity among the citizenry on the desirability of imposing forced loans upon the clergy. A letter written by Gherardino di Niccolò Gherardini Giani, a man well informed on the subject of communal finance, to his friend, Tommaso di Piero di messer Ridolfo de' Bardi, states that, if *prestanze* had not been exacted from the clerics, it would have been necessary to raise the taxes of the citizenry.[67] Another unpopular alternative would have been to impose the dreaded *estimo* upon the real property of the city's inhabitants. During March and April 1375 this form of taxation was twice proposed but failed to obtain the necessary two-thirds majority.[68] By February of the following year the need for communal revenue encouraged the advisors to the Signoria to suggest that the *prestanze* against the clergy be tripled.[69] Four months later Iacopo di Piero Sacchetti, a leading political independent and spokesman for the *Gonfalonieri,* advocated that the commune sell or temporarily alienate ecclesiastical property in order to raise additional revenue.[70] Shortly thereafter the Signoria elected *Ufficiali dei livellari e dei preti* to perform this function. The holdings of the church were placed on the open market, and in January 1377 the *Camera del Comune* records the first payments.[71] Members of the lower orders, as well as patricians, took advantage of this opportunity to increase their patrimony at the expense of the church. The Alberti, Albizzi, Bardi, Bondelmonti, Cambi,

---

66. The licensing of Jewish pawnbrokers in Florentine territories was a particular case in point. This important violation of the Bishop's Constitution occurred in 1375 and not at the end of the century as modern scholars have contended. *Cam.,* 168, unnumbered folio (31 October 1375); U. Cassuto, *Gli Ebrei a Firenze nell' eta del Rinascimento* (Florence, 1918), 15; *I Capitoli del Comune di Firenze,* ed. C. Guasti (Florence, 1893), II, 39 ff.

67. G. A. Brucker, "Un documento fiorentino sulla guerra, sulla finanza a sulla amministrazione," *Archivio Storico Italiano,* cxv (1957), 165–76.

68. *L. F.,* 40, f. 139 (28 March 1375); f. 141 (17 April 1375).

69. *C. P.,* 14, f. 18 (25 February 1376).

70. *C. P.,* 14, f. 57r (26 June 1376); Stefani, rub. 731.

71. *Cam.* 176, unnumbered folio (20 January).

Medici, Morelli, Pazzi, Peruzzi, Strozzi, and Tolosini clans could be counted among the more notable beneficiaries. These numerous transactions, which continued to take place until June of the following year, fill eight large volumes of the treasury records and reveal the extent and diversity of ecclesiastical property.[72] Long after the conclusion of the Otto Santi war, the issue of restitution of this property remained unresolved and continued to plague relations between church and state.

During this turbulent interval the state also seriously challenged the juridical authority of the church when it decreed that any citizen who had suffered an injustice in an ecclesiastical court might appeal to the Signoria for a redress of grievances.[73] Shortly thereafter the building that housed the Court of the Inquisition was destroyed, and the authority of the Holy Office was rendered ineffectual within Florence. Even more significant was the commune's assumption of jurisdiction over crimes against religion. The most ancient Florentine statutes gave the state tribunals authority to try only cases involving a charge of blasphemy; other crimes against religion (such as black magic, witchcraft, and sorcery) came under the purview of the Bishop's Curia and the Tribunal of the Inquisitor. After 1375, however, charges of this type became a matter of communal concern.[74]

III

The bitter conflict between church and state (1375–78) precipitated tensions in the lives of the Florentines. Prominent political figures, such as Simone di Rinieri di Peruzzi, who ten years earlier had been in the vanguard of those advocating return of the papacy to Rome as the best remedy for the many ills that beset Italy, were now coming to the conclusion that the church was, at best, a negative force in the temporal life of the peninsula and, therefore, a citizen's primary political obligation was to his native city.[75] This view was not confined to the Florentine

---

72. Ibid., 176–83.

73. *P.*, 63, f. 73; *L. F.*, 40, f. 150 (12 July 1375).

74. U. Dorini, *Il diritto penale e la delinquenza in Firenze nel sec. XIV* (Lucca, 1916), 67.

75. S. Morpurgo, "La guerra degli Otto Santi e il tumulto dei Ciompi nelle ricordanze di Simone di Rinieri Peruzzi," *Miscellanea fiorentina di storia e erudizione* 2 (1894): 10–13. For Simone's earlier statements, see *C. P.* 6, f. 37 (13 January 1365).

laity: Giovanni delle Celle, famous ascetic of Vallombrosa and scion of a noble Tuscan family, in a letter to Guido di Neri del Palagio, a leading patrician, contended that citizens of the republic should not hesitate to serve in the government or to pay taxes in support of the war effort. He also stated that the excommunication launched against the Florentines by the pope was unjust and, therefore, not binding.[76] This same Guido was the recipient of a letter from the Florentine humanist priest Luigi Marsili, who felt that, while the government did not have the right to harm those clergy who performed their sacred offices, it certainly was not obliged to suffer the few who meddled in communal politics. Marsili, an Augustinian, was bitterly hostile toward Avignon, and during the Otto Santi war he transcribed Petrarch's anti-papal sonnets. His teachings were to have a profound effect upon such early Florentine humanists as Salutati and Bruni. Prior to the outbreak of the Otto Santi war, Coluccio Salutati was elevated to the post of chancellor of the republic; it was in this capacity that he heartily championed the nomination of Luigi Marsili for the episcopal bench. In so doing, he castigated the corruption of the church by pointing out that the Augustinian had earned his doctorate in theology at the University of Paris by virtue of intellectual merit and not because of his connections with the ecclesiastical hierarchy.[77]

Coluccio's writings not only reflect the teachings of the pious priest Marsili, who, as the intellectual heir of Petrarch, scourged those modern sophists who were neglecting the *studia humanitatis* in order to pursue the hollow study of dialectic, but they also bring to mind the attacks of Marsiglio of Padua against the unwonted preponderance of the church in civic life. It is of interest to note that in 1363, when the governmental advisors were becoming particularly vocal in their criticism of the church's liberties, Marsiglio's *Defensor Pacis* was translated into the vernacular in Florence.[78] In this provocative work we witness an integral

76. F. Tocco, "I Fraticelli," *Archivio Storico Italiano* 25 (1905): 349–51.

77. E. Gartin, "I cancellieri umanisti della Repubblica Fiorentina da Coluccio Salutati a Bartolomeo Scala," *Rivista Storica Italiana*, LXXI (1959), 190–91; U. Mariani, *Il Petrarca e gli agostiniani* (Rome, 1946), 66ff.

78. E. Garin, op. cit., 191. This date coincides with the outbreak of the Florentine-Pisan war and all potential sources of revenue had to be tapped. The advisors to the Signoria proposed that a forced loan be imposed upon the clergy and that they be subjected to extensive communal levies. Cf. *C. P.*, 4, fols. 43, 64r, 69, 72. See also notes 98 and 99. It should be noted that Salvestro de' Medici

humanization of the state, anchored, as a modern commentator has indicated, not upon religious presuppositions but upon the specifics of
man's experience and the concreteness of human values.[79] In Coluccio's
writings a strong emphasis is also placed upon the "terrestrial nature of
the human vocation" and man's sacred obligation to his earthly city.[80] In
his correspondence as chancellor, he depicts the men of Florence as the
heirs of the Romans, and he draws analogies between the sacred duty of
the Romans to defend their *libertas* and that of their latter-day counterparts who were obligated to defend *Florentina libertas* against the hosts
of "avaricious Babylon."[81] In his opinion the Florentines were not only
duty bound to defend their *patria*, but they were also charged with the
divine mission of destroying "la chiesa carnale" and erecting in its place
"la terza chiesa spirituale."[82] Specifically, he sees the artisans and merchants as the champions of Florentine liberty and he speaks of them as
"benignissimi homines quos michi videtur divine potentie digitus
eligesse." He goes on to eulogize the socioeconomic base of Florentine
society—the guilds, "per quas sumus quod sumus," and on which the
grandeur and majesty of the city is predicated. Very significant in the letters of Coluccio looms the fact that Florence is a free city in which *il popolo*
are sovereign. It is this *popolo*—the *mercatores* and *artifices*—who are the
anchor of the state, for without them, "we cannot live."[83]

   The years following the Otto Santi war were troubled ones for the

---

made his radical proposals on ecclesiastical questions during that same year. Cf.
footnote 89.

   79. E. Garin, *La filosofia dal medio evo all' umanesimo* (Milan, 1947), I, 78.

   80. E. Garin, *L'umanesimo italiano* (Bari, 1952), 38. This same point of view is
manifested in his earlier writings. See especially his letter to his friend, Ser Andrea di ser Conte, in *Epistolario di Coluccio Salutati*, ed. F. Novati (Rome, 1891), I,
26–29 (8 June 1366).

   81. For a consideration of the millenarian milieu in Florence at this time, see
M. B. Becker, "A Comment on 'Savonarola, Florence, and the Millenarian Tradition,'" *Church History* 27 (1958): 306–7.

   82. H. Grundmann, "Die Papst-prophetien des Mittelalters," *Archiv für Kulturgeschichte*, XIX (1928), 122; N. Sapegno, *Storia letteraria d'Italia: il Trecento* (Milan, 1934), 528–40; N. Valeri, *L'Italia nell' età dei principati dal 1343 al 1516* (Milan,
1949), 206; E. Garin, op. cit., 38ff.; M. Meiss, *Painting in Florence and Siena After
the Black Death* (Princeton, 1947), 80–93.

   83. E. Garin, "I cancellieri umanisti della Repubblica Fiorentina da Coluccio
Salutati a Bartolomeo Scala," op. cit., 195. The term *popolo* used here refers to
some 2,500 non-*magnati* guild masters.

republic. A violent revolution (the *Ciompi*) catapulted *il popolo minuto* into power in the summer of 1378, then there ensued a turbulent era of popular government, and finally, in 1382, a severe oligarchical reaction set in, displacing many of the *novi cives* from communal office. With the resumption of the undisputed rule of the oligarchs, the church recovered certain of its ancient prerogatives. But, for the most part, these concessions were peripheral in character. The Signoria remained adamant on such fundamental issues as making restitution of ecclesiastical property, canceling legislation that called for the imposition of forced loans upon clerics, revoking *gabelle* on church foundations, abandoning communal jurisdiction over the last wills and testaments of usurers, and recognizing clerical immunities from the decisions of secular courts. Gradually, these matters had come under the purview of the state, and the oligarchs did little to reverse this trend.[84] Moreover, by the end of the fourteenth century the scope of secular political power had evolved to the point where the government could actively intervene in the area of relations between the papacy and the clergy of Florence. The government assumed the role of defender of the Florentine clergy against the fiscal exactions of Rome; it justified this course of action on the grounds that it was necessary to conserve the wealth of the local clergy "in abundance."[85] The government of what by this time was obviously a prototype of the territorial state expressed, in no uncertain terms, its desire to have a territorial clergy. Opposition in the government was mounting against the traditional papal practice of giving certain ecclesiastical

---

84. For the suspension of legislation requiring the commune to restore church property, see *P.*, 73, f. 121r; *L. F.*, 42, f. 26r (12 October 1384); *P.*, 76, f. 39 (17 May 1387); *L. F.*, 43, f. 4 (22 May 1387); *P.*, 77, f. 202; *L. F.*, 43, f. 77 (26 November 1388); *P.*, 78, f. 283; *L. F.*, 43, f. 137 (10 December 1389); *L. F.*, 43, f. 180 (16 November 1390); *P.*, 80, fols. 171–73r (20 November 1391). The outbreak of the war with the Visconti intensified the republic's need for additional revenue "pro defensione libertatis" and, as in the past, the Signoria imposed *prestanze* and other imposts upon the clergy. For a discussion of this question by governmental advisors, see *C. P.*, 24, fols. 4–30r (November, 1384–February, 1385). On the assessment of *gabelles* upon ecclesiastical establishments, see *Statuta Populi Communis Florentiae*, III, 402–05. On the question of communal jurisdiction and the weakening of the authority of the church courts, see ibid., I, 123–29; III, 370. For an evaluation of the landed patrimony of the clergy, made by the commune for the purpose of tax assessment, see G. Canestrini, *La scienza e l'arte di stato dagli atti ufficiali della repubblica fiorentina e dei Medici* (Florence, 1862), 152.

85. *C. P.*, f. 165 (20 January 1388).

benefices to foreigners.[86] For the first time in communal history, provisions were enacted giving the Signoria authority to take over the income from ecclesiastical benefices held by non-Florentines, since these men had frequently neglected the property of the church and permitted it to fall into decay.[87] Rectors of the republic were to act as protectors of ecclesiastical properties and vacant churches; no individual was to be permitted to accept any ecclesiastical title for benefice without the consent of the Signoria. Finally, communal officials were empowered to remove any interdict that might be laid upon the city as well as to revoke any excommunication launched against a citizen.[88]

By the beginning of the fifteenth century the bitter antithesis between church and state had lost most of its sharp edge. The republic had appropriated to itself many of the functions that had formerly belonged to the mediaeval church. The Great Schism and the Conciliar Movement were certainly factors that weakened the ability of the papacy to check these intrusions. The Tuscan clergy had themselves become more reconciled to a subordinate role. Fra Giovanni Dominici and his renowned disciple, San Antonino, responded to these historical mutations by encouraging the faithful to be more mindful of their responsibilities toward secular society; while San Bernardino of Siena extolled the active civic life as opposed to that of contemplation.[89] This trend was also encouraged by Coluccio's successors in the Florentine chancellory, Bruni and Poggio, who proclaimed man's sacred obligation to civil society and polemicized against sterile asceticism and the monastic ideal of withdrawal.[90]

The years that separated the decade of the 1340s from the advent of the Medici (1434) not only witnessed the emergence of a territorial state and church from the matrix of a citizen commune, but they were also the setting for the development of a *Weltanschauung* that caused men to see politics as an activity divorced from traditional moral considerations. One of the most eminent Florentine statesmen of the early fifteenth century, Gino di Neri Capponi, hero of the republic's great vic-

86. C. P., 31, f. 45r (5 June 1396).

87. P., 83, fols. 212r–15 (10 December 1394). The Signoria was empowered to elect six officials who were to oversee the enforcement of this provision. Cf. *Statuta Populi Communis Florentiae*, 3:347.

88. Ibid., 1:125–27.

89. E. Garin, *L'umanesimo italiano*, 51–53.

90. Hans Baron, "Franciscan Poverty and Civic Wealth as Factors in the Rise of Humanistic Thought," *Speculum* 13 (1938): 1–37.

tory over Pisa, drawing upon his long experience with communal affairs, composed a set of political maxims for his son in which he urged him to avoid entanglements with priests and "not to bother with churches unless for the purpose of sacraments and divine offices." He further admonished the young man to do his best to see that the church remains interested in purely spiritual matters. The memories of Gino's childhood were vivid when he recalled how the Albizzi liaison with the church had undermined the unity of Florence and made its citizens the prey of contentious factions. Finally, he advised his son to vote always for that candidate for high communal office who possessed the most important of all qualifications—a deeper concern for the welfare of the commune than for the salvation of his own soul. This remark was to lead Francesco Guicciardini to tell Gino's great-grandson that his forebears knew that it was not possible "to rule domains and states according to the precepts of Christian law."[91]

---

91. R. Sereno, "The Ricordi of Gino di Neri Capponi," *American Political Science Review* 52 (1958): 1118–22.

5

A Study in Political Failure:
The Florentine Magnates (1280–1343)

No order in Florentine society is more complex and various than the magnates. My purpose is to trace out their history from the last two decades of the thirteenth century, to the year 1343. The earlier limit is dictated by the fact that documentary evidence toward a definition of this order appears only with the late Dugento, while the year 1343 marks the beginning of a concerted and sustained effort to bring this patriciate under the force of public law. After completing this inquiry, I hope to be able to draw certain inferences that may be of some use to cultural historians of the later North Italian Middle Ages.

I

The term *magnate* first appears in a public document in the year 1281 and is employed to designate a specific category of citizens who were to be required by law to post security for their good behavior.[1] This caution-

Reprinted from *Mediaeval Studies* 27 (1965): 246–308, by permission of the publisher. © 1965 by the Pontifical Institute of Medieval Studies, Toronto.

I wish to thank Professor Wallace K. Ferguson for reading this essay and making valuable suggestions.

1. Definitions of the term *magnate* are legion. Words such as *nobiles, milites,* and *magnates* were frequently used interchangeably. Cf. G. Fasoli, "Ricerche sulla legislazione antimagnatizia nei comuni dell'alta e media Italia," *Rivista di Storia del Diritto Italiano* 12 (1939): 241ff. No attempt will be made in the present study to comment upon the origins of those classified as "milites vel magnates." For examples of disquieting evidence that makes generalization difficult, see J. Plesner. *L'émigration de la campagne à la ville libre de Florence au XIIIᵉ siècle* (Copenhagen, 1934). For a cautious and sensitive appraisal of the inadequacies of precise socioeconomic distinctions between classes in a late medieval commune, see E. Cristiani's recent study of Pisa: *Nobiltà e popolo nel comune di Pisa* (Naples, 1962), 13–63. The socioeconomic background of the Florentine patriciate-noble and commoner alike—is treated by E. Fuimi in "Fioritura e decadenza dell'economia fiorentina," *Archivio Storico Italiano* 116 (1958): 443–509.

94

ary measure came as a result of a general pacification of the city bravely initiated by the pope's representative, Cardinal Latino. In 1280 His Holiness was vitally interested in establishing concord among the feuding factions and contending orders in the Arno city. Rome stood much in need of Florentine support if the papacy was to realize its grand North Italian political objectives, and as long as the pontiff's great Guelf ally was torn by internecine strife, Florence would be less than useful to him. The need for public order and the desirability of being concerned with the good of the commonwealth rather than with one's private interests was not only a persistent theme in the sermons of such great preachers as Cardinal Latino, but it was also at the heart of the thirteenth-century classical revival, and indeed it is entirely fitting that Cicero's and Aristotle's political teachings should have been incorporated into the civic humanism of the medieval commune. The same message prompting men to maintain a well-ordered state peopled with a law-abiding citizenry was also proclaimed by communal artists whose frescoes praising "buon governo" were soon to adorn the walls of the many town halls of Tuscany.[2]

The legislation of 1281 differed markedly from its medieval forebears: first, in that it required magnates to post a money bond that would be confiscated in case of a serious breach of the law, rather than merely waiting for a crime to be committed and then assessing the penalty according to the gravity of the offense. Second, this law was an innovation in that it required a certain segment of the citizenry to take an oath of peace, instead of resorting to the traditional medieval remedy of calling upon all men to exchange the kiss of peace in the cathedral.[3] Cardinal Latino's program was directed toward the pacification of long standing and fierce quarrels, especially among the *grandi* and *possenti* of such aristocratic families as the Adimari, Donati, Pazzi, and Tosinghi. It was these clans from the highest echelons of the patriciate

---

2. N. Rubinstein, "Political Ideas in Sienese Art," *Journal of the Warburg and Courtauld Institute* 21 (1958): 179–207; H. Wieruscowski, "Art and the Commune in the Time of Dante," *Speculum* 19 (1944): 14–33.

3. N. Rubinstein, "La prima legge sul sodamento," *Archivio Storico Italiano* 93 (1935): 161–72. The council of *i savi* was to deliberate on the posting of security by magnates and to settle problems pertaining to the practical application of the statutory disposition. The *sapientes* were to determine who was to post "satisdationem." Cf. *Le Consulte della Repubblica fiorentina dall'anno 1280 all'anno 1298*, ed. A. Gherardi (Florence, 1896–98), 1:33.

whose lawless behavior the cardinal and the commune were determined to check. The persistence of "broils, discords," and even "great wars" among these *consorterie* encouraged the chief magistracy of the republic to designate as magnates the feuding families of the Adimari, Bardi, Buondelmonti, Bostichi, Cavalcanti, Donati, Foraboschi Frescobaldi, Gherardini, Giandonati, Malispini, Manieri, Mozzi, Rossi, Tornaquinci, Tosinghi, and Visdomini. "Guerre et scandala" perpetrated by these magnates are to be a recurring motif in the annals of the city, and the aforementioned families were singled out by the Florentine chroniclers as being most prone to respond to the vendetta.[4] Although the contentions of a Giovanni Villani or a Dino Compagni cannot be accepted uncritically, the fact remains that only one of the long list of fierce and lawless families mentioned in their chronicles was to escape the harsh restraints imposed by the Ordinances of Justice in late 1293. Perhaps that family—the Falconieri—whose proclivity for the blood feud was as pronounced as any clan in Florence, evaded the rigors of this ordinance because they had supported Giano della Bella, the leader of the popular revolution of that year.[5] It would appear then that the term *magnate* came to be applied to many individuals from the city's leading families who chronically practiced the time-honored and customary act of private vengeance during the years between 1281 and 1293.

The consummation of peace, so devoutly to be wished, was fervently sought throughout the world of the late Middle Ages; and the he-

---

4. G. Villani, *Cronica,* ed. F. Dragomanni (Florence, 1845) 8:1; D. Compagni, *Cronica,* ed. I. del Lungo (Florence, 1889), 1:22. For a discussion of *vindictae* and *guerr(a)e* as a general European phenomenon, with special emphasis on the Florentine experience, see N. Rubinstein, *La lotta contro i magnati a Firenze* (Florence, 1939).

5. R. Davidsohn, *Forschungen zur Geschichte von Florenz* (Berlin, 1896–1927), vol. 3, n. 23. The Falconieri were active in England as merchants and bankers; with the early *Trecento,* however, the men of this clan demonstrated an appetite for violence and soon were outlawed as Ghibellines. On 12 September 1304 Schiatta was condemned by the vicar of the podestà to decapitation and destruction of his property for raiding the contado and killing, robbing and kidnapping "populares florentinos." Others were convicted for similar crimes in the Mugello and finally, on 15 October 1315, the family was banished. See *Camera del Comune,* 1 bis, f. 70. (Henceforth this source will be abbreviated as *CC.* All documents cited are to be found in the *Archivio di Stato* in Florence.) They were back in the city even before their ban was removed and serving in the government. *Libri Fabarum,* 13, f. 1 (Henceforth abbreviated as *LF.*)

roes of those days were saints like Francis, who exorcised the demons of discord from the towns, or blessed kings like St. Louis, whose life stood as a religious monument to be worshiped by the many who hungered for peace. But the peace associations, so encouraged by the church, and the peace guilds, sponsored by the lay rulers, could only achieve their sacred ends when an effective machinery for enforcing public law came into being. Only then would the rule of law be a viable alternative that could compete effectively with the ancient and honorable form of gaining revenge. It is worth noting that to a Dante the ultimate and all-consuming purpose of peace was religious. When this blessed goal was reached, men would be liberated from the cares of this world and permitted to contemplate their true end—the salvation of their souls. To the men of letters of the early *Quattrocento,* the ends of peace were secular. Leonardo Bruni Aretino, foremost humanist of his generation, and Florentine chancellor, believed that the fruits of peace would enable man to cultivate his personality and to pursue virtue through the active political life. To the men of Dante's time the state, metaphorically speaking, was "a mystical body"—an expression frequently used to characterize the Eucharist—and the *Signoria* was hailed as "savior" and "redeemer," while to the later humanists, governments and societies were man-made, and their ends were secular.[6]

Much could be done to temper the violent and impulsive medievals who thought more of honor than they did of that brief moment of life granted to man before he crossed over into eternity. The cult of the Virgin, the promptings of chivalry, the subtle teachings of the Romance, the psychologizing of the new Italian poetry, each sought to instill compassion and the quality of introspection in the men of the late medieval world. And these cultural developments can be viewed with profit within the context of the pervasive yearning for peace so much in evidence in this society. While Florence was certainly not isolated from these grand European cultural movements, her experience and success with the repression of extreme antisocial behavior were to play a part in

---

6. C. T. Davis, "An early Florentine Political Theorist: Fra Remigio De' Girolami," *Proceedings of the American Philosophical Society* 104 (1960): 671; E. Kantorowicz, *The King's Two Bodies* (Princeton 1957), 193–232. The chief magistrates of the commune were the priors, and, according to Giovanni Villani, the term *prior* was taken from the passage in the Holy Gospel where Christ says to His disciples: "Vos estis priores." *Cronica,* 7:79. For an example of the use of religious metaphors in an important public document, see E. Cristiani, op. cit., 500.

creating a particular regional political milieu that came to rely upon law
rather than on the sermons, the religious pageants, and the civilizing
nightly rituals of the waning Middle Ages. The Florentines came to
know that the demons of discord would inevitably return to mock the
efforts of the saint and that therefore the greatest possibility for security
rested in a government before which all citizens were equal. This ideal,
however, was only to become explicit in the new civic humanism of the
early *Quattrocento*.[7]

One might begin with a paradox: In order to achieve equality it
would be necessary first to have inequality, and this is something of a
truism throughout the history of thirteenth- and fourteenth-century Florence. In 1282 Cardinal Latino's program of pacification collapsed, and
the leaders of the city's mercantile and industrial patriciate inaugurated
a new *Signoria* founded upon the primacy of the seven major Florentine
guilds. For the next century and a half this magistracy was to insist repeatedly that its sacred duty was the maintenance of "veram et perpet-
uam concordiam et unionem conservationem et augmentum pacifici et
tranquilli statuts artificum et artium et omnium popularum et etiam
totius comunis et civitatis et districtus Florentie."[8]

---

7. E. Garin, "I cancellieri umanisti della Repubblica fiorentina da Coluccio
Salutati a Bartolomeo Scala," *Rivista Storica Italiana* 71 (1959): 200; H. Baron, *Humanistic and Political Literture in Florence and Venice at the Beginning of the Quattrocento* (Cambridge, Mass., 1955). All the major chroniclers of the fourteenth
century, from Dino Compagni through the Villanis and Stefani, were bitter critics of those whose behavior was factious, and each attributed the misfortunes
of the city to the machinations of these intractable citizens. Cf. Marchionne di
Coppo Stefani, *Cronica fiorentina*, ed. N. Rodolico, *Rerum Italicarum Scriptores*,
new ed., 30, pt. 1 (Città di Castello, 1903–55), rub. 775, 790; G. Villani, *Cronica*,
9:271. Donato Velluti contended that the virus of factionalism served to encourage the political aspirations of the lower orders, since the vying cliques each bid
for their support. *Cronica domestica*, ed. I. del Lungo (Florence, 1914), 241. Compagni observed that the nobility of the contado "who obey her [Florence] more
from fear than love," enjoyed the spectacle of discord since it humiliated the ar-
rogant Florentines. *Cronica*, 1:1.

8. G. Salvemini, *Magnati e popolani in Firenze dal 1280 al 1295* (Florence,
1899), 384. The tendency in the twelfth and thirteenth centuries was to use ecclesiastical authority to buttress the cause of peace. In commenting on the peace
of Cardinal Latino, Compani says, "they [the Guelfs and Ghibellines] wisely
agreed to come to terms . . . under the yoke of the church, in order that the bonds
of the agreement might be maintained by the church's power" (trans. of *The
Chronicle of Dino Compagni* by E. Benecke and A. Howell [London, 1896], 8).

Not only were certain of the magnates to be an integral part of this regime, but particular members of this class were to be among the warmest champions of its efforts to preserve public order. Just as these men had supported Cardinal Latino in his ill-fated endeavors, so now they were to give encouragement to the new regime and call upon the *Signoria* to intervene and pacify the feuding families of their own class. Many were to be as anxious as the humblest burghers for protection against the violence of the lawless *consorterie*. At least one-half of the city's magnate families were matriculated in the greater guilds between 1282 and 1293, and these men differed little in outlook, interests, and patrimony from the great burghers. During this interval it was generally considered to be unnecessary for men of this stripe to post security for their good behavior since they were reputed to be law-abiding citizens who followed a respectable economic calling.[9] Furthermore, the fused elite of the greater guilds—magnate and commoner alike—were in agreement on fundamental issues from the complex coinage question, to the working out of the intricate details of the republic's ambiguous foreign policy, and, if one confines his researches to the abbreviated minutes of the various communal council meetings where these matters were discussed, then, indeed, the relations between magnate and great burgher appear to be most idyllic during the decade after 1282. Recent scholarship has made much of this concord and demonstrated that the ruling families of Florence were composed of men who rose to eminence as a result of the economic revolution which transformed Tuscany in the late twelfth and early thirteenth centuries. Few of these clans were feudal in origin and the overwhelming majority were distinctly nouveaux—scions of houses of "modest beginnings."[10]

---

9. G. Salvemini, op. cit., 187; R. Ciasca, "Dante e l'arte dei medicie e speciale," *Archivio Storico Italiano* 89 (1931): 91–95.

10. Marc Bloch's treatment of the French nobility suggests that this cadre was being transformed into a legal class during the later Middle Ages. We find "what had long been by mere convention a hereditary vocation," being transformed "into a legalized and jealously-guarded privilege" (cf. *Feudal Society,* trans. L. Manyon [Chicago, 1961], 322). The import of this would be that it became increasingly difficult to pass into the ranks of the French nobility after the twelfth century. Moreover, there was a marked tendency to associate the term *nobility* with the exercise of specific juridical prerogatives. For an assessment of recent literature on this theme, see Georges Duby, "Une enquête à pour-suivre: la noblesse dans la France," *Revue Historique* 226 (1961): 1–22. The North Italian

That certain of these "boni homines" were magnates was, to a large extent, a juridical matter, for wherein did the Bardi or Frescobaldi *magnati* differ from their fellow bankers, the great *popolani* of the houses of Peruzzi and Acciaiuoli? Without minimizing present-day historical descriptions of this quasi fused patriciate, and acknowledging that the great magnate bankers and wool merchants were to continue to serve the commune as wise counselors and responsible bureaucrats over the next centuries, it should be emphasized that the problem of the magnates has another and most sorely neglected side.

Florentine chroniclers and those versed in the prevailing Aristotelian political theory were quick to suggest that no good regime could deny representation to the magnates; never at any time, no matter how democratized civil life became, were these men excluded from all public offices.[11] Not only was their talent and rich experience indispensable to the *Signoria*, but the very tenure of any regime depended upon winning the consent and support of a majority of the great *popolani* and *magnati*. This does not preclude the existence of dissident elements, however, and it is precisely here that the current historical view of the magnates falls short. One cannot assess correctly the character of the

---

situation was not comparable, since there had been extensive interpenetration between noble and commoner, and many nouveaux clans had risen to the top echelons of communal society. Social mobility was pronounced and economic distinctions tended to blur from the eleventh through the thirteenth century. Cf. G. Luzzatto, *Studi di storia economica veneziana* (Padua, 1954), 125–65; E. Cristiani, op. cit., 129–34. To argue, however, that because of this socioeconomic interpretation the North Italian urban patriciate achieved homogeneity would be fallacious. See Jacques Heers's incisive discussion of "Le divorce entre les deux aristocraties est très net," in *Gênes au XVe siècle* (Paris, 1961) 511–62; M. Rabozzi, "Lotte in Novara fra antica e nobilità," *Bollettino Storico per la provincia di Novara* 1 (1948): 5–20. No study comparable to that of Heers's exists for Florence. Cf. E. Fiumi, op. cit., 443–509.

11. Villani, *Cronica*, 11: 118; Compagni, *Cronica*, 2:12. Speakers before the *Signoria* never tired of advocating that Florence's neighbors—Siena, Volterra, Pistoia—could cure all varieties of civic maladies if they would only grant the magnates a larger share of offices. *Consulte et Pratiche*, 10, f. 93r; ibid., 11, f. 105r; ibid., 12 f. 149; ibid., 14, fols. 14r–31r. (Henceforth this source will be abbreviated *CP*.) Magnates were in fact excluded from office in only a few of the North Italian towns. Cf. G. Fasoli, "La legislazione antimagnatizia a Bologna fino al 1292," *Rivista di Storia del Diritto Italiano* 6 (1933): 351ff. Frequently, "the ferocious dispositions" of the statutes were confined to the realm of theory.

magnates by merely reading minutes of the communal councils, for throughout Florentine history those men who were brought into the government were in fact the ones who tended to be sympathetic with the objectives of the ruling *Signorie*. Nowhere is this practice more obvious than during the decade of the 1280s; those magnates who were co-opted were of course in fundamental agreement with the great *popolani*. By 1285, however, it had become apparent that there were other magnates, even kin of those holding high office, who, in the language of the day, "were not content to live *la vita civile*."[12] Because of the continued lawless behavior of these men, the *Signoria* felt compelled to convoke a general parliament. The first speaker at this citizen assembly, an eminent lawyer, maintained that since the discords which embroiled the city had been provoked exclusively by unruly magnates, this order should be forced to settle its differences so that the city might once again have peace. The next counselor, the hosier, Nerio, advocated that the *Signoria* itself reduce the *discordia* so prevalent among this class.[13] Despite the sage advice and the repeated efforts of the *Signoria* to terminate private warfare among the magnates, strife appears to have intensified during the ensuing years. Giovanni Villani was of the opinion that the collapse of this regime and the rise of the popular *Signoria* of 1293 was occasioned by the unabating civil wars within the ranks of the magnates.[14] Only too seldom was the *Signoria* able to make peace prevail between the warring families. When this was accomplished, however, there was ample cause for joyous festivals and colorful public pageants; even the parsimonious communal councils enthusiastically voted subsidies to commemorate these rare instances in order to impress the

---

12. Salvemini, op. cit., 308.

13. The jurist was Dominus Raynerius del Sasso. Cf. *Le Consulte*, 1:169–70.

14. *Cronica*, 8:1. Despite concerted effort during the 1280s, the regime had been unable to dissuade the magnates from recourse to the vendetta. As early as 1281, the magnates were prohibited from exercising this prerogative. Worth noting is the fact that this right was guaranteed to all the other orders of society. It would seem then that vendetta among classes other than the magnates did not pose so great a problem for a *Signoria* concerned with the keeping of public order. Among the top echelons of communal society it was thought to be dishonorable to resort to public courts for vindication. It should be remembered that in the early commune the aristocracy was distinguished by two ancient and related privileges: the right to bear arms and the right to execute justice. Cf. N. Rubinstein, *La lotta contro i magnati a Firenze* (Florence, 1939), 50–54; E. Cristiani, op. cit., 82–89.

volatile populace with memories of the blessings of harmony and the triumphs of public law.[15]

These victories of public law over private prerogatives could not be insured through government by exhortation or admonition; as early as 1281, a special citizen militia had been organized composed of one thousand men, "amatores et zelatores boni et pacifici status dicte civitatis," to assist the republic's magistrates in performing their official duty against lawless *magnates et potentes*.[16] At first this militia was the responsibility of the greater guilds, and they alone were permitted to assemble under the standards of their *arti*, but soon the five middle guilds were granted this privilege, and, finally, the honor was bestowed upon the nine lesser guilds of the city. By 1288 the force behind public law had gained momentum and was now rooted in the guild corporations of the city.[17]

And yet even this more broadly based *Signoria* was unable to quell the chronic violence. The arrest and condemnation of a great magnate would be enough to trigger public rioting and aristocrats such as Corso Donati, offspring of a family Dante was to call "the outrageous tribe that playeth dragon," could marshal the city mobs against the troops of the podestà or the capitano and prevent them from arresting a high-born culprit; then when the melee was over, and the minions of the law were frustrated, Corso and his cohorts would go unpunished.[18] Figures like Corso filled their countrymen with equal parts of fear and fascination: those who damned him went on to praise him in the same breath for his fatal gifts of beauty and charm. He, in the company of other patricians, was to constitute that core of rugged individualists who made the Flor-

---

15. The *Signoria* expended two thousand lire for the celebration of a marriage that reconciled the feuding houses of the Lamberti and the Della Tosa. At a meeting of the communal councils shortly thereafter, a speaker proposed that a vote be taken "super eo quod libre 2,000 que possunt expendi in matrimoniis contratendis pro pace facienda inter Tosinghos et Lambertos possint expendi occasione matrimoniorum et occasione pacis." *Le Consulte*, I, 360, 372 (11 April 1290). The *Signoria* was anxious to offer every inducement to those who would make peace. Cf. *Le Consulte*, I, 372; *Archivio Notarile*, A. 983, f. 25r, C. 102, f. 82. The one act of the despised tyrant Walter of Brienne that was to win him kudos was his pacification of contentious magnate clans. For copies of peace pacts signed by these houses, see *Balìa*, 1.

16. G. Salvemini, op. cit., app. 4, 337–46.

17. R. Davidsohn, *Storia di Firenze* (Florence, 1957), vol. 2, pt. 2, 294–96, 419; *Forschungen zur geschichte von Florenz*, vol. 3, n. 1197.

18. Villani, *Cronica*, 7:114; Davidsohn, *Storia di Firenze*, vol. 2, pt. 2, 417.

entine politics of the late *Dugento* so unpredictable. If prediction were in order, one might suggest that it was the suppression of this type of individualist that was to make possible the more collectivized Renaissance state with its more cohesive ruling class.[19]

Just as troublesome to the regime was the regular practice of commuting sentences and laying aside verdicts against magnate families such as the Pazzi or Frescobaldi.[20] Here again we can observe something of the division, or better still the tension, between magnates who sat in the government and those who remained outside. A Della Tosa might warmly support severe legislation enacted by the *Signoria* prohibiting the granting of judicial dispensation for high crimes, while one of his own clan or class might suffer the consequences of this Draconian measure.[21] No single medieval practice did more to impede the attempts of magistrates to bring the *potentes* and *magnates* of the city to justice than did repeated grants of judicial dispensation. And yet these enactments reveal something of the dualism implicit in medieval ways: either the culprit would be visited with a vengeful justice or be graced with merciful compassion. Thirteenth-century sentimentality was especially drawn to the plight of the mighty whose horrendous fall from high estate could evoke the extremes of laughter or tearful pity. Therefore, the emotions of *il popolo* made the ministrations of justice against the overmighty a precarious venture at best. Finally, there was no such entity as an independent judiciary in the Italian city-state, and the *Signoria* could and did either prompt or set aside court verdicts. Chroniclers bemoaned this practice and lamented that the powerful were able to commit the greatest atrocities with impunity, while the poor and the

---

19. In speaking of "how the great man of the people, Giano della Bella, was driven out of Florence," Villani opines that the leader of the popular revolution "was presumptuous and desired to avenge his wrongs." Then he draws the moral for his audience: "And note that this is a great example to those citizens who are to come, to beware of desiring to be lords over their fellow-citizens or too ambitious; but to be content with the common citizenship." *Cronica*, 8:8. Dino Compagni's chronicle is replete with vivid descriptions of political individualism whose quest for "vainglory" debased communal politics. No portrait is more striking than that of the Black Guelf leader, the magnate Corso Donati, who is depicted as a later-day Catiline. Compagni's sympathies, like those of Villani, are with "la gente comune"; only those men had the public good at heart. D. Compagni, *Cronica*, 2:20; 2:9; G. Villani, *Cronica*, 8:13; 8:69.

20. *Provvisioni Protocoli*, 1, fols. 60r–61r; *Le Consulte*, 1:347, 360.

21. Ibid., 1:308 (2 October 1285).

weak were hanged, broken on the wheel, or decapitated for every trifling misdemeanor.[22] The irony was that the same men who were appalled by these conditions were not above using their political influence to assist magnates who sought to escape the rigors of communal law.[23]

Much more matter of fact as a cause for obstructing justice was the persistent communal need for revenue and the dilemma of the *fideius-sores*. Pardons were granted regularly, depending upon the needs of the *Camera*, at a rate of 15 percent of the original condemnation. Such a pardon liberated those who had gone surety (the *fideiussores*) for a lawless magnate. There were in the city numerous magnates who either would not or simply could not afford to post bond, and, since the well-being of the republic depended upon the suppression of crime among the magnates, *fideiussores* were to be sought among the affluent of any class.[24] This meant that great *popolani* were much involved in the fate of lawless magnates and, therefore, ambivalence tended to be nurtured. There was also the troublesome question of the liability of the *consorteria* itself, intensified by the tangle of medieval property laws. In addition, there loomed the awesome prospect of the destruction of the homes of the tainted families. Problems of dowry and the plight of children made any reprisal a matter of grave concern to those magnates and *popolani* who served in the councils of the republic at this time. Their vote for or against judicial dispensation was cast not only in light of this knowledge but very frequently on the basis of intimate personal experience. Florence was governed by a closely knit elite and tragedy was rarely a private matter. Men were seldom alone, and this absence of privacy was reflected in the display of life in the streets, the sidewalk business transaction, the open markets and broad piazzas, and the autobiographical celebrations of the loves and hates of a Dante or a Boccaccio. Only much later were the Renaissance architects to be concerned with the modern notion of privacy.

The role of the *Signoria* as peacemaker was further complicated by the mixed reception which greeted its efforts. The overall tendency of Florentine legislation was to intrude more and more into matters formerly decided by the councils of a *consorteria*, or a tower society, and

---

22. Stefani, *Cronica fiorentina*, rub. 555; Villani, *Cronica*, 3:58; Compagni, *Cronica*, 1:5.

23. Velluti, *Cronica domestica*, 20–21.

24. *Le Consulte*, 1:376.

some among the magnates welcomed this intervention. Once vendetta was proclaimed, its reverberations affected the guilty and innocent alike, and the blood-stained torso of Mars was more than an image from *The Divine Comedy.* Certain magnates accepted the decisions of communal arbitrators, rather than lay down their lives before "that mutilated stone." In other instances, where private justice was a fait accompli, the parties involved willingly subscribed to a settlement dictated by a public magistrate and signed peace pacts guaranteeing that they would desist from further vengeance. Often judicial dispensation was not granted by communal courts until these conditions were met.[25] Soon the commune demanded half the property of the aggressor and sought to limit the right of vendetta to the individual who had personally suffered insult or injury; in this way the *consorteria* was to be prevented from seeking revenge in the name of some distant kinsman. The magnates both desired and despised the intervention of the *Signoria* in this sensitive area, but the cumulative effect of repeated legislation by successive *Signorie* accustomed them to turn to the state for settlement of feuds. The only action of the loathed despot, Walter of Brienne (1342–43), to receive unanimous acclaim was the establishment of peace pacts among the warring magnates. After 1343 stringent enforcement of communal law was to do much to tame the more obdurate elements and to engender a deeper respect for the authority of public law. The continued growth of communal bureaucracy also would serve to reduce the incidence of crimes of violence among all classes and produced an environment in which the ties of community were strengthened at the expense of private loyalties.[26]

---

25. M. Becker, "Gualtieri di Brienne e l'uso delle dispense giudiziarie," *Archivio Storico Italiano* 113 (1955): 245–51; A. Enriques, "La vendetta nella vita nella legislazione fiorentina," *Archivio Storico Italiano* 91 (1933): 85–146.

26. M. Becker, "An Essay on the Novi Cives and Florentine Politics, 1343–1382," *Mediaeval Studies* 24 (1962): 35–82. Later in the Trecento, when a public luminary was slain in a vendetta, the Signoria would decree "quod acerrima vindicta fiat" against the assassin. Furthermore, his consorts were to be punished, their property to be devastated, and the entire clan to be visited "cum perpetua ruina." The regime would then sponsor a lavish state funeral for the victim "in order to honor his memory." *CP.,* 19, f. 63r (16 September 1380). The public figure in this instance was Giovanni Mone, grain merchant and one of the "Eight Saints" in command of the war against the papacy. Cf. *Provvisioni,* 64, f. 19. (Henceforth this source will be abbreviated *P.*)

Until 1292 the magnates held 12 percent of the seats in the priorate, and this statistic has been utilized by recent historians in an attempt to demonstrate that Salvemini's and Davidsohn's descriptions of the preceding decade, as an interval characterized by class conflict between the entrepreneurs of the guilds and the landholding magnates, are fallacious. Unfortunately, however, the newer arguments are not altogether convincing.[27] Already it has been suggested that those magnates co-opted for the priorate were not entirely typical of their class; nor was 12 percent a very sizable representation for this order. Such an apportionment was actually discriminatory since the magnates numbered approximately one-quarter of the more affluent citizens of the commune, and their membership was about equal to that of the *popolani* matriculated in the greater guilds.[28] If one adds the 6 percent representation accorded the lesser guilds to the 12 percent granted the magnates, then one has a *Signoria* composed of 82 percent *popolani grassi* who, for the most part, were great bankers, industrialists, and international traders. As has been indicated previously, the 12 percent of the magnates who sat in the *Signoria* were great capitalists of the same stripe, but two troublesome questions yet remain: How representative were these men of the many included in this heterogeneous group juridically defined as magnates? And how enthusiastically were the policies, sponsored by the elite of the greater guilds, received by those magnates excluded from the *Signoria?* The older accounts by Salvemini and Davidsohn erred in attempting to uncover evidence of magnate dissent in the abbreviated minutes of the council meetings, but the modern revisionists, Ottokar

---

27. The leader of the revisionists who led the critique of the older views was Nicola Ottokar. For a survey of his writings and a sympathetic analysis of the weaknesses inherent in his philosophy of history, see E. Sestan, "Nicola Ottokar," *Rivista Storica Italiana* 71 (1959): 178–84.

28. This rough figure is derived from a statement in *Le Consulte,* 1:202. Ser Arrigus Gratie proposed that a *prestanza* be exacted from six thousand two hundred of the citizenry. Of this number, one thousand five hundred or so were magnates. The ratio of magnates to affluent *popolani* rate payers was not altered substantially in the subsequent period. The *Monte,* or funded communal debt, was composed of outstanding *prestanze* accumulated between 1326 and 1343. The total number of rate payers was eight thousand, and, if we subtract the names of petty rate payers from this figure, our ratio of affluent *popolani* to *magnati* is still roughly four to one. Cf. *Monte, campione dell'impianto del 1345,* S. Giovanni, S. Spirito, S. Maria Novella, S. Croce.

and Fiumi, have also erred in presuming that the harmony that existed between a small segment of the Florentine magnates of the greater guilds and their commoner confreres can be projected to include that remaining half of the city's magnate families not inscribed in any guild as well as that large group of magnates who inhabited rural Tuscany.

That magnates participated in the *Signoria* from 1282 to 1292, and that they were to continue to serve each succeeding regime, must be taken into account by anyone desirous of understanding the rise of a heightened sense of civic consciousness within this group. As to the unrepresented majority, it will be necessary to examine the effect of public policy upon their great variety of interests. The magnates in the *Signoria* were part of the world of the guilds, and the dominant trend was toward a highly economically regulated society. Like neighboring city-states, Florence was profoundly concerned with achieving the goal of economic self-sufficiency. This entailed extensive legislation fixing dates for the planting of crops and their harvest, restricting the flow of agricultural labor, insuring the cultivation of idle lands, regulating the prices of agricultural commodities, checking the illegal export of foodstuffs, establishing the terms of tenement; the commune was now intervening in the most intimate details of rustic life.[29] All of his was to be done so that agrarian production might increase and the republic might then achieve a higher degree of self-sufficiency. Control over rural markets, the fisheries along the Arno, the cattle trade, as well as over the distribution of such essentials as salt, was accompanied by the imposition of a host of indirect levies on foodstuffs and wines. The extension of communal gabelles into remote territories under Florentine jurisdiction meant that state courts had to be established to enforce collection of imposts and that a multitude of fiscal practices had to be regularized. To the seventy or so magnate families of the *contado*, this signified an encroachment upon ancient prerogatives and traditional ways. The triumph of communal sovereignty was to be a gradual and uneven process, but the result was certain—the slow dissipation of the seigneurial power of unfriendly magnates. At first the commune did little to interfere with the ancient rights of those lords whose loyalty to the republic had been demonstrated, and even in 1289, when the *Signoria* proclaimed an end to serfdom in Florentine dominions, the tenurial

---

29. I wish to thank Dr. Philip Jones, of Oxford, for permitting me to read his manuscript on the agrarian history of Italy in the late Middle Ages.

nexus between these lords and their serfs remained unbroken.[30] The regime did, however, assert the principle that the men of the *contado*, no matter what their status or condition might be, were to be amenable to communal levies, and that all rustics were to be liable for service to the commune. The tendency was, then, to replace the suzerainty of the lord with that of the commune, and to require that the men of the *contado* do castle guard, repair bridges and walls, maintain roads, and, in fact, be responsible for that great variety of other public services so augmented during the course of the *Dugento*. Similarly, Florentine sovereignty impinged upon the lordship of magnates over rural communes and *popoli*, and soon these hamlets were being assessed, taxed, and judged according to the prescriptions of Florentine statutes rather than by more traditional formulas. This latter development, involving the abrogation of private feudal rights, lasted well over a century and resistance to it was tenacious. The growth of territorial law and its final victory over more personal types of medieval jurisdictions was haphazard, and what the commune could not achieve legally, she gained through purchase and adroit diplomacy.[31]

The initiative for regulating the magnates of the *contado* came not only from the *Signoria* but also from the rectors of the rural communities as well. Tearfully they besought the priors of the republic to put an end to the chronic violence perpetrated by certain *magnates et potentes*, calling upon the government to prevent these lawless men from acquiring property in the vicinity and contending that, if these "evil men" were allowed to extend their holdings, it would not be long before the villagers would find themselves under their "heel." The *Signoria* frequently heeded the petitioners and announced that magnates might not

30. E. Besta, *Le persone nella storia del diritto italiano* (Padua, 1931), 99ff; R. Caggese, *Classi e comuni rurali nel medio evo italano* (Florence, 1908), 2:227; L. Simeoni, "La liberazione del servi a Bologna nel 1256–1257," *Archivio Storico Italiano* 109 (1951): 3–26. The liberation of the *manentes* did not imply the ceding of the land on which they worked. Cf. E. Cristiani, op. cit., 151–56; and the important study of R. Romeo, "La Signoria dell'abate di S. Ambrogio di Milano sul comune rurale di Origgio nel secolo XIII," *Rivista Storica Italiana* 69 (1957): 340–77, 472–506.

31. *Delizie degli toscani*, ed. I. di San Luigi (Florence, 1770–89), 7:191. See legislative debate of 5 September 1380: Quod fiat ita quod Tarlati et Ubertini stent in devotione communis. Quod cito nox viva mittatur ad filios domini Magii et alios Ubertinos et Petramalem ad exhortandum cos. Et cum pecunia subveniatur. *CP.*, 19, f. 63.

purchase estates in particular areas "pro bono et quieto statu districtus."[32] In 1286 the podestà and capitano were authorized by the *Signoria* to force the most unruly of the *potentes* to sell their properties and thus relinquish their extra legal dominion. Rural communities were urged to take action against these transgressors, "maxime magnates," and to confiscate their lands. Gradually, there emerged in the *contado* a highly integrated regime whereby the syndics of country parishes came to assume greater responsibility for the actions of their constituency. In the case of the magnates this meant that the rural parishes were now liable for their unpaid gabelles and subject to fine if criminous citizens or banished magnates were found in the region. Moreover, rural magistracies were also to be condemned if they failed to report crimes to the Florentine judiciary.[33] The problem of brigandage remained chronic, and, as the city and the *popoli* of the *contado* became mutually interested in the construction of roads, the rustic *popolares* entreated the *Signoria* to protect them from the many extortions and larcenies committed by magnates against those *contadini* transporting goods to market.

The monasteries, abbeys, and pious foundations of Tuscany also turned to the *Signoria* for redress of grievances, for they suffered not only from the usurpations of their magnate neighbors but also from the numerous peculations and appropriations of church property by magnates such as the Aliotti, Buondelmonti, Girolami, Tosinghi, and others. Especially notorious were the Della Tosa and Visdomini clans who used their ancient authority as patrons and defenders of the bishopric to sequester church revenues whenever the See was vacant. Dante's taunt "So did their fathers who, whene'er your church is vacant, stand guzzling in consistory" could have been directed against any number of high-born patricians.[34]

---

32. *Statuti della Repubblica Fiorentina*, ed. R. Caggese (Florence, 1910–21), 100 (1284); G. Salvemini, op. cit., 356–57; G. Rondoni, *I più antichi frammenti del costitito fiorentino* (Florence, 1882), 43.

33. The first extensive records concerning the activities of the Florentine magistrates are to be found in the *Camera del Comune, Entrata, 1 bis*. This particular volume of the treasury records of some 350 folios is dated from October 1342 to July 1343 but contains transcripts of many cases of a much earlier vintage.

34. *Paradiso*, 16:112–15. For a summary of the role of the Florentine patriciate in the Tuscan church, see R. Davidsohn, *Firenze ai tempi di Dante*, trans. E. Theseider (Florence, 1929), 1–18.

Not only was it commonplace to find these great clans encroaching upon the prerogatives of the church, but the unanimous opinion of *Trecento* chroniclers was that these *potentes* used their ecclesiastical influence to intimidate and oppress the poor and the weak.[35] During intervals when the political power of these magnates was at a low ebb, both the clergy and laity, who administrated ecclesiastical estates, pressed suit against these aristocratic despoilers. The position of the church, however, remained ambiguous because, while, on the one hand, many of the Tuscan prelates were themselves magnates, on the other, there was widespread trepidation at the prospect of allowing church property to slip away. The ecclesiastical hierarchy was itself torn on the question of whether to support popular *Signorie* in their policies designed to recover church properties from the usurpers or to ally with the oligarchical opposition. Popular regimes frequently protected church estates only to levy taxes on them, while oligarchical governments were more mindful of ancient ecclesiastical liberties where taxation was involved.[36]

The view of the *Signoria* toward the magnates of the church was equally as troubled since there was a mounting concern that the great feudatories of the *contado,* such as the Ubaldini, the Ubertini, the Pazzi of Valdarno, and the Counts Guidi, would use their enormous ecclesiastical *auctoritas* to undermine the republic and make it the victim of the vagaries of ever-shifting Italian church politics. Over the next century a variety of communal statutes were enacted calculated to prevent just such a horrendous eventuality.[37] Clearly, this was an invasion of ancient

---

35. Marchionne di Coppo Stefani, op. cit., rub. 616; Villani, *Cronica,* 12:43; N. Rodolico, *I Ciompi,* 42. Cf. also M. Becker, "Some Economic Implications of the Conflict between Church and State in Trecento Florence," *Mediaeval Studies* 21 (1959): 1–16.

36. M. Becker, "Church and State in Florence on the Eve of the Renaissance," *Speculum* 37 (1962): 511–14. During intervals when the Signoria was democratized, monasteries and pious foundations made accusations against magnates who usurped church property. The culprits were prosecuted vigorously under the appropriate provisions of the Ordinances of Justice. Cf. R. Davidsohn, *Forschungen zur geschichte,* 4:164–65; J. Plesner, op. cit., 104–69. Frequently, clergy had reason to fear the vendetta of irate magnates. Religious establishments were willing to concede prerogatives and jurisdiction to Florence in return for the Signoria's pledge to defend the clergy from their enemies. P. Santini, *Documenti dell'antica costituzione del comune di Firenze* (Florence, 1952), 253.

37. *Statuti della Repubblica Fiorentina,* 273–74; A. Panella, "La guerra degli

feudal prerogatives, and it was accompanied by the erosion of imperial privileges until, by the end of the *Trecento,* even the overweaning Counts Guidi, so remote from the city, were now subject to communal levies. During the 1280s, assessments on the lands of the Ubaldini were raised three times, and, while certain great lords were able to conserve specific feudal rights, the trend was clearly in the direction of mounting state sovereignty. Communal commissions were certainly not unsympathetic to these time-honored privileges, but they were guided by scrupulously legalistic criteria, and in the absence of compelling evidence the decision went against the accused. Not infrequently, tortuous litigation culminated in communal purchase of property and rights.[38]

The magnates of rural Tuscany were as little united as their urban counterparts, and communal rectors were called upon repeatedly to make peace between contentious clans. Sometimes state intervention was blatant, and the militia of the republic did battle with the warring feudatories. Upon occasion peace was restored only after the beleaguered nobles formally submitted to the jurisdiction of the commune on the condition that the *Signoria* cancel all outstanding condemnations against the clan "sine aliqua solutione."[39] The net public power was further extended into the far reaches of Florentine territory when the great feudal magnates were compelled to have city dwellers post security for their continued good behavior.

The law was becoming increasingly discriminatory against those judged by their contemporaries to be the most energetic harbingers of "raw egoism"—the antisocial magnates. And that this repression should occur at a time when these magnates were still the backbone of

---

Otto Santi e le vicende della legge contro i vescovi," *Archivio Storico Italiano* 99 (1941): 36–49. For disquieting evidence of usurpations of ecclesiastical prerogatives by such magnate families as the Aliotti, Della Tosa, Gherardini, and Visdomini, see *Manoscritti varii,* 46. For the influence of the great feudatories on the Tuscan Church, see F. Schneider, *Die Reichsverwaltung in Toscana von der Gründug des Langobardenreiches bis zum Ausgang der Staufer (568–1268)* (Rome, 1914), 299–346.

38. For an inquest conducted by communal magistrates pertaining to certain properties "qui occupata erant . . . per quosdam potentes et magnates contra communem Florentie," see *Atti del Esecutore, 33.*

39. In this instance the object of the Signoria's benevolence was the Pazzi of the Valdarno, who acknowledged "sint et esse debeant ad honorem subiectionem et obedientem et servicium communi." *Le Consulte,* 1:347 (12 January 1290).

the Florentine armies is itself noteworthy. In fact, it was to be less than four years after that glorious 11 June 1289, when the charge of the elite magnate cavalry won the day against Arezzo at the Battle of Campaldino, and long before citizen troops were rendered obsolete by foreign mercenaries, that the magnates were to be struck by the cruelest measures in the republic's annals—the discriminatory Ordinances of Justice of 1293.[40]

Over the next generation, despite the incessant pleas of magnates, who continued to serve in the vanguard of the city's host, that their bravery and patriotism should be rewarded with the abrogation of these dread ordinances, newer and harsher restraints were placed on this class by the *Signoria* in 1309, 1321, and 1324. It would seem that facile generalizations attempting to correlate anti-magnate laws with the dwindling military importance of the magnates are overhasty; severe constraints long antedated the decline in military contribution of this order.

The regime of 1282–92 lacked precise objective criteria for defining the magnates. The *Signoria* was itself a composite of the urban aristocracy and in its actions toward the magnates it made numerous exceptions to the general provisions of the law. Theoretically, an entire family might be required to post security, but in practice important exemptions were granted.[41] To the men governing the city during this critical decade there was no proper definition of the term *magnate,* and, therefore, public policy was as inconsistent as it was pragmatic. Beyond the statement that certain individuals whose behavior was a threat to the peace and tranquillity of the city would be compelled to post bond as magnates, little can be said. Nor was there a precise notion of the membership of a *consorteria* until 1293: it is only then that magnate clans were defined and fused into an order now designated as the Florentine nobility. The movement toward a more exact description of the nobility occurs between 1289 and late 1292 when specific criteria are formulated to distinguish commoner from noble. Hitherto, this imprecise and vaguest

---

40. N. Ottokar, *Studi comunali e fiorentini* (Florence, 1948) 86ff.

41. Salvemini, op. cit., 186–87. Nicola Ottokar has demonstrated that Davidsohn's reading of *Diplomatico S. Spirito* (31 January 1289) is incorrect and that magnates judged to be "impotentie" were released from this onerous obligation. Cf. *Il comune di Firenze alla fine del dugento* (Florence, 1926), 249. Finally, even the Draconian Ordinances of Justice of January 1293 permitted the Signoria to treat separately with those magnates "qui eisdem dominis Prioribus insufficientes et impotentes videbuntur." Cf. Salvemini, op. cit., 407.

of all medieval social designations was bestowed upon those who held certain feudal estates, or had received the accolade from the church, the emperor, a foreign lord, or even from the Florentine *Signoria*, which had held regalian rights since 1260.

The *Signoria*, in the years immediately before the enactment of the Ordinances of Justice, was confronted with the problem of financing protracted and, for the most part, ill-starred military ventures. That this policy culminated in the debacle of 1292 did much to discredit those who had been responsible for formulating foreign policy. During those four critical years the *Signoria* relied heavily upon the magnates for counsel since these men were most experienced in military matters and most familiar with the intricate workings of Italian diplomacy. The records of the council meetings disclose that there was no division among the elite on foreign policy questions, and the regime blundered ahead with a high degree of unanimity.

There is some justice in blaming the magnates for certain disasters that befell the republic and later there was sentiment charging the great houses with conducting foreign affairs in accord with their own private interests rather than out of concern for the general welfare. When the list of magnates was drawn up in 1293, it included the names of those who had directed the disastrous war effort, and the framers of the ordinances were not influenced by the prior juridical status of a given individual. Families such as the Acciaiuoli, Medici, Peruzzi, and Strozzir, great commoners who had less political influence at this time and were little implicated in the war effort, were to profit most from the restraints placed upon such clans as the Bardi, Cerchi, Mozzi, and Spini who had been deeply involved. It was the latter who were reckoned among the Florentine nobility in 1293 and, therefore, were rendered ineligible for the highest elective offices. Many other families who would have been regarded as "noble" by Dante's contemporaries, by virtue of their claims of lineage and ancient title, were not inscribed upon the rolls as "magnates et nobiles." Among their number were the Altoviti, Baldovinetti, Della Bella, Chiermontesi, Guigni, Importuni, and Pagolotti. Not only were they not so closely identified with the calamities of those years, but certain of them proved to be warm supporters and even leaders of the popular revolution of 1293.[42]

---

42. Villani, *Cronica*, 4:2, 13; *Paradiso*, 6:127ff.; Ottokar, op. cit., 174ff.

From 1289–92 Florentine legislation revealed certain characteristics that were to be of consequence to the magnates. Under the pressure of war and the attendant need for revenue, the *Signoria* tightened lax administrative practices, introduced reforms into the treasury system, and revised the tax structure.[43] No longer could the city afford the casual controls over communal property and rights nor the loose accountability of government officials so prevalent in easier days. Now it was imperative that the city act to conserve its wealth and augment its income so that it could support the military campaigns in progress. Actions such as the liberation of the serfs in Florentine territories have not been viewed within this context, but, if they are placed within the sequence of the legislation of these years, then this measure stands as one of a series of enactments designed to extend public control in order to increase state funds. Upon being freed, the serf was immediately subject to communal imposts. Public authority was also strengthened at the expense of private rights when communal syndics and foreign magistrates were appointed to put an end to the many frauds and abuses of office holders and overmighty citizens.

This trend toward a more impersonal and impartial type of regime was also to be much in evidence during 1323–25, 1328–29, and after 1343. During each of these intervals comparable developments culminated in the foundation of a popular *Signoria*, and fundamental to the establishment of this democratized regime was the vigorous enforcement of the *divieto*. This law prohibited members of the same family from holding high office simultaneously and required that an individ-

---

43. For the most recent analysis of those alterations in the communal fiscal structure, see N. Ottokar, op. cit., 216ff. Beginning in April 1289 and continuing throughout the fall of that same year, the *Signoria* created new offices such as the "sei rationerii," enjoined to control the "pecunia communis," and appointed foreign rectors "ad reinveniendum iura communis." The special purpose of these latter officials was to prevent "fraus, dolus aut symonia in averi communis." Apparently, abuses in the public sale of communal lands and the auctioning of taxes to farmers of these levies was rampant. Cf. also Davidsohn, *Forschungen,* 4:304–5; B. Barbadoro, *Le finanze della repubblica fiorentina* (Florence, 1929), 253–55.

Controversy has centered around communal grain policy and the extent to which it was regulated by harsh governmental decrees at this time. It should be noted that the *Signoria* was much concerned with the grain trade, since this traffic yielded the republic substantial income; gabelles were the principal source of communal revenue. *Le Consulte,* 1:4ff. For bibliography, see D. Herlihy, *Pisa in the Early Renaissance* (New Haven, 1958), 110–12.

ual could only stand for reelection to the *Signoria* after a suitable lapse of time (usually two or three years).

The chronicler, Dino Compagni, much immersed in city politics, and several times prior of the republic, contended that the rulers of the commune, the great *popolani*, co-opted certain of their magnate kinsmen and together they constituted an elite whose membership was repeatedly reelected to the *Signoria*.[44] In November 1292, when the reaction against this elite had gained momentum, the councils met to discuss the ever vexing question of the *divieto*. The speakers expressed fresh political sentiments: in addition to advocating the strict enforcement of the *divieto*, Ubertino Strozzi and Bonisegna Becchinugi proposed that each guild be limited to a single seat in the priorate.[45] Iacopo de Certaldo made the radical suggestion that all who had previously served as prior should be henceforth barred from this office. He then went on to offer another novel view: let there be twelve priors, four from the major guilds, four from the *populares*, and a like number from the lesser guilds of the city.

What these speakers were committed to was the concept of a guild government as opposed to the rule of the great families of the *arti*. Before 1292 no serious effort had been made to equalize representation among the guilds, now offices were to be distributed, at least in theory, upon a corporate rather than a personal basis. An even bolder suggestion was made by Tiero Burbassi, no friend of the magnates: let the *Signoria* be elected by the representatives of the seven major and five middle guilds. He then added this startling proviso: no one may be chosen to the priorate who is himself a knight or has a relative who has received *la dignità cavalleresca*. The prohibition was to apply to all families who had received knightly honors over the past thirty years. With slight modifications, this was to be the formula incorporated into the Ordinances of Justice of 1293. Those who held patents of nobility were now to be included among the city's magnates and to be compelled to post security as well as to suffer disfranchisement from the highest communal offices.

It is evident from the speeches of Burbassi and others that the introduction of this new juridical category was intimately connected with

---

44. Compagni, *Cronica*, 1:5, 8, 20; Villani, *Cronica*, 7:131; 8:39; 10:128; 11:59; *Le Consulte*, 2:671–72.

45. *Le Consulte*, 2:225.

the problem of reducing the political influence of the great families. This end was to be achieved through the strict enforcement of the *divieto* and the application of a more specific definition of the term *magnate*. Communal society was moving toward the rule of the guilds and away from domination by individual entrepreneurs. Offices were to be distributed so that representation would be accorded, more or less proportionately, to the various corporate guilds of the city, and, with the enactment of the legislation of 1293–95, this ambitious plan was realized. For the first time the nobility, magnates and knights alike, were excluded from the *Signoria,* certain of the communal councils, and high guild office. In this way the hegemony of the Adimari, Bardi, Cavalcanti, Donati, Frescobaldi, Mozzi, Rossi, and others over civic life was disrupted. This new nobility created by the Ordinances of Justice was now to feel the full force of anti-magnate legislation, and no longer were individual members of these clans, who incidentally happened to be great guildsmen, exempted from the restraints imposed upon their order.

The new government was grounded in the collectivized world of the twenty-one guilds, but the footing was far from secure, for its tenure depended upon the suppression of the intense political individualism of the older families. Just as the earlier regimes had endeavored to restrain the lawlessness of men by designating them as magnates, so the new *Signoria* of twenty-one *arti* sought to check the ascendancy of particular clans over public life by placing upon them the disability of noble status. Liabilities upon this group were enlarged in April 1293, when they were excluded from the Council of One Hundred, the Council of the *Capitano,* the consulship of the guilds, and, finally, the priorate itself. This disfranchisement was accompanied by a substantial increase in the number of magnates required to put up bond for their continued good behavior.[46] No longer were exemptions granted, but now the entire *consorteria* was to be included—even down to the least legitimate of its offspring. One could dwell at great length upon the many onerous measures enacted between the years 1293 and 1295 and easily lose sight of an essential feature of civic life as it developed over the next half century. While it is true that the nobility were deprived of the right to hold a variety of offices, they did continue to occupy critical posts and to exert much influence over public policy.

At the outset it should be understood that the *Signoria* was deeply

---

46. R. Davidsohn, *Storia di Firenze* (Florence, 1957), 2, 2, 633.

conscious of the differences between noble families as well as the dis-similarities among members of the same clan. The Ordinances of Justice permitted the priorate to exempt certain less menacing members of no-ble families from their inhibiting provisions and set forth the formula that magnate houses that had not been required to post security over the past five years were to be reclassified as *popolani* or commoners.[47] With-out minimizing the possibility of political favoritism, and the abuses in-herent in any such policy, it can be suggested that while on the one hand the ordinances increased the size of the Florentine nobility by declaring that any clan that included a knight was ipso facto noble, the more co-operative members of a family could be disassociated from the order. Much more significant is the fact that many magnates could and did have impressive public careers between 1295 and 1343. These men demonstrated strong sympathies for the policies of the ruling oligarchy and many of these politically trustworthy men were eventually allowed to assume commoner status. They, unlike such magnates as Corso Do-nati, were to shun the individualistic political act and follow the labyrinthine path dictated by ever shifting communal interests. A his-tory of a few of these noble families should suffice to suggest the extent of their participation in public life and to indicate the possibilities still open to members of this class desirous of serving the commune.

The magnate house of Adimari was typical of that large group of patrician families so useful to the regime in its relations with the church.[48] Over the first four decades of the fourteenth century Florence tended to rely heavily upon the Guelf system of alliances with the pope and king of Naples. The Adimari held high ecclesiastical office in Tus-cany and were well represented in the captaincy of the Guelf Party. Therefore, it is not surprising to find many Adimari serving as commu-nal ambassadors to the papal curia. Regularly Adimari were sent on sen-sitive diplomatic missions to neighboring communities and to far off Guelf cities. Like so many others from their order, this family also sup-plied numerous captains and podestàs to enforce Florentine jurisdiction in the *contado*. Magnate status was no disadvantage when one exercised authority over the rustics. Similarly, it was commonplace for a member

---

47. Salvemini, op. cit., 406–8.

48. *Estimo*, 1, f. 29; *CC.*, 1 *bis*, fols. 55r–56; *Libri Fabarum*, 13, I. f. 24r (hence-forth this source will be abbreviated as *LF*). *LF.*, 16, II, f. 21r; *LF.*, 19, f. 104r; *Diplo-matico*, S. Maria Novella (13 April 1287).

of such a clan to serve as judicial officer over a large town in the Florentine domain. This most affluent family, great realtors in both the city and countryside, were frequently members of special committees selected by the government to make recommendations in the critical area of communal finance. Here there was no unanimity of opinion, and the Adimari, like other patrician houses, fell out among themselves.

It is ironic to note that the government and its advisors were in substantial agreement on the objectives of Florentine foreign policy and yet reluctant to vote taxes necessary for its implementation. The Adimari were well versed in the twin questions that were of utmost concern to the various *Signorie* throughout this trying period—foreign policy and state finance. Especially vexing was the decline of citizen armies and the coming of mercenaries and military protectors. The Adimari favored the remedy espoused by an overwhelming majority of the men then in power: when the military situation had deteriorated and communal debts mounted until the republic's credit was in jeopardy, then the *Signoria* should call in a foreign lord who would bring victory to Florence on the battlefield and restore stability in the counting house.

Contemporary chroniclers singled out the magnates and charged them with being subverters of the republic and champions of despotism. A more objective appraisal indicates that while one of the Adimari was indeed appointed as communal syndic to bestow the lordship of the city on Charles, duke of Calabria in 1326, and another Adimari stood up in the Council of the Podestà and spoke on behalf of a provision to grant additional powers to the then despot of the city, Walter of Brienne in 1342, the fact remains that the tendency to embrace despotism at moments of fiscal and military crises was also pervasive among the great *popolani* who ruled the city until 1342.[49]

Not only did the Adimari support despots and military protectors,

---

49. Messer Tommaso Altoviti counseled that Brienne be made captain and protector of the city. Further, he spoke in favor of the prorogation of the despot's tenure. *LF.,* 21, fols. 95–108 (May–June 1342). Taddeo Antella and Salvestro Baroncelli likewise favored the establishment of Brienne's *Signoria. Duplicati Provvisioni,* 3 fols. 21r–22r (September 1342). The Guicciardini, Lotti, and numerous other popolani championed Brienne's cause. Ibid., 3, fols. 17–18; *LF.,* 21, f. 91r. Taddeo Adimari spoke in the Council of the Podestà for conferring additional powers on Brienne; shortly thereafter he was in the service of the despot as ambassador to Volterra. Another Adimari was both ambassador to Bologna and vicar of Pistoia during Brienne's tenure.

but they, along with other leading magnates and commoners, held high office under these foreign lords. Their response was to the exigencies of the moment and their view of politics pragmatic and adaptable. In their actions they conformed to the pattern of an oligarchy and for this they were justly rewarded. In January 1338 five members of the clan were granted the dignity of knighthood in the name of the commune and *il popolo*. It should be borne in mind that after the early 1330s one could enjoy the status of knighthood without being subject to the disabilities imposed upon magnates by the Ordinances of Justice.[50] Perhaps these Adimari were a trifle too successful politically and too well identified with the ruling oligarchy of the 1330s, for soon they came to commit the same type of offense that was to discredit the patriciate in 1343. Over the years they practiced the sins of a self-assured ruling class during an era when the boundary between private and public rights was barely discernible; they proceeded to appropriate state property and usurp communal prerogatives, and, finally, they converted certain influential offices in the *contado* into a family preserve.

If many of the Adimari had become an integral part of the confident elite that governed the republic until the early 1340s, others of this house not only stood outside this circle but even placed themselves beyond the pale of communal law. The enactment of the Ordinances of Justice in 1293 and their periodic revisions over the next half-century made the penalties for magnate violence ever more severe; even so, the rate of crime among this order was little diminished.

During the 1330s, of the seventy-two city families inscribed among the magnates, forty-six stood convicted by the republic's magistrates for serious breaches of the law.[51] This means that approximately two-thirds of the city's magnate families contributed to the pervasive lawlessness of these times. Each house averaged four condemnations for high crimes, ranging from assault to homicide, and, for the most part, their victims were commoners. The Gherardini led the way with thirteen con-

---

50. G. Salvemini, *La dignità cavalleresca nel comune di Firenze* (Florence, 1896), 65. Mediaeval legislation is characterized by its imperfect implementation and even before the decade of the 1330s, perhaps as early as 1315 or 1316, upon occasion knighthood was conferred upon certain eminent popolani such as the Acciaiuoli, Medici, Peruzzi, and Strozzi for service to the commune and *il popolo*. Neither the recipients of this honor or their kinsmen were barred from the *Signoria*. Cf. *Delizie degli eruditi toscani*, 12, 262–73.

51. *Guidici degli Appelli*, vols. 121–25.

victions, followed by the Aleis and the Frescobaldi with ten apiece; the Giandonati amassed eight, while the Buondelmonti and Cavalcanti were charged with seven each. This list is far from complete since it only records those crimes for which judicial dispensation was granted. From 1339 to 1341 the *Signoria* permitted payments to be made into the communal treasury in return for the cancellation of condemnations. Therefore, when it is suggested that the magnates who constituted less than 6 percent of the population perpetrated 146 high crimes over a single decade, this figure actually represents a tiny fraction of the total, for we have only sparse records of those crimes committed by magnates against whom the commune was able to enforce the court's mandate.[52]

The persistence of violence in a family so nearly assimilated into the arena of public life as were the Adimari suggests that the enforcement of law was less than forthright and that communal councils and rectors were not unmindful of the status of these patricians. The general practice of granting judicial dispensation for serious offenses was a regular feature of oligarchical rule; only during brief intervals before 1343, when the base of the regime was sufficiently broadened, and popular government held sway, was this deeply rooted custom reversed.[53] Of the forty-six magnate families granted dispensation, thirty-five were related to the great *popolani* who held high public office, and many among the beneficiaries were from clans regularly serving in the government. The Frescobaldi, second only to the Gherardini in number of remissions received, provided the republic with numerous podestàs and captains for the *contado* and cities under Florentine dominion. Moreover, they furnished the regime with military officers, captains of rural leagues, and officials over fortifications.[54] Invaluable was their activity as syndics in

---

52. Court records before 1342 are sparse and discontinuous; therefore, in addition to the source cited here, the earliest volumes of the *Camera del Comune* provide us with the only extensive documentation on magnate crimes. Had the *Atti* of the executor of the Ordinances of Justice been preserved, this figure would have been much greater, for this official had major jurisdiction over criminous acts of magnates.

53. Cf. M. Becker, "Florentine Popular Government (1343–1348)," *Proceedings of the American Philosophical Society* 106 (1962): 375–77.

54. *LF.*, 13, I, f. 18r; *LF.*, 17, fols. 155r, 186r; *LF.*, 19, fols. 48r–51, *LF.*, 20, f. 3r; *P.*, 14, f. 19r; *Capitoli Protocoli*, 12, f. 68 r. This same family that provided the republic with some of its ablest civil servants also sired some of the most committed traitors. Rebellious Frescobaldi gave aid (in the form of grain) and comfort (in

charge of hiring mercenaries, but even more vital was the role they played in the many diplomatic missions dispatched to the papal curia and the other great courts of Europe. This was a family whose commercial and personal contacts spanned the continent, and from the many branches of their firm came pertinent news from distant points which benefited the *Signoria*. They, like the Buondelmonti and Gherardini, stood high in the Tuscan church, the captaincy of the *Parte Guelfa*, and the councils of the pope.

Very like these families were the Bardi, and perhaps this most ubiquitous of all magnate clans best illustrates the extent of power and influence still concentrated in the hands of the nobility.[55] A detailed description of the activities of the Bardi would be similar with that of the house of Adimari: the law abiding and the lawless, the public spirited and the indifferent—all would exist side by side in the *consorteria*. At critical moments in the history of this clan, communal councils saw fit to grant errant Bardi judicial dispensation and to absolve them from the onerous verdicts of the republic's courts. After 1343, and then only for a brief interval, was this most prominent of all Florentine families to be struck by the full force of communal law. When these condemnations were leveled, virtually every member of the house was affected since, according to the reformed version of the Ordinances of Justice of 1344, liability for crimes by magnates was extended to include very distant kinsmen. At this time Bardi influence over communal politics was negligible; only the year before *il popolo* had burned many of the finest Bardi palaces, and their company was on the verge of bankruptcy. In earlier days, when they were respected and feared, the regime would have been very reluctant to take reprisals against sixty-two members of this family in the space of a month. Before 1340 Bardi were the principal consultants to the *Signoria* on financial matters, and along with their banking confreres, the *popolani* house of Peruzzi, they were the mainstay of Florentine treasury operations. They acted as bankers for the commune,

---

the form of lances) to the enemies of the Parte Guelfa and the republic. *CC.*, 1 bis, f. 185.

55. This proud family boasted some seventy or so separate households. Cf. *Estimo*, 306. Twenty-four men from this clan were required to sign peace pacts with rival consorterie. Cf. *Balie*, 1 (18 September 1342). For materials on their role in public life, see *P.*, 9, f. 140r; *P.*, 13, f. 59r; *P.*, 14, fols. 138, 188; *LF.*, 14, fols. 3, 187; *Capitoli Protocoli*, 12, fols. 48, 187; *LF.*, 21, f. 52r; *Duplicati Provvisioni*, 4, fols. 1r, 116r.

conducted complex foreign credit transactions, imported needed grain from the republic's great Guelf ally, the Angevin Kingdom of Naples, served as paymaster for troops, hired mercenaries, loaned money to the *Camera del Comune* so that the city could honor its treaty commitments, and were among the most experienced of Florence's tax farmers and the most trusted of the diplomats. While the Bardi themselves were unable to hold office in the priorate of either of its colleges, their commoner partners did so and, according to the chronicler, Giovanni Villani, acted as spokesmen for the interests of their company. This, coupled with the repeated appearance of Bardi before the *Signoria* when crucial public questions were being debated, and the inclusion of magnates from this clan in the various *balìe* (extraordinary commissions), meant that the claims of their kinsmen for preferential treatment were not likely to be overlooked.

Instance after instance, comparable to those cited from the history of the Bardi, could be offered to illustrate the persistent duality of magnate behavior. Similar inferences could also be drawn from the abundant data pertaining to the actions of individual members of such great commoner families as the Acciaiuoli, Alberti, Altoviti, and a host of others. What was clearly in evidence by the 1330s might best be characterized as a government staffed by a fused patriciate, and this type of regime drew heavily upon the talents and resources of the Florentine aristocracy. When it acted in this decade to remove certain disabilities from the knights of the city so that now they were permitted to sit in the *Signoria* and to serve as consuls of the guilds, the regime was giving form to this imperative.[56]

Throughout the early decades of the Trecento the various *Signorie* had regularly distinguished between the law abiding and the lawless magnates, frequently rewarding the former by conferring commoner status upon them. These men joined the knights, and together they were restored to full participation in political life. Moreover, the regime differentiated between the great and powerful magnate clans and those of slight affluence and little prestige. Soon the latter were juridically dissociated from the former and numbered among the *popolani* of the city. The *Signoria* was consistently responsive to petitions from lesser mag-

---

56. This step merely afforded legal recognition to a practice that had been indulged in before. Cf. n. 50; *P.,* 27, f. 51; Salvemini, op. cit., 105.

nates who asserted that they had much more in common with the peaceful and law-abiding artisans and shopkeepers of the city than they did with their dissolute and reckless *consorteria.* Finally, the commune expressed its gratitude to the great magnates who served the republic so generously when it granted them subsidies, immunities, and tax exemptions. Often they were the central figures in patriotic ceremonies and festivals.[57]

From the foregoing it would be possible to project the conclusion that the machinery of state would continue to operate smoothly. Pragmatically, and with great circumspection, communal political society would also gravitate toward the formation of a homogeneous oligarchy whose membership would no longer be differentiated by the legalistic distinctions between magnate and *popolano.* Not only do the events of the 1340s indicate this projection to be erroneous, but even the earlier history of Florence reveals the presence of fissures in the governing classes. Each succeeding regime, until 1343, was plagued by violence among the patriciate, and in part the continuance of these criminous acts was encouraged by the preferential treatment accorded the magnates. The *Signoria* played a dual role: on the one hand, it granted judicial dispensation to habitual offenders, while, on the other, it persisted in attempting to make the time-honored goal of an orderly and peaceful city a reality. It was responsive to the influence of patricians anxious to escape the rigors of communal law and yet aware of the pressing need for public order. The inconstancies of the political scene did not escape the attention of such keen observers as Dante, who never tired of exposing the fickleness of priors bent upon enacting "such subtle provision that to mid-November reaches not what thou in October spinnest." A generation later Dante's insight had become proverbial in

---

57. Magnates who desired *popolano* status averred that they were *debiles et impotente.* Cf. *P.,* 15, f. 174r (9 May 1318). For honors visited upon a single magnate family, the Della Tosa, see Dino Compagni, *Cronica,* 3:38. At the death of Rosso della Tosa, three of his kin were made "cavalieri del popolo" and the deceased was accorded a magnificent public funeral. The heirs of Gottifredo were awarded exemptions from communal imposts because of their sire's prowess in battle. Cf. *P.,* 15, f. 6 (27 July 1316). See *Le Consulte,* 1:47, for a proposal of a communal counselor: "quod in adventu ipsius Cancellerii [refers to the officer of King Rudolph] Potestas, Capitaneus et milites et magnates civitates Florentie vadant sibi . . . alacriter videndo et recipiendo."

Florence so that whenever Giovanni Villani wanted to declaim against
the city's greatest vice—*incostanza*—he would quote this line from the
Divine Comedy.[58]

While poets and chroniclers emphasized the pendulum-like quality of Florentine government, and were always quick to point out its erratic nature, they were unaware of the cumulative effect of public policy as it inexorably intruded into certain areas of patrician life. Despite
remissions of condemnations and annulments of sentences, the direction was toward an ever closer regulation of the lives of the *potentes et
magnates.* Special *balìe* were established with extraordinary powers to
compel magnates to underwrite the peace of the city; eminent officials
were commissioned to pacify contentious clans, and if reconciliation
failed, they were empowered to take swift and severe reprisal.[59] Feuding Guelf magnates were exhorted to settle their differences, and truces
were imposed by the *Signoria* with the proviso that additional security
be posted by the more belligerent. Particular magnate families such as
the Cavalcanti, with a *consorteria* of eighty-one men and numerous retainers, were repeatedly called upon to exchange the kiss of peace.[60] The
role of government was expanded and new magistracies were created
whose techniques were sometimes at odds with the imperatives of earlier chivalric codes of honor. These new officials, concerned with maintaining peace and issuing numerous public pronouncements proclaiming the need for tranquillity, posed a serious threat to traditional
mores.[61] Nor should we consider the magnates themselves as being extraneous to this movement. Both before and after the passage of the Ordinances of Justice many among this order staunchly supported the re-
solve of successive regimes to create a pacific environment in the city.[62]
And yet it would be an error to exaggerate the scope of the victory of
public law. Attempts to limit the right of vendetta to those who had per-

---

58. *Purgatorio,* 6:142–44.

59. Cf. *Delizie degli eruditi toscani,* 10, 92, 117, 281, 289–91, 341. The incidence
of such *balìe* was much greater through the first half of the Trecento; the possible implications of this fact will be considered in the next part of this study.

60. *P.,* 15, f. 24; *balìe* 1; *P.,* 13, f. 128r. For the size of certain magnate consorterie, see *Capitano del Popolo,* 463. The Adimari totaled forty-three, the Bardi
eighty-one, and the Rossi seventy-seven.

61. Cf. *P.,* 15, fols. 20r 24; *P.,* 16, fols. 66–67; *P.,* 23, f. 87r; *P.,* 25, f. 90.

62. Leading magnates from the houses of Bardi, Bondelmonti, and Tornaquinci served as peace officials (Paciarii). *Delizie degli eruditi toscani,* 11, 288.

sonally suffered some outrage to their honor or assault upon their person do not imply a wholesale condemnation of this practice, but rather reveal a mentality that recognized the need, even the sacred duty, for avenging certain indignities. The desire of the *Signoria* was to impose bounds upon appeals to arms, for *popolani* were also not immune to the call of honor, and any assessment of a burgher ethic must take this into account.[63] The literature, art, the very culture of the *Trecento* and *Quattrocento* will lose much of its dramatic dimension if we do not recognize the durability of deep sentiments of private honor. Few areas of Florentine experience reveal more clearly the interaction between the medieval honorific code and the ethic of the burgher.

Older values, then, were not crushed but, rather, were contained, and the reduction of the magnates was a long-term process that never denied the claims of honor. After the middle of the *Trecento,* however, the government was called upon less frequently to pacify obstreperous magnates and restore peace among contentious families. This would seem to indicate that certain volatile strains in the aristocratic temperament had been refined. The way was prepared when the *Signoria* acted to circumscribe vengeance and vendetta by a rule of law: the crime for which revenge was sought had to be "clarus et manifestus," two witnesses were required to attest to the enormity of the offense, and the punishment exacted was to be proportional to the injury suffered. In the 1330s new legislation was passed that seems at first to be at odds with this trend, for it removed certain fundamental limits from the right of vendetta. But a closer examination of these enactments suggests that their purpose was to enlist the support of a larger segment of the citizenry in the suppression of crime. Homicides by magnates were especially rampant at this time, and the *Signoria* placed the culprits under what amounted to a ban of outlawry; now they were to be treated like those who had been banished for crimes against the state and to be deprived of the protection of law. The consequences were that any citizen could join forces with the *consorteria* of the injured party and strike down the malefactor. Under these conditions the conduct of a vendetta was virtually impossible, and private citizens were identified with public law. Soon fines were imposed upon any individual who did not assist communal officials in the apprehension of criminals. Finally, a judicial

---

63. G. Bruckner, *Florentine Politics and Society, 1343–1378* (Princeton, 1962), 38–40.

commission drew up a new criminal code increasing threefold penalties for misdeeds against person. Within a few years, however, these harsh measures were modified; between 1339 and 1343 the practice of judicial dispensation blunted the impact of the law upon the wayward scions of the great houses.[64]

II

The extent to which the *novella* reflected the practices rather than the aspirations of this society is of course conjectural, but the overwhelming acceptance of such works as Boccaccio's *Decameron* indicates that the Florentines had a sympathy with those who could overcome an opponent with wit and cunning, rather than with buckler and sword. No one would have denied the exquisite pleasure that followed revenge, and Sacchetti, in his 111th tale, praises the sensible Venetian law permitting a citizen, upon payment of fifty soldi, to clout a clergyman who has offended the honor of his wife or daughter. The author then laments the impossibility of such a delicious vendetta in the city of Florence. Paolo di Pace da Certaldo's opinion is less intriguing but perhaps it is more representative of popular thinking on the theme of outraged honor: indeed, "La prima allegrezza del mondo si e fare sua vendetta," but upon sober reflection he offers this caution to his son: Not only is such an act an offense in the sight of God, but it is usually carried out so ineptly that the whole affair wins reproach rather than praise. One's fame is almost always tarnished because either the revenge taken is excessive and therefore you are judged to be cruel, or the vengeance is inadequate and thus you are esteemed a cowardly fool.[65] If we hold that the persistence of vendetta and the claims of honor were directly proportional to the place one occupied in the Florentine patriciate, and if we agree that the lure of vendetta was felt throughout Florentine society and yet responded to more frequently by the magnate members of the enormous *consorterie,* then we might concur in the judgment that when the community exerted an inhibiting influence upon this ancient practice, the ef-

---

64. *CC,* 1 bis. Cf. also M. Becker, "Gualtieri di Brienne e l'uso delle dispense giudiziarie," *Archivio Storico Italiano* 11 (1955): 245–51.

65. Paolo di Messer Pace da Certaldo, *Il libro di buono costumi,* ed. S. Morpurgo (Florence, 1921), 270; F. Sacchetti, *Il Trecentonovelle,* ed. V. Pernicone (Florence, 1946), nov. 111.

fects were most strongly felt among the magnate class. Again, the humor of Boccaccio implies that the thing that citizens most feared was appearing ridiculous in the eyes of their neighbors, and a true gentleman was distinguished from a clod by the elegance and subtlety of his reprisals. The difference between the *Decameron* and the earlier collections of vernacular tales, and even between it and later French imitators, is that Boccaccio's world is characterized by its delicate blending of bourgeois craftiness and aristocratic style, while the others are marked by a coarseness of provocation and a crudeness of retaliation displayed against a background of secondary characters almost insensitive to the sufferings of others.

If in the thousand incidents of everyday life there was the possibility of giving offense or suffering an indignity that would diminish one's status, how tender and raw must the feelings of those who suffered some terrible political outrage have been? If the bonds between men gradually strengthened, and the multitude of subtle interrelationships and dependencies accumulated so that in the intricate social world the plane of competition was becoming more intellectual than physical, then what can be said about the mode of conduct of those patricians who were so involved in the bitter political rivalries of the early years of the *Trecento?*

Boccaccio and his audience believed in the durable nature of the social world; how different were the conceptions and commitments of those who theorized on the politics of this era. From the humblest chronicler to the writer of the most original political tract of the period, overwhelming emphasis was placed upon the fragile structure of the state. So delicate was this political mechanism, in the opinion of Marsiglio of Padua, that the main work of those who governed must always be its preservation: "Because among men thus gathered together there arise disputes and quarrels, which if not regulated by the norm of justice would cause battles and the separation of men and thus finally the destruction of the state, there had to be established in this association a standard of things just and a guardian or maker thereof."[66] Politics it-

---

66. A. Gewirth, *Marsilius of Padua* (New York, 1951), 1, 106. It is worth noting that in Giotto's allegorical figures personifying the "Virtues" in the Scrovegni Chapel at Padua, the one figure to wear a crown—for she is queen of all—is Justice. It was justice that was the protector of all earthly possessions and the guarantor of their equitable distribution.

self in the hands of men like Marsiglio came to be a theoretical science
that sought to establish the necessary conditions for the preservation of
the state, and *Signorie* existed "to moderate the excesses of men's tran-
sient acts" by reducing them "to equality or due proportion." In terms
of Florentine experience the *maximum inconveniens* of the state was to be
achieved by the strict and impartial enforcement of the *divieto* as well as
the rigorous implementation of the Ordinance of Justice. No matter how
often these laws were violated in practice, they managed to retain a
forceful hold upon the popular imagination, and each time the *Signoria*
was democratized, their precepts were reasserted. There was, then,
strong support for a political leveling of the magnates, but, despite this,
and critical for subsequent developments in Florentine cultural history,
a deep respect—even a sympathy—for their past accomplishments and
their present style of life endured. Seldom were penalties and restraints
transposed from the realm of politics to that of society. Notwithstanding the many legal disabilities placed upon the Florentine nobility, magnates and knights alone were exempted from a variety of the republic's
sumptuary laws. They and their wives were therefore permitted to
adorn themselves with numerous luxury items, ranging from gaudy
headdresses to bejeweled gowns and furred mantles.[67] Such finery was
explicitly denied *il popolo* who were expected to be more frugal and less
ostentatious. The Statutes of the *Capitano* of 1322–25, decried the fact that
many Florentine citizens, especially *artifices*, no longer lived according
to the dictates of reason, but rather now sought to imitate magnate style
and, as a result, contracted large debts. Such a mode of living, contended
the framers of the statutes, was appropriate only to *magnates et milites*.[68]

In 1349, when a strong oligarchical reaction had set in and the *Signoria* was anxious to placate the magnates, the *Esecutore* of the Ordinances of Justice conducted an investigation for the purpose of punish-

---

67. *Statuti della Repubblica Fiorentina*, 222. D. Compagni (*Cronica*, 1:111) observes that knights, "set under bounds," were granted more money than
popolani who suffered the same fate. Cf. also Paolo di Messer Pace da Certaldo,
op. cit., 150, for a statement of the perquisites and prerogatives of the various
orders in society.

68. G. Salvemini, op. cit., 53; *Statuti della Repubblica Fiorentina*, 226–27. "Quia
plerumque florentini cives et artifices non ad rationem sed ad similitudinem
magnatum vivere volunt et sic dispendia expensarum incurrunt, statutum et or-
dinatum est quod nulla persona civitatis Florentie possit vel audeat mictere ul-
tra decem domina cum ea domina vel puella que ad maritum mandat."

ing those *artifices* who habitually violated communal sumptuary laws.[69] Upper-class sympathies stood squarely against these upstarts—the nouveaux riches of the city—who arrogated to themselves the hallmarks of noble status, for they were men without lineage or renown. Precedence was given to magnates and knights at most public ceremonies, and only jurists and high government officials could vie with them for this honor. Throughout the fourteenth and fifteenth centuries literary men continued to squabble over which order was entitled to receive this token of esteem. From wedding to funeral a noble was secure in his privileges: he was free to invite more guests to the nuptials, serve a more elegant repast, have more mourners follow his bier from a service ablaze with more candles and conducted by more clergy.

The organic character of the Florentine social world during the early years of the *Trecento*, where each class or order knew well its place, stood as the *paideia* of the patriciate. But this self-same patriciate so socially secure and certain of its values, was divided into contentious political factions. The biological metaphor running through Marsiglio of Padua's political writings emphasizes the inevitability of this strife in the body politic by likening the tenure of the state to the life cycle of a plant or animal and thus bringing to the fore a realization of instability inherent in the nature of man and his institutional creations. It is to the fifth book of Aristotle's *Politics* that Marsiglio turns, for he, like so many of his contemporaries, was concerned with the preservation of the tender body politic, and this of course involved the prevention of revolution.[70] It is fear of the state's subversion at the hands of the great and powerful clans that pervades the writings of communal political thinkers during this era. Their conception of good government stresses the need for moderating political excesses and dispensing what Aristotle called "rectificatory justice." They are not interested, as later humanists are to be, in educating men to pursue the moral good within the framework of civic life but, rather, with promoting the very minimal objective of encouraging the citizenry to shun intense partisanship and despise factionalism.[71]

---

69. *Atti Esecutore* 211 (9 August–27 December 1349). This volume contains "Inquisitiones contra artifices contrafacientes ordinamentis communis Florentie."

70. Gewirth, op. cit., 1, 34–106; *Defensor Pacis*, 1:1, 3.

71. Cf. esp. *Defensor Pacis*, 1:1, 7; 1:12, 5–8; 1:13, 5; 1:19, 2.

The blight of factionalism was everywhere in evidence in the North Italian communes, and the Florentines and their neighbors regularly saw a variety of contentious cliques struggling for dominion over the state. In order to understand this chronic contest, due weight must be given to the fact that neither of these vying groups differed substantially in its social commitments or its economic orientation from its rival. Therefore, in Florence one finds magnates and *popolani* in one party contending with magnates and *popolani* of the other party for control of the *Signoria*. And yet some explanation must be offered for the persistent observations of contemporary chroniclers who blamed the curse of factionalism, as well as most of the other ills that befell the republic, upon the machinations of the seditious and conspiratorial magnates. One of the serious omissions of modern scholarship in assessing the political role of the magnates is its failure to place sufficient stress on *Trecento* explanations of political events. It would not be difficult it is true to show that Giovanni Villani and his fellow chroniclers depicted the magnates in a false light and that this order was certainly innocent of many of the political crimes so laboriously catalogued by contemporaries. And yet, if we were to follow this tack, then we would be neglecting what is in itself a most crucial piece of historical evidence—the almost unanimous judgment of contemporaries who correctly or incorrectly saw the magnates as the principal agents of rebellion and discord. This reluctance to try to see the magnates as their contemporaries saw them is much in evidence in the writings of present day social and economic historians who have shown that magnate demands for power and preferential treatment were frequently based upon false claims of ancient lineage and manufactured connections with high-born feudal nobles. One could readily establish the fact that many magnate families were indeed nouveaux and that their claims of ancestry were mythical, but by the early years of the fourteenth century they and their neighbors had come truly to believe in these genealogies. Time and human memory were malleable in the *Trecento;* what was ancient and remote might have transpired only a short time before, and men forgot family history when it was to their advantage.[72] Therefore, when factions fought for dominion,

---

72. In referring to events that occurred only fifty years before his birth, the chronicler Compagni states that it is not his intention to write about things "long past." Cf. *Cronica,* 1:2. On the general and most relevant theme of "The Folk Memory," see M. Bloch's chapter in *Feudal Society,* trans. L. Manyon (Chicago,

there might be little socioeconomic difference between the contending parties, and yet one might come to embody certain qualities and characteristics considered by contemporaries to be aristocratic.

Since the Florentine patriciate was so little differentiated on economic grounds, neither party constituted a threat to guild society. The leadership on both sides was sympathetic to the aspirations of the greater guildsmen and in fundamental accord on communal fiscal policy. Neither proposed startling innovations in any area of public life, and both repeatedly announced their intention of conserving traditional institutions and time-honored political practices. Even when the Donati faction won its substantial victory in 1301, little was done to alter the forms of civic life. The threat to the *libertas* of the city, then, stemmed not from those who would make constitutional innovations but, rather, from single families or small cliques who would use the *Signoria* for their own aggrandizement. Coups by such factional chiefs were of course commonplace at this time, and one can be reasonably certain that if they had succeeded in Florence the results would have been the lordship of a single family presiding over a mixed communal constitution. The family that would have ultimately gained dominion would have differed little from its mighty counterparts who led the opposition party.

Since city magnates and high *popolani* were not divided on socioeconomic issues, and contending factions also concurred in this area, there was much political mobility. Magnates could and did shift their allegiances in this power struggle. During the early Trecento vying factions were anxious to gain magnate support since this order could easily tip the political balance. Florence's ancient experiences with the political maneuvers of the Uberti clan were reinforced by the recent machinations of the Donati at a time when despotisms were emerging in so many nearby territories. These were the last days for the com-

---

1961), 88–108. The question of whether a clan was considered to be nouveau or ancient is certainly, to some extent, a cultural one. No amount of socioeconomic history can establish the parvenu character of a clan without considering the criteria implicit in contemporary historical consciousness and in "the folk memory." E. Fiumi employs only economic criteria to determine the antiquity of Florentine nobles. This would not have been the way in which most Trecento Florentines would have judged themselves, nor would their concept of the "antique" be commensurate with that held by a twentieth-century man. Cf. "Fioritura e decadenza dell'economia fiorentina," *Archivio Storico Italiano* 115 (1957): 385–439.

munes at Bologna, Milan, Orvieto, and Rimini, and many Florentines attributed the destruction of *libertas* to factionalism promoted by the inordinate ambitions of illustrious clans.[73]

In Florence the Bordoni faction, so sympathetic to the magnates, led a patrician clique which came to prominence soon after the ouster of the Donati. Like their magnate predecessors, they, too, were suspected of harboring dictatorial ambitions. *Il popolo* entertained the same opinion of the enemies of the Bordoni—the Serraglini faction.[74] As early as 1321, disaffection was mounting against these factions and their magnate allies, and soon a reaction set in against the rule of this patrician elite. The few Florentine families who had controlled city politics for almost a generation now found the extralegal position they had so carefully constructed seriously threatened. The popular reaction of 1322–25 aimed to reduce special privilege and restrict political individualism; in its stead it sought to institutionalize a broad guild rule. Such a *Signoria* entailed the regular syndication of office holders in general and particularly the judicial review of the political activities of those Bordoni who had used public power for private ends. The *Esecutore* of the Ordinances of Justice found Bernardo di Pagno di Bordini guilty on a charge of peculation of communal funds, and for this he was fined two thousand lire and excluded from public office. His brother, Chele, was convicted on the same count and sent into exile. Shortly thereafter a cohort, the former prior

---

73. M. Becker, "Florentine 'Libertas': Political Independents and 'Novi Cives,' 1372–1378," *Traditio* 18 (1962): 393–407.

74. This family contracted marriage alliances with the Adimari, Tornaquinci, and the Villanuzzi. Moreover, according to Compagni, they had a great rural following and would appear in the city with their "gran seguito" and "pennoni di loro." *Cronica*, 3:1920; Villani, *Cronica*, 9:271. Because the Bordoni were considered to be wholly sympathetic to the magnates, they were deprived of *popolani* status and made magnates. A bit later they were restored to popular status, but this did not preclude the use of knightly titles by certain Bordoni after 1330, or perhaps even a bit earlier. *P.*, 15, f. 120r (23 December 1317); *Delizie degli eruditi toscani*, 3, 351; *CC.*, 26, f. 118; *CC.*, 29, 278r. After 1343 at least one of the Bordoni was inscribed among the magnati and condemned for assault. *CC.*, 54, f. 153r.
This family furnished the republic with treasury officials, purchasers of communal gabelles, castellani, and ambassadors. Men from this house were especially prominent as leaders of the republic in its disastrous war with Pisa in 1341 and in the entourage of the despised despot, Brienne, in the following year. Cf. *LF.*, 15, f. 23r; *LF.*, 17, f. 57; *LF.*, 18, f. 5r; *P.*, 12, f. 95; *Capitoli Protocoli*, 12, fols. 116, 119, 176, 283; *P.*, 31, f. 7; *LF.*, 21, f. 46; *CC.*, 2 bis, f. 200.

Zanobi Corsi de' Borghi, was also convicted for abusing his authority when he placed the troops of the commune at the disposal of Chele.[75]

The ouster of the Bordoni was accompanied by a democratization of the *Signoria;* substantial numbers of *novi cives* were brought into the government. It was at moments such as this that the nebulous term *il popolo* acquired a more definite political meaning, and a concern for the "common good" was more in evidence. This was an interval rather like that of 1293–95 when the Ordinances of Justice were enacted and the *Signoria* stood as the defender of *il popolo.* While a definition of this term did not necessarily exclude the magnates, and the *Signoria* was looked upon as the protector of guilds whose membership included so many from the magnate order, an awareness was developing of what can best be described as a "status popularis." Under this type of popular regime, law-abiding magnate families were to be rewarded with grants of commoner status, while their more obstreperous peers were to suffer the harsh visitations of communal law. Neither of these policies represented an innovation, but not since the tenure of the popular *Signoria* of 1293–95 had they been implemented so enthusiastically. In 1324 a dramatic step was taken: a third of all the magnate families of the republic were declared to be *popolani.* With a single measure the *Signoria* had succeeded in depleting substantially the ranks of the nobility and strengthening the forces of *il popolo.*[76] By means of this political device, the norm of conformity to communal law was proclaimed on a massive scale, and it was announced that all who obeyed its dictates could now aspire to the highest honors of public life.

This emphasis upon cooperation was to be given impetus by the republic's magistrates who were now urged to enforce the law with vigor against the city's remaining magnate houses. When the judge Piero Landolfi condemned two magnates from the house of Somaia to a heavy fine for assaulting a commoner, *il popolo* were overjoyed, and, as soon as Landolfi finished his term of office, they bestowed upon him the title of "cavaliere del popolo." The crowd was especially impressed with this

---

75. R. Davidsohn, *Storia di Firenze,* 3, 992; Villani, *Cronica,* 9:294; Marchionne di Coppo Stefani, op. cit., rub. 382. For an attempt to arrive at a pragmatic definition of popular Signorie, see M. Becker, "Some Aspects of Oligarchical, Dictatorial and Popular Signorie in Florence, 1282–1382," *Comparative Studies in Society and History* 2 (1960): 421–39.

76. G. Capponi, *Storia della repubblica di Firenze* (Florence, 1930), 1, 165; Villani, *Cronica,* 9:287.

magistrate because he referred to his term in office as "la sua rude Signoria" and thus advertised his willingness to bring the overmighty to justice.[77] The popular *Signoria* was deeply concerned with enforcement of existing legislation against the magnates and in 1324–25 encouraged the communal courts to convict all *potentes* who had failed to post security for their continued good behavior. Reprisals were also taken against dissident magnates of the *contado* who showed so little regard for communal law.[78]

The chronicler Giovanni Villani, active in government at this time and present during many crucial sessions of the communal councils, was convinced that certain magnates in key military positions, as well as others who advised the *Signoria* on critical foreign policy matters were seeking to discredit this popular government by urging a program that could only culminate in disaster.[79] Villani believed that these magnates pursued these reprehensible tactics in order to undermine public support and bring the *Signoria* into disfavor; then the regime would have to win the adherence of the magnates by conceding to them what they had so ardently desired since 1293—the abrogation of the Ordinances of Justice. Not only did the *Signoria* remain undaunted, but it even went so far as to strengthen the Ordinances and to call for a general revision of all Florentine statutes.[80]

Perhaps the most noteworthy action of this *Signoria* in the eyes of its contemporaries was the reduction of magnate representation in the captaincy of the *Parte Guelfa*. This organ of communal government played a pivotal role in the conduct of foreign policy, and for years its

---

77. Davidsohn, op. cit., 3, 992.

78. The Corbizzi were fined on 8 October 1325 for failing to post security as *magnati*. On that same day they were condemned for not appearing in court to defend themselves. Cf. *CC.*, 1 bis, f. 78. For comparable charges against other magnates during this interval, see ibid., f. 79r (Pazzi); and ibid., f. 175 (Miglore).

79. Villani, *Cronica*, 9:214. In an earlier era (1293–95), when popular discontent was directed against the magnates, a disposition of the Ordinances of Justice was enacted in an effort to eliminate the intrusion of single powerful citizens in the conduct of the republic's foreign affairs. Cf. Salvemini, op. cit., 426–27.

80. Penalties against criminous magnates were tripled at this time. Cf. *LF.*, 12, II, fols. 88r, 109 (7 November–3 July 1325). A sweeping revision of communal statutes took place between 16 March 1322 and 6 April 1324. This was the first general reformation of Florentine law to occur since the popular *Signoria* of 1293–95, and very few changes were to be made until the outbreak of the next of the republic's great revolutions in October 1343.

councils had been dominated by nobles such as Betto de' Brunelleschi, Rosso della Tosa, Geri Spini, Pazzino de' Pazzi, Bernardo de' Rossi, and a host of others. Foreign lords and princes were well advised to treat privately with the Guelf captains for they were judged to be the most influential men of the community.[81] In 1323, when the commune added several eminent commoners to the captaincy, it was displaying a distrust of magnate loyalty and a suspicion of magnate motives.

At precisely the moment when *popolani* were admitted into the sacred captaincy, the city was being threatened by a coalition of exiled nobles and seditious urban magnates. Their vain attempt to overthrow the regime was to provide the patriotic Villani with another opportunity to laud the vigilance of *il popolo*, who once again had rescued the republic from the grasp of the tyrannous magnates. Three members of this order, Amerigo Donati, Tegghia Frescobaldi, and Lotteringo Gherardini, great Guelf captains, were seriously implicated in this conspiracy, but they inspired such fear among the citizenry that none could be found who would dare accuse them. It was then that the communal councils took the untoward step of indicting them and placing them on public trial. Although they were condemned, their sentences were very light and few criticised this turn of events. Villani even came forward and praised the *Signoria*'s moderation and temperateness, for only in this way could amity come to the city. Many other magnates were implicated in this abortive coup, but, wisely, the *Signoria* chose to overlook their complicity in the interest of peace and tranquillity.[82]

The addition of three great *popolani* to the captaincy of the *Parte Guelfa* did little to alter the overall program of this most aristocratic of all communal institutions; for the newcomers differed very little from their magnate counterparts in social status, and patrimony. Perhaps the subtle difference between these two orders rested in the area of public opinion. In blaming the magnates for the difficulties that befell the republic during these years, Villani oversimplified the causes of the communal dilemma; his approach, however, was similar to that of the popular *Signoria*. The government acted to reduce the influence of the magnates in the councils of the *Parte Guelfa*; this effort suggests a decline of public confidence in the political reliability of this class. Moreover, the inference can be drawn that *il popolo* felt better served by *popolani* in mat-

---

81. Davidsohn, op. cit., 3, 460.
82. Villani, *Cronica*, 9:219.

ters of foreign policy. No vital issues were in dispute and very few questioned the almost universally held principles of Guelfism. Florence's ties with the papacy and its loyalty to Naples were secure, and its hostility to the Ghibelline lords of Italy was unwavering. What was in doubt was the durability of magnate allegiance to the city of Florence.

Any search for the historical antecedents of this widely held suspicion must take into account the role played by magnates at certain critical moments in communal history. The sympathy of the Della Tosa and Frescobaldi for the despotic intervention of Charles de Valois into communal life in 1301, the persistent alignment of the Pulci with the Tuscan Ghibellines, who periodically raided the *contado*, the adherence of the Circuli to the cause of the tyrannous lords of Pisa and the alacrity with which they betrayed public trust, the many Amadori, Lucardesi, Falconetti, Homodei, Nerli, and Russoli, who took up arms in 1312 and raised the banner of the Ghibelline lord, Emperor Henry VII, were not easily forgotten. These and many other magnates stood condemned for their numerous treasons, and in 1323, when these nobles assembled and shouted such battle cries as: "Death, death to the commune and to *il popolo* of Florence and to the Guelfa and long live the Ghibellines," few in the city were reassured.[83] Nor was the magnate insurrection in the *contado* or the overthrow of the popular *Signoria* at San Miniato to inspire public confidence in the reliability of this order.[84]

Like virtually all other North Italian communes Florence saw the magnates as the principal threat to *libertas* and to the constitutional stability of the republic. No demonstration of the compatibility of the socioeconomic interests of magnate and commoner should obscure this fact. And yet once again only modest inferences can be drawn from this assessment since despite the blatant individualism of defiant magnates, *il popolo* were not eager to stifle the legitimate aspirations of those who were cooperative and civic minded. In part this attitude is explicable in terms of the frailty of communal constitutional structure and the regime's need to obtain the consent and support of those referred to as "boni et sufficentes homines civitatis." To the medievals in general and the Florentines in particular, it would have been unthinkable to exclude the prominent and affluent from the decision-making process. This commitment was reinforced by another consideration: prowess at arms

---

83. Davidsohn, op. cit., 3, 323.
84. Villani, *Cronica*, 8:98.

was highly regarded and, more than this, was viewed as one of the essential elements of good citizenship. Civic humanism was to make much of the antique heroes whose soldiery and bravery on behalf of the Roman republic gave it its grandeur; this was indeed a quality worthy of *emulatino*. Soon the Florentines were to pay a bounty to those who assumed the onerous burdens of knighthood. While the realities of military practice were eventually to stand at variance with this ideal and the Florentine militia was to be disbanded, the theme of citizen chivalry proved to be durable and reappeared after a brief hiatus in the writings of Leonardo Bruni Aretino.[85] The profession of arms and the cult of the hero must be studied so that men will desire to gain glory in the name of the state. No regime, until that of 1343, seriously challenged this ideal, and even then the attempt was far from effective.

Even at the height of the popular reaction in 1324 the *Signoria* was willing to open up new offices to the magnates.[86] To the men of the *Trecento* the term *status popularis* implied that representation must be accorded to the eminent men of the community, no matter what their juridical status might be. Even later when the *Signoria* was further democratized and hostility against the magnates ran high, no one in the council halls objected to sharing certain offices with the magnates. Moreover, proposals were made to augment magnate representation in critical posts. Giovanni Villani, surely no friend of this order, steadfastly upheld their political rights and vigorously contended that by all the canons of *buon governo* they were entitled to a share in the government.[87] The communal political ideal continued to be that of a civil society in which all the affluent and high-born were to have a voice. In the 1360s and 1370s, when there was another outburst of anti-magnate feeling, the regime and its advisors were not dissuaded from this commitment. They clung tenaciously to this principle and even upheld it as a remedy for the many political ills that beset neighboring cities. They were unanimous in proposing that constitutional adjustments be made to equalize representation between magnates and *popolani*. For did not this for-

---

85. C. C. Bayley, *War and Society in Renaissance Florence* (Toronto, 1961), "De Militia," 369–87.

86. Davidsohn, op. cit., 3, 991. The facts pertaining to this interval of popular government are presented by Davidsohn, but his interpretation is colored by his strong commitment to the idea of class conflict.

87. Villani, *Cronica*, 11:118.

mula for resolving civic quarrels have the weighty authority of Aristotle behind it? His teachings in the *Politics* and the *Ethics* were now
widely read in the vernacular and stood at the core of the theory of *buon
governo.* Just as popular was Cicero's program envisioning a *concordia
ordinum* between the nobility and the *populares* against those *improbi*
who would bring the state to ruin.

The entry of *novi cives* into the *Signoria* of the early 1320s did not result in the denial of such fundamental magnate prerogatives as the right
to occupy certain public offices, nor was the influence of the magnate
order diminished. But what did occur might best be described as the
resurgence of a more impartial and impersonal type of regime. Once
again the ruling patriciate was confronted with mounting governmental expenses at a time when confidence in the fiscal strength of the republic was dwindling. In February of 1322 the *Signoria* was unable to
make restitution to communal creditors and therefore was forced to de-
clare a moratorium on public debts.[88] A crisis of this order that was to
recur so frequently after 1342 could only be met with radical tributary
reforms which would curtail many traditional immunities and deny
certain privileges to the older patriciate. For the *Signoria* simply could
not afford to permit the continuation of longstanding abuses so costly
to the republic. In 1315 the patriciate had succeeded in divesting themselves of a large measure of their tax responsibility; now direct taxation
on all real estate in the city and *contado* was reinstated.[89]

The same patriciate had sorely neglected a much needed revision
of communal statutes and ordinances. Not since the last interval of popular rule (1293–95) had any regime looked to these perplexing legal matters. Now, three times between March 1322 and March 1325, judicial
commissions were appointed by the democratized *Signoria* to correct
and amend Florentine law so that glaring inconsistencies and ambiguities might be removed. Interest in legal reform, so essential, considering
the ad hoc character of Trecento government, was always at its height
when the *novi cives* entered public life in substantial numbers, and it is
worth noting that the next great reexamination of laws and statutes was
to take place immediately after the popular revolution of late September 1343.[90] Strict syndication of public officials and severe enforcement

---

88. *P.,* 18, f. 65 (25 February 1322).

89. Barbadoro, op. cit., 148–59.

90. R. Palmarocchi, "Contributi allo studio delle fonti statutarie fiorentine,"

of the *divieto* was once again an integral part of this movement to exalt public authority at the expense of personal influence.[91] The end product of this trend was to control the extralegal behavior of the entrenched patriciate—magnates and commoners alike. In no sense can such an effort be judged discriminatory against the nobility since the tendency was to apply the same norms to the other Florentine orders. Once again we witness an attempt to enforce rules which stemmed from collective needs, and this entailed the repression of the political individualism of the great and overmighty. In this context we see that the *Signoria*'s reforms of the *Parte Guelfa* represented a purposeful effort to curb the inordinate influence of the dynasts in the captaincy over the formulation of public policy.

III

The effects of political experimentation during the years 1322–25 were insubstantial, and despite a renewed flurry of reform in 1328–29, Florence was very soon to reorient its politics around a more personal type of *Signoria*. In the 1330s the commoner aristocracy and the affluent magnates of the greater guilds again came to treat public office as if it were their own private preserve. Among the best represented of all the city's families were the Bardi, Cavalcanti, Frescobaldi, Gherardini, Rossi—magnates all. It was to these nobles that the regime turned for advice in matters of foreign policy and communal finance, and when special *balìe* (extraordinary commissions) were founded, their names were among the most prominent. Soon the most pressing public problems were dealt with by these *balìe* and the bankers of the house of Frescobaldi and Bardi joined their *popolani* counterparts, the Acciaiuoli and Peruzzi financiers, in directing affairs of state.[92] During this decade there was a marked ten-

---

Archivio Storico Italiano 88 (1930): 56–57; P. Santini, "Le più antiche riforme," *Archivio Storico Italiano* 79 (1921): 224–26. Cf. n. 81.

91. G. Masi, *Il sindacato delle magistrature comunali nel seculo XIV* (Rome, 1930). On the complex question of syndication, see Becker, op. cit., 427–29.

92. In the early months of 1336 the war against Martino della Scala was directed by the "Sei sulla guerra." Among their number was Ridolfo de' Bardi, Simone della Tosa, Acciaiuoli Acciaiuoli, Giovenco de' Bastari, Celle Bordoni, and Simone Peruzzi. Bardi, Peruzzi, and Acciaiuoli were also well represented in the Balìa authorized to raise revenue. Cf. A. Sapori, *La crisi delle compagnie mercantili dei Bardi e dei Peruzzi* (Florence, 1926), 107–8.

dency to grant concessions to the magnates and to be generally mindful of the claims of the Florentine aristocracy. This regime represented
the interests of a handful of the city's most prestigious guilds, and the
dominant families matriculated in these corporations were to form a homogeneous patriciate.[93] Until 1340 the *Signoria* was secure and self-
confident, and, except for sporadic instances of seditious activity by
such magnate families as the Caponsacchi in 1329, who attempted to
open the city gates so that rebels and exiles might enter and bring down
the regime, or the treasonous negotiations of a Della Tosa with the chancellor of Mastino della Scala, tyrant of Verona to convey the lordship of
the city to the despot, domestic tranquillity prevailed.[94] In this atmosphere of relative internal accord and burgeoning communal prosperity,
the trend was toward a fusion of magnate and *popolano grasso* into a social amalgam best described by the term *aristocracy*. This tendency had
long been in evidence, and upon occasion had almost been realized, but
disunity among the Florentine elite, the surge of new men, the intervention of pope or Angevin monarch, humiliating military debacles,
and declining public revenues, each in turn, at critical junctures, had
prevented the consolidation of an aristocracy after all. The interests of
the urban magnates were almost identical with those of the wealthy
popolani, and, except for the persistence of violence, little seemed to
stand in the way of this amicable fusion.

Soon this government of the guild patriciate abandoned the strict
interpretation of the Ordinances of Justice and decreed that those who
held the dignity of knighthood and had not been classified as magnates
since 1293, were to be declared eligible for the highest elective offices in
the republic. Shortly thereafter, a special commission was established
with authority to create new knights and in 1335 the statutes of the *Parte
Guelfa* empowered the captains to bestow a bounty of fifty florins upon
anyone deemed worthy who would be willing to assume the honors
and burdens of knighthood.[95] Throughout its tenure the *Signoria* was

---

93. For an assessment of certain features of oligarchical *Signorie,* see Becker,
op. cit., 429–34.

94. *Guidice degli Appelli,* 124, I, f. 25r (20 February 1329). Feo della Tosa, one
of the many condemned on this count, paid two hundred lire on 20 September
1337 for judicial dispensation. Cf. ibid., 124, I, f. 22.

95. F. Bonaini, "Statuto della parte guelfa di Firenze," *Archivio Storico Italiano*
5 (1857): 41.

extremely solicitous of the welfare of all sectors of the Florentine nobility. At no time in communal history were more *grandi* to escape the rigors of communal law through grants of judicial dispensation than in those halcyon years immediately preceding the democratization of the Florentine state in 1343.

Clearly, the regime was concerned with the problem of staffing the officer cadre of the citizen army, and the benign policies it advocated were intended to encourage the high-born to serve as knights in the elite cavalry. Despite the lure of subsidy and civic honor, this program was fated to fail, and yet we must not be misled by our knowledge of the unfortunate outcome into underestimating the enthusiasm with which the *Signoria* embarked upon this venture. The regime of the 1330s was willing to recall exiled magnates and restore them to full citizenship if they would put their arms at the disposal of the republic. Grave doubts were voiced concerning the efficacy of mercenary troops, and men remembered that Rome had been great when citizen armies commanded by public-spirited generals had taken the field. Its decline ensued with the enlistment of foreign contingents who fought for gold rather than love of *patria*. A few among the city's magnates were responsive to this type of appeal, and still Brunelleschi, Della Tosa, and Ricasoli led the republic's host, but these nobles were the exception rather than the rule.[96] As in earlier days, public policy was predicated upon a curious duality that did little to encourage the maintenance of a military caste. Knighthood and service to the state were accorded their niche in the pantheon of civic virtues, but those who followed these noble callings still found themselves bound by the harsh restraints of collective life. Judicial dispensation and preferential treatment might be meted out to certain nobles, but the Ordinances of Justice remained in effect. Granted the hyperbole of this magnate complaint: "If a horse is running along and hits a *popolano* in the face with its tail; or if in a crowd one man gives another a blow in the chest without intending harm; or if some children of tender age begin quarelling, an accusation will be made. But ought men to have their houses and property destroyed for such trifles as these?" the emotion from which it stems is real enough.[97]

---

96. G. Villani, *Cronica*, 1:134. At this time over six hundred affluent Florentines maintained horses and weapons, and, while they did not usually serve in person, they did send hired replacements. Bayley, op. cit., 8.

97. Compagni, *Cronica*, 1:12.

In his justly famous description of "the greatness and state and magnificence of the commune of Florence," Giovanni Villani laments the fact that in 1336–38 there were only "seventy-five full-dress knights." "To be sure, we find that before the second popular government now in power was formed (before 1293) there were more than 250 knights, but, from the time that *il popolo* began to rule, the magnates no longer had the status and authority enjoyed earlier, and hence few persons were knighted." The observation, "i cavallieri non ebbono stato," was commonplace at this time.[98] To the good burgher Villani who only despised the lawless among the magnates, this was a tragic portent of military disasters to come.

The need for law and order, the desire to preserve Florentine *libertas* against the machinations of the powerful clans, and the persistence of certain features of impartial and impersonal government, led to the accumulation of numerous judicial and political restraints upon the magnates. Indeed, these restrictions were lessened during the decade of the 1330s, but still no one gained any ostensible civic advantage from magnate status. Therefore, nobles continued to petition the government for the privilege of becoming commoners.[99] No attack was made upon the social prestige of the nobility and yet men were anxious to abandon their magnate status; this type of action demonstrates the incommensurate magnitudes of the *Trecento* social and political universes. The guild aristocracy that so admired the code of the nobility was unwilling to abrogate the dread Ordinances of Justice. Nor were they eager to restore all magnates to their full political rights; they were, however, desirous of imitating the way of life of this order and happy to receive the benefits of noble martial prowess.

Giovanni Villani's so oft-quoted observations pertaining to Florentine magnates and knights are of course relative, based as they are on a comparison of status and authority enjoyed by the nobility in 1336–38 with that of the era before 1293. As informative as this comparison is, it tells us very little about the degree of influence the magnates still exercised during the 1330s. The history of this era suggests that statements by chroniclers that magnates had little status and less authority must be

---

98. *Delizie degli eruditi toscani*, 12, 352; Villani, *Cronica*, 11:94.

99. Cf. requests of magnates from Certaldo and Colle for popular status; identical petitions were submitted by the house of Galigairi, the Counts Alberti, and the Vecchete, *P.*, 32, fols. 1–2; *LF.*, 21, f. 87r (14 May 1342).

challenged. Granted that there was something of a decline, still we see affluent commoners of the guilds eagerly seeking to marry into magnate families and priding themselves on kinship with the mighty feudatories of the Tuscan *contado*. Nor can we doubt the civic pride taken by these burghers in the most aristocratic of all Florentine organizations—the *Parte Guelfa*. Did not these self-same commoners consistently elect the scions of magnate houses to represent the commune in the most solemn of public ceremonials? When visiting dignitaries arrived in the city, were they not graciously welcomed and entertained by noble patricians? The very forms and amenities of communal life were replete with the ethos of chivalry, and the artisan and merchant guilds were a part of its pageantry, with their costumes, military companies, coats-of-arms, and processionals.[100] The one glaring exception was the diminishing interest in the play of knightly arms. Less and less were the Florentines gratified by the medieval tournament and soon this spectacle was to be greeted with apathy, if not scorn.[101]

It would appear, then, that communal society had made a selection from among the many knightly virtues, retaining only those compatible with the need for public order. Now men were knighted not for their

---

100. State ritual prescribed that *milites* should represent the commune. During a later interval, when communal legislation was restrictive, and the nobles lost ancient prerogatives, the *Signoria* still insisted that important embassies be captained by a *miles:* "Atque fiat responsio per unum militem antiquum qui bene sciat totum et res antiquas." Cf. *Consulte et Pratiche*, 19, f. 16 (21 July 1380). This is, of course, not surprising since Florence was not isolated from the chivalric currents of Trecento Europe. Even the working class desired to emulate the bachelorhood of knights; in 1343 Walter of Brienne permitted them to have their own coats-of-arms, to form squads attired in special livery, and to fly banners bearing their insignia. Thirty-five years later, all of this was to be revived by the Ciompi revolutionaries. Upon seizing power, these humble woolcarders were to create *milites* of their own. Cf. C. Falletti-Fossati, *Il tumulto dei Ciompi* (Rome, 1882), 172; Marchionne di Coppo Stefani, rub. 566; A. Doren, *Le arti fiorentine* (Florence, 1940), 2, 230–31.

101. The last great tournaments staged in Florence during the Trecento appear to have been those of Easter 1343. No mention is made of major jousts in the writings of Giovanni Villani, which treat the subsequent period of Florentine history (to 1348), nor in the massive chronicle of his kinsmen, Matteo and Filippo, which runs through 1363. Likewise, Marchionne di Coppo Stefani does not note the occurrence of a major tournament, and his chronicle concludes in 1385. Literary men before 1343 referred consistently to the tourney. Among the more prominent literati were Francesco da Barberino (*Documenti d'Amore*), Fol-

valor of arms but, rather, so that they might inspire awe among the inhabitants of the countryside when they went out to serve as communal officials. More and more, high civil servants and bureaucrats bore the honorific title of "knight." This designation seldom failed to elicit the admiration of *il popolo,* and soon it was to be conferred on the many men who responsibly governed the state and bravely directed the many wars of the second half of the *Trecento.*

Earlier in this study it was suggested that the decline of the Florentine knight is not explicable in terms of the communal attitude toward the magnate, but an explanation must be sought, rather, within the context of startling changes in methods of warfare. The heroic work of the army in the early years of the fourteenth century had been the suppression of insurrection and the defense of the Florentine *contado.* For the most part this had been accomplished by a series of relatively brief campaigns waged within easy distance of the city. The militia of the *contado,* while far from trustworthy, frequently proved to be quite useful, and this force in combination with citizen armies, captained by nobles and great feudatories, achieved a succession of notable victories. Long-range campaigns in distant places were beyond the competence of such troops; subsidies and foreign military commanders who led their own contingents seemed an adequate alternative.

During the decade of the 1330s the remedy of the citizen militia and the communal knight became obsolete; no longer could they be relied upon to realize the ambitious schemes envisaged by the new Florentine imperialism. Until this moment the *Signoria*'s policy had been largely defensive, and only mildly interested in expansion. Most of the republic's military energies over the past thirty years had been expended in fending off dissident exiles, rebellious feudatories, and meddling German emperors. For such purposes foot and mounted militia had been indispensable, but now Florence was promoting a grand design that involved alliance with far-off Venice, the dispatch of troops into Lom-

---

gore da San Gimignano (*Le Rime*), and Giovanni Villani (*Cronica*, X, 128). The tourney of 1343 failed to elicit the enthusiasm of the citizenry. Cf. Villani, 12:8.

Much later, in the early Quattrocento, when literary men such as Leonardo Bruni Aretino were trying to revive certain of the military virtues associated with knighthood, they were contemptuous of the ornamented knight of the mock tournament (the *miles gloriosus*). Cf. Bayley, op. cit., 379. The *dignitas* of knighthood came to be intimately connected with civic virtue.

bardy, and all this was to be done so that Pisa might be defeated and Lucca conquered and annexed. These plans could only be executed by mercenary armies capable of waging protracted warfare in foreign lands. The issue at stake was no longer the reduction of a single castle in rural Tuscany but, rather, large-scale warfare throughout North Italy. In the major battles of 1341 fewer than a score of Florentine knights saw action, and, while the treasury records do indicate that certain *grandi* did continue to serve as captains, the terms of their employment had altered dramatically.[102]

By 1342 they were being hired under the same type of contract that prevailed for the city's other mercenaries, and thus native *milites* had lost their grandeur and become pensioners of the state. All occasional Bondelmonti, Della Tosa, or Ricasoldi might win the acclaim of the crowd for his daring at arms, but it was to the office of the *condotta* that the *Signoria* looked for victories over the numerous free-booting companies that streamed into Italy during the middle years of the *Trecento*. Soon this office, along with special commissions, was in the business of enlisting the city's would-be enemies under the Florentine banner and paying marauding companies to evacuate Tuscan territory. The warfare of those years seldom brought honor but frequently resulted in victory. The military virtues associated with knighthood found little expression on the battlefield, and in the closing years of the *Trecento* they even elicited scorn from such writers as Sacchetti. Fools and knaves, parvenus and the vulgar, were awarded the golden spurs, but one must not conclude that all Florentines denigrated the virtues of a militant nobility.[103]

The humanist chancellor Leonardo Bruni Aretino implored the Florentines to restore the republic's militia; to him, the year 1351 had been disastrous for his beloved adopted city, for it was then that the *Signoria* abolished the last vestiges of the citizen army.[104] Machiavelli's well-

---

102. Among the magnates who filled military posts at this time were Adimari, Agli, Bardi, Bordoni, Cavalcanti, Mozzi, Spini, and Tornaquinci. Cf. *CC.*, 1, fols. 2r–36; *CC.*, 11, fols. 13r ff.; *CC.*, 24, f. 48; *CC.*, 28, fols. 628–42. These magnates received a stipend from the commune for recruiting and leading Florentine troops in battle. *Popolani* from high-born families also served in the same capacity. Albizzi, Bastari, Guicciardini, Mazzingi, Raffacani, Rimbaldesi, Rondenelli, and even Medici were included among their number. *CC.*, 1, f. 28r; *CC.*, 4, fols. 68ff.; *CC.*, 11, fols. 10r–11r; *CC.*, 21, f. 40; *CC.*, 24, fols. 40–41.

103. Sacchetti, op. cit., nov. 168, 213.

104. Bayley, op. cit., 21.

known views were much more extreme: he attributed the decline of civic virtue itself to *il popolo*'s repression of the nobility. This oppression had resulted in the death of martial spirit among the citizenry, and he saw the reconstruction of the militia as a means for reviving this antique virtue.[105]

The literary tradition that found expression in the writings of the Quattrocento humanists failed to take into account the fundamental changes in military tactics that caused the city to have recourse to mercenaries. The Ordinances of Justice and the other repressive enactments of *il popolo* had done far less to discourage Florentines from assuming the burdens of knighthood than had the new strategies of war itself. The remedies of the 1330s that sought to restore the *milites* to full political rights proved ineffectual because citizen knighthood had become militarily obsolete.

IV

Any consideration of the role of the Florentine nobility during the years immediately preceding the establishment of the popular *Signoria* in the autumn of 1343 must treat the degree of political influence exerted by this order during this interlude. Once again we are confronted with Giovanni Villani's assertion that the fifteen hundred "cittadini nobili et potenti" (magnates) who were required to post security for their continued good behavior and the seventy-five knights of the elite cavalry were without "stato ne Signoria" in the years 1336–38.[106] It has already been suggested that this statement can only be interpreted relatively since the chronicler is comparing the degree of status and power enjoyed by the nobility before 1293 with that of his own day. Two questions remain, however: first, can we equate the magnates with the knights? and, finally, does not the evidence presented by Villani indicate that the magnates continued to play a crucial role in Florentine politics until at least the 1340s? The leading nobles of the city in those years were not *cavalieri*, and the history of this interval demonstrates that these men could still dominate public life even though they made no appreciable military contribution. That Villani casts these aristocrats in the role of

---

105. N. Machiavelli, *History of Florence*, trans. F. Gilbert (New York, 1960), 107–11.
106. Villani, *Cronica*, 11:94.

arch villains bent upon subverting the state, and that he holds them responsible for the many political tragedies that befell the city, signifies that magnates from the house of Bardi, Frescobaldi, Neri, and Rossi did indeed wield an inordinate influence over the government. The very argument offered in Villani's chronicle would be unintelligible if this were not taken into account. No single observer of the Florentine political scene attributes more influence to the magnates during those years than does Villani. Nor was this view confined to the pages of a single chronicle: this was the very interpretation subscribed to by the popular *Signoria* established in October 1343.[107]

The magnates held one-third of the positions in the special commission formed in 1336 to direct the war against Mastino della Scala, lord of Verona and Padua, and the Bardi took charge of the disbursement of monies to the Florentine troops. They were well represented on every diplomatic mission of consequence and ubiquitous in the communal councils of this time. It would appear, then, that Villani's estimate of magnate power cannot be accepted uncritically.[108] One might argue, however, that the power exercised by a Bardi or a Della Tosa stemmed from his position in the guild aristocracy and that he, along with other magnates, had become a part of the oligarchy of the *arti* inseparable from the great burghers. If this were the case, then the patriciate would be a collectivity, and single houses would tend to shun acts of political individualism and recourse to violence in the interests of the whole. Moreover, they would abjure the divisive slogans of the past that made so much of the differences between magnates and *popolani grassi* and be willing to live within the communal constitutional framework. Instead, the magnates were repeatedly to attempt to overthrow the popular constitution and annul the despised Ordinances of Justice.

---

107. Cf. M. Becker, "An Essay on the 'Novi Cives' and Florentine Politics, 1343–1382," *Mediaeval Studies* 24 (1962): 56–58.

108. Filippo Bardi was elected to the Dieci—a special *balìa* authorized to conduct complex diplomatic negotiations with Venice. *Capitoli Protocoli*, 12, f. 242r (26 September 1336); *LF.*, 17, f. 39r (29 July 1338). Ridolfo Bardi was appointed to a committee empowered to raise revenue and handle delicate foreign policy questions. *LF.*, 17, f. 39r (29 July 1338). Andreas Bardi was a member of a special *balìa* of eight. *LF.*, 17, 176 (9 December 1339). Cf. also n. 55. The magnate houses of Adimari, Brunelleschi, Forabosci, Gherardini, and Gianfigliazi were extremely active in the government during the late 1330s and early 1340s. *CC.*, 1, f. 206r *LF.*, 141, fols. 141–69r; *Capitoli Protocoli*, 12, fols. 143–238; *LF.*, 19, fols. 104r; *LF.*, 21, fols. 52r ff.

In November 1340 the Bardi joined with the still powerful feudatories of Tuscany to make armed insurrection. Their fellow conspirators the
Ubertini, the Ubaldini, the Counts Guidi, the Tarlati of Arezzo and the
Pazzi of the Valdarno, ancient Italian nobles all, had support in the city
among those magnates who desired to undo the hated ordinances that
discriminated against their class. The conspiracy failed but the discontent that provoked it was soon again to express itself in 1342 and 1343.

Armando Sapori, twentieth-century historian of medieval Florence,
has studied this insurrection in great detail and concluded that it demonstrates the absence of divisions among the various orders of Florentine
society at that time. His researches indeed disclose that economic differences between magnates such as the Bardi and Frescobaldi on the one
hand, and the *popolani* Peruzzi and Acciaiuoli on the other, were insignificant.[109] But once again the same dilemma recurs: to what extent
does the absence of economic distinctions imply the eradication of other
differences? First, it should be noted that the Bardi gained their principal
military support from those feudal nobles least assimilated into communal economic life and, second, that the conspirators were joined by
dissident magnates—members of the city patriciate—who still strained
under the yoke of the Draconian Ordinances of Justice. Many of this latter group were certainly members of the mercantile oligarchy as Sapori
has shown; this does not mean, however, that these men were willing to
observe the many onerous provisions of the republic's constitution.

Sapori rejects Villani's account of this uprising, and chooses to assert the homogeneity of the Florentine oligarchy on economic grounds.
Surely Villani was well versed in the economic facts of life for he was
a partner and agent of the most prominent banking establishment of
his day. No medieval chronicler was more knowledgeable or more lo-
quacious about business matters than was Villani, and yet he observes
crucial distinctions between *popolani* and magnates. His narration of
the Bardi conspiracy not only lays stress upon the enthusiasm of magnates for the overthrow of the dreaded ordinances, but also emphasizes the reluctance of particular members of this eminent clan to submit to the dictates of communal justice. There were of course strong
economic motives that occasioned the abortive revolt, but in no way
do these preclude the play of traditional forces which encouraged the

---

109. A. Sapori, op. cit., 146ff. For communal posts held by Frescobaldi at this
time, see *LF.*, 17, fols. 155r–86r; *LF.*, 19, fols. 49r–51.

magnates to rebel. When Piero de' Bardi was sentenced to pay a fine of six thousand lire for an offense committed against one of his vassals of the Castle of Vernio, and Andrea, his brother was obliged to surrender the fortress of Mangona to the republic, the Bardi had ample justification for recourse to arms. Further provocation was added when the *Signoria* enacted severe legislation directed against those Bardi who had acquired other fortified properties in the *contado*.[110] Over the next few years magnates were to demonstrate their antipathy toward measures such as these and demand the abrogation of all legislation considered to be discriminatory.

Any analysis of the political role of the magnates in the 1340s must avoid imposing a logic upon events alien to the men of the times. Recent scholarship has reached the conclusion that, because certain magnates had interests in common with *popolani*, class distinctions were rendered meaningless.[111] The presumption here involved is that a rationally organized and highly efficient society existed that in turn produced an integrated culture where men were guided in critical matters by reason rather than emotion. But the facts of *Trecento* experience belie such an oversimplified hypothesis: despite the high degree of economic and social cooperation so evident between magnates and *popolani*, the violence and discord were endemic to the former. It was easier for the ruling oligarchs to agree upon matters of economic policy than it was for them to be in accord on such questions as the renunciation of the vendetta by a particular magnate clan, or the desirability of compelling warring *consorterie* to exchange the kiss of peace and post sizable security. Any study of the patrimonies of the elite of Florentine society will not disclose significant differences between those of the magnates and those of the affluent commoners, and yet, this notwithstanding, more subtle distinctions did exist. The Bardi and Frescobaldi were considered magnates because they were required by law to post security for their continued good behavior. The men of the *Trecento* had a juridical mentality that made much of this: status at law was a mode of demarcation and a source of identity. This preoccupation was implicit in their most rudimentary social perceptions. Repeatedly, chroniclers were to insist that Florence was divided into three classes: magnates, *popolani*, and *il*

---

110. *Manoscritto varii*, 501, f. 159r; Sapori, op. cit., 124.

111. For a summary of research on this question, see E. Fiumi, "Fioritura e decadenza dell'economia fiorentina," *Archivio Storico Italiana* 115 (1957): 385–91.

popolo minuto.[112] Within this social universe men's identities depended upon membership in certain legally constituted orders; legal personality was bestowed only on guildsmen who were matriculated in a specific corporation juridically accredited by the commune. It is not necessary to mention the legal distinctions between master, apprentice, and journeyman any more than it is required to enumerate the gradations between the orders of clergy. Law was a psychological category, and a scrupulous regard for legality pervaded the political milieu. Later, when *il popolo minuto* wished to change their status, they petitioned the *Signoria* for the right to found a new legal order, that is, to establish artisan corporations.

The city's magnates were not a socioeconomic class, but rather a juridical cadre, and this classification had an absolute relevance in the eyes of their contemporaries. The patriciate was then divided juridically and no amount of socioeconomic cohesion should cause us to overlook this fact. Modern scholarship which tends to neglect this penchant for legality so deeply imbedded in the Florentine mentality, presents a rational view of social change and human motivation based upon a compatibility of economic interests. Such a description cannot account for the persistence of magnate antisocial behavior and political antagonism. Mutual suspicion and distrust between the magnates and *popolani* were much in evidence in 1340. The Bardi and Frescobaldi appealed to their fellow magnates to avenge insults, real or imagined, and to overthrow that *Signoria* which enforced the ordinances so cruelly. The chroniclers of Florence, *popolani* all, saw the magnates bent upon destroying the political order of the city. They came to believe that these nobles were seized with an inordinate ambition to dominate public life.[113] If these opinions are oversimplifications of complex interaction between the two top echelons of Florentine society, they should nevertheless not be discounted, since these convictions influenced men and their actions.

---

112. This view of society was to persist in the writings of historians and diarists throughout the Trecento. Cf. G. Scaramella, *Firenze allo scoppio del tumulto dei Ciompi* (Pisa, 1914), 26–36.

113. Cf. Becker, op. cit., 44–45, 80–82. In order to check the magnates, it was desirable to staff the *Signoria* with a majority of *popolani*. See the prescription of the Dodici for maintaining the peaceful *status* of Arezzo: "Et quod populares maior pars remittantur in civitatem," *Consulte et Pratiche*, 19, f. 44 (31 August 1380).

V

The early 1330s were years of relative harmony between magnate and *popolano,* and the *Signoria's* policies reflected this cordiality. Only the most affluent sat in the communal councils and very few new men were able to win entry into this charmed circle. And yet this accord was as precarious as it was fragile. By 1338 we can observe a hardening of communal policy toward the magnates and a general transformation of the regime's program that was to have serious repercussions for the entire privileged class.[114] What was to dissolve might best be described as the easy laissez-faire conduct of public life. The world of Florentine business was to undergo its most severe crisis, and the public revenue was to decline until it was no longer adequate for the ambitious imperialistic plans of the republic. Under the impact of these twin pressures, the regime found it necessary to reduce the privileges and immunities of the entrenched classes. Vigorous tax reforms were proposed to revive a declining treasury, but few who sat in the councils were willing to support them.[115] Cooperation among the patriciate was pervasive in periods of prosperity, but with the onset of adversity the bonds became strained. The ruling elite were now sharply divided on the issue of the feasibility of maintaining the costly alliance with the papacy. Furthermore, they were split on the question of the desirability of pursuing the expensive war against Lucca. Many were reluctant to see direct taxes imposed upon their capital and lands.[116] As to the role of the magnates in these troubled years, they ignored so many vital communal needs and continued to press for the repeal of the Ordinances of Justice and

---

114. The basis for this change was the pressing communal need for revenue in order to mount an offensive against neighboring Pisa. This demand for additional revenue came at a moment when the yield from gabelles (the republic's principal source of income) had declined precipitously. By 1341 the *Signoria* was exerting every effort to recover communal property, and, according to a provision enacted in May of that year, much of the *bona et iura communis* had been usurped by "magnates et potentes," and, since the citizenry was afraid of these haughty and powerful lords, no effort had been made to wrest the property from them. Now the Officials of the Towers were to have extraordinary authority to recover state property and any citizen was to have the right to make secret denunciations (*in tambure*) against predatory "magnates et potentes." Cf. *Duplicati Provvisioni,* 2, fols. 12–12r.

115. *LF.,* 19, fols. 29–187r (8 June 1340–20 May 1341).

116. Barbadoro, op. cit., 125ff.; *LF.,* 17, f. 90.

the establishment of a *Signoria* that would be solicitous of their private interests.

In September 1342 the overwhelming majority of affluent *popolani* and magnates championed the desperate remedy of establishing a dictatorship. Walter of Brienne was installed as lord of the city for life, and granted sweeping powers. In one of his first acts he demonstrated his sympathies toward the magnates by absolving the Bardi, Frescobaldi, Nerli, Pazzi, and Rossi from the condemnation they had incurred as a result of their leadership of the abortive revolution of November 1340. Eminent members of these families were now permitted to return from exile and soon they numbered among Brienne's most trusted counselors. Adimari, Bardi, Donati, Rossi and others undertook far-flung diplomatic missions for the new lord of the city. Adimari, Cavalcanti, Rossi, and Tornaquinci held high administrative posts in the Florentine *contado*.[117] Numerous magnates were granted judicial dispensation from convictions on charges of treason; the Falconieri and Guidolotti had been declared enemies of the Holy Roman Church and rebels against the state in 1304. Now these clans, but recently listed among the despicable Ghibelline nobles of the city, had their citizenship and property restored. The Pulci and Circuli, who had attacked their native city in the company of the perfidious Ghibellines of Pisa, were likewise granted dispensation from these high crimes. A host of rebel magnates soon were to have condemnations for capital offenses annulled.[118]

The most vital concern of the Florentine magnates was the abrogation of the Ordinances of Justice, and here, too, their desires were given serious consideration. Although Brienne did not acquiesce completely, he did make substantial alterations in one of its most vexatious clauses: the degree of responsibility for crimes of kinsmen was drastically reduced so that now only close blood relations were liable.[119] Unfortu-

---

117. Cf. CC., 1 bis, fols. 130r–249; *Atti Esecutore*, 17, f. 17r. For the despot's decree absolving the Bardi, Frescobaldi, Nerli, Pazzi, and Rossi from condemnations incurred as a result of their participation in the rebellion of 1 November 1340, see C. Paoli, *Delle Signoria di Gualtieri Duca d'Atene* (Florence, 1862), 76. The citation given by Paoli for the document should read, *Balìe*, 2, fols. 12–13, instead of, *Provvisioni*, 32, f. 12.

118. Other ranking families of magnate status granted dispensation for comparable crimes were the Amadori, Corbizzi, Falconetti, and Visconti.

119. On 10 June 1349 an advisor to the *Signoria* proposed that the Ordinances of Justice be reestablished as they had been before Brienne had tam-

nately for Brienne, the very magnates so frequently recipients of his largesse, were at best only mildly enthusiastic in their support of his *Signoria*, and, as soon as popular rebellion erupted in July 1343, they joined the surging mobs in the streets and attacked his *palazzo*. Immediately upon regaining its ancient liberties, the government of the republic was taken in hand by a coalition of magnates and *popolani grassi*. The office of Prior was now open to the Florentine magnates. For the first time since the winter of 1292, Adimari, Bardi, Cavalcanti, Foraboschi, Mannelli, Pazzi, and Spini entered the highest magistracy of the republic. For almost two months these scions of the best families met with their commoner peers to treat the great public questions of the day. *Il popolo* was not ungrateful to these aristocrats for their heroism on that glorious St. Anne's Day, 26 July, when they came to the fore and provided leadership so that an undisciplined demonstration could become a successful revolution. It was therefore fitting that these aristocrats should be allocated a generous share of high communal offices. Not since the thirteenth century had such an opportunity been presented to the magnates.

This aristocratic coalition had an unparalleled chance to demonstrate its qualifications for political leadership. The prestige of such magnate families as the Adimari, Bardi, Cavalcanti, Donati, Frescobaldi, Pazzi, Rucellai, and others was at its apogee.[120] Certainly, high-born *popolani* and *magnati* had previously proven their ability to cooperate politically. There was even some sympathy with the demands of magnates for the cancellation of the Ordinances of Justice. Based upon the performance of this patriciate, however, one must conclude that few *Signorie* in the annals of the republic showed themselves to be so inept and short-sighted. Granted that the circumstances were hardly propi-

---

pered with them. This counselor suggested that all magnates to the sixth degree had been responsible for their kinsmen before the coming of Brienne. *Consulte et Pratiche*, I, f. 6.

120. It appeared reasonable to Giovanni Villani—no warm friend of the magnates—that they should have a share of political offices since they had been the "principali" in the July revolution against Brienne. The chronicler added that the *popolani grassi* "accustomed to governing," supported the "grandi co' quali aveano molti parentadi." Cf. *Cronica*, 12:18. Seven magnates were chosen to serve in the highest communal magistracy (the *Quattordici*) along with seven *popolani*. The magnates were Ridolfo Bardi, Pino Rossi, Giannozzo Cavalcanti, Giovanni Cianfigliazzi, Testa Tornaquinci, Bindo della Tosa, and the ubiquitous Talano Adimari.

tious, that the city was faced with a staggering public debt, and that confidence in the Florentine business world was at its lowest ebb, that unrest among the many workers of the city's *Lana* industry was widespread, still, the uncreative and pedestrian quality of this regime's policies must remain striking. The legislation enacted during its tenure represented a response to the narrowest of interests and reflected the egoism of the highest echelons of communal society. In their actions the ruling patriciate expressed their desire to return to the easy laissez-faire program of earlier days that at best was suitable only for intervals of great general prosperity. At these times the tendency was to minimize the role of government so that few fiscal burdens and restraints would be placed upon the patriciate. The tax structure was adjusted to increase the income from direct levies that fell on the population as a whole, while imposts on capital and property, which struck the patriciate, were cancelled.[121] Such an approach was bound to fail at this time because communal needs far exceeded the ever dwindling tribute collected from direct levies. No longer was it possible to finance the business of government in the traditional and time-honored manner; new and daring techniques were imperative if the *Camera* was to be rescued from the limbo of bankruptcy. In the face of this challenge, the aristocrats of August 1343 saw fit to increase the retail sales tax and to reapportion the city so that their own tax assessment would be drastically reduced. This failure to respond to communal needs surely was a factor in demonstrating the unfitness of the magnates to govern.[122] Their political partners, the great *popolani*, so closely bound to the magnates by kinship and business interests, were faced with a stark and painful alternative. Since November 1342, the treasury had been unable to amortize or even pay interest on the public debt, and, therefore, the great *popolani* who were the principal creditors of the republic were denied the use of their capital as well as the return from their investment. Fiscal reforms, even if they involved sacrifice, were, then, mandatory at this time, but, judging from the policies pursued by those controlling the *Camera,* only the most

---

121. CC., 2 (this volume of the treasury records covers the tenure of the *Signoria* of the *Quattordici*).

122. For an assessment of the communal fiscal dilemma in August–September 1343, see M. Becker, "Florentine Popular Government (1343–1348)," op. cit., 360–65. This aristorcratic regime was unable to pay salaries to communal retainers or honor the republic's commitments to its citizens living in Verona as hostages. P., 32, f. 60 (16 September 1343).

fatuously sanguine could have believed that they would be initiated by this particular coalition.

The incapacity of magnates to govern effectively was also evidenced by their judicial policies—or lack of them. Much more significant than the annulment of the Ordinances of Justice was the fact that the high crimes of magnates went virtually unpunished during the summer and early fall of 1343.[123] The authority of the Florentine courts was made almost ineffectual and as a consequence, private rights repeatedly triumphed over public law. Communal properties were widely appropriated by the great clans for personal use, and this was symptomatic of what might be described as the beginnings of a systematic dismemberment of the Florentine state. The bonds of community were in the process of being severed, and the tendency was unmistakably toward the dissolution of the commune. The great work of the next regime would involve the successful repression of these centrifugal forces and the containment of the egoism of the powerful clans.

Giovanni Villani contends that at first il popolo were satisfied to see the Signoria in the hands of those magnates who had been so instrumental in the ouster of Brienne, believing them to be peaceful and law abiding. Soon, however, this fund of good will was dissipated, and the superbia of these men became quite evident.[124] The chronicler Stefani observes that the popolani grassi were now thoroughly disenchanted with their magnate confrères and quickly came to the realization that their interests could be better served if they aligned themselves with the masters of the lesser guilds, for these minori could be counted upon to be "subservient and reverent" and do the bidding of their social superiors. According to Stefani, the great popolani who assumed office after the overthrow of Brienne, 1343, were accustomed to holding the lion's share of public posts, but it was not long before they found themselves relegated to a subordinate role. This seemed unjust since there were twenty

---

123. Giovanni Villani's contention that the high crimes of magnates were not prosecuted by this aristocratic regime (Cronica, 12:19), is borne out by the appropriate volume of the Camera del Comune. Cf. CC., 2.

124. Moreover, suspicion among the populace mounted because of the pervasive fear that the magnates were conspiring with neighboring tyrants to the detriment of the city's liberty. Marchionne di Coppo Stefani, rub. 599; Giovanni Villani, Cronica, 12:21. Very shortly certain Bardi, Frescobaldi, and Rossi were exiled because they had been convicted of plotting with Pisa. A Donati was condemned on a similar charge. Stefani, rub. 599, 605; G. Villani, Cronica, 12:32.

thousand *popolani* and only one thousand or so *magnati*.[125] Their loss of
representation appeared to be an inevitable consequence of their unfortunate alliance with magnates who would be satisfied with nothing less
than complete hegemony over the *Signoria*. Subsequent communal history was to demonstrate that Stefani's assessment was not far from the
truth: the *popolani grassi* did indeed find the lesser guildsmen to be much
more cooperative as political partners than the magnates.[126]

Certainly popular feeling against the magnate rulers cannot be an
entirely reliable guide in the fixing of responsibility for the misrule of
Florence during August and September 1343. When the rancor of *il
popolo* exploded and the mob joined forces with the republic's militia to
besiege the palaces of the Bardi, Cavalcanti, Donati, Frescobaldi, and
Pazzi, certain of the magnates supported the popular cause. Moreover,
many *popolani* had sided with the nobles and as office holders had
shown the same incapacity to lead the republic in its desperate hour. The
fact remains, however, that the deepest resentments were harbored
against the magnate class, and the contempt and disloyalty of leading
magnates toward the popular regime of October 1343–48 did little to re-
pair this opinion. Stefani notes that so intense was the distrust of *il popolo*
that "almost all the grandi" fled the city and "retired to the *contado* and
remained there."[127]

VI

Florentine experience until October 1343 had revealed the irrepressible
capacity of the magnates to reassert their political virility. Their prestige
had fluctuated; but this order had always been an integral part of civil
life, and never were they disbarred from certain critical offices. Fundamental to communal life was the principle of according representation
to affluent men—be they noble or commoner, and successive regimes
availed themselves especially of the valuable services of magnates. For
the most part, state tribunals contented themselves with taking reprisals
against only the most lawless of the magnate class. Even here the *Sig-*

---

125. Stefani, rub. 588.

126. Cf. M. Becker, "Florentine *Libertas:* Political Independents and *Novi
Cives, 1372–1378," Traditio* 18 (1962): 393–407.

127. Stefani, rub. 599. The chronicler also notes that many disgruntled magnates entered the service of foreign governments.

noria was especially mindful of the prestige and dignity of these aristocrats and frequently mitigated the harsh verdicts of the courts. Few magnate families were not the beneficiaries of cancellations of sentences and dispensations from verdicts. During periods of prosperity, which usually coincided with times of political calm in Italy, magnates and *popolani grassi* blended their talents to rule the city. It was only when foreign enemies appeared before the walls, or the *Signoria* was confronted with conflicting alternatives in the area of foreign policy that this coalition collapsed. Then the magnates, along with certain *popolani,* would assert their political individuality and embrace causes that threatened the *libertas* and sovereignty of the republic.

At these moments they tended to disregard what a Villani or Stefani or Compagni would have considered the good of the collectivity, in favor of their own egotistical interests. Every time Florence was confronted with a threat to its dominion, there were magnates who would desert the republic and enlist under the banner of a foreign prince or an Italian lord. Their persistent antipathy toward the Ordinances of Justice also indicated that they stood as the greatest single challenge to the constitutional order of the republic.

Social unrest is, after all, a relative concept, and, when the magnates are marked as the one order that did most to disturb the equilibrium between classes, it should be borne in mind that neither the workers of the city nor the small guild masters posed any serious threat to the prevailing socioeconomic system during the first four decades of the fourteenth century. The lower strata of Florentine society were fairly quiescent during those years, and, therefore, discontented segments of the magnate world stood out in bold relief against the background of a social universe bereft of revolutionary ardor. Later in the century *il popolo minuto* were to be the class that demanded radical revisions of the constitution, and they were then to constitute a seditious menace and to stand condemned in the eyes of their guild master contemporaries as the sowers of discord and treason. In the absence of other disaffected strata of society before 1343, the magnates, never as pernicious or despicable as *il popolo minuto,* were an order to be feared, placated, and even emulated. The desire of the *popolani grassi* to work in harmony with the magnates was everywhere in evidence, and the latter suffered no appreciable attrition of political influence between 1295 and 1343. Actually, they were presented with an unparalleled opportunity to govern the state as late as the summer of 1343. The conclusion that can be drawn is that this juridical order could retain an identity, not only in its own eyes, but even in those of its contemporaries in an environment where the social and economic forces all favored assimilation. It would appear, then, that the forces in operation were not sufficiently powerful to tame the political individualism of the magnates and cause their fusion with the burgher class. Occupation, comparable economic interests, and even intermarriage were not enough, and a new ingredient was essential.

Florentine communal society was fragmented and there were numerous pockets of legal authority and a plethora of foci of power. The commoner patricians respected this myriad of entities and generally displayed an overrefined regard for *status ordinum*. In such an atmosphere the rights and privileges of a legal order like the magnates were given every consideration. The subduing of the magnates came only after the Florentine patriciate had failed to provide leadership during the protracted crisis from 1338–43. It was to be the great work of the regimes after 1343, culminating in the formation of the territorial state of the late *Trecento*, that repressed the obdurate magnates. In the course of this process, traditional forms, intimately associated with the era of the commune dissolved, and successive *Signorie* replaced private immunities with public law. Out of this experience emerged a cohesive aristocracy quite different from the patriciate of the communal age. The issues dividing these *optimates* concerned the procedures of communal finance, the techniques of diplomatic maneuver, and the conduct of the interminable wars of the early *Quattrocento*. Sedition and violence were now more sporadic and the disputes between aristocrats revolved around the management of the funded communal debt or the extent to which the *Signoria* should sponsor mercantilistic programs. The ties of *consorteria* and even of guild slackened, and an intimate nexus developed among the great oligarchs who were now virtually stockholders in a giant corporation called the state. Less and less did the *Signoria* have to play its great medieval role of peacemaker. A canopy of law and bureaucracy was constructed, and the intrusion of public power into the recesses of private life became ever more apparent.

If one comes to accept the Burckhardtian, vitalistic and rationalistic historiographical approach to the Renaissance, and, if one entertains his commitment to an interior ideal unity of historical personality as a hallmark in defining the ethos of this era, then the taming of the Florentine magnate looms as a significant datum. To argue that the Florentine Renaissance is characterized, at least in part, by the citizen's discovery of his persona or ego is to suggest that what came to be unveiled was a new self-consciousness of will and personality. In other words, the individual approached society in a new guise. To capture this self-consciousness, one must attempt to recognize and understand the kind of presuppositions with which the individual approached himself.

In the interval of Florentine experience we have considered, the fused patriciate (half-burgher, half-magnate) failed to furnish leadership and as a consequence confidence in personal government, with its reliance upon exhortation, admonition, and political magnanimity, ebbed. In its stead we witness the rise of a sterner *paideia* that exalts the power and majesty of communal law. No longer is the *Signoria* to be so responsive to the perquisites and prerogatives of the magnate. This means that the development of the persona or citizen ego as well as the cultivation of citizen perspective will acquire a new creative and resilient adaptability. The *bonus civis* must suppress all proclivities for violence. If he is to compete, it must be through shaping his compulsions to the norms of a burgeoning civic humanism rather than to the promptings of a chivalric code. Essentially, then, the period after 1343 marks the triumph of the imperatives of the collectivity over the impulses of the magnate individual. In this latter sense, then, the repressive quality of civic life represents a slightly different emphasis than that accorded to the Italian experience by Jacob Burckhardt in his masterpiece, who may have underestimated the role of public law in tightening the bonds of society.

Finally, there remains the stylistic changes so thoughtfully examined by Millard Meiss in his *Painting in Florence and Siena after the Black Death* (Princeton, 1951). There he observes the repressive quality of Tuscan painting after the early 1340s. Gone is the spontaneous, the elegant, and the chivalric. Dissipated also is that easy confidence which prompted so much of the protohumanistic art from Cimabue through Giotto—a faith that the individual could achieve self-mastery and interior reform (*renovatio*) in the easy, casual world of the gentle communal *paideia*. Occasionally, and then only in time of crisis, would it be necessary to apply the enduring external compulsions of the rule of law. After the 1340s the art and even the literature would become increasingly puritanical, extending as it did the norms of communal law into the most intimate recesses of private life. The new sterner *Signoria* would now become the great engine of compulsion, and the consequence would be a more civic persona. Much later with Machiavelli, the demands of this engine would become self-justifying.

6

Economic Change and the
Emerging Florentine Territorial State

Even at the height of Florentine prosperity, the total income of the commune was barely sufficient to cover half of the republic's ever-mounting expenditures. This circumstance stemmed from the costly wars that Florence was compelled to wage throughout the fourteenth century.[1] Earlier, the armies of Florence had been drawn from the populace, and the budget had reflected this fact. In 1303 the communal debt was a trifling sum, but within a generation it had increased to the grand total of 450,000 florins, and this was in excess of the amount that the city could hope to raise from all revenue sources over a sixteen-month period. Giovanni Villani tells us that the outlay for troops averaged 140,000 florins for the years between 1336 and 1338. As a bitter afterthought he adds that this exorbitant sum did not include the pay for those mercenaries hired by the republic to fight the disastrous campaigns in Lombardy. By 1342 this public debt had reached 800,000 florins. In that same year the number of mercenaries enrolled in the Florentine armies was twenty times greater than the citizen levies. These military expenses, more than any other single factor, brought on the formation of the consolidated public debt, and their continued incidence

---

From *Studies in the Renaissance* 13 (1966): 7–39. Reprinted with permission.

This is an expanded version of a paper read at the North Central Renaissance Conference, which met on 16 February 1962 at Cleveland, Ohio.

1. On the origins of the *Monte,* see B. Barbadoro, *Le finanze della repubblica fiorentina* (Florence, 1929), 629–87. For a treatment of the *Monte* in the *Quattrocento,* see L. Marks, "The Financial Oligarchy in Florence under Lorenzo," in *Italian Renaissance Studies* (New York, 1960), 123–45. Cf. also G. Brucker, "Un documento fiorentino sulla guerra, sulla finanza e sulla amministrazione pubblica (1375)," *Archivio Storico Italiano* 115 (1957): 169; E. Fiumi, "Fioritura e decadenza dell'economia fiorentina," *Archivio Storico Italiano* 117 (1959): 427–502; A. Sapori, *L'età della rinascita* (Milan, 1958), 149–54. For the military background, see C. C. Bayley, *War and Society in Renaissance Florence* (Toronto, 1961), 3–58.

caused this debt, or *Monte,* to surge ever upward. By the end of the fourteenth century this communal debt totaled over 3,000,000 florins, and
by the middle years of the fifteenth century, when Florence incurred
new liabilities through the formation of the *Monte delle doti,* it climbed
to the astronomical figure of 8,000,000 florins. The way in which this
communal debt was accumulated, and its sharp ascent, remain neglected facets of Florentine history, and yet, if we aspire to understand
the emergence of new loyalties and the rise of a new political mentality,
we must treat the *Monte* with the respect it merits.

An increase of public indebtedness from 47,275 florins in 1303 to
3,000,000 florins in 1400, and finally 8,000,000 florins just two generations later, did irreparable damage to medieval political and economic
structures. New allegiances and bonds were created; private interests
diminished in the face of a mounting concern with state affairs. In communal society, the church, the nobility, the confraternities, the *Parte
Guelfa,* and the great guilds with their affluent burghers had provided
capital and credit; money and credit were almost exclusively in the
hands of these orders and medieval corporations, for the commune had
little wealth. By the fifteenth century, however, the state had become the
largest consumer of capital and a rentier class had invested heavily in
the interest-bearing public debt. The movement was from a private system of multiple economies—lay and ecclesiastical—toward the formation of a unitary public fiscal structure. The management of this debt affected not only the fortunes of the citizenry but even the well-being of
the Florentine business community, which was using *Monte* shares as
negotiable instruments.

The story of this funded communal debt occupies a central position
in the writings of the most important of all the chroniclers of the second
half of the *Trecento,* and it is not surprising to discover that the author
was also a *Monte* official.[2] The chronicler, Stefani, our best source for the
events of the 1370s, believed that the reduction of interest rates on the

----

2. G. Brucker, "The Ghibelline Trial of Matteo Villani (1362)," *Medievalia et
Humanistica* 13 (1960): 52–54. For materials pertaining to Matteo's political career and patrimony, see *Libri Fabarum,* 34, f. 26[r] (11 September 1355). (All documents cited in this essay are to be found in the *Archivio di Stato* in Florence.) Cf.
also *Estimo,* 8, f. 77; *Prestanze,* 83, f. 18; *Monte,* 442, f. 59. His experience with the
Monte adds dimension to the observations he makes in his chronicle (M. Villani,
Cronica, ed. F. Dragomanni [Florence, 1844–45], 8:71). Another chronicler much
involved in state fiscal matters was Donato Velluti, keeper of the best domestic

debt was the single most important measure to be taken by the government in over a century.[3] In the *Quattrocento*, when the communal councils spoke of the *Monte* as "the heart of this body that we call city . . . [which] every limb, large and small, must contribute to preserving," and described the same *Monte* "as the guardian fortress, immovable rock and enduring certainty of the salvation of the whole body and government of your state," they were indulging in much more than ponderous metaphors.[4] This was indeed an exact, if flowery, description of the economic heart of a new organism—the Renaissance territorial state. We might begin by asking this question: how much was the sum of 8,000,000 florins? The answer, if we employ the tax returns of 1427, would be that it was an amount of money approximately equal to the total wealth of the Florentine populace. In other words, the state debt had grown until it was equal to the entire capital of the Florentine citizenry; the entire state budget would not suffice to pay the carrying charges on this grand total.[5] Next we might inquire into how and why

---

chronicle for the middle years of the *Trecento*. Cf. *La cronica domestica,* ed. I. del Lungo and G. Volpe (Florence, 1914); *Libri Fabarum,* 23, f. 15^r (26 May 1344).

3. Marchionne di Coppo Stefani, *Cronica fiorentina,* ed. N. Rodolico (Città di Castello, 1903–55, *Rerum Italicarum Scriptores,* vol. 30), rub. 883–84. For Stefani's career as a communal financial official, see *Prestanze,* 368, f. 1^r, *Consulte et Pratiche,* 14, f. 87. (Henceforth this source will be abbreviated as C.P.) Cf. also *Camera del Comune,* 158, unnumbered folio (27 February 1374). (Henceforth this source will be abbreviated as C.C.) For additional bibliographical detail, see A. Panella, "Per la biografia del cronista Marchionne," *Archivio Storico Italiano* 88 (1930): 241–53; M. Becker, "Un avvenimento riguardante il cronista Marchionne di Coppo Stefani," *Archivio Storico Italiano* 117 (1959): 137–46.

4. Marks, op. cit., 127–28. The number of citizens inscribed in the various *Monte* of the *Trecento* ranged from approximately five thousand to eight thousand, the high point being reached just prior to the onslaught of the Black Death. Virtually every Florentine of substance had money invested in the *Monte.* There was a tendency, however, for the wealthy speculators to buy up large blocks of shares, and this was certainly true of such families as the Medici, Da Panzano, Panciatichi, Rinuccini, and others. Cf. P. J. Jones, "Florentine Families and Florentine Diaries in the Fourteenth Century," *Papers of the British School at Rome* 24 (1956): 196–97.

5. P. J. Jones, op. cit., 197 n. 113, presents the most recent evaluation of the total capital of Florentine citizens as being between 8 and 9 million florins, of which business capital amounted to 1,100,200 florins. (The statistics cited for the Florentine *Quattrocento* are from G. Canestrini's *La scienza e l'arte di stato* [Florence, 1862], 151ff.)

this curiously modern system of deficit finance gained such momentum in the years just before the Black Death.

The medieval system of gabelles, or indirect taxes, was simply inadequate to underwrite the military expenses of the commune, and what is more, between 1339 and 1342, the years immediately preceding the founding of the *Monte*, the returns from the gabelles were decreasing alarmingly.[6] It was evident that the days of the ever-expanding medieval economy were at an end. This is not to suggest, as several modern economic historians have done, that Florence was caught in the irreversible grip of a terrible depression. Nothing could be farther from the truth: rather, it is to propose that the halcyon days of the medieval upswing were waning. It is important to realize that the economy remained viable and was in fact to demonstrate an astounding capacity for resiliency. But beginning in 1339 we witness a general deterioration in the returns from the gabelles. The republic's revenue from her single most important impost, the customs toll, had reached 90,200 florins by the year 1337. Very soon, however, it tapered off and then plunged precipitously. In the following year it returned 83,500 florins and by 1343 the income had fallen to 68,000 florins. The city's second most lucrative tax was the levy on the sale of wine: it averaged 58,000 florins for the years between 1336 and 1338, but by 1342 it had dropped to 36,000 florins. The returns from the gabelle on contracts show a similar fluctuation during these critical years: for the biennium 1336–38, it had totaled 20,000 florins annually, but within four years it had lost two-thirds of its value. The impost on salt averaged 14,450 florins for the interim 1336–38, but by 1342 it had plunged to 4,679 florins. Comparable patterns of steep decline are evinced by the many other communal levies, and, judging from these crucial indicators of communal well-being, we can conclude that the bottom of the curve of state finances was reached late in 1342.[7]

---

6. Evidence for this statement is derived from the figures presented by Giovanni Villani in his *Cronica*, ed. F. Dragomanni (Florence, 1844–45), 11:92, for the biennium of 1336–38. For returns from the customs toll for 1343, see *C.C.*, 5, f. 18. It is important to note that, when this gabelle was sold on 13 January 1339, it brought in 14,200 florins less than it had yielded in 1336–38. Figures for the gabelle on wine, contracts, salt, and other communal levies are taken from *C.C.*, 2 bis.

7. The records of the *Camera del Comune* indicate that this occurred in November of that fateful year, and it was at that time that Walter of Brienne, short-lived despot of the city, enacted a decree declaring a moratorium on communal

The decline in public revenues is but one of the many indices that can assist us in determining the locus of the darkest part of the communal depression. As early as 1339, the Signoria had found it extremely difficult to farm out Florentine taxes. The auctions that were held annually had been able to turn up very few publicans willing to advance money to the treasury for the right to collect certain of the imposts. Moreover, many of those who had purchased this right were now unable to make payment because the yield had fallen far below its anticipated level. Therefore, the Signoria was compelled to establish special commissions for the purpose of collecting those taxes that could no longer be farmed out. The yield from rural imposts was also dwindling, and groups of tradesmen and shopkeepers, such as the vintners and butchers, tearfully petitioned the Signoria for tax relief. Villages and hamlets were likewise unable to fulfill their obligations to the commune, and their syndics railed against the evil times, lamenting the failure of crops and calling for a redress of grievances. The number of small landowners in the *contado* had declined, and as a result the commune acted to reduce the rural property tax by some seventy-five thousand lire.[8]

By 1341 it had become apparent that unless the fiscal structure of the Florentine commune was altered drastically the state faced bankruptcy. In January of that year the government announced that revenues from indirect taxes were no longer adequate to finance the republic's military ventures. At this moment it was suggested that lands and capital be taxed. The overwhelming resistance to this proposal is a fact of particular significance for an understanding of the economic mentality of the Florentines represented in the government at this time.[9] Tradition

---

debts. The treasury balance was just above 15,000 florins, barely enough to meet the daily exigencies of government. Cf. A. Sapori, *La crisi della compagnie mercantili dei Bardi e dei Peruzzi* (Florence, 1926), 148–51; C.C., 2 bis, f. 7.

8. Barbadoro, op. cit., 616; Sapori, *La crisi*, 138. Among purchasers of communal imposts who were unable to meet their obligations to the treasury were the buyers of the *gabella portarum*, the gabelle on wine, cattle, mills, hawkers of foods, and the levy on communal property. Cf. C.C., 2 bis, fols. 157^r–158^r, 187^r, 219, 313.

9. After 1315 the dreaded *estimo* was suppressed, and only under the despotisms of Charles of Calabria (1325–28) and Walter of Brienne (1342–43) was it revived. Cf. M. Becker, "Some Aspects of Oligarchical, Dictatorial, and Popular *Signorie* in Florence, 1282–1382," *Comparative Studies in Society and History* 2 (1960): 434–38. The greater guildsmen who completely dominated the Signoria

and economic interest dictated a policy that was at the base of the formation of the Florentine Renaissance state. The elite—both new and old—held strongly to conservative communal fiscal thinking. The government must be financed through indirect taxes and *prestanze*.[10] The latter were loans made by private citizens at rates of interest well above those realized from landed investment. Fifteen percent was not at all uncommon. Instead of paying taxes, then, an affluent Florentine lent money to the republic and gained a sizable income. The irony of the situation was that the government could not hope to repay the principal on these loans unless new sources of taxation were unearthed. Much has been made of the feeble efforts to discover these new sources, but the fact remains that even after they were found they were not tapped appreciably.[11] This essentially is the way the *Monte* came into being and grew until it became the very "heart" of public life.

After 1345, when the consolidation of the public debt was achieved, this mountain of indebtedness came to dominate the formulation of public policy. As a result of its establishment, a new relationship emerged

---

at this time repeatedly rejected the imposition of the *estimo* as well as any levy on the guilds themselves. Cf. *Libri Fabarum*, 14, ff. 41ʳ–43, 45; 19, f. 118; 20, f. 59.

10. Time and time again, advisors to the Signoria urged the government to impose new gabelles or to ask for voluntary loans; only when these remedies were exhausted would the speakers consent to discuss more drastic alternatives. In the matter of gabelles the tendency was to oppose the *gabella mercantie* and other imposts that fell most heavily upon the *arti maggiori* and to favor levies on such commodities as wine, bread, or meat. In 1351 Uguccione Ricciardi made a novel suggestion to the Signoria: instead of imposing a tax on *mercantie*, compel the citizens to serve in the Florentine garrisons without pay. Iacopo Banco Puccio, another speaker, much preferred exacting money through voluntary loans and then hiring mercenaries. When the most democratic of all Florentine regimes (1378–82) was finally able to enact direct taxation, the advisors to the Signoria demanded that taxpayers be given interest; in effect, this converted an *estimo* into a *prestanza*. Cf. *C.P.*, 1, pt. 1, and *C.P.*, esp. 17.

11. The *catasti* of Florentine citizens in 1427 yielded 25,341 florins, of which less than a quarter was contributed by commercial wealth. The *contadini* paid in over three times this amount. See Jones, op. cit., 187; G. Cavalcanti, *Istorie fiorentine*, ed. G. di Pino (Milan, 1945), 4:8; P. Berti, "Nuovi documenti intorno al catasto fiorentino," *Giornale Storico degli Archivi Toscani* 4 (1860): 32–62. The text of the enabling act founding the *catasto* was published by O. Karmin, *La legge del catasto fiorentino del 1427* (Florence, 1906), 11ff. It should be noted that the interests of the major guildsmen were insured by the proviso that eight of the ten officials in charge of assessing this tax were to be elected by the major guilds.

between the affluent citizen and the political community. No longer were his concerns explicable merely in terms of clan loyalty, guild affiliation, or membership in a tower society. Now he became involved—as he never had before—with the life of the republic. As the communal debt grew, so did his interest in politics, and in 1425, when the *Monte* for dowries was founded, his very progeny depended upon the ability of the state to weather the Milanese onslaught and Italian wars. At a time when a suitable dowry was a necessity, the winning of a husband depended upon the ability of the state to meet its commitments. It seems to me that the *Monte* had much to do with the creation of an audience for the civic humanists and the artists of the early *Quattrocento*. The Florentines wanted to believe in the durability and magnificence of this new entity—the state. The novel type of political discourse that comes to fruition with Machiavelli reflected the interests of men in the cult of the state. The citizen's well-being and his very economic survival were inexorably bound to this new organism, and if one views the enthusiasm with which increases in the value of *Monte* shares were greeted, and the grief when decreases were announced, then one comes to understand that the state was no mere abstraction in the *Quattrocento*.

In medieval Florence one's destiny was little influenced by government fiscal policy and the bonds of society were personal; at the upper level there was a bedazzling configuration of loyalties frequently in conflict. But with the rise of public indebtedness these tended to be dissipated. In the thirteenth and early fourteenth centuries the republic could and did borrow money from the guild corporations and the *Parte Guelfa*, but now the sums that could be garnered from these sources were trifling in the face of the huge budgets that Florence was compelled to underwrite. Medieval corporations and political organizations lingered, but they contributed less and less proportionately to the state's fiscal problems. Private fortunes continued to rise and decline, and, just as state consumption of capital increased, so too did the ratio of public to private expnditures—and the shift was inexorable.

To anticipate our story, it was to be the *Monte* and its management that became the single most important determinant of public policy. No longer could private citizens or medieval corporations be called upon to alleviate substantially the now perennial fiscal dilemma. As we shall see, during the 1360s, a system of deficit spending insinuated itself into the scheme of budget operations. The Florentine treasury now began to borrow large sums of money from the *Monte*, and this bookkeeping device was to be resorted to with ever-mounting frequency over the next century. Faced with staggering military commitments, the Signoria would propose legislation authorizing the officials of the *Monte* to make loans to the *camera*, and these credits were to become the mainstay of the republic's budgetary program.[12] By the end of the century the Signoria was paying interest on the debt only sporadically, diverting these funds to finance the costly wars against the Visconti of Milan. Public life began to center itself on the funded communal debt until the officials of the *Monte* came to be numbered among the most important of the republic's elected officers. The state had become a giant corporation in which the citizenry had invested a very substantial part of its patrimony. Anything that adversely affected the welfare of the republic would also deal a cruel blow to the fortunes of the citizenry, for, in fact, the two were now inseparable.

I

In the year 1342, as has been said, the communal revenues of Florence struck their nadir. In November of that year the newly installed despot of the city, Walter of Brienne, issued a decree suspending payment of interest to communal creditors. Formerly, the revenues from customs and the imposts on wine, salt, and contracts had been assigned for this purpose. Now the income from these levies was to revert to the communal treasury so that Florence might be able to meet her most pressing obligations. The *camera* had a balance of only 15,138 florins—barely enough to meet the most commonplace costs of government. Moreover, Brienne

---

12. For example, from 1 September 1368 to 31 August 1369 the treasury borrowed 77,556 florins from the *Monte*. This sum was approximately equal to the revenue from indirect taxes pledged for interest payments to communal creditors. What occurred, then, was that the capital of the *Monte* was being depleted, while the income from gabelles was being used to pay the interest. Cf. *C.C.*, 127–32. A similar situation obtained from July 1372 to August 1373, when 74,457 florins were transferred from the coffers of the *Monte* to the officials in charge of hiring troops for the republic. During the war with the Ubaldini, which broke out shortly thereafter, the amount involved reached almost 100,000 florins. Cf. *C.C.*, 149–63. Preliminary researches indicate that, beginning in November 1378, the treasury officials borrowed large sums from the *Monte*, usually at the end of their tenure of office, so that their accounts would balance and the republic would be able to pay its mercenaries. Cf. *C.C.*, 186, 190, 193.

was compelled to resort to numerous forced loans, and although he imposed direct levies on property and capital, he was unable to resume payment of interest to communal creditors. In fact, these desperate measures only succeeded in enlarging the public debt, since the recent forced loans merely added to the total, and the returns from the direct levies were being dispensed to mercenaries and communal functionaries almost as soon as they were received by the *camera*. In the immediately ensuing years, however, we witness a startling upsurge in communal revenues, so that by 1348 some of the more lucrative of the gabelles had almost recovered their optimum yield. The salt tax, for example, fell short of its 1336–38 return by only 450 florins, while the customs toll gained 11,000 florins during an interval of less than five years. A similar increment was registered by the wine tax, while the gabelle on contracts was to triple in value during that same period. Comparable gains were also registered by the levies on cattle, markets, mills, oil presses, and fisheries.[13]

Contrary to the conclusions of economic historians who depict the middle years of the fourteenth century as a kind of economic wasteland, state finances demonstrated amazing recuperative power. As we shall observe, this same vitality will reassert itself in the years immediately following the onslaught of the Black Death. Statistical evidence does not assist us in verifying the contentions of present-day Florentine economic historians who portray this era as one of economic stultification. So committed are they to this view that they are unwilling to acknowledge the relevance of the data presented in their own studies that indicate a trend toward recovery.[14] Receipts from the customs toll contin-

---

13. For returns on the salt tax, see *C.C.*, 6, f. 45^r; 9, f. 59^r; 14, f. 77^r. For the customs toll, see *C.C.*, 5, f. 18; 6, f. 47; 7. f. 115; 14, f. 18; 18, f. 102; 25, f. 104^r. Returns from the gabelle on wine rose from 36,000 florins in 1342 to 45,000 florins just before the Black Death. Cf. *C.C.*, 9, f. 394; 10, f. 84; 11, f. 33^r, 25, f. 104^r. For the gabelle on contracts, see *C.C.*, 10, f. 108^r, 11, f. 34; 14, f. 18; 17, f. 6. For the yield of the lesser gabelles, see *C.C.*, 12, f. 41^r; 11, f. 34; 23, f. 26; 10, f. 107; 16, f. 102^r, 10, f. 9. Since these taxes were auctioned off during this interval, the increased income that accrued to the commune resulted from the judgment of buyers who believed that economic conditions were going to improve. I have been unable to find significant increases in the rates of the gabelles that would account for their greater yield between 1343 and 1348.

14. For example, E. Fiumi in "La demografia fiorentine nelle pagine di Giovanni Villani," *Archivio Storico Italiano* 108 (1950): 78–158, presents population statistics indicating that the period prior to the Black Death was one of urban

ued to increase throughout the decade of the 1350s and 1360s, and, furthermore, an identical upsurge is recorded by the other principal gabelles.[15] The recovery after 1343 and the remarkable resurgence after 1348 demonstrate the resiliency of the Florentine economy. At a time when other north Italian cities lost their preeminence and commenced to live on their past glories, Florence was proving its durability. This fact is vital for an understanding of the persistence of public confidence in the funded communal debt, for, without a viable and healthy economy, investment in the *Monte* would have been an act of charity hardly characteristic of the Florentine.

We must realize that the citizens of 1343—the makers of the glorious revolution that drove Brienne from the city—addressed themselves to problems of government without the knowledge that with each succeeding generation the public debt would mount ever higher. Hence we must view these men and their actions in terms of their day-to-day confrontation of the perplexities of communal finances. And, while their actions had unforeseeable consequences, their intent was communal fiscal

---

growth, and yet he views these years as an interval of unmitigated decline. Similarly, his study of the number of rate payers in the Florentine *contado*, during the 1350s and 1360s, presents statistics indicating an increase, rather than a decline (90–94). Also, as we shall see, data from the treasury records, concerning the yield of the *estimo* on the *contado*, challenge Fiumi's conclusions on Florentine tax policy and reveal that the Signoria's regimen of the *contado* grew substantially harsher during the 1350s. In 1356 it produced 35,065 florins; this increase suggests that his contention about the symbiotic relationship between city and *contado* is inexact. Cf. E. Fiumi, "Sui rapporti tra città e contado nell'età comunale," *Archivio Storico Italiano* 114 (1956): 18–68; C.C., 57–62 (January–December 1356). A. Sapori in his study, "La gabella delle porte di Firenze" in *L'età della Rinascita* (Milan, 1958), p. 139, speculates about how Florentine revenues could have held up so well in the second half of the *Trecento* despite the onslaught of the Black Death and the veritable cyclone of business failures. His statistics, coupled with data from the treasury records, demonstrate that income from the *gabella portarum* increased sharply during the decade of the 1350s and the early 1360s, leveling off in 1365 and then undergoing a severe decline beginning in 1371. From May 1357 to April 1358 this *gabella* brought in 47,021 florins; the following year it rose to 56,570 florins. By 1364 it had climbed to 87,563 florins, and it remained on this plateau throughout most of the 1360s. Cf. pertinent treasury records for the years in question; and also n. 57.

15. Returns from the salt tax, imposts on cattle and meat, markets in the *contado*, and levies on hawkers of foodstuffs demonstrate comparable gains during the 1350s and early 1360s.

solvency. The rule of the city during the forty years after 1343 was in the hands of an uneasy coalition of affluent new citizens (i.e., the first of their clan to hold high communal office) and members of the old patriciate. For much of this time leaders of these two not unrelated strata of society were concerned with bringing in the revenues necessary for the work of government and the funding of the burgeoning communal debt. The net effect of these efforts, however, was little understood by this fragile coalition that dominated the councils of the Signoria. Piecemeal, and ever so gradually, the *novi cives* and their patrician colleagues acted to tighten the structure of communal politics. Although they failed to solve fundamental nagging fiscal problems, their efforts were not without result. Under their aegis the commune underwent a subtle transformation, for their policies did much to destroy the easy laissez-faire political morality of earlier days. Perhaps one illustration will suffice to suggest something of the character of this change. Earlier communal society was marked by its persistent reliance upon judicial dispensation. Sentences of great severity were decreed against those who failed to pay taxes or evaded customs, only to be reversed or annulled by action of the communal councils.[16] Now, between 1343 and 1348, such a setting aside of the verdicts of tribunals was rare. Justice was executed because the treasury could ill afford the loss of revenue.[17]

Other forces were also at work contributing toward a more impartial administration of the law, and these were equally vital to the transformation of the commune. The new citizens were champions of a more impersonal type of regime. Over the centuries their aristocratic predecessors had created a variety of organizations that were staffed and controlled exclusively by the patriciate, and these corporate bodies had become a law unto themselves. After the popular revolution of 1343, however, the new citizens sought to bring these aristocratic organizations under governmental surveillance. First, they insisted that their

---

16. Cf. *Guidice degli Appelli*, 122, pt. 2, for the many revocations of sentences and the numerous grants of judicial dispensation issued in 1341.

17. Severe condemnations were launched against the Bondelmonti, who paid fines totaling 5,161 lire, 16 soldi. Cf. *C.C.*, 6, f. 72ʳ (19 June 1344). The Cavalcanti were fined 3,000 lire, as were the Gherardini and the Giandonati. The family hardest hit by this vigorous enforcement of communal law was the Bardi, with sixty-two members of this house convicted on a variety of charges. The Donati, Frescobaldi, Pazzi, and Rossi were but a few of the many magnate houses who were dealt with severely at this time. Cf. *C.C.*, 4–19.

financial records be subject to review by communal officials.[18] Then they asserted the right of the Signoria to oversee the election of officers and demanded that they submit to Florentine jurisdiction.[19] Finally, the new men used the law as a wedge to achieve equality. The most exclusive of these medieval corporations that had previously been closed to the parvenus were now opened to the newcomers. As a result of the actions of the councils of the republic, the venerable *Parte Guelfa* was compelled to grant entrée to newcomers, just as the sacrosanct Court Merchant was forced to bestow representation upon these upstarts.[20] This successful quest for equality was duplicated in the guild world where the balance between the major and minor *arti* was redressed and both were afforded equal treatment in the matter of the enforcement of antimonopoly legislation.[21] Over the course of the next century state power intruded more and more into areas formerly the exclusive concern of the major guilds.[22]

Perhaps the tendency of the Signoria to assert its authority at the expense of the church best illustrates this shift from commune to territorial state. The fiscal dilemma of the city after 1342 did not permit the Signoria to recognize traditional medieval claims for clerical immunity. Here again the *Monte* played its part, for the more the clergy was taxed,

---

18. The Signoria was authorized to elect officials who would review the accounts of the *Parte Guelfa*. Cf. *Provvisioni*, 38, f. 226. (Henceforth this source will be abbreviated as *P.*) The Signoria also made important reforms pertaining to bequests to pious foundations. Cf. *C.P.*, 4, ff. 87–89.

19. The Signoria elected captains and treasurers of certain religious confraternities and established a special commission to oversee the management of their assets. Cf. *P.*, 36, f. 34^r; *C.C.*, 32, f. 50^r; *P.*, 37, f. 70; 39, f. 105^r. Especially significant were the efforts of the Signoria to compel the captains of the *Parte Guelfa* to make restitution of communal property and to obey the mandate of the Florentine courts. Cf. *C.P.*, 3, f. 92; 4, f. 47^r; 5, f. 7.

20. For the bitter debate over the question of admitting minor guildsmen to the captaincy of the *Parte Guelfa*, see *C.P.*, 8, ff. 1–53 (November 1366–March 1367). Throughout this interval the *Parte* vigorously resisted this proposal. The chronicler Marchionne di Coppo Stefani blamed the admission of minor guildsmen to the *Marcanzia* on factionalism and contended that such a step lowered the dignity of this high office. Cf. Stefani, op. cit., rub. 734.

21. M. Becker, "La esecuzione della legislazione contro le pratiche monopolistiche delle arti fiorentine," *Archivio Storico Italiano* 117 (1959): 8–28.

22. M. Becker, "The Republican City State in Florence: an Inquiry into Its Origin and Survival (1280–1434)," *Speculum* 35 (1960): 49–50.

the more revenue the republic would have on hand for its creditors. Intimately connected with the fiscal crisis was the republic's withdrawal from her traditional Guelf alliance with the papacy. The Signoria's reason for this radical shift of loyalties was that the republic could no longer afford to assume the strenuous financial commitments required by the old ties.[23] In terms of the reorientation of Florentine political thinking and the rise of civic humanism, the new foreign policy looms especially large. Medieval allegiances to pope and emperor tended to pass out of the political dialogue, and the civic humanists who were to become chancellors of the city formulated their discourse in terms of Florentine *libertas* rather than within the framework of traditional ideology.

What the government of 1343 desired was to extricate the city on the Arno from the costly Guelf alliance system so that sizable savings could be effected in the military budget. Only then would the *camera* have the funds necessary for meeting the interest payments on the republic's staggering debt. The new men were certainly not averse to this drastic change in communal foreign policy since they had little memory of the benefits, political and commercial, that had accrued to the city and its bankers from these ancient ties. Later in the 1350s Florence demonstrated the same reluctance to assist her old Guelf allies because such an adventure was too extravagant. Finally, in 1375 Florence went to war with the papacy and financed this ill-fated venture by confiscating large tracts of church land and auctioning them off to her citizenry.[24]

The dynamics that lay behind this cooling of affection for Avignon were also in evidence in the relations between the republic and the Tus-

---

23. Cf. A. Sapori, *La crisi*, 141–42. It was at this time that the republic dispatched ambassadors to the imperial court of Lewis the Bavarian. In a letter to the king of Naples—Florence's longtime Guelf ally—the Signoria stated that it was compelled to seek "other friends" even if they were Ghibellines, such as the emperor (*Missive*, 5ff. 98–99). See also the king of Naples' letter to the Florentines in which he reproves them for not taking counsel with him on foreign policy questions (C. Paoli, *Della Signoria di Gualtieri Duca d'Atene in Firenze* [Florence, 1862], 63).

24. Members of the lower orders, as well as patricians, took advantage of this opportunity to increase their patrimony at the expense of the church. The Alberti, Albizzi, Bardi, Bondelmonti, Cambi, Medici, Morelli, Pazzi, Peruzzi, Strozzi, and Tolosini clans were numbered among the more prominent beneficiaries. The holdings of the church were placed on the open market, and in January 1377 the first payments were recorded in the *Camera del Comune*. Cf. C.C., 186, unnumbered folio (20 January 1377).

can church. In 1345–46 legislation was enacted designed to bring the clergy under Florentine jurisdiction and to limit the authority of ecclesiastical tribunals. Each of the contemporary chroniclers contends that the animus of the populace was in part directed against the Tuscan church because noble and powerful Florentines were using their clerical status to aggrandize themselves and to oppress *il popolo*.[25] Added credence can be given to these observations since the legislation of those years against "ecclesiastical liberties" was proposed by the captains of the guilds, two-thirds of whom were new men. These new men deeply resented the fact that high church office had become the exclusive preserve of the patriciate, and persistently over the next forty years, when they were well represented in the Signoria, the government acted to destroy the medieval liberties of the clergy until, by the early *Quattrocento*, the church had become territorialized. The Signoria undermined the authority of the Inquisition, denied the right of sanctuary, demanded that it be consulted in the selection of high church dignitaries, and asserted the right of its courts to try criminal clergy.[26] The purview of state law was extended until it encompassed many matters that, in the medieval world, had been dealt with by the Courts Christian. Now breaches of morality, charges of blasphemy, and cases of sorcery and witchcraft had become the concern of the state.

One of the most sensitive areas into which state power intruded was that of usury. After 1343, according to communal law, victims of usurious contracts were not permitted to sue for damages in church courts; the state assumed a responsibility the medieval world clearly had bestowed upon the church.[27] The regulation of the pawnbroker—the most notorious of the manifest usurers—affords an insight into the political mentality of those Florentines called to govern the city over the next century and a half. Pawnbroking continued to be regarded as a sinful profession, and thus the Signoria felt a sacred obligation to punish

---

25. Cf. M. B. Becker, "Church and State in Florence on the Eve of the Renaissance (1343–1382)," *Speculum* 37 (1962): 509–27.

26. For attacks upon the prerogatives of ecclesiastical courts, see *P.*, 63, f. 73; *Libri Fabarum*, 40, f. 150 (12 July 1375). For severe regulations against the right of sanctuary, see *P.*, 60, f. 148; *Libri Fabarum*, 40, f. 52 (21 January 1373). The Signoria also demanded a voice in the selection of high church dignitaries. Cf. *P.*, 63, f. 70ʳ (7 July 1375).

27. M. Becker, "Some Economic Implications of the Conflict between Church and State in Trecento Florence," *Mediaeval Studies* 21 (1959): 5–6.

these *feneratores* so hateful in the sight of man and God. Since, after all, men could not be dissuaded from this most reprehensible of activities through fear of divine wrath, it was necessary for the Signoria to compel them to pay a sizable fine. Only those who did pay this fine into the *camera* were to be licensed, and they formed a cartel that had a monopoly over pawnbroking in the territories of the republic. Further, they were to be immune from prosecution as long as they were in good standing with the *camera*. Upon occasion the Signoria was to use these funds to staff an embassy at the papal curia. The government was loath to overlook any potential source of revenue, but it should be understood that Florentine attitudes toward these manifest usurers were not prompted by economic considerations alone, for there were deep-seated religious imperatives that generated moral ambiguities which continued to endure even in the *Quattrocento*. These were troubling enough to disturb the conscience of even the sturdiest of citizens; nevertheless, they did not have the requisite force to deter the Signoria from declaring the shares in the funded communal debt both interest-bearing and negotiable. These measures were accomplished in the face of stiff ecclesiastical opposition, and there were many who considered them to be a grievous breach of canon law.[28] Nor did these moral scruples dissuade the Signoria from designating the officials of the *Monte* as executors of the wills of manifest usurers. Again this move occasioned bitter clerical protestations. But the Signoria was not to be discouraged, and the authority of the officials of the *Monte* was further extended to include even

---

28. M. Villani, *Cronica,* 3:106; R. de Roover, "Il trattato di fra Santi Rucellai sul cambio, il monte comune e il monte delle doti," *Archivio Storico Italiano* 111 (1953): 3–34; J. T. Noonan, *The Scholastic Analysis of Usury* (Cambridge, Mass., 1957), 121–28. The Franciscans tended to defend the institution of the *Monte,* while the Dominicans and the Augustinians were bitterly critical. Cf. Barbadoro, op. cit., 666–69. It is interesting to note that the leading Dominican in Florence at this time was Piero Strozzi, who preached vehemently against the *Monte* on the grounds that it was usurious. Members of his family suffered a crisis of conscience at this time and made large-scale restitution of usury. This was the family who commissioned Orcagna and Nardo to do the altarpiece and murals for the Spanish Chapel in S. Maria Novella. The fact that restitution of usury was made before the advent of the Black Death should be taken into consideration when reading Millard Meiss's *Painting in Florence and Siena after the Black Death* (Princeton, 1951), 72–73. For the document concerning the restitution on behalf of the deceased Rosso di Geri Strozzi, see *Diplomatico,* S. M. Novella (12 July 1345).

the patrimonies of minors. Soon the *Monte* officials were to displace the clergy as guardian and protector of the estates of widows and orphans. Inexorably, the state was invading the clerical domain; not only was it assuming a variety of roles hitherto reserved for the great prelates of the medieval church, but it was also displaying a new political morality. Medieval misgivings persisted and restitution of usury continued, but, when the Signoria sanctioned dry exchange in return for a fee to be paid into the *camera,* there were few dissenters in the state councils, despite the fact that this form of exchange ranked as one of the most serious breaches of canon law.[29]

There were other areas of moral ambivalence, and in these we witness a tension between the state's need for revenue and the persistence of medieval attitudes. What emerges, however, is a Renaissance tendency to separate the ethically good from the politically necessary. This view, frequently taken with great anxiety, was to find expression in the early *Quattrocento* in the book of maxims of a Gino Capponi who was to advise his son to vote only for those men who cared more for their country than for the welfare of their own souls. It was precisely this doctrine that permeated the tragic view of politics so elegantly expressed by Guicciardini and Machiavelli.[30]

For the state to command the attention and occasion the moral anxieties of its citizenry, many of the intimate bonds of communal life had to be loosened. The great fount from which men had drawn their identities was the *consorteria.* It was this kindred group or clan to which one owed one's most fierce and abiding loyalty. Never displaced from Florentine life, but much weakened by the various Signorie after 1343, the *consorteria* began to lose certain of its medieval features. The new men favored the extension of communal law into the far reaches of the coun-

---

29. On 15 and 16 July 1329 the communal councils enacted legislation imposing a tax of one-half percent on "cambium siccum." There was considerable opposition in the councils. Cf. *Libri Fabarum,* 55, f. 54. In 1435 this law was suspended for two years, and citizens were permitted to engage in dry exchange operations. Cf. *P.,* 126, f. 313ʳ (22 November 1435); *Libri Fabarum,* 57, f. 42. For an extensive bibliography on *cambium siccum* and other varieties of exchange, see R. de Roover, *L'Evolution de la lettre de change* (Paris, 1953), 170–216. Cf. also R. de Roover, "What Is Dry Exchange?," *Journal of Political Economy* 52 (1944): 262–64; Noonan, op. cit., 182–87, 315–34.

30. Renzo Sereno, "The *Ricordi* of Gino di Neri Capponi," *American Political Science Review* 52 (1958): 1118–22.

tryside and enforced the verdicts of the courts against the great lords of the *contado* with a zeal that had not been much in evidence among their aristocratic predecessors.[31] As the burden of the state debt grew heavier, the popular government felt obliged to bring in more revenue from the countryside. Feudal privileges and the immunities of the great families tended to decline and state power replaced private justice throughout the Florentine territories.

After the 1350s the republic began to acquire dominion over much of Tuscany and for the next half-century, until the conquest of Pisa, state bureaucracy was to proliferate. The ties that had previously bound men to their overlords were gradually replaced by bonds—sometimes very onerous—between city and rural inhabitant. Steep communal taxation did much to destroy the old nexus and encourage the dissipation of the authority of the old families of the *contado*.[32] Later we shall consider in detail the effects of the Signoria's deep concern for the acquisition of military subsidies from the territories and the establishment of a regular schedule of levies. It was seldom, in the second half of the *Trecento*, that the great lords of the district marshaled the host; rather, it was the republic's bureaucrats who efficiently collected payments in lieu of military service.[33] Further, the government was much interested in systematically recording title to property and rights so that they might be directly amenable to state imposts. The republic was becoming the intermediary between the inhabitants of the *contado* and the old rural lords. Finally, after many false starts, beginning in 1345 and concluding with the *catasto* of 1427, the first complete state register of real and personal property since antiquity was drawn up by the city's tax officials.

Within the city walls the influence of the great clans was also substantially reduced. Severe prohibitions against multiple office holding by members of the same family were rigorously enforced. The new men were particularly harsh in their treatment of the Florentine magnates after 1343, and the law was interpreted so that these houses were subject to both heavy fines and political ostracism. More than any other single factor, the motive force for these repressive measures stemmed from the

---

31. Cf. M. Becker, "The *Novi Cives* in Florentine Politics (1343–1378)," *Mediaeval Studies* 24 (1962): 35–82.

32. Cf. E. Fiumi, "Fioritura e decadenza dell'economia," *Archivio Storio Italiano* 116 (1958): 484–87.

33. Bayley, op. cit., 7ff.

desire of the citizenry to curtail the violent behavior of an aristocracy who eagerly sought to emulate the vendettas and blood feuds of the ancient *consorteria*. The government acted to compel individual members of a *consorteria* to settle in different quarters of the city, and many *magnati* who obeyed the laws of the republic were rewarded with grants of bourgeois status.[34] By the middle years of the fourteenth century noble status had become a detriment, so hedged in was it by legal restrictions. Numerous petitions were presented by clan members beseeching the Signoria to separate them from their *consorteria*, permit them to change their family names, and even abandon their coat-of-arms. All this was to be done so that they might have bourgeois status in order to be eligible for high public office and free from the many restraints placed upon *magnati*.[35]

When the new men were well represented in office, there was a marked tendency to extol public law at the expense of medieval prerogatives. Nowhere was this more in evidence than in the valiant efforts of these popular regimes to recover and protect state property. Here we have an index of the character of this type of regime. It attempted to defend the possessions and rights of the state from the usurpations and appropriations of the great and the powerful.[36] Again the motivation for this policy is mixed: on the one hand, the new citizens desired to curb the lawlessness of their social superiors, and, on the other, both patrician and newcomer were anxious to safeguard all possible sources of revenue. This was imperative in the face of an ever-increasing public debt.

II

That the generation of Florentines called upon to govern their beloved native city during the tense years between the onslaught of the Black Death and the outbreak of worker revolt in the summer of 1378 faced problems of unprecedented complexity in the area of communal finance

---

34. *P.,* 42, 113 (21 August 1355); *P.,* 49, f. 1 (11 August 1361). In October 1343, 530 *magnati* were declared *popolani,* and the chronicler Marchionne di Coppo Stefani states that these men were from the less powerful and less criminal *magnati* families. Cf. rub. 616–17; Villani, *Cronica,* 12:22.

35. The highest incidence of these petitions was between 1349 and 1363. Cf. *P.,* 36–51.

36. Cf. M. Becker, "Some Aspects of Oligarchical, Dictatorial and Popular *Signorie* in Florence, 1282–1382," op. cit. (n. 9), 421–34.

is everywhere in evidence in the minutes of the advisory councils to the
Signoria. Despite the many bold reforms and the general assertion of
state power initiated by the new men and their civic-minded patrician
colleagues, the public debt multiplied fourfold over this thirty-year
period. Despite the efforts of this coalition to move Florence out of the
orbit of the costly papal alliance system, the burden of military expenditures grew ever more irksome until it threatened to topple the intricate
structure of public finance and even destroy popular confidence in the
fiscal reliability of the state. The bulk of the republic's income accrued
from indirect levies such as the gabelles on wine, salt, and meat, as well
as the customs toll, and these were now pledged, with increasing frequency, for the hire of mercenary soldiers or for the restitution of outstanding governmental debts. No sooner were these gabelles collected
than their disbursement began. State income was no longer sufficient to
meet the daily expenses of government. The old remedies of a happier
day, when budgetary deficits were minute, were now pitifully inadequate. By the late 1360s and early 1370s the treasury was prone to be in
arrears some 300,000 florins a year. As has been previously noted, a loan
from a guild of a few thousand florins or a subsidy from the *Parte Guelfa*
of not much more or a grant from the Tuscan clergy would hardly make
a dent in this by now imposing figure. Governmental expenditures were
running twice the total of the treasury's intake.

Communal counselors were well aware of the most effective solution to the republic's fiscal dilemma: extricate Florence from the costly
wars and expensive diplomatic maneuvers endemic to Italy at this time.
Only in this way could the city be rid of "intolerable expenses."[37] There
had been a day when the budget of the *camera* was balanced, but this
desideratum had been achieved only when Florence had been able to
cut ties with the papacy and Naples and successfully isolate itself from
the intrigues and conflicts of its neighbors (1343–48). Moreover, it had

---

37. During the Pisan War such prominent patricians as Carlo Strozzi repeatedly exhorted the Signoria to terminate hostilities with a peace treaty, thereby
freeing the city from the burden of "intolerable expenses." The blunt Salvestro
de' Medici urged the Signoria either to raise the necessary revenue or make
peace with Pisa. *C.P.*, 4, f. 94ʳ (4 September 1363). As soon as the exigencies of
war diminished, speakers appealed to the government to reduce substantially
the number of mercenaries in the republic's employ. Cf. statements by Messer
Niccolò Alberti in *C.P.*, 5, f. 116ʳ (5 August 1364). For a comparable situation during the Otto Santi War (1375–78), see *C.P.*, 14, ff. 52ff.

renounced its old imperial ambitions; after making these sacrifices, it was able to reduce military expenditures by two-thirds.[38] Immediately after the Black Death, however, outlays for mercenaries doubled, and this was only a prelude of things to come. By the end of this century, when Florence fought for her *libertas* against the Visconti lords of Milan, these costs had increased some 2,000 percent.[39] Even the staunchest proponents of Florentine isolation were unable to prevent the city from becoming embroiled in the incessant power struggles continually raging in north Italy throughout the troubled years of the second half of the *Trecento*.[40] Costs escalated even more sharply after the decade of the 1360s; less and less frequently did citizens take up arms in behalf of the republic, until only a single family, the Agli, regularly followed the profession of soldiery. The brief campaigns of the early fourteenth century, waged by citizen militia with a liberal sprinkling of mercenaries, had worked little hardship on the Florentine treasury and, therefore, required only slight alterations in the tax system.[41]

---

38. M. Becker, "Florentine Popular Government (1343–48)," *Proceedings of the American Philosophical Society* 106 (1962): 363–64. During the year 1345 the republic's military budget totaled 75,000 florins. This figure is derived from the *Camera del Comune*. Each volume covers a two-month interval; therefore, disbursements averaged 12,500 florins for each two-month period. In the following year expenditures were only 11,534 florins for a comparable interval. In 1347 they averaged 10,080 florins, and for the first half of 1348 until the onset of the Black Death they totaled 29,125 florins for a half-year, or 1,708 florins for each two-month period.

39. In May and June 1349 expenditures for mercenaries rose to 17,391 florins, their highest figure since the halcyon days of empire building in the early 1340s. By March and April 1350 they were up to 30,833 florins. Treasury officials were now borrowing regularly from the receipts of the gabelles. Customs revenues and money from the impost on wine were diverted to pay mercenaries; formerly, this income had been used to retire the public debt. Soon the gabelle on salt was assigned to the *Capsam conducte,* and even the revenues obtained from farming lesser imposts were pledged for this purpose. Cf. *C.C.* 32 (March–April 1349).

40. There was strong sentiment among the advisors to the Signoria for adhering to the terms of the Treaty of Sarzana. This accord, signed with Milan in 1353, bound Florence to strict neutrality in matters north Italian. Communal counselors therefore tended to argue that an alliance with the papacy would be a violation of the provisions of this treaty. In practice, then, those who espoused this position were hostile to any commitments to major Italian powers. Cf. M. B. Becker, "Church and State in Florence on the Eve of the Renaissance (1343–1382)," op. cit. (n. 25), 509–27.

41. Bayley, op. cit., 3–58. In May 1302 five hundred Florentine horse and six

Try as they would, the rulers of the republic could not free Florence from the burdens of war. Those men who entered the Signoria after the Black Death were faced with the nagging problem of finding revenue without jeopardizing the city's credit. In July 1351, at a time when the effects of the war with the Ubaldini were still being felt, and the drain to be incurred by hostilities with Milan was becoming apparent, the Signoria convened an advisory council. The first speaker urged the Signoria to raise revenue in the time-honored fashion, through the imposition of gabelles. He reasoned, as so many others were to do, that indirect levies on foodstuffs and other necessities would occasion less dissension among the citizenry than direct levies on capital and property. Only by shunning the dreaded *estimo* could the unity of the citizenry be ensured.[42] The principle of direct taxation had been abandoned in 1315, and only twice since then had an *estimo* been exacted. Moreover, in both instances it had been effected during the tenure of a well-hated despot: first, Charles of Calabria had resorted to it in 1325, and then Walter of Brienne had enacted it in 1342. Therefore, past history and public opinion conspired to make recourse to this remedy as difficult as it was unpopular. It was not that the priorate and its colleges were unwilling to propose its implementation at desperate moments when the treasury was virtually insolvent but, rather, that such a suggestion could rarely be expected to win the necessary two-thirds vote in the communal councils for its passage. Much later, regimes committed to the principle of direct taxation were reluctant to enforce the *estimo* for fear of alienating their more affluent adherents. Those who sat in the highest communal offices and were most experienced in matters of public finance would propose such a direct levy only to be forced to make major concessions. So damaging were these concessions that the law that finally emerged bore little resemblance to the original proposal. The Signoria obligated the treasury to pay interest on the individual's contribution and even agreed to return the tax payment at some future date when the commune prospered.[43] In this way the *estimo* came to be converted into a forced loan (*prestanza*).

Despite the unpopularity of the *estimo*, the Signoria continued to debate its merits, and once during this thirty-year interval it was actu-

---

thousand Florentine foot soldiers besieged Pistoia for twenty-three days at a cost of only 12,093 florins.

42. *C.P.*, 1, 1, f. 22 (30 July 1351).
43. *C.P.*, 11, f. 134; *Libri Fabarum*, 41, f. 32; *C.P.*, 18, ff. 6–91.

ally put into effect. In 1352, under pressure of war with the Visconti, the tax was imposed and brought revenue into the treasury over the next few years.[44] Again in 1355, when Tuscany was menaced by the awesome prospect of a German emperor and his hosts, an *estimo* was enacted and officials were appointed to supervise its collection. This time, however, resistance proved too formidable and the books of assessments for this direct levy were now used to determine the rates for a series of interest-bearing forced loans.[45] Once more, at the height of the costly war with Pisa (1363), the Signoria reactivated the *estimo*. Furthermore, they established the intricate machinery for its collection and took the serious, and rather expensive, step of hiring a foreign judicial official "ad faciendum extimum civitatis Florentie."[46] Again at the critical moment the direct levy was abandoned, and the records of the treasury show that the Pisan War continued to be financed by interest-bearing forced loans. Hostilities against S. Miniato at the end of the decade of the 1360s occa-

---

44. Cf. G. Brucker, *Florentine Politics and Society, 1343–1378* (Princeton, 1962), 93. In support of Brucker's contention that this levy was a direct one, cf. *C.C.*, 47, f. 50: "Leonardus Bartholini camerarius gabelle fumantum et extimi civitatis Florentie." The *camera* continued to collect belated returns from this direct impost until May–June 1361. Donato Velluti was particularly well informed upon communal fiscal matters, and he reveals that in July and August 1349, when his brother Piero sat in the Signoria, payment of interest to holders of *Monte* shares was prorogued. Only in March–April 1351, when Donato himself became *gonfaloniere di giustizia* was legislation enacted authorizing revenue from the *gabella portarum* to be used to pay interest to these creditors. The implication then would be that, without the enactment of an *estimo*, the *gabella portarum* would necessarily be diverted to meet the current expenses of the commune. Cf. Donato Velluti, *Cronica domestica* (n. 2), 38–39.

45. *C.C.*, 68, f. 127^r (November–December 1357). Notation is made here that on 29 April 1355 officials were appointed to draw up lists of rate payers to be liable for an *estimo* in the city. Matteo Villani's observations on the background of this legislation and reactions to it suggest something of the pressures brought to bear upon the Signoria to abandon the principle of direct taxation. According to his testimony, and he was himself a minor official of the *Monte*, those who made payment into the *camera* were to be assigned revenue from incoming gabelles at the rate of 10 percent a year. The well-to-do paid the assessments of the "impotenti" and were to receive interest at the same rate. An important and little studied traffic in the buying and selling of *prestanze* comes to be increasingly evident for the balance of the *Trecento*. See M. Villani, *Cronica*, ed. F. Dragomanni (Florence, 1846), 4:83.

46. The magistrate elected was Messer Pino Charde (*C.C.*, 99, f. 189 30, December 1364).

sioned debate on the merits of this direct tax, but the proposal suffered its usual fate.[47]

Indirect levies were as popular with the membership of the communal councils as the idea of the *estimo* was repugnant, and from records of the earliest meetings in July 1351 until the summer of 1378 stolid Florentine guildsmen continued to suggest that the Signoria add new gabelles and increase the rates of existing ones.[48] Perhaps mounting military budgets could be met with this commonplace remedy so favorable to the interests of the well-to-do. Revenues from the customs toll and the levies on wine, salt, contracts, and meat could be assigned to the officials in charge of making disbursements to troops. At first this expedient seemed especially promising. The crucial gabelle, the customs toll, was the mainstay of the Florentine treasury, accounting as it did for almost one-fourth of the *camera*'s cash receipts. As we have observed, it suffered a marked decline in 1338 and continued to plummet until 1343, when it staged a noticeable recovery. Just before the onslaught of the Black Death it was only 11,200 florins shy of its highest yield. It dipped during the plague but again recouped, and during the 1360s, despite the lingering effects of the plague, it began to climb and its phenomenal ascent continued through the next decade.[49] Comparable gains were registered

---

47. *C.P.*, 10, f. 110^r (15 May 1369).

48. From the early 1350s until the late 1370s the question of whether or not to augment communal gabelles was related to the need to satisfy state creditors. Cf. *C.P.*, 1, 2, f. 83 (21 October 1354); 2, f. 41 (16 February 1359); 4, f. 126^r (24 November 1363); 12, ff. 10^r–12^r (March 1372). Also it would be possible to use additional revenues from increased gabelles as collateral for new communal loans. One type of gabelle was certain to elicit opposition from government counselors: the gabelle on wool and cloth. Cf. *C.P.*, 1, 1, f. 22 (30 July 1351).

49. M. Becker, "Florentine Popular Government (1343–1348)," op. cit. (fn. 38), 361–62. It rose from 47,021 florins (May 1357–April 1358) to 56,570 florins (May 1358–April 1359). By 1364 it was yielding 87,563 florins a year, and it remained at approximately this level until 1368, when it declined to 60,682 florins. If we use the *gabella portarum* as an index of communal prosperity, we can suggest a recovery in the 1350s, a high order of prosperity in the 1360s, and then a contraction in the 1370s. Conditions in the early 1370s seem to have been comparable to those of the 1350s. The *gabella portarum* returned 50,012 florins from March 1370 through February 1371. The following year showed a gain of 8,672 florins. It is well to remember that the substantial increase in the rate of key imposts such as customs, wine, and salt occurred in 1351; therefore, fluctuations cannot be explained in terms of modifications in rates. Moreover, it is possible to correlate these fluctuations with returns from other gabelles and establish cer-

by other gabelles, and the Signoria added to the Florentine bureaucracy in the hope of regularizing tax collection. Unfortunately, however, even the resilient economy, which could produce a customs toll that averaged 85,320 florins a year between 1364 and 1367—only 4,000 florins less than the top yield achieved in the halcyon biennium of 1336–38—could do little to assuage the crushing fiscal burden.[50] At first, income from the principal gabelles could be used for the hire of mercenaries, but, with the coming of the decade of the 1360s, the funds were pledged, with increasing frequency, for the payment of interest on outstanding government loans. During the latter years of that decade the bulk of the mounting receipts was committed, and the spectacular gains registered by the *gabella portarum* could not be utilized for military purposes. The action of the communal councils aggravated the problem. In a moment of fiscal irresponsibility, unparalleled in the annals of the republic, the councils tripled the interest rates paid to many of the state's creditors. The implications for the already overburdened treasury system were grave: now additional income from the gabelles would be consumed by the increased carrying charges. The question of amortization of the communal debt was disregarded and only came to the fore during the revolutionary crisis of 1378.[51] The yield from such gabelles as the impost on contracts was designated for the maintenance of communal fortifications and by the middle 1350s was devoted exclusively to this cause.[52]

---

tain communal fiscal trends. Perhaps the best single indicator is the gabelle on contracts, which brought in 22,894 florins in 1356, rose during the 1360s, only to drop precipitously in 1370, and then, like the gabelle on customs, to recover substantially in 1371. See also n. 21.

50. Brucker, op. cit. (n. 44), 95. According to the provision of 1358, loans of communal creditors were to be inscribed immediately in a 15 percent *Monte.* Cf. C.C., 71, ff. 166–66ʳ (May–June 1358).

51. A petition presented to the Signoria during the July days of the Ciompi revolution proposed that the government make provision for the amortization of the *Monte* over a twelve-year interval and that the interest rate be pegged at 5 percent. The first suggestion was not seriously entertained, while the second did in fact become official government policy over the next four years. Cf. N. Rodolico, *I Ciompi* (Florence, 1945), 122–23; C.C., 184–210.

52. At first the commune added approximately one-third to the revenues from the gabelle on contracts to keep state fortifications manned and in repair. Soon, however, expenditures from the treasury were reduced, and it is possible that additional labor services and castle guard were being demanded from the *contado.* Cf. C.C., 41–42. In the early 1350s treasury disbursements for this purpose averaged some 4,000 florins a month.

It would be possible to add picayune sums to the communal treasury by imposing gabelles on baked goods or taxes on weights and measures, but the returns would do little to ease the strain of spiraling treasury deficits.[53] A few among the many advisors to the Signoria advocated a tax on wool and cloth, but the overwhelming majority of greater guildsmen vehemently contested this proposal. Furthermore, they were equally hostile to suggestions that the guilds should submit to communal levies. Long ago the *arti maggiori* had won immunity from these exactions, and they did not intend to yield the precious fruits of this glorious victory. Instead, they championed gabelles on pawnbrokers and counseled the Signoria to impose stiffer fines upon the city's prostitutes. Despite the prevalence of both of these trades, contributions from usurers and women of ill repute would be trifling.[54] Still, when special commissions were appointed to investigate the question of securing additional communal revenues, they came forward with the same ancient remedies. Spokesmen for these *balie* were to drone on in the same tiresome vein over the next thirty years: add new gabelles, end tax leakage, and practice the strictest economies in government. But, even if the Signoria had followed this sage and conservative advice, it would not have led to the alleviation of the fiscal bind.[55]

---

53. The impost on the retail sale of baked goods—a most unpopular levy—yielded only 1,350 florins a year. Cf. *C.C.*, 39, f. 101^r (2 April 1350). The return from the tax on weights and measures was a trifling 304 lire. Cf. *C.C.*, 71, f. 153^r (15 May 1358).

54. The license charge on pawnbrokers—a fee in the form of a fine—brought in about two thousand florins a year during this period. On 1 September 1371 Lucia Giorgio, prostitute, was condemned for soliciting in Florence without wearing the seal of her profession. Her fine, seven lire, ten soldi, was paid directly into the "capsam quattuor clavium," a special division of the treasury designated for money to be applied toward *Monte* interest payments. On the subject of pawnbrokers, see M. Becker, "Nota dei procesi riguardanti prestatori di danaro," *Archivio Storico Italiano* 114 (1956): 736–46.

55. In 1373, when the commune was warring against the Ubaldini and hard-pressed for funds, the Signoria received this perplexing advice from the spokesmen for the colleges: suspend restitution of interest to *Monte* creditors while at the same time make certain that the public retains confidence in communal fiscal integrity (*C.P.*, 12, f. 121 [5 July 1373]). The entire question of responsible fiscal leadership among the governmental personnel remains to be investigated. In March 1372 communal councilors were faced with a grave dilemma; in order to pay interest to communal creditors it would be necessary to borrow money from these self-same individuals in the form of a *prestanza*. Among the futile propos-

With the conclusion of the Pisan War, treasury deficits had become a regular feature of communal finance, so chronic was the discrepancy between ordinary revenues and extraordinary military expenses. The reluctance of the communal councils to impose levies on capital and property compelled the Signoria to resort to forced loans. Fourteen times during the course of the Pisan War (1362–64) tribute was gained through *prestanze*. As early as June 1358, these loans were systematically being converted from short-term debts to long-term obligations. The government was acting to incorporate these *prestanze* into the funded communal debt. To the names of the many original holders of *Monte* shares, their heirs, and the purchasers of titles to this first indebtedness were added new accounts of recent government creditors. Furthermore, by creating new *Monti* and engaging in a variety of fiscal stratagems, the Signoria was able to boost the interest rates so that government creditors after 1358 could collect from 10 to 15 percent on their holdings.[56] Needless to say, such steps were welcomed enthusiastically by the principal creditors of the commune. The fact that these creditors were the self-same individuals who staffed the Signoria at this time may help us to account for the inauguration of such a costly policy. The most affluent of the new men joined forces with the scions of the old houses to advance money for the recruitment of troops. These loans to the *camera armorum* by dyers, vintners, druggists, as well as by the patrician clans of Alberti, Albizzi, Bardi, Peruzzi, Ricci, and Strozzi, were now incorporated into the public debt, and it was these particular creditors who sat as fiscal advisers to the Signoria. It was their protestations that echoed in the council halls admonishing the Signoria to keep faith with the republic's creditors.[57]

---

als designed to forestall this necessity was a tax on Florentine prostitutes. The old chestnut, a gabelle on baked goods, was also boldly advanced. Cf. *C.P.*, 12, ff. 10^r–38.

56. Matteo Villani's comments on this legislation assume new meaning in the light of the fact that he was one of the officials in charge of the management of the public debt. Added credence must also be given to the remarks of Stefani for the same reason. Cf. *Cronica*, ed. F. Dragomanni (Firenze, 1846), 8:71; Marchionne di Coppo Stefani, *Cronica*, rub. 520, 799, 882.

57. Those *novi cives*, who were among the principal creditors of the republic, were Pace Brunetti, tanner (697 lire); Mone Fantini, vintner (1,395 lire); Giovanni Goggio, used clothing dealer (174 lire); Pasquino Telli, blacksmith (139 lire), and numerous others. Cf. *C.C.*, 54, f. 174^r. For additional names, see *C.C.*, 66, 68–71. Other patrician families not mentioned in the text include the Del Bene (1,032),

The inscription of the many *prestanze* of the late 1350s and early
1360s into the books of the *Monte* posed a formidable problem for those
managing public finance. Although the state was not liable for the restitution of principal in the near future, it was responsible for the interest.
This obligation had become more and more onerous with the raising of
rates by 100 or 200 or even 300 percent. Moreover, the communal debt
had increased approximately threefold in the short span of a decade and
a half after the Black Death. And, as we have seen, this was but a prelude, for by 1380 the debt had reached 2,500,000 florins. From this time
on, as has been noted, its ascent was even more spectacular, until it was
reckoned at the towering figure of 8,000,000 florins.[58] And in the main
this massive obligation had been incurred as a result of the frequency
with which the Signoria resorted to the *prestanze.*

III

As early as 1365, shortly after the conclusion of the costly Pisan War,
communal councilors were anxious about the ability of the government
to meet its fiscal commitments.[59] The question plaguing the Signoria
concerned the unearthing of new sources of revenue to help defray the
spiraling costs of the *Monte.* Men with limited vision might advocate the
strict enforcement of communal sumptuary laws or the closer supervision of communal food markets, but the returns would be petty. What
was clearly the greatest single little-tapped fiscal resource of the republic were the numerous territories under its sovereignty—the countryside and the Tuscan towns. Very recently, economic historians have
sought to discredit the thesis advanced by Salvemini and others that

---

Covoni (3,416 lire), Guidalotti (3,269 lire), Guicciardini (3,406 lire), among
others.

58. Marks, op. cit., 123–47; Brucker, "Un Documento fiorentino," op. cit. (n.
1), 169.

59. This war added something over a million florins to the public debt. The
wars of the early *Trecento* left only a small residue of indebtedness. Even a
conflict with so formidable an adversary as Castruccio increased the debt by
only 50,000 florins. Cf. Barbadoro, op. cit. (n. 1), 630. *Prestanze* were levied at a
frantic pace throughout the Pisan War. Cf. *Prestanze*, 13 (June 1362) through volume 109 (July 1364). In June of the following year advisors to the Signoria expressed concern about whether there were sufficient funds in the treasury to pay
interest on the public debt. Cf. *C.P.*, 7, ff. 87–89.

Florence exploited her domains. The revisionists, instead, have depicted the relationship between city and *contado* as being little short of idyllic. And, indeed, there is something to be said for this interpretation if we limit its application to thirteenth- and early fourteenth-century experience when communal budgets were minimal and the citizenry took up arms in their own defense.[60] The dominant economic tone of this communal society was laissez-faire, and, since wars fought by a citizen militia were relatively inexpensive, the republic could well afford a loosely administered and lightly taxed *contado*.[61] The rise of the public debt and extravagant warfare did much to destroy this gentle regime.

Beginning in the 1350s and gaining momentum over subsequent decades was the implementation of a rugged program designed to increase Florence's share of *contado* wealth. First, the rate of the rural *estimo* was revised. In the biennium 1336–38 it had been only 10 soldi per lira. By 1353, however, it was being assessed at 15 soldi per lira; five years later the figure was 20 soldi, and in the sixties it fluctuated between 30 and 40 soldi.[62] The return from this rural *estimo* averaged 30,100 florins during the years 1336–38, and complaints from the countryside indicate that many believed this tax to be oppressive.[63] Shortly after the Black Death, with country population diminished by one-third to one-half, and a substantial decline in productivity, the exaction of the rural *estimo* yielded the Florentine treasury 35,355 florins. The burden of taxation of those who had survived the plague had risen by almost one-half. Nor was this dramatic increase an isolated phenomenon. The old rate of the gabelle on wine produced in the *contado* underwent a similar revision; the rate went up from 10 soldi in 1336 to 20 soldi in the decade of the 1350s and finally reached 30 soldi in the subsequent decade.[64] The

---

60. For the most recent summary of the revisionist view of the Tuscan *contado*, see E. Cristiani, *Nobiltà e popolo nel comune di Pisa* (Naples, 1962), 151–61.

61. *C.C.*, 2 *bis*. This volume of the treasury records contains numerous citations against *popoli* and rural communes for failure to honor their commitments to the republic. Unpaid *estimi* and condemnations for negligence dated back into the 1320s and were collected in 1342–43. This was the period of Walter of Brienne's Signoria.

62. *C.C.*, 45, f. 14ʳ (January–February 1353); *C.C.*, 70, unnumbered folio (March–April 1358); *C.C.*, 139, unnumbered folio (16 December 1370).

63. G. Villani, *Cronica*, 11:92; Barbadoro, op. cit., 201; E. Fiumi, "Sui rapporti tra città e contado," op. cit. (n. 14), 36–37.

64. *C.C.*, 30, f. 255ʳ (November–December 1348). The rate was unchanged

yield from the gabelle on meat in the *contado* had averaged 4,400 florins
for the prosperous years of the early *Trecento;* now rates were augmented, and, if we take into account the decline in population, the return of 5,716 florins for the year 1357 represented an increase of over a
hundred percent. Comparable gains were registered from a variety of
other rural imposts, ranging from the levy on country markets to the
gabelle on rural nobility.[65] In 1364, as the debt from the Pisan War
mounted, the Signoria resorted to the expedient of imposing a forced
loan on the *contado.* This *prestanza* was assessed at approximately three
times the urban rate and enriched the *camera* by 19,175 florins in a single month.[66]

Communal policy toward the republic's territories was, then, increasingly dictated by budgetary deficits and the pressing need to underwrite the inflated state credit structure. If sufficient funds from the
contado could be collected to pay mercenaries, then the customs toll and
other gabelles, formerly used for this purpose, could be placed at the
disposal of the *Monte* treasurer for restitution to communal creditors.
One technique for achieving this end was to extract money in lieu of rustic militia duty. This rarely exacted obligation now became a regular fea-

---

throughout the decade of the 1340s; it was only with the advent of the 1350s that
this gabelle on the *contado,* like so many others, was raised dramatically. Cf. C.C.,
45, f. 75ʳ (January–February 1353); 77, unnumbered folio (May–June 1359).

65. The gabelle on nobles had been 2,000 florins in the biennium 1336–38. On
22 December 1351 it was doubled by action of the communal councils. The tax
on rural markets was 3,400 lire in 1351; three years later it was up some 600 lire,
and by 1360 it totaled 5,277 lire. Cf. C.C., 45, f. 84 (30 January 1353); 53, f. 107
(April–May 1354); 83, unnumbered folio (May–June 1361). The date 1351 is a
critical one in the history of Florentine taxation. In that year there was a general
upward revision of all gabelles. Cf. Villani, *Cronica,* 2:46.

66. C.C., 103, unnumbered folio (2 August 1364). A certain Niccolò Cassini
was elected treasurer of this *prestanza,* and it was assessed at 30 soldi per lira.
The rate of the *estimo* on the *contado* was soon upped to 40 soldi per lira. The old
rate (1336–38) had been only 10 soldi per lira. Cf. Villani, *Cronica,* 11:92; C.C., 139,
unnumbered folio (16 December 1370). At the close of the decade of the 1370s,
an *estimo* levied on the *contado* at the rate of 40 soldi per lira was expected to produce 20,000 florins in revenue. The same amount could have been garnered by
the state in the biennium 1336–38 with an *estimo* imposed at only 10 soldi per
lira. In order to obtain the same yield, the Signoria had quadrupled the rates and
this burden was to be borne by a much depleted population. For a study of rural population at this time, see E. Fiumi, "La demografia fiorentina," op. cit. (n.
14), 89–94.

ture of fiscal policy, and after 1351 the rate was progressively raised.[67] Despite these stiff payments, the men of the *contado* were not freed from militia duty, and throughout this period rural communes and *popoli* were continually being fined for failure to dispatch troops or supplies to distant outposts.[68] Other onerous obligations were pressed with ever more efficiency by an expanded communal bureaucracy. If a country parish failed to furnish a contingent for castle guard or neglected to re-pair walls and maintain fortifications, the *regulatores* were prepared to impose fines. Income from these condemnations was specifically desig-nated for payment of interest on the *Monte*. The Signoria continued to urge the *regulatores* to seek additional revenue in the *contado*, and these officials began to prosecute rural communes for ancient delinquencies. By the late 1360s, hundreds of these hamlets were forced to pay a cer-tain percentage of their *estimo* for past breaches of the law: offenses ranged from failure to send candles to the Baptistry in honor of Flor-ence's patron saint to usurpations of public property. These fines helped to defray the carrying charges on the *Monte*.[69]

Much more lucrative were the myriad of assessments placed on the subject cities. At first they were required to maintain garrisons of knights and foot soldiers and to furnish military subsidies. Soon these obligations were converted into cash payments; between 1353 and 1368 Pistoia's contribution increased by 50 percent. San Gimignano was even less fortunate, since its tax was doubled over the same interval. Bibbi-ena's tribute soared by one-half over a mere two years.[70] By the early

---

67. *Provvisioni*, 39, f. 75^r (29 December 1351): "Tassatio quinque peditum pro centenario"; *C.C.*, 57, f. 2 (23 February 1353). Giovanni Catallini Infangati was *camerarius tassationis peditum*, which was imposed at a rate of 15 soldi per lira. The return from this tax was 20,915 lire during the first two months of his tenure.

68. Condemnations were visited on country communities by a variety of communal officials, from the captains of war to the regular city magistrates (*C.C.*, 53, f. 89 [16 May 1353]; 85, f. 133 [19 September 1361]).

69. Cf. *C.C.*, 137 (July–August), section entitled, "Introytus quatuor clav-ium." Also registered in this portion of the volume are the numerous fines paid by *castellani* and other state functionaries resident in the *contado*.

70. In the early 1350s Pistoia was supporting a garrison of forty *equites Ul-tramontanni*. The stipend for each knight was 26 lire a month, and the total dis-bursement, including that to foot soldiers, was approximately 2,800 lire for a two-month interval. Soon Pistoia was making additional payments into the *cam-era* in the form of subsidies for defense. In 1354 these totaled 7,000 lire (*C.C.*, 52, f. 70^r [1 April 1354]; f. 215 [22 December 1354]; 69 [January–February 1358]). Pro-

1370s these subject cities had come to be virtually incorporated into the Florentine fisc. The treasurers of San Miniato were now Florentine citizens who paid receipts directly into the *camera* of the republic. Revenues from customs tolls, gabelles on wine, and levies on contracts were now transferred to Florence. Over the next years the rate of taxation doubled and sometimes tripled. The subject cities could not hope to meet their crushing responsibilities to Florence, and soon their treasuries began to run sizable deficits.[71] New taxes, new debts, and a stern program of Florentine mercantilism did little to encourage the economic growth of these towns.[72] Out of the ever-widening claims of the Florentine treasury

---

posals that Florence should exact special imposts and levy *prestanze* on such communities as Pistoia and Volterra were justified in the light of the "multa beneficia" conferred by the republic's benign rule. The subject people ought to be grateful and Florence "cum iusticia pecuniam procuretur ab eis." Cf. *C.P.*, 15, f. 116 (19 May 1378). On Bibbiena, see *C.C.*, 119, unnumbered folio (27 June 1369). San Gimignano is the subject of a recent monograph by Enrico Fiumi, *Storia economica e sociale di San Gimignano* (Florence, 1961). Fiumi demonstrates the profound crisis Florentine fiscal policy induced in that small community. The incidence of taxation increased almost threefold from the late *Duecento* to the early *Quattrocento*, and San Gimignano incurred severe budget deficits. The author wryly observes that by 1435 imposts were being placed even on locks and keys. Cf. 160–64, 189–91. For San Gimignano's earlier tax assessments, see *C.C.*, 106, entire volume; 118, entire volume.

71. Soon after the thwarting of the rebellion of San Miniato, Florentine officials were empowered to collect all the important gabelles and to supervise the fiscal administration of this subject town. By 1371 revenues from the courts of San Miniato were being paid directly into the Florentine treasury. Cf. *C.C.*, 135–40 (1370–71). The communities under Florentine dominion were consistently incurring debts by their steady borrowing from the *camera* of the republic. On the subject of mercantilism, see R. Davidsohn, "Blüte und Niedergang der fiorentinischen Tuchindustrie," *Zeitschrift für die gesamte Staatswissenschaft* 85 (1928): 225–55. For additional bibliography, see M. Becker, "The Republican City State in Florence," op. cit. (n. 22.), 50. By the end of the *Trecento* a tax was being placed on each piece of imported cloth. Even inexpensive varieties were being excluded from the Florentine market. E. Fiumi has graphically described the impact of Florentine legislation that imposed gabelles on goods exported by citizens of San Gimignano to any other town than the Arno republic. Cf. E. Fiumi, *Storia economica*, 185.

72. Neither Fiumi nor any other investigator of Tuscan rural history has drawn inferences about the possible effects of Florentine economic policy upon the *contado* and its many towns. In the case of San Gimignano the one community whose *Trecento* history has been carefully analyzed, the heavy tax burden

were forged the links of empire, and the pattern of exploitation of the *contado* hastened this transition.

The search for revenue led to the integration of Florentine territory and the rise of empire, but the fiscal dilemma of the treasury persisted. In the early 1370s the customs toll and returns from other major imposts declined precipitously at the very moment when Florence embarked upon a series of wars, each of which proved more costly than its predecessor. The War of the Eight Saints occasioned expenditures of over two and a half million florins, and these outlays were soon dwarfed when hostilities erupted with Milan. By the early *Quattrocento* approximately 850,000 florins were being expended annually for the hire of mercenaries; moreover, when the tempo of warfare heightened, the outlay would increase by as much as 50 percent. At best, communal levies could be expected to cover only one-fourth of this expenditure. The yield from gabelles still lagged and tax returns were barely sufficient to meet the commonplace demands of government.[73] In the early 1370s a new practice was initiated that was to continue for the remainder of the century: the treasurer of the *Monte* was authorized to lend sums averaging 200,000 florins a year to the *Camera del Comune*. This practice, coupled with the ever more frequent recourse to the interest bearing forced loan, caused the public debt to soar into the millions.

IV

The late years of the *Trecento* and the early *Quattrocento* witnessed acceleration of trends already prominent in the 1360s and 1370s. During

---

laid on this subject town by its masters certainly discouraged economic development. Florentine tax policy also resulted in ever stricter regulation of those who plied minor trades in the *contado*. Cf. *C.P.*, 14, 89^r (3 October 1377). Here we find a discussion of these regulations as they pertained to innkeepers. Cf. also *C.P.*, 15, f. 100 (10 April 1378) for discussions concerning vintners and butchers.

73. This average for governmental expenditures was frequently exceeded. In 1391, for example, outlays for the hire of mercenaries approached 800,000 florins, while in 1414 they exceeded 1,000,000 florins. By 1424 these disbursements had risen above the 2,500,000 florin mark. Cf. *Proveditore di Camera*, 7, f. 45 (1391), "Somma tutte uscite di chondotta." Cf. also ibid., ff. 336–37; 25, ff. 20–43 (1414); 29, ff. 34–81^r (1424). (Henceforth this source will be abbreviated as PC.) Over the entire period expenditures for the maintenance of Florentine castles and fortifications climbed steadily from an annual figure of 90,000 lire in the 1390s to 150,000 in the 1430s.

these war-torn years the government was compelled to resort again to forced loans, and millions of additional florins were added to the public debt. The intake of the treasury averaged slightly better than 300,000 florins a year, while government outlays totaled some 800,000 florins annually. Therefore, the commune was obligated to borrow almost a half-million florins each year from the denizens of the city.

With such a heavy incidence of forced loans it was difficult to set money aside for the amortization of the public debt. Traditional revenues were already committed to the war effort, and, if monthly interest payments on the new forced loans were to be made, additional sources of public revenue would have to be unearthed. By the early *Quattrocento* carrying charges on these *prestanze* alone amounted to 280,000 florins per annum.[74] Communal councilors were still reluctant to levy direct taxes on urban real estate or capital. Thus, once again the Signoria resorted to the stratagem of increasing the fiscal burdens of the *contado* and the subject domains. By 1402 the *contado* was contributing approximately 140,000 florins in tribute to the Florentine *camera*. Such a sum was equal to almost one-half of the treasury's intake from gabelles and was much in excess of earlier receipts from rural imposts.[75] The bulk of *contado* revenue was of course consigned to the treasurers of the *Monte,* and they in turn disbursed it to communal creditors in the form of interest payments. Over the next two decades the Signoria was also to extract substantial income from its newly acquired domains. Arezzo, Volterra, Pisa, and Cortona were each obligated to underwrite a part of the carrying charges on the public debt. In 1408 Pisa paid the very ample sum of 200,000 lire into the treasury of the *Monte,* and, while it is not possible to make long-range assessments of the fiscal advantages won by Florence as a result of the domination of the seacoast town, certainly during these years it was a source of substantial profit.[76]

Meanwhile, there was a continuation of the erosion of traditional medieval immunities. Now the Florentine clergy were regularly re-

---

74. *PC.,* 21, ff. 250–68 (1408).

75. *PC.,* 17, ff. 157^r–202^r. Returns for 1404 and 1405 remained at the same high level (*PC.,* 19, ff. 166^r–213 [1404]; 20, ff. 167–203 [1405]).

76. *PC.,* 22, ff. 181–96 (1408). Surviving records for other subject cities are much less complete, but for Arezzo, see ibid., 34, ff. 193–93^r, 197–97^r; for Volterra, see ibid., 27, ff. 311^r–12; for Cortona, see ibid., 28, f. 375^r; 29, f. 344. Imposts on Prato were levied directly by the officials of the *Monte.* Cf. ibid., 28, f. 413; 29, f. 332.

quired to contribute large subsidies to the *camera*. Medieval guilds, religious confraternities, and a spate of other tax-exempt bodies also lost their antique privileges. In the 1380s the communal *estimo* was extended into the territories of the Counts Guidi and Ubaldini so that the last great Tuscan feudatories were now liable for state levies. Finally, by 1427 a single tax system had been forged for the whole of the republic's lands.[77]

It was the government's desperate need for revenue that was weakening the private system of multiple economics—lay and ecclesiastical—and prompting the formation of a unitary public structure. Over the first quarter of the fifteenth century greater sums of citizen money found their way—albeit reluctantly—into the Florentine treasury. The mounting pressures of warfare accelerated the flow of capital into the public fisc, until by 1427 virtually no Florentine with a modest patrimony (2,000 to 3,000 florins) was without holdings in the public debt.[78] The number of *Monti* had multiplied, and now even the dowries of Florentine girls were invested in public stock.[79] The state was rapidly becoming the proverbial economic Leviathan, and this transformation cannot be overlooked by historians who seek the boundary line between economics and intellectual life. Private fortunes and personal prosperity were now linked with the well-being of the body politic. Each time a Florentine military victory was announced or an important diplomatic advantage won, the value of shares in the *Monte* ascended. Every chronicler, from the humblest *anonimo* to the most celebrated humanist, was aware of the state's crucial economic role in civic life. Sermons, letters, and diaries are replete with the anxieties and the hopes occasioned by

---

77. Cf. E. Fiumi, "Fioritura e decadenza," op. cit. (n. 1), 492–93; and also "La demografia fiorentina," op. cit. (n. 14), 127–35.

78. This statement is based upon a survey of rate payers listed in volumes 64 to 72 of the *Campioni del Catasto dei cittadini*.

79. L. Marks, op. cit., 127–29. The particular *Monte* in question, called "Monte delle Doti," was founded in 1425 at the time of the wars against Filippo Maria Visconti to alleviate pressure on the public debt. Within a generation the annual obligation of the state to those who had invested in this *Monte* was 199,000 florins. When this indebtedness is added to the republic's other liabilities to *Monte* shareholders, a grand total of 347,000 florins would be required simply to meet the annual interest payments. This figure is in excess of annual revenues by some 129,300 florins. Cf. G. Canestrini, *La scienza e l'arte di stato* (Florence, 1862), 1: 163ff.

the effect of public policy on private well-being.[80] Florentine chancellors and men of letters, from Leonardo Bruni Aretino to Poggio Bracciolini, saw clearly the connection between the affluence of citizens and the splendor, culture, and durability of the city-state. Moreover, they encouraged the appetite for private gain since, in the end, such an appetite must redound to the advantage of the state.[81]

New loyalties, new concerns, and a new consciousness of the role of the public economy had emerged. The historian Francesco Guicciardini quotes the *Quattrocento* chancellor Leonardo Bruni Aretino as saying that by the end of the fourteenth century the destiny of Florence and its denizens was tied irrevocably to the *Monte*.[82] Out of the communal chrysalis had emerged a viable political entity—the Renaissance state—governed by an aristocracy whose private fortunes were dependent upon the durability of the republic. Without such a dependency, the audience for the pronouncements of the civic humanists would not have been so ample, nor would Florentines have been so appreciative of a civic art that extolled the integrity and vitality of the state. That this state held powers and exercised a sway over an integrated territory made those who thought about politics feel much closer to the polis of antiquity than to that loosely knit bundle of privileges—the medieval commune.

80. Cf. Giovanni di Morelli, *Ricordi,* ed. V. Branca (Florence, 1956), 251–65; Ser Lapo Mazzei, *Lettere di un notaro a un mercante,* ed. C. Guasti (Florence, 1880), 1, 9, 45–48; F. Sacchetti, *Sermoni evangelici,* ed. O. Gigli (Florence, 1857), 111; Vespasiano da Bisticci, *The Vespasiano Memoirs* (London, 1926), 159.

81. E. Garin, *L'umanesimo italiano* (Bari, 1952), 59–60; H. Baron, "Franciscan Poverty and Civic Wealth as Factors in the Rise of Humanistic Thought," *Speculum* 13 (1938): 16ff.; R. Roedel, "Poggio Bracciolini nel quinto centenario della morte," *Rinascimento* 11 (1960): 51–67.

82. F. Guicciardini, *Le Cose fiorentine,* ed. R. Ridolfi (Florence, 1945), 109: "e el Monte disfara Firenze e Firenze disfara el Monte." (I wish to thank Mr. Anthony Molho, Brown University, for this reference.)

7

The Florentine Territorial State
and Civic Humanism in the
Early Renaissance

The two most penetrating and sensitive commentators upon the early Florentine Renaissance are Hans Baron and Eugenio Garin.[1] Each of these scholars has argued persuasively for a connection between cultural developments and Florentine public life. The present inquiry follows this same tack but with a slightly different perspective. It is not the wars against the Visconti of Milan in the late Trecento and early Quattrocento that will be stressed as being solely responsible for that outburst of intellectual and artistic activity commonly described by the term *civic humanism* but internal political and economic developments. Therefore, foreign policy and foreign affairs will be dealt with only insofar as they serve to create chronic political problems and persistent budgetary difficulties. Further, it will be suggested that the impetus in encouraging the rise of civic humanism was furnished by a new type of political organism—the territorial state. No effort will be made here to suggest its origins or attempt to delineate its genesis. Instead, I shall try to indicate something of the scope and authority of this new variety of regimen and to point up certain problems peculiar to this type of polit-

---

From *Florentine Studies: Politics and Society in Renaissance Florence*, ed. Nicolai Rubinstein (London, 1968), 109–39. Reprinted with permission of Faber and Faber, Ltd.

1. Baron's writings are numerous, but see especially, "Das Erwachen des historischen Denkens im Humanismus des Quattrocento," *Historische Zeitschrift* 147 (1932): 5–20; *The Crisis of the Early Italian Renaissance*, rev. ed. (Princeton, 1966). Garin's works represent the most compelling composite of Italian Renaissance thought in general and Florentine thought in particular. See especially, "I cancellieri umanisti della repubblica fiorentina da Coluccio Salutati a Bartolomeo Scala," *Riv. Stor. Ital.* 71 (1959): 185–208; "Umanesimo e vita civile," *Atti della Accademia Fiorentina di Scienze Morali*, 16 (1947–50): 57–104; *L'umanesimo italiano* (Bari, 1952; Engl. transl., Oxford, 1965).

ical entity. This was a polis markedly different from that of the early fourteenth century, and it made very different demands upon the Arno citizenry. Civic art and the civic humanism of a Salutati or a Bruni or a Poggio gave voice to these new demands. Few men of this generation remained immune to the promptings of a new polis, and this distinguished assembly was to include the foremost classicists in all Europe along with Franco Sacchetti and the artists, Donatello, Ghiberti, Masaccio, Brunelleschi, and a score of other luminaries.

I

In the late 1370s there was to be an outburst of patriotic poetry. An anonymous enthusiast was to call his fellow citizens "true Christians elected by God" to undo the heinous work of the "carnal church."[2] These were the difficult times of the War of the Eight Saints. Soon afterwards, Franco Sacchetti, the leading Florentine poet and writer of *The Three Hundred Tales*, was to compare the twelve labors of Hercules with the glorious victories of his beloved native city.[3] Florence was "Fiorenza santa," and it had been divinely elected to initiate a spiritual *renovatio*. Such flowery language was not altogether unfitting if one were paying tribute to a new political entity that had gone far in the usurpation of powers once held exclusively by the medieval church.

---

2. *Diario d'anonimo*, ed. A. Gherardi, in *Documenti di storia italiana* (Florence, 1876), 5:308. Substantial numbers of prophecies uttered in the 1370s entertain the hope of imminent religious reform under the aegis of the Arno republic. This "bella città" will bring happiness to those opposing the hosts of evil. Amid the tribulations of the Antichrist, Florence emerges "pregnant with the hope of a new era." Cf. D. Weinstein, "The Savonarola movement in Florence," *Comparative Studies in Society and History*, suppl. 2 (1962): 198 (and n. 1); N. Rodolico, *I Ciompi* (Florence, 1945), 53–62, 142–43. (I wish to thank Professor Donald Weinstein for making available to me certain unpublished materials on the subject of prophecy and the commune.)

3. One of his sonnets contains the line, "Florentina civitas Dei et domina libertatis." This new "civitas Dei" must install a regimen designed so that the clergy can again follow the precepts and life of Christ, and in this way truly minister to the needs of mankind. Cf. Franco Sacchetti, *Il libro delle Rime*, ed. A. Chiari (Bari, 1936), nos. 179–94. On the general question of the writer's civic morality, see L. Caretti, *Saggio sul Sacchetti* (Bari, 1951), 86–139.

Notable is the fact that by the 1370s the Florentine Signory had become sufficiently powerful to be cast in the role of savior. For an illustration of the use of the word *salutificator* (savior), see M. Becker, "An essay on the 'novi cives,' and Florentine politics, 1343–1382," *Medieval Studies* 24 (1962): 75.

By the early 1380s the Tuscan clergy had been stripped of most of its medieval immunities and liberties. The Florentine government had succeeded in even wresting away control of the inquisition, and it had almost become a state tribunal.[4] Such ancient rights as benefit of clergy and sanctuary had been systematically denied. The Tuscan church was now making regular contributions to the public fisc. Enormous tracts of ecclesiastical lands were confiscated by the state, and, while the government did assume liability for some of this clerical patrimony, restitution was made infrequently and in paltry amounts. Most telling of all, however, was the growing power of public courts at the expense of ecclesiastical tribunals. By the early Quattrocento it was virtually impossible to prosecute anyone on a charge of usury in an ecclesiastical court, since the plaintiff would be required to deposit an amount of money exactly equal to that which he was suing for. Such a sum was to be deposited in the coffers of a state court, and if the plaintiff won in the church court, the money would be forfeited to the defendant.[5]

Two organizations closely associated with the Italian church were likewise much reduced in stature. Starting in the middle years of the fourteenth century, the Signory began to hedge the authority of those quasi-political bodies, the religious confraternities, until they were almost under state domination. Not only did the Signory appoint captains to govern the most prominent of these groups, but the communal councils enacted laws putting the public treasurer in charge of the assets of

---

4. The spiritual milieu of these troubled times is treated by M. Meiss, *Painting in Florence and Siena after the Black Death* (Princeton, 1947), 80–93; N. Sapegno, *Il Trecento* (Milan, 1934), 528–40; H. Grundmann, "Die Papst-Prophetien des Mittelalters," *Archiv für Kulturgeschichte* 19 (1928): 120–23; Garin, op. cit., 38ff.; M. Becker, "Florentine Politics and the Diffusion of heresy in the Trecento: A Socioeconomic Inquiry," *Speculum* 34 (1959): 60–75.

Too frequently, the middle years of the Trecento have been depicted as being full of sound and fury, signifying at best the indeterminacy of transition. What has been neglected are the creative social and economic impulses that served to transform the relaxed regimen of the medieval commune into the commanding rule of a Renaissance polis. The most telling decade for the enactment of legislation hostile to the church, the magnates, and the *Parte Guelfa,* and therefore favorable to the growth of the territorial state, was 1372–82. Cf. M. Becker, "Florentine 'libertas': political independents and 'novi cives,' 1372–1378," *Traditio* 18 (1962): 393–407.

5. *Statuta Populi et Communis Florentie* ("Friburg," 1778), 1:124–25 (bk. 2, rub. 19: "Quomodo procedatur quando instrumentum vel aliud dicitur usurarium").

the confraternities. By the 1370s direct fiscal supervision was the order of the day.[6] With the advent of the fifteenth century, these lay religious companies were expressly prohibited from engaging in any political activities, no matter how trivial. If this proviso were violated, then the chancellor of the republic was to confiscate all the confraternities' assets and distribute them among the poor.[7] Much more significant than the extension of state hegemony over the many confraternities was the reduction of the power of that most intractable of medieval organisms— the *Parte Guelfa*. The religious confraternities could, upon occasion, be used by those who sought to undo a communal statute against the Tuscan church, but the *Parte Guelfa* could and did serve as the arm for the city's nobility and the papacy of Avignon. By the late 1370s many of the great nobles of Florence had come to champion a pro-papal policy. Further, they employed the *Parte Guelfa* to check those political activities conducted by the Signory against the interests of the Holy See. When war erupted between Florence and the papacy, the *Parte* stood in direct opposition to the bellicose program. So intransigent was the *Parte* and so obdurate its enemies that revolution ensued. The events of the late 1370s and early 1380s encouraged public-minded Florentines to deni-

---

6. Severe regulation of the confraternities began at the height of the Pisan War, when the *Camera* was sorely pressed for funds. Cf. A.S.F., Provv. 51, fols. 7–7v (21 August 1363). (All unpublished documents cited in this study are to be found in the Archivio di Stato, Florence.) The connection between the growth of government regulation and the rise of the public debt becomes increasingly clear when we learn from this provision that all bequests from last wills and testaments made to these bodies were to be paid into the Florentine treasury, and certain of their assets were to be sold by the state. Monies realized were to be used to satisfy the claims of communal creditors. Two years later the government reserved the right to examine the accounts of these bodies, even though they were under the direct jurisdiction of the Bishop of Florence. Provv., 52, fol. 151 (30 May 1365). For examples of statutes of these confraternities, see *Testi fiorentini del dugento e dei primi del trecento*, ed. A. Schiaffini (Florence, 1926), 34–54. On the general theme of these organizations in north Italian history, see G. Monti, *Le confraternite medievali dell' Alta e Media Italia* (Venice, 1927), 1:147–93; 2:23–25.

7. R. Caggese, *Firenze della decadenza di Roma al Risorgimento di Italia* (Florence, 1913), 2:360. For instance, earlier than that cited by Caggese, see Lib. Fab., 41, fol. 90 (18 February 1383). After 1415 it was necessary to have the permission of the Signory before a religious company could be organized. Cf. *Statuta Populi* cit., 3:42.

grate the role of this most venerable of medieval quasi-public organizations until its functions had become almost purely ceremonial and administrative. No longer were the aristocratic captains to be privy to the great public decisions.[8]

The second half of the Trecento is also the scene for the final triumph of public rights over the medieval prerogatives of the great feudatories of remote Tuscany. With the advent of the 1380s, such patrimonies as those held by the Counts Guidi and Ubaldini were finally declared subject to direct public levies. Just as telling were the many usurpations of seigneurial rights by the republic—this despite older treaties between commune and feudal lord in which the former agreed to respect the prerogatives of the latter.[9] Starting in the 1340s and gaining momentum over the next two decades was the inauguration of a program to regain "iura communis"; such an effort entailed the scrupulous implementation of public law against feudatories alleged to have usurped "bona et iura communis."[10]

While the Signory never abolished legislation permitting injured Florentines to have recourse to vendetta, there is no question but that this honorable response to outrage tapered off after the 1330s. The lawlessness of the Florentine nobility was such that a walk along the Arno in the late Dugento was almost as dangerous as an evening stroll in Central Park. The crimes of the Bardi, Cavalcanti, Nerli, Rossi, and others—magnates every one—fill hundreds of folios of court records. The re-

---

8. Judging from representation accorded the *Parte,* it reached the apogee of its *auctoritas* in the late 1360s and early 1370s. Cf. Cons. Prat., 9–12. Shortly before, legislation had been enacted requiring that the Guelf captains be present at all important sessions of the communal councils. Cf. U. Dorini, *Notizie storiche sull' università di Parte Guelfa in Firenze* (Florence, 1902), 28–39.

9. In a single month the Counts Battifolle were fined the grand total of 52,473 lire 10 soldi for usurping public property. Formerly these extensive holdings spread over three rural parishes and had been acknowledged by the commune as the private patrimony of these feudatories. C.C.E., 161, unnumbered fol. (7 July 1374). In the territories of the Counts Guidi (the Commune of Romena) and those of the Ubaldini (the Podere Fiorentino) the *signori* enjoyed jurisdiction and exemption from the communal *estimo.* In the early 1380s these lands were subject to all obligations. Cf. E. Fiumi, "L'imposta diretta nei comuni medioevali della Toscana," *Studi in onore di Armando Sapori* (Milan, 1957), 1:338; P.C., 1 (1384).

10. M. Becker, "Florentine popular government (1343–1348)," *Proceedings of the American Philosophical Society* 106 (1962): 373–77.

public acted to limit the right of vendetta, and, since this form of revenge was most status worthy among magnates and haute bourgeoisie, this restriction tended to alter the behavior of the highest stratum of patrician society. No longer was it considered disgraceful to seek vengeance in the courts of law rather than in a street brawl. There was a marked trend among the patriciate to turn more enthusiastically toward state courts. In addition, some of the most lawless of the magnates literally became pensioners of the commune, and their arms and good will were at the disposal of the republic.[11]

Numerous rural nobles went even further than becoming public pensioners. The rural socioeconomic landscape had been transformed over the later Middle Ages. In Tuscany the status of "vassal" had virtually disappeared from *contado* life by the last part of the Trecento. There had been a time, two generations or so before, when such a juridical designation was economically advantageous to the individual in question. Now, however, as taxes tended to become territorial rather than personal, there was little to be gained from such a status. With the mid-1360s local communities were held liable for almost all imposts; the nexus between rural inhabitant and urban government was growing tighter. The great fiefs of Tuscan antiquity were now responsible for the

---

11. Many of the feudatories of the great Tuscan house of the Ubaldini were to become pensioners of the commune shortly after the republic waged her last great war against these nobles in the early 1370s. C.C.E., 169, unnumbered folio (21 November 1375). For arrangements between Florence and other Signori during these years so critical for the formation of the territorial state, see C.C.E., 171, unnumbered folio (12 April 1376); Lib. Fab., 41, fol. 101r (28 April 1383). On this general but neglected theme, see G. Soranzo, "Collegati, raccomandati, aderenti negli stati italiani dei secoli XIV et XV," *A.S.I.* 119 (1941): 3–35. What the commune could not gain through coercion, it was to achieve with subsidies. In a discussion held by the advisory councils before the Signory on 5 September 1380, speakers suggested that the Tarlati clan and other great feudal lords in the vicinity be visited by discreet diplomats "ad exhortandum eos. Et cum pecunia subveniatur." Cons. Prat., 19, fol. 63. Cf. also *Delizie degli eruditi,* ed. Ildefonso di San Luigi (Florence, 1770–89), 7:191.

On the problem of magnate lawlessness, see Giudice degli Appelli, 121–25. During the decade of the 1330s there were seventy-two Florentine families inscribed among the city's *magnati.* Of this number forty-six stood convicted of grievous breaches of communal law. Each of these houses averaged four convictions for high crimes ranging from assault to homicide and treason.

exaction of gabelles on wine and even on the rural nobility.[12] Little wonder that scores of Tuscan noble clans deserted their *consorterie* beginning in 1342–43. They stood up in communal court and renounced their ancient ties and lineage, then the Florentine councils declared them to be *populares et non magnates*. In this way did the Pazzi of Valdarno, the Counts of Certaldo, the Becchi of Castro Fiorentino, and hundreds of others ask to be included among *il popolo* of Florence. The ancient *consorterie* were collapsing, and new bonds between men and their state were being forged.[13]

Exactly the same pattern can be discerned among the city's magnates. There the noble house of Ricasoli renounced its magnate status, changed its name to Bindacci, and were declared *populares*. The Della Tosa became the Bilisardi, the Donati the Bellincioni, the Bondelmonti the Montebuoni. This is but a fraction of the shift from partially disfranchised magnate to fully participating citizen.[14] Many magnate individuals petitioned the Signory, stating that they had always been "peaceful and law-abiding men"; some beseeched the governors of the city to take cognizance of the fact that they and even their forebears had been "law-abiding merchants" properly matriculated in one of the city's guilds. Because some consort of theirs had committed a crime, they were being made to suffer. Now they looked to the state to offer them redress of grievances and afford them protection.[15] Progressively over the course of the fourteenth century, fewer and fewer individuals peti-

---

12. The advantage accruing to those declared "homines alterius," and thus being declared exempt from certain Florentine imposts, was to disappear almost entirely over the first years of the Trecento. Cf. E. Fiumi, "Fioritura e decadenza dell' economia fiorentina," *A.S.I.* 116 (1958): 482–83. Significant was the fact that tributary obligations were now becoming territorial rather than personal and that increased communal income was being employed to pay interest to communal creditors, C.C.E., 130 (March–April 1369).

13. *Statuta Populi*, cit., 1:446–47; Balìe 5 (1349). For a discussion of taxation as a force in encouraging magnates to seek *popolani* status, see E. Fiumi, *Storia economica e sociale di San Gimignano* (Florence, 1961), 189ff.

14. Very important were the payments made into the treasury by many who were granted the coveted *popolani* status. Again the monies accruing from these former magnates were diverted to communal creditors. Cf. C.C.E., 89–95 (May–June 1362–May-June 1363).

15. Cf. G. Brucker, *Florentine Politics and Society, 1343–1378* (Princeton, 1962), 155–56.

tioned the government for the right to bear arms. The noble activity of jousting and swordplay had fallen into disrepute. Later, when this sport was revived, it was the ceremonial and decorative aspects that enticed Quattrocento Florentines.

The city's guilds, like the magnates, were transformed over the second half of the Trecento. Egalitarianism triumphed among the *arti* just as it had among the *grandi*. Granted that such a victory was largely juridical, yet it is no less important for that reason. All guilds and guildsmen became liable for prosecution on charges of violating communal statutes against monopolies after 1343. No longer were the city's seven major guilds virtually exempt from these stern ordinances. Moreover, the imbalance between major and minor guild representation in the Court Merchant was substantially corrected in the early 1370s. At that same time, lesser guildsmen were permitted to have complete recourse to both the Court Merchant and the state tribunals. This was a great advantage, since litigation was frequently tortuous in guild courts.[16]

It is ironic that at the very time when legal parity was coming into being, the political system of the guilds was entering a decline. First, the by now familiar pattern of state intrusion into another facet of the medieval order was evolving. Officers of the republic were charged with responsibility for the communal food supply. They not only undertook to import certain commodities but even to fix prices and arrange for their sale.[17] In the 1380s—only a decade after the installation of such officials—a special commission (*balìa*) was founded to regulate guild matters. With the advent of the Quattrocento, those bastions of the pluralistic medieval political universe began to lose prestige, and, even more significant, they suffered an attrition of revenue. Only a century before, these artisan, mercantile, and industrial corporations had been the principal bulwark of Florentine public life. They, like so many other quasi-political medieval institutions such as the *Parte Guelfa* and the religious confraternities, could provide fiscal support for communal ventures. During the first third of the Quattrocento the treasury of the guilds was so meager that now no reliance could be placed upon the *arti* by the

---

16. M. Becker, "La esecuzione della legislazione contro le pratiche monopolistiche delle arti fiorentine alla metà del secolo quattordicesimo," *A.S.I.* 117 (1959): 8–28; A. Doren, *Le arti fiorentine,* ed. G. Klein (Florence, 1940), 2:70.

17. For a description of the authority of these officials, see Cons. Prat., 21, fols. 53, 56–56r; C.C.E., 230, fol. 4r (21 April 1386); A. Doren, op. cit. 2:105.

state.[18] The coming of the Medici in 1434 heralded a decline of the jurisdiction of both the Court Merchant and the guild tribunals. In their stead, state courts assumed control. Finally, by the end of the Quattrocento the entire elaborate system of guild matriculation was undermined. Again, state authority intruded rudely.[19]

Such an intrusion might well be described as an expression of proto-mercantilism, for there were deep economic needs that were becoming more dependent upon state power for their satisfaction. If one reads the correspondence of the Florentine chancellery for the second half of the fourteenth century (Missive), then one is struck by the great abundance of letters dispatched by the Signory in support of the myriad of enterprises of Florentine merchants who traded and banked from the Balearic Islands to the exotic capitals of Eastern Europe. More and more, the precarious but profitable activities of these businessmen required state support. This is particularly in evidence in the correspondence beginning in the late 1370s, when Florence's favored position was put in jeopardy; foreign competition and the hostility of the papacy were handicaps too severe for the republic's traders to overcome.[20]

Increasingly, the city's manufacturers called upon the Signory to afford them protection from ruinous foreign competition. In October 1393 the first general legislation was enacted establishing a sizable duty upon the importation of fine foreign cloth. Over the next years the consuls of the once so proud wool guild acknowledged that further state action would be necessary if the guild and its membership were to prosper.

---

18. G. Canestrini, *La scienza e l'arte di stato* (Florence, 1862), 156.

19. R. Pöhlmann, *Die Wirtschaftspolitik der florentiner Renaissance und das Prinzip der Verkehrsfreiheit* (Leipzig, 1878), 48–49; A. Doren, *Die florentiner Wollentuchindustrie von vierzehnten bis zum sechzenten Jahrhundert* (Stuttgart, 1901), 418ff.

20. The concern of the Signory for winning advantages for Florentine bankers, merchants, and industrialists is indicated by the ever greater number of discussions on this topic as well as the growth of communal diplomatic correspondence devoted to promoting the republic's mercantile interests abroad. Cf. especially Missive della Prima Cancelleria, 17–35. On the decline of Florentine foreign trade during the 1370s, see *Cronica fiorentina di Marchionne di Coppo Stefani*, ed. N. Rodolico, *R.I.S.*, vol. 30, pt. I (Città di Castello, 1903–55), rub. 765. The best available index for assessing the vigor of this foreign trade are the receipts from the customs toll. In 1368 they stood at 196,395 lire, while in 1377 they totaled only 93,806 lire. For the figures on the earlier year, see C.C.E., 122–27, and for the latter year, see C.C.E., 176–81.

Similar requests were made by other cloth guilds during the first part of the Quattrocento.[21] Certain of the leadership of the major guilds had concluded that the guilds could not sustain their competitive position on the European market unless they were propped by rigorous tariff systems. That the first such system was introduced in October 1393, during the tenure of Maso degli Albizzi as Gonfalonier of Justice, when he first came to dominate the political scene, indicates that the most powerful elements in communal politics responded enthusiastically to the imperatives of protomercantilism. Moreover, two of Florence's major wars, one against Pisa in the 1360s and the other against the same adversary in the early fifteenth century, were in response to the exigencies of manufacture and trade. These conflicts were enormously costly, but finally Florence wrested control of the littoral from its sturdy neighbor and soon was building ports and constructing galleys to further the Mediterranean interests of its great merchants.[22]

Not only did Florentine protomercantilism entail a sustained response to the needs of her business community—a response the once powerful guilds were unable to effect—but it also came to embody an even more telling awareness to the needs of the state itself. Exactly in the same year, 1393, laws were enacted prohibiting Florentines from insuring any merchandise borne on foreign ships. The public interest could best be served if money were prevented from leaving the country. Simultaneously, a law was passed designed to keep hard money in the Florentine domain. Anyone who exported more than fifty gold florins at one time was liable for prosecution.[23] This was an expression of the same impulse that had animated Florentine legislation framed to prevent any citizen from alienating shares of public stock *(Monte)* to foreigners. The state was reluctant to pay interest to noncitizens who would take money outside the Florentine territories.[24]

---

21. C. C. Bayley, *War and Society in Renaissance Florence* (Toronto, 1961), 71–72. R. Davidsohn's "Blüte und Niedergang der florentinischen Tuchindustrie," *Zeitschrift für die gesamte Staatswissenschaft* 85 (1928): 225–55, so frequently cited as an authoritative study on the Florentine cloth industry, is much in need of revision. For evidence pertaining to demands by the consuls of the wool guild for protection, see Lib. Fab., 51, fol. 203 (30 May 1418); ibid., fol. 206r (9 June 1418).

22. For appropriations devoted to these ends, see P.C., 27–40.

23. L. Piattoli, "Le leggi fiorentine sull' assicurazione nel medioevo," *A.S.I.* 90 (1932): 208–11. For a discussion of this problem, held by the advisers to the Signory in August 1395, Cons. Prat., 31, fol. 107r.

24. Canestrini, op. cit., 131.

Increased state participation in economic life occasioned an enlargement of communal bureaucracy. Over the fifty years between the popular revolution of 1343 and the oligarchical reaction of 1393, the number of officials hired by the Florentine treasury quintupled. In addition, an abundance of new fiscal posts were created. In the 1340s the numerous officers in charge of funding the communal debt were authorized to regulate the intake of certain gabelles. As the century advanced, their number and responsibilities multiplied.[25] Another set of officials most conspicuous after the 1350s were the *regulatores*. These key appointees met with the Signory to decide critical matters pertaining to tax assessments and the intake of gabelles. Soon they and their many notaries and scribes were conducting inquiries into problems of rural quotas, making surveys and collecting unpaid obligations from great feudatories. By the early 1370s they were meeting with the Signory and appearing before the communal councils, where they explained the merits of a particular tax bill or discussed the need for recovering public properties.[26] On this score, dozens of new positions were being created so that public properties could not only be recovered but even profitably managed. Special judges were appointed along with notaries and bailiffs to oversee the collection of the principal communal gabelles.

---

25. By the 1360s their number had quadrupled, and by the 1370s they were handling such diverse matters as the licensing of pawnbrokers and the operation of a credit bank for the republic's mercenaries. By 1377 these officers in charge of the communal debt were also serving as guardians of orphaned minors. At a meeting of the advisory councils to the Signory, it was suggested "pro utilitate pupillorum" that the patrimony of these children should remain "in the hands of the commune." It would then be invested in the funded communal debt "cum interesse." It should be observed that earlier the role now performed by the state was filled by one of the city's many confraternities. Cf. Cons. Prat., 15, fol. 54r (13 November 1377).

26. On the early history of the *regulatores*, see Archivio dei Sindaci, B., IV, 5, fol. 1r. The date given for the beginnings of effective administration by the *regulatores* in this source is 1352. On their participation in sessions of the government, see especially Cons. Prat., 6, 12, and 14.

The office of *defensor* was originally created by the Signory to check the spoliation of the *contado* by *magnates* and *potentes*. By 1367, however, the function of this vastly expanded office had been altered: now its members were being regularly dispatched to the environs of the city in order to punish tax delinquents and protect communal property. Cons. Prat., 12, fol. 57. The office of *bargellino* underwent a similar evolution. Cons. Prat., 8, fol. 28r (11 January 1367). On the fiscal role of the *Capitano della Custodia* and his staff, see C.C.E., 33, fol. 71 (14 May 1349).

No longer was one set of officers sufficient, but appointments were made for wine, salt, customs tolls, and many others. Especially effective were the officers in charge of that veritable army of *castellani*. These *offitiales castrorum* were busily engaged in supervising the public monies that went to maintain state forts and battle stations.[27]

One would hardly have to dwell upon the vast expansion of the vicariate and the captaincy throughout the burgeoning Florentine empire in order to be convinced of the movement toward the bureaucratization of the polis. Further, the increased use of complex techniques of syndication starting in the 1340s would bedazzle even the most technically minded of modern lawyers. By the 1370s a review of the financial activities of a vicar or a captain had become a notarial tour de force.[28] In point of fact, so many aspects of communal life were coming under closer supervision and regulation, while at the same time the state was performing a myriad of new functions, that it was becoming extremely arduous to locate qualified personnel. The bulk of the new officialdom were responsible for the manifold activities of the public fisc.

As early as the 1380s, the main feature of communal debate was governmental fiscal policy. The problems of rule were becoming more and more managerial. The tendency had been to move away from selecting communal officeholders by lot or even by popular election. Instead, crucial positions in the treasury or in charge of the public debt *(Monte)* were now filled by appointment. What was required was technical knowledge. Problems were not those that stemmed from efforts to implement new policies but, rather, from the attempts to underwrite the far-flung and enduring commitments of the republic. The medieval ideological content of politics was slowly dissipated until popes, emperors, Guelfs, and Ghibellines were seldom the topic of heated debate in communal councils after 1382. Well before that date, however, extraordinary commissions *(balìe)* did most of the administrative work of government.

---

27. Cf. P.C., 1ff.

28. The treasury records indicate that the number of officials compelled to make restitution of communal monies increased tenfold over the generation since the early 1340s. If one looks into the many volumes of the *Atti dell' Esecutore,* one is immediately struck by the long and involved procedure that comes into vogue in the mid-Trecento. On the theme of syndication, see G. Masi, *Il sindacato delle magistrature comunali nel secolo XIV* (Rome, 1930). There are special runs of documents housed in the Florentine archives yet to be examined on this neglected theme. Cf. Sindacato del Capitano e Podestà, 1ff.

These *balìe* provided the regime with continuity of action. Their function was to minister to the persistent problems confronting each and every Signory from the 1360s on: the apportionment of revenue and the hire of troops. The same personnel moved from *balìa* to *balìa*, and as far as communal fiscal policy was concerned, there was precious little alteration. Even during intervals of revolution the direction of the public fisc was not substantially modified. Too frequently, historians have relied upon new and spectacular legislation enacted by communal councils at dramatic moments without seeking to discover whether these radical innovations were indeed implemented.[29]

The work of these *balìe*, then, involved, first, drawing up propitious contracts with mercenary troops and, second, managing the public fisc so that disbursements could be made and communal creditors repaid. Needless to say, such functions could only be filled if the membership were given expanded powers. As early as the 1350s, the ancient system of farming taxes was abandoned, and the commissioners supervised the collection of many gabelles.[30] In the following decade they were authorized to provide certain revenues for the holders of public stock *(Monte)*. To this end they were charged with the obligation of finding new sources of revenue. Fines against violators of the city's food laws were increased. Under the aegis of this *balìa*, new communal grain mills were to be constructed so that the state might enjoy a higher income. Stricter ordinances were passed regulating the use of public fisheries and fulling mills. Mounting public indebtedness, occasioned almost exclusively by the phenomenal escalation of war costs since the 1350s, was making the regime of these *balìe* both more necessary and more brutal.[31]

---

29. The test period might be 1378, when a radical revolution was waged and won. The victors announced a fiscal program. The treasury records indicate that little or none of the proposed reforms were in fact implemented. The same was true of the subsequent regime. Cf. C.C.E., 185–87. For a study of intent, the works of Niccolò Rodolico are invaluable, especially *I Ciompi* (Florence, 1945), but an analysis of the practices of revolutionary regimes still remains to be done.

30. The treasury records reveal that the shift from private collection of communal imposts to public exaction occurred in the interim 1348–49. The last year, then, the *gabella portarum* and other principal levies were farmed was 1348. Cf. C.C.E., 25–31. Again the middle years of the Trecento prove to be crucial for the transformation of the commune into a territorial state.

31. For a record of the enormous disbursements of certain of these *Balìe*, see P.C., 1, fol. 425; ibid., fol. 336; ibid., fol. 337. On the general subject of rule by

II

With the advent of the 1380s, it can be suggested that the exigencies of the public economy were becoming the dominant consideration in Florentine civic life. Perhaps the following somewhat oversimplified description of the transformation of the commune into an entity approximating a Renaissance territorial state would not be altogether amiss. Until the 1320s the intake of the treasury and its outlay were in balance. The public debt for the first decade and a half of the fourteenth century stood somewhere between 47,500 florins and 50,000 florins. This was a petty sum, and it was relatively easy to meet interest payments.[32] Further, expenditures for warfare could be covered by the income from such taxes as customs tolls and the gabelles on wine and salt. Neither state credit nor government spending were critical to the communal economy. In this type of society the foci of wealth and of credit were principally in the hands of private investors, and, while the impact of communal spending was not altogether negligible, it could hardly inspire new directions in civic life. But, beginning with the 1320s, the delicate equilibrium between the *entrata* and the *uscita* of the *Camera* was disturbed, and over the next twenty years the treasury ran sizable deficits. Finally, by the early 1340s public indebtedness reached a considerable sum. Yet, compared with the totals attained in the late fourteenth century, the amounts were trifling. The formation of the floating communal debt in 1345 marked the beginnings of a gradual transformation in communal society. The *Monte* came to be so embedded in civic life that it was to assume the role of determinant in the formulation of public policy. Moreover, the total indebtedness of the *Monte* was never to be reduced; over each decade there were to be substantial increments occasioned by the costliness of war.

Contemporaries regarded these expenditures, which threw the budget out of balance, as being the result of temporary conditions. They would attribute these substantial outlays to the machinations of a faction or the connivance of self-seeking and unscrupulous men, rather

---

these extraordinary commissions, see Giovanni Antonelli, "La magistratura degli Otto di Guardia a Firenze," *A.S.I.* 112 (1954): 3–29.

32. A. Sapori, *L'età della rinascita* (Milan, 1958), 149–54; E. Fiumi, "Fioritura e decadenza," loc. cit., 427–502; M. Becker, *Florence in Transition* (Baltimore, 1967), 1:4.

than to the product of a situation now endemic. The advent of the emperor into Tuscany and the granting of subsidies to the marauding companies added sizable amounts to the public debt in the 1350s, while the war with Pisa and the campaigns against San Miniato al Tedesco had a comparable effect in the subsequent decade. Finally, the intervention of the Visconti lords of Milan, the conflict with the Tuscan feudatories of the Ubaldini clan, and the costly War of the Eight Saints with the Papacy (1375–78) prompted this public debt to soar still higher. During the forty years since the decade of the 1340s, state fiscal policy came to be the most absorbing of all public concerns. No longer were chroniclers satisfied merely to describe families and enumerate their patrimony; now they came to place strong emphasis on public economic life. Before war was declared or peace treaties confirmed, it became mandatory for the treasurer of the *Monte* to render an opinion. The chronicler Filippo Villani narrates an instance of just such an occurrence, and opines that the Florentines got the better of Pisa (1362–64) simply because the Florentine treasury could better afford the brunt of the campaigns.[33] In the 1360s–70s the treasurer of the *Monte* did make enormous loans from the principal of the public debt so that Florence might hire mercenaries. In fact, without these loans the special branch of the *Camera* that was authorized to hire troops would have been unable to function.[34]

Gradually, then, the Arno republic was moving away from a private economy in which government intake and outlay was a negligible causal force, toward the formation of an economic system in which government spending and borrowing was to play a decisive role. During the middle years of the fourteenth century, when successive regimes searched energetically for revenue, medieval immunities, privileges, and liberties had tended to erode. As we have seen, the Tuscan church came to be heavily taxed, and the guilds, along with the Court Merchant, lost many of their ancient prerogatives. The church, the *Parte Guelfa*, the guilds, the Court Merchant, and the religious confraternities were no longer potent political entities by the 1380s. The pressing needs of the republic's treasury could no longer be satisfied by a small subsidy from the clergy or a loan from the *Parte Guelfa*, or even a direct levy on

---

33. F. Villani, *Cronica*, ed. F. Dragomanni (Florence, 1845), 11:82.

34. This practice was first recorded in the treasury records of May 1368 and was to continue over the entire period treated in this study. Cf. C.C.E., 125, fols. 11r–12r, and subsequent volumes.

the city's guilds. The private wealth of Florence was being increasingly syphoned into the burgeoning communal debt. So large had this indebtedness become that no small group of families or merchant corporations could underwrite any but the smallest part of it. Unlike the situation in the early Trecento, when a family like the Bardi could alleviate substantial fiscal pressure by making a loan of about 30,000 florins, such a sum would be minute in the face of early Quattrocento demands. Now virtually every affluent Florentine had a sizable portion of his patrimony invested in one or more of the several funded communal debts. In 1345 less than a hundred families had large-scale *Monte* holdings; by 1427, however, this number had increased more than twentyfold and in most instances the amounts involved were thirty and forty times as great as investments in the original *Monte* of 1345. The *Catasto* of 1427 demonstrates compellingly that virtually every Florentine whose patrimony exceeded 3,000 florins was a shareholder in the republic's funded debt.[35] No longer, then, could any one of these thousands of investors in public securities (the political elite of the city) disregard the operation of the public sector of the economy.

By the 1380s the public debt had become the pivot around which the treasury revolved. Simply to meet the minimal interest payments on the *Monte* would require approximately half of the commune's total tax revenue. So unwieldy and inflated had the *Monte* become that amortization could scarcely be more than a pious hope. In 1387, carrying charges on the *Monte* stood at more than 150,000 florins, but this was only a harbinger of things to come. By 1394 the total had reached almost 190,000 florins. Ten years later, just after the outbreak of the Pisan War, it had increased to approximately 250,000 florins. As an aftermath of the war the total rose by another 25,000 florins. During the course of the conflict a special *Monte* was established for the sole purpose of financing hostilities against Florence's neighbor. Over the course of the following two decades, the *Monte* totals remained fairly constant; new funded debts were created out of special forced loans *(prestanzoni)*, and these were to be interest bearing at rates of either 7 or 8 percent.[36]

---

35. P. J. Jones, "Florentine families and Florentine diaries in the fourteenth century," *Papers of the British School at Rome* 24 (1956): 197–98. The figure three thousand florins is derived from a survey of *Monte* holdings of the citizenry in the year 1427. This sum represents an average.

36. P.C., 4, fols. 272–76r; ibid., 10, fols. 245–65; ibid., 19, fols. 256r–69.

With the creation of new funded debts, the operations of the *Monte* and its officers began to expand into new fields. Now they concerned themselves with the funding of special loans from merchants, or with the consolidation of *prestanze* on the countryside. For many years they had been in charge of the restitution of interest to those clergy whose properties had been confiscated during the War of the Eight Saints (1375–78). Sixteen years after the conclusion of this conflict, the officials of the *Monte* were still delaying the payment of 15,000 florins a year interest to Tuscan ecclesiastics.[37] Among their other functions were the drawing up of contracts with pawnbrokers, the prosecution of manifest usurers, and the protection of the patrimonies of Florentine orphans. They were also charged by the communal councils to finance the building of a Florentine fleet as well as to underwrite the activities of the republic's university (the *studio*). When the chronicler Gregorio Dati spoke of the officials of the *Monte* as having great power and authority ("grande balìa e autorità"), he was not exaggerating in the least, for he was well aware that "almost all the income of the commune comes into their hands."[38]

Beginning in 1390, forced loans *(prestanze)* came to be exacted at a frantic pace. In that year alone they were to total a half-million florins. In the following year they rose to 673,937 florins, and the next year saw a return of a little over 600,000 florins. By 1393, however, the total soared above 1,200,000 florins, and this figure was soon to be reached again during the early years of the Quattrocento. Moreover, special *prestanze* were leveled against the inhabitants of territories under the republic's rule. Many of these *prestanze* were interest-bearing at rates of 7 or 8 percent; in the year 1407 the treasury set aside approximately 85,000 florins for payment of interest. In that same year the treasury was dispensing 11,584 florins for interest to those who paid *prestanze* in the recent war against Pisa. Rate payers had an option: they could pay a smaller assessment and lose both interest and capital, or they might pay a heavier assessment and receive interest and eventually regain their capital.[39]

It is not possible always to have a precise estimate of these *prestanze*, since the communal system of treasury bookkeeping was exceedingly

---

37. P.C., 10, fol. 260.

38. *Istoria di Firenze di Gregorio Dati dal 1380 al 1405*, ed. L. Pratesi (Norcia, 1904), 153–54. Cf. also 117 n. 4.

39. For the year 1390, see P.C., 8; for 1391, P.C., 7; for 1393, P.C., 9; for 1407, P.C., 21.

complex. Sometimes balances were not struck, and, upon occasion, the statistics are less than complete. Bearing this in mind and making the most conservative estimate, the total for all *prestanze* during the decade of the 1390s would be approximately 5,000,000 florins. The first five years of the Quattrocento would see this total augmented by 3,500,000 florins. Judging from the tax returns of 1427 (the *Catasto*), this astronomical figure would be at least seven times the total of all the commercial wealth in the city. Although these returns did not provide an altogether candid presentation of the taxpayers' patrimony, the amount of private capital now being absorbed by the state was staggering by any standard. Nor was there to be any respite: in 1424 *prestanze* amounted to 560,912 florins; in 1426 they stood at 888,309 florins; in 1427 the figure was 439,590 florins; and, finally, in 1431 they reached almost 600,000 florins. If we were to add all the *prestanze* exacted by the government from 1390 to 1427, we would discover that the grand total would be an amount equal to the wealth of the entire citizenry as recorded in the *Catasto*. Of course, the major portion of these *prestanze* soon came to be incorporated in the *Monte*. Not only did this inflate the public debt; it also served to increase substantially the number of citizens who were state creditors. In addition, the size of individual holdings in the public debt was augmented.[40]

Starting in 1388, with the first war against the Visconti, military expenses began to spiral; in that year the outlay for hiring troops was just under 300,000 florins. By 1391 it reached more than 750,000 florins. In 1400 it was almost 500,000 florins, and it sustained this level over the next half-decade. Clearly, a substantial part of the increment in the public indebtedness was occasioned by expenditure for warfare; over the next quarter of a century these outlays were not diminished, since Florence continued to wage war against its neighbors. In a single year, 1424, the total exceeded 2,500,000 florins. Expenditure for troops (only a single item in a military budget) between the early 1390s and the late 1420s would reach the grand sum of about 10,000,000 florins. If one adds the *Entrata delle Castelle* and the outlay for provisions and arms, not to speak of subsidies to emperors and princes, then perhaps another million florins can be tacked on to this already imposing figure. Such a sum is again higher than the total capital of all Florentines, which, according to

---

40. Cf. P.C., 6–37.

the *Catasto* records, stood at from eight to nine million florins.[41] Certainly this would stand as the most convincing instance of massive state intervention in communal life. Over an interval of only slightly more than a generation, government spending and public fiscal policy had conspired to precipitate an unprecedented acceleration in the flow of capital from private investment into the public sector of the economy.

This redeployment of capital into the hands of the state was further intensified in 1425 when the *Monte delle Doti* was founded. This credit institution served as a type of insurance bank in which deposits were made by families so that their daughters might be guaranteed a dowry and might be assured a progeny. In an age when a girl without a dowry had virtually no opportunity to marry, this ingenious plan would appear to have been a boon to the unfortunate. It was possible to make arrangements with the officials of this *Monte* whereby one could deposit a fixed sum over a specified number of years and thus obtain a suitable dowry. The term of the normal contract ran from seven to fifteen years; if one selected the shorter term, then one paid a larger annual payment. If the daughter died or entered a convent before the term expired, part of the deposit went to the commune; if, however, she had marriageable sisters, then the capital could be transferred and a new contract drawn up under less favorable conditions. This particular *Monte* was to add substantially to the obligations of the republic, for Florence was committed to pay 3.375 percent on all deposits. By 1470 the liability of the republic for the *Monte delle Doti* was 198,000 florins yearly, and this figure was well over one half the annual revenue of the city.[42] The republic was now responsible not only for the defense of the Florentines but even for the proper marriage of their children. As much as any single fiscal stratagem, the foundation of this *Monte* induced the citizenry to look toward the state for its well-being. When Cosimo de' Medici postponed making payments on the *Monte delle Doti*, the chronicler Giovanni Cavalcanti averred that he had broken the bond that tied "la grandezza della Repubblica colla libertà del Monte."[43] So tight was the

---

41. P.C., 5–29. Jones presents materials on the extent of Florentine wealth in "Florentine Families," loc. cit., 197.

42. L. Marks, "The Financial Oligarchy in Florence under Lorenzo," in *Italian Renaissance Studies*, ed. E. F. Jacob (London, 1960), 128–29.

43. *Istorie fiorentine*, ed. F. Polidori (Florence, 1839), 2:203. Much later, Francesco Guicciardini was to quote a saying recorded in 1457, "el Monte dis-

nexus between the grandeur of the state and the integrity of the *Monte* that in the mind of this chronicler they had become inseparable.

III

The problem of finding fiscal support for this inflated credit structure was indeed the most pressing to confront Florentines who sat in the *balìe* (extraordinary commissions) over the years. That their efforts met with some degree of success is attested by the fact that the value of shares in the public debt did not decline appreciably over the years between the 1380s and the 1430s. They were traded on the market at a price that varied between 25 and 35 percent of their face value, and this quotation differed little from that of the decade of the 1370s. For tax purposes they were assessed at from 50 to 60 percent of their value. As to the *Monte delle Doti*, despite the abuse heaped on Cosimo when he prorogued payment, this institution continued to prove extremely popular. There is little to indicate that Florentine confidence in the fiscal reliability of the state diminished over this sixty-year period. Rather, the alacrity with which the citizenry made short-term loans to the *Camera* suggests that faith in the integrity of the public fisc was durable. Despite a myriad of complaints, lampoons, and even invective, Florentines continued to underwrite the burgeoning expenses of war through numerous forced loans. Gregorio Dati enumerates the republic's outlays for warfare during the years 1375–1405, arriving at the sum 11,500,000 florins. Then he expresses the naive doubt that no one would have believed that there was so much money in the world. Indeed, how could the Florentines have raised such a staggering amount? The answer for Dati was divided into two parts: first, much of the money lent to the republic was inscribed in the *Monte* and, second, the wars themselves were a boon to the Florentine economy. The mercenaries spent much of their pay in the city, Florentine merchants imported provisions, and businessmen made all manner of profit on government contracts. Even more telling, however, for the state of the economy and public morale, were the fruits of the victories. The conquest of Pisa in the early Quattrocento both expanded opportunities for Florentine capitalists and augmented the gen-

---

farà Firenze o Firenze disfarà el Monte." Cf. *Le Cose fiorentine*, ed. R. Ridolfi (Florence, 1945), 109; and *Ricordi*, ed. R. Spongano (Florence, 1951), 126. (I wish to thank Anthony Molho and Nicolai Rubinstein for these references.)

eral revenue of the republic.[44] Guido Cavalcanti emphasizes identical points in his chronicle. This he does in the form of an oration delivered by the city's political leader, Rinaldo degli Albizzi. After extolling Florence's ancient forebears, "our fathers the Romans," and eulogizing the citizenry's love for their republic, he says he intends to speak with candor: To tell you the truth, during periods of warfare our city is crowded and everyone profits from our successful martial undertakings.[45] Finally, there was yet another reason for public support; even in the darkest days of the conflict with the Visconti, when all seemed hopeless, Florentines could believe sincerely that the duke of Milan "was only an *uomo mortale.*" When he died, then, "finito [era] lo stato suo," but, as for Florence, it would endure and thrive again because "il Comune non può morire."[46]

General confidence in the reliability of officials over the *Monte* appears to have been well placed; the treasury records indicate that these public servants were scrupulous in the performance of their arduous tasks. That the state frequently was compelled to suspend interest payments to *Monte* shareholders does not gainsay the fact that, as soon as conditions improved, the treasury would resume its accustomed disbursements. Every month a certain portion of the customs toll, the gabelles on wine, salt, contracts, the *estimo* on the *contado,* and a host of other levies would be assigned to a special section of the *Camera* for the purpose of restitution. Each *Monte* and many of the larger *prestanze* were supervised by a staff of accountants and financial rectors. These men kept meticulous accounts, and the monies were set aside regularly for the republic's creditors.

In the last analysis, both the psychology and mechanics of this complex system of deficit financing depended upon general business conditions, for it was the state of the economy that would determine the amount of revenue available to the treasury. Unless Florentine prosperity could be sustained at a reasonable level, the intake of the *Camera* would fall and the inflated credit structure must collapse. There were times when the Signory was forced to cut rates, but, as soon as the cri-

---

44. *Istoria di Firenze,* 136–39.

45. *Istorie fiorentine,* 1:75, 79. When Florentine foreign policy met with success, the value of *Monte* shares rose. Cf. D. Buoninsegni, *Storie della città di Firenze dall' anno 1410 al 1460* (Florence, 1637), 93.

46. Dati, *Istoria di Firenze,* 74.

sis had passed, the old rate would be restored. Florentines firmly believed that the state would soon recover its vigor and creditors would be paid in full.

This faith was amply justified by the intake of the *Camera* from the traditional gabelles.[47] Judging from the returns from the customs toll, Florence remained a vigorous commercial city, and the treasury collected even more revenue than it had garnered in the prosperous years of the early Trecento. The yield of this gabelle had never been higher than 90,100 florins. Beginning in 1384, however, the return was 119,133 florins, and it rose still higher in the following year, when it registered 132,475 florins. While it is true that it declined to 82,496 florins at the height of the Visconti war, it soon recovered and stood almost at the same level it had attained in 1384. By 1394 it recorded a total of 115,667 florins. In the decade of the 1410s it went above 120,000 florins, reaching 127,421 florins. Over the next few years there was a sizable decline, and in 1424 the figure was only 94,732 florins. It sustained that low until 1427; then once again recovery set in, and the customs toll shot above the 100,000 florin mark.

Despite the vicissitudes of war and the vagaries of diplomatic maneuvering, despite the invasion and occupation of Florentine territories, despite plague and famine, this most critical barometer of the republic's well-being never experienced dramatic fluctuations, indicating that both foreign trade and communal customs receipts remained vigorous and thriving.[48] Certainly, the rates of the customs tolls must have been

---

47. This statement has validity only if we recall that until 1427 the enormous forced loans collected by the treasury were used to underwrite the costs of war and diplomacy. Therefore, it would be possible to use the yield from the gabelles to pay interest on *Monte* stock. After 1427, returns from direct taxes on property and capital would bring in sizable returns. In 1429 the yield from the *Catasto* was 168,502 florins, and in the following year it rose to 414,758 florins. This type of levy did not increase the public debt as did a *prestanza*, which was interest bearing and inscribed in the *Monte*. The *Catasto*, then, relieved much of the fiscal pressure on the treasury and would serve to inspire confidence in communal creditors. A preliminary investigation suggests that it was not until the 1470s that the value of *Monte* stock declined. Cf. L. Marks, op. cit., 129–30. It may be that this decline was much accelerated in the 1380s by the sharp decrease in gabelle returns. Cf. L. Marks, "La crisi finanziaria a Firenze dal 1494 al 1502," *A.S.I.* 112 (1954): 60–72.

48. The statistics on the *gabella portarum* are virtually continuous for the period under consideration. My position is that the economy remained vigor-

adjusted periodically, but the tenacity of this gabelle is attested to by the constant yield over a period of almost a half-century. Nor was this an isolated phenomenon; comparable patterns of behavior were registered by other economic indicators. The return from the levy on salt evidenced more erratic behavior. It would plunge precipitously in a single year and then recover its value and finally surge upward. Overall, however, it did not diminish during the years from 1384 to 1427 (the year the *Catasto* was founded). In the earlier year it stood at 63,870 florins, while in the latter it totaled 82,150 florins. Other returns did not differ markedly from the customs and the salt gabelle.[49]

The republic could then be assured of an income almost identical to that enjoyed in the middle years of the Trecento or even during the apogee of Florentine prosperity, the biennium 1336–38. There was no more reason for men to doubt the fiscal potency of the state in 1430 than there had been in 1360 or even 1330, if we measure fiscal potency in terms of communal income. Moreover, the returns from indirect taxes proved almost constant, accounting as they did for approximately 270,000 florins a year. It was not until the late 1480s that they began to tumble, and it is worth noting that the late fifteenth century marks the beginning of a failure of public confidence in the fiscal integrity of Florence. At this point, the psychological imperatives that gave durability to the Florentine economy and inspired faith in the economic capabilities of the state remain elusive, but surely the steady decline of returns from indirect levies did little to shore up civic confidence. In 1487 income from these levies was only 160,000 florins, and by 1490 it had dropped to 105,000 florins.[50]

That the state was assured of a substantial income from gabelles and customs tolls meant that in periods of peace the returns could be pledged for payment of interest to communal creditors. Customs tolls and the gabelles on wine and contracts, in addition to the *estimo* on the *contado*, were assigned to the creditors of the *Monte Comune* (the largest

---

ous and that there was no sharp and sudden drop. Cf. P.C., 34, fols. 56–59; P.C., 35, fols. 69–74; P.C., 36, fol. 61r; P.C., 38, fol. 97 for returns of this gabelle in the early 1430s. Again the statistics demonstrate that it sustained its vigor.

49. The same contention as was made concerning the *gabella portarum* has validity for most of the other communal levies. Also there was little change in their yield immediately after 1427. Cf. P.C., 30, fols. 76–112; P.C., 32, fols. 74–112r; P.C., 33, fols. 70–113.

50. Cf. n. 1 and previous discussion.

of all *Monti*, bearing 5 percent interest). The gabelle on salt was pledged to those who made 8 percent *prestanzoni*, while the tax on mills and fisheries went to those who made special loans for the Pisan War. Such a system may have done much to reassure the creditors of the republic, and to sustain their morale, but it left almost no monetary residue with which to support the expenses of government and the waging of war.

As we have seen, with almost all the republic's regular income already committed to the satisfaction of the claims of the shareholders in the public debt, the Signory had to resort to numerous forced loans. But such a tactic merely increased the communal debt, and, therefore, it would be necessary to extract additional revenues. At this juncture we can observe the acceleration of a trend already in progress since the middle years of the Trecento. This trend, perhaps as much as any other, was to be responsible for the development of a highly specialized and more imposing form of state organization. Subject territories, rural parishes, and country villages had already lost much of their autonomy during the middle years of the fourteenth century. This movement toward greater dependence on Florence was largely a resultant of the pressing demands made upon the city's domains by the public fisc. Further, Florentine bureaucracy had expanded and the city was now assuming the role of guardian and sometimes spoiler of rustic wealth. The *contado* of the later Middle Ages was little taxed, and, because communal budgets were small, there was little reason for exploitation. The very citizens who staffed the Signory were owners of extensive rural patrimonies. There was always opposition to the levying of direct taxes on the countryside, and, in the early Trecento, Florentine regimes were reluctant to incur the enmity of the communal councils even in times of budgetary crisis.[51]

As we have seen, the shift to a sterner regime over the *contado* began in the middle years of the Trecento; what had begun gradually was to become intensified and by the late 1380s had reached considerable magnitude. The contribution of the *contado*, the rural districts (the outlying reaches), and the subject cities bore perhaps one-fifth of the brunt of all imposts. This was a substantial increase over the figure of a half-

---

51. For evidence of hostility to the enactment of the *estimo* on the *contado*, see Capitoli, Protocolli, 12, f. 173 (1 February 1337); Lib. Fab., 14, fols. 41–45 (18 December 1329); ibid., 16, pt. 2, fol. 77r (8 November 1335); ibid., 17, fol. 90 (19 January 1339).

century before, when the fraction was perhaps no more than 10 percent. Moreover, the levy on such commodities as meat and wine in the *contado* continued to rise.[52]

The *estimo* on rural wealth was a regular feature of the Florentine tributary system, and, where earlier there had been only a single direct levy in the course of a year, now there were sometimes two and often three. Even during the 1360s and 1370s it was not unusual to find this harsh expedient resorted to. Beginning in the 1380s, the commune levied not only an *estimo* but what was described as an "extraordinary impost" on the countryside. By 1388 this latter assessment became a regular feature of the Florentine system and continued to be collected throughout the early Quattrocento. In addition to this, starting in 1393, the republic placed an "extraordinary *estimo*" on the rural regions; this, too, came to be a permanent feature of the Florentine tributary system. By 1395 the *estimo* was bringing in just over 17,500 florins to the *Camera*, while the extraordinary *estimo* was yielding approximately 31,500 florins. Moreover, the extraordinary imposts were returning almost 15,500 florins.

The tax on wine produced in the *contado* stood at 17,000 florins. The sum of all these rural imposts reached the very impressive figure of 85,000 florins, and this at a time when intake from general taxation was just above 300,000 florins.[53] By 1402 the figure had ascended until the *contado* was contributing almost 140,000 florins a year to the Florentine treasury, and during the early Quattrocento this amount was not infrequently exceeded. Soon fixed payments were substituted for some of the old levies, and the rate of the extraordinary imposts was much augmented. Now the wealth of the countryside contributed almost one-half to the general revenues. Special taxes were being placed on rural communes and country parishes, and Tuscany was being called upon to pay forced loans. By 1431 approximately 80 percent of all monies collected

---

52. By 1388 the levy on meat slaughtered in the *contado* had reached 6,979 florins; this figure was over one-third higher than that cited by Giovanni Villani for the prosperous biennium 1336–38. Cf. *Cronica*, 9:92; and P.C., 5, fol. 238r (1388). For the 1380s the tax on wine in the *contado* averaged 15,000 florins, and this figure was at least one-third higher than that collected during peak years of the middle Trecento. C.C.E., 80–86.

53. For the *entrata dell'estimo ordinario del contado* in the year 1395, see P.C., 11, fol. 267. For the *entrata dell'estimo straordinario del contado* for the same year, see P.C., 11, fol. 205. The returns for the gabelles on wine and meat are reported in the same volume on fols. 227 and 278, respectively.

from rural localities were being distributed to the treasurers of the various *Monti* so that interest payments to the communal creditors could be met. From 1427 on, the wealth of the environs and districts of Florence were inscribed in the *Catasto:* each time the *Catasto* was imposed (and it could be exacted several times during a year) the contribution of the *contado* was to be 18,594 florins, while the city's was to be 25,341 florins. Considering the disparity in wealth, the *contado*'s share seems disproportionate.[54]

During the late Trecento and the first quarter of the Quattrocento, fixed payments were substituted for some of the old levies, and the rate of the extraordinary imposts was raised. All of this occurred at a time when the countryside was suffering the ravages of war, and the probabilities are that rural population was on the decline. Almost every year the Signory enacted special legislation encouraging immigration into rural Tuscany. The government promised immunity from seizure for debt as well as important tax concessions to those who would take up residence in the countryside and work the land.[55]

While no precise picture can be drawn of economic conditions, certainly the harsh regime of the *contado* could not have come at a more unpropitious moment. Likewise, it is not possible to ascertain with exactitude the effects of the republic's stern program on long-range rural developments; but when we note that Florence's intake from the *contado* reached the staggering sum of 150,000 florins in 1405, and when we observe that in succeeding years new assessments were levied on the countryside with monotonous frequency, we can suggest that the fiscal demands of the city hardly stimulated the vigor of the rural economy. Furthermore, in the 1420s numerous *prestanze* were being collected from the environs and districts of the city. It goes without saying that the bulk of the revenue from the *contado,* some 80 to 90 percent of the total, was assigned to the treasurers of the various *Monti* for payment of interest to communal creditors.[56]

---

54. G. Canestrini, *La scienza e l'arte di stato* (Florence, 1862), 122–25.

55. For a model for such a type of provision, see Provv., 72, fol. 1614; Lib. Fab., 41, fol. 116 (21 October 1383) and Provv., 80, fol. 197; Lib. Fab., 43, fol. 232 (15 December 1391). The reason given by the Signory for the enactment of such measures is that the lands of the *contado* are not sufficiently cultivated. The greater incidence of such provisions occur over the late Trecento and early Quattrocento.

56. Cf. P.C., 34, fol. 154; P.C., 35, fol. 141.

This Spartan regime, in its search for money, was acting to integrate rural territories into a political complex that can perhaps be best described as a Renaissance state. So different was this type of regime from its medieval predecessor of the thirteenth and early fourteenth centuries, that, while terms like *republic* or *commune* might continue to be employed to describe the Florentine political configuration by men from the thirteenth through the fifteenth centuries, the fact was that the entity described in the later period differed markedly from that of the earlier time. The lax and easy government of the Middle Ages had receded, and in its stead emerged a strict, almost exploitative type of regime. By the fifteenth century the term *commune* no longer signified a government characterized by a relaxed rule over its rural domains. Instead, the government was anxious to garner substantial tribute from the countryside. In time of peace this revenue could be disbursed to the republic's creditors, while in time of war it could be employed for the hire of mercenaries. The laissez-faire rule of a medieval commune was replaced by the strict rule of a Renaissance territorial state, and this change was dictated, at least in part, by the pressing economic exigencies of the world of the late Trecento and early Quattrocento.

We have seen that the stringent control of subject cities began in the second half of the Trecento and that this development paralleled the emergence of the republic's sterner policy for the *contado*. Florentine officials were being appointed by the Signory to oversee the collection of gabelles in certain districts. By the 1360s and 1370s direct payment of taxes collected by subject cities were being made into the Florentine treasury. These returns were then utilized either to hire troops or to pay interest to communal creditors.[57]

Florence won much territory during the second half of the Trecento and the early Quattrocento; prizes such as Volterra, Arezzo, Pisa, Cortona, and, finally, Livorno were attained. Pisa, conquered in 1406, is the city for which the most abundant treasury records survive, and therefore it can be used as a test case. Almost immediately after occupying the territory of its neighbor, the Florentine Signory established a special section of the *Camera* to be expressly devoted to handling Pisan fiscal affairs. In 1407 an itemized account of the income of Pisa was drawn up by the officials of the Florentine *Camera*. All gabelles of the subject city were turned over to her conqueror. By 1408 the Florentines were mak-

---

57. Cf. C.C.E., 135–53.

ing a substantial profit on the Pisan tax intake. The *Entrata* of the treasury exceeded the *Uscita* by approximately 200,000 lire.[58] It is not possible to make long-range assessments of the fiscal advantage won by the
Florentines as a result of their domination of Pisa, but certainly during
the early years the conquest was not unprofitable. Beginning in 1414,
special military levies were placed on Pisa, amounting to between
33,000 and 56,000 florins a year. In addition, an *estimo* of thirty soldi per
lira, rather high by Florentine standards, was levied on the Pisan *contado*. Further, a tax was placed on Pisan grain. The major part of all this
revenue was diverted to the *Monte* and used for restitution to communal creditors. In 1428 Pisa, in the company of so many other Florentine
subject cities, was made liable for the *Catasto*.[59]

A comparable but less amply documented history can be narrated
for such prize Florentine possessions as Arezzo, Cortona, and Volterra.
These places also rendered their income from customs and the gabelles
on wine, salt, meat, and contracts to Florentine treasury officials. The
greater part of these monies were employed for the usual purposes, either the hire of mercenaries or for supporting interest payments on the
Monte. While figures are scattered and records discontinuous, it would
seem that the *Entrata* of these towns did exceed the expense of administration and defense, and therefore Florence, at least during the early
Trecento, did realize a profit. In addition, there were the numerous special levies placed on the subject cities; in the case of Cortona such a levy
was often in excess of that commune's total *Entrata* for a given year.
Prato was a special case and as early as 1420 was being assessed extraordinary taxes by the officials of the *Monte*. Very soon all income from
gabelles collected by Livorno were placed at the disposition of these
Florentine officials.[60]

There were of course the numerous levies upon lesser places and
more remote rural regions. During the course of the 1380s these imposts
were increased by some 70 percent, and the added intake was to be utilized for defense. Beginning with 1393 there was a further increment in
these imposts, when they were boosted from approximately 18,000

58. P.C., 22, fols. 181–96.

59. G. Canestrini, op. cit., 127ff. On diversion of revenues from Pisa into the
hands of the treasurers of the *Monte*, see P.C., 38, fols. 168ff.

60. P.C., 27, fol. 311r (1419); P.C., 28, fol. 375 (1420); P.C., 29, fols. 332–413
(1424); P.C., 30, fol. 259 (1426).

florins to 28,000 florins. Further, these same communities were subject to heavy fines if they did not comply with Florentine regulations.[61]

IV

With the establishment of the *Catasto* in 1427 certain problems in communal finance were altered. The treasury records indicate that from the date of its establishment until 1431, this direct tax was exacted some thirty-three times, and, while several of these exactions were not for the full value of individual assessments, still in a single year, 1429, the republic realized about 170,000 florins in revenue from this source. The following year the intake was well above 400,000 florins, and in 1431 it totaled more than 700,000 florins. That the government could rely upon such a substantial income did not, however, relieve the tax payers from the obligation of paying *prestanze*. In 1431 these forced loans amounted to close to 600,000 florins.[62] This meant that the indebtedness of the *Monte* continued to increase despite the imposition of direct taxes. Nor was the total indebtedness of the commune to diminish over the balance of the Quattrocento, for the Signory was to impose regularly special *prestanze*, sometimes at 12 percent interest, which were in fact short-term war loans. The difference perhaps between the credit structure of the early Quattrocento and that of the later years stems from the sharp decline in communal income from gabelles. In the years covered by the present study, income from indirect taxes remained vigorous and served to shore up public confidence in the fiscal reliability of the state. The discussions of the advisory councils to the Signory in the late Quattrocento suggest a precipitous decline in public trust.[63] The fact was that the *Monte* had become inflated at a time when communal income was reaching its nadir.

It is worthy of note that the interval treated in this study coincides with the era alleged to be the apogee of civic humanism. Certainly, any discussion of this intellectual movement must take into account those

---

61. P.C., 8, fols. 374–78; P.C., 9, fols. 375–89r.

62. Cf. "Ritratto dei Catasti," P.C., 34, fols. 303–66. Many of the *catasti* imposed were for a fraction of the total evaluation of citizen patrimonies. Cf. P.C., 32, fols. 332–38 for revenues from the *catasti* of 1429. For the year 1330, see P.C. 33, fols. 332–78. For a summary of *prestanze* levied in the year 1431, see P.C., 31, fols. 202–24.

63. Cons. Prat., 61, esp. fols. 51–98.

economic factors that encouraged the growth of empire, transformed relations between city and *contado*, and, finally, bound the destinies of the
affluent to the public fisc through the institution of the *Monte*. It was at
exactly this time that Florence's chancellor, Leonardo Bruni, asserted the
positive value of wealth, averring that it is to the city as blood is to the
individual. A little later, another chancellor and an equally eminent humanist, Poggio Bracciolini, was to extol trade and commerce because it
was only through these vital activities that cities gained the wealth that
made possible their splendor, beauty, and art.[64] These men, deeply civic-
minded, were not speaking in a vacuum but, rather, were responding to
the exigencies of their times. The nexus between private wealth and civic
well-being was apparent, and perhaps it would be fair to say that a new
economy had emerged that was now dependent upon government
spending and government credit. Under the sway of this new economic
system affluent citizens had become the major shareholders of a giant
corporation that might be termed the "Renaissance state." This entity
had come into being in the early Quattrocento, and, while it was not until 1470 that a piece of Florentine legislation spoke of the *Monte* as "the
heart of this body which we call city" and argued that "every limb, large
and small, must contribute to preserving the whole body: as the guardian
fortress, immovable rock and secure strength of the salvation of the
whole body and government of our state," this was but a much delayed
recognition of the most imposing of Florentine institutions.[65] In fact, exactly the same statement could have been made two generations earlier.

V

Some inferences should be ventured as to the implications of this transformation of the medieval polis into the Renaissance territorial state.[66]

---

64. Garin, *L'umanesimo italiano*, 59–60; Baron, "Franciscan Poverty and Civic
Wealth as Factors in the Rise of Humanistic Thought," *Speculum* 13 (1938): 16ff.;
R. Roedel, "Poggio Bracciolini nel quinto centenario della morte," *Rinascimento*
11 (1960): 51–67.

65. "Il cuore di questo nostro corpo, che si chiama città . . . ogni membro pi-
cholo et grande contribuischa quanto commodamente ciaschuno può alla conservatione di tutto il corpo: come presidi et roccha firmissima et stabilimento certo
della salvatione di tutto il corpo et governo di stato nostro." Quoted, in English
translation, by Marks in "The Financial Oligarchy under Lorenzo," op. cit., 127.

66. Perhaps this quotation from the writings of Eric Voegelin can serve as an

If one argues that the shifting of what Marc Bloch called "the ties of obligation" precede and encourage the "transvaluation" of the consciousness of one's identity, then the citizen of the new Renaissance state was responding to very different imperatives than his forebears of the medieval commune. In the medieval commune this sense of identity had essentially its place in the asymmetrical combination of private loyalties and multiple allegiances to quasi-public bodies such as guild, religious confraternity, and *Parte Guelfa*. It was laced with civic pride and patriotism. Neither communal art nor public rhetoric sought to coerce the citizen into constricting his loyalties or focusing these vague sentiments. Instead, there was the easy, happy belief that these loyalties and emotions were somehow compatible and in the end would further the well-being of the commune. Admonition and exhortation framed to effect the spiritual regeneration of the citizen were the hallmarks of the communal *paideia*. The demands of the city and the requirements of citizenship were minimal, and thus the calls for public sacrifice were modest. The rule of law was gentle, marked as it was by extreme solicitude for the well-being of the noble and the burgher patrician. Judicial dispensation, remission, and pardon were the order of the day. The incidence of taxation both on city and *contado* was light, and the loan of a few thousand florins from guild or *Parte Guelfa* might sustain the public fisc.

Giovanni Villani and his contemporaries of the first part of the Trecento were spokesmen for the rule of law only in a theoretical sense. They would extol the advantages of strong government and yet condemn a particular regime for infringing upon the ancient liberties of the church or the time-honored rights of the nobility. Further, they would denounce communal magistrates as "tyrants"; upon closer inspection, however, these tyrants can be shown merely to have engaged in the enforcement of statutes prohibiting the carrying of deadly weapons or the smuggling of salt and grain.[67]

---

introduction to these inferences: "Human society is not merely a fact, or an event, in the external world to be studied by an observer like a natural phenomenon. Though it has externality as one of its important components, it is as a whole a little world, a cosmion, illuminated with meaning from within by the human beings who continuously create and bear it as the mode and condition of their self-realization" (*Philosophy of the Social Sciences: A Reader*, ed. M. Natanson: [New York, 1963], 3).

67. See G. Villani, *Cronica*, 11:16, 39, where he contends that the law should be enforced and then assails the regime for *uficiali arbitrari*. In point of fact these

Beginning in the mid-Trecento, however, a new and sterner regime emerged, and with it the gentler *paideia* receded. Now chroniclers extolled, both in fact and in theory, the sway of communal law. No exceptions were to be made for nobility or clergy.[68] Moreover, coupled with the mounting demands of law we witness the intensification of the incidence of fiscal burdens upon the citizenry. To those concerned with the problem of the culture of this polis there looms the challenge of a paradox. The nascent civic humanism defined by Hans Baron and Eugenio Garin is as much a description of the realities of civic life as it is of the myth of the polis. Bearing this paradox in mind, it may be that certain ambiguities of civic experience can be more clearly comprehended. Thus, with the burgeoning of the territorial state and closer supervision of public life the republic came to require hundreds of additional civil servants. While the literature and the art of the period proclaim the glories of serving the state, the records of the Florentine treasury disclose that thousands of ordinary citizens preferred to pay the substantial fine of twenty-five lire rather than assume the responsibility of public office. Similarly, many office holders made sizable payments into the *Camera* for absenting themselves from key posts over extended intervals. An identical situation occurred in the councils of the republic, where dozens of elected members were regularly fined for failure to attend sessions.[69] If the expanding polis required citizen talent and participation, it had still greater need for citizen revenue. Again, we observe the same ambiguity: on the one hand, protestations of civic generosity were intoned, while, on the other, literally thousands of petitions were received by the Signory requesting a substantial reduction in an individual's tax contribution.[70]

---

magistrates searched for arms, ousted the banished from the Florentine *contado*, and attempted to control street brawling. Cf. C.C.E., 1 *bis*, fols. 37ff., for a record of the pedestrian activities of these law enforcement officers. Cf. also Stefani, *Cronica fiorentina*, rub. 505.

68. Cf. Becker, "An Essay on the 'Novi Cives,'" cit., 59–82. It should also be observed that, with the closing years of the Trecento, the state became increasingly capable of offering protection to the citizenry. Therefore, the Signory received fewer and fewer petitions from individuals requesting the right to bear arms because of long-standing family feuds and vendettas.

69. The number grew especially formidable during the 1380s. Cf. C.C.E., 210ff. Yet concern for political reputation and pride of office are absent from none of the major chroniclers: Iacopo Salviati, Giovanni di Paolo Morelli, Buonaccorso Pitti, Stefani, etc.

70. Again we observe that during the 1380s, while requests for preferential

It would seem that the new *paideia* is as much a product of the reality as of the myth. Students of domestic chronicles, manner books, and diaries are struck by the persistent ambiguity of civic sentiment. The self-same writer who composes a panegyric on his beloved native city also concocts ingenious recipes for defrauding the treasury of the republic. Indeed, one discovers an inordinate number of stratagems designed to minimize civic responsibility. And yet, because the power of the state looms ever more formidable, the sterner *paideia* achieves momentum. This more impersonal *paideia* voices the exigencies of the state. It will become a persistent element of civic life, not by virtue of bland acceptance but, rather, by dint of the intense conflict it provokes in the Florentine mentality. The same diarist who advises his progeny to shun public life will laud the value of high office only a few pages later. That chronicler most critical of the Signory's fiscal policy will be the warmest advocate of continuing the costly war against Milan.[71]

Myth and reality had blended, and, while one could not be substituted for the other, each would lose meaning without its counterpart. Art and literature ministered to that twilight zone where ideal and real converged. It was in the area of this ambiguity that civic rhetoric gained cogency and the civic humanists acquired an audience. Patriot and egoist, the Florentine citizen desired to believe in the durability of the polis. His patrimony, the dowry of his daughters, and thus his progeny were hostages to the well-being of the state. Exactly at this time emerges the first great profusion of civic monumental art since the times of ancient Greece and Rome.[72]

Some impressionistic fragments of evidence and a skeptical dis-

---

treatment in matters of taxation increased markedly, so too did the number of bequests to the republic as well as the number of state funerals. Payments are now made to the state "pro honorando corpus" by patriotic relatives. For an early notation in the treasury records of such a payment, see C.C.E. 223 (27 March 1384). There is also a notable augmentation in the number of individuals receiving state pensions commencing in the 1370s. Finally, there is a substantial jump in the number of patents of knighthood conferred upon "honorable citizens" by a grateful republic.

71. Giovanni di Pagolo Morelli, *Ricordi*, ed. V. Branca (Florence, 1956), 317, 333–34. (I wish to thank Professor Anthony Molho for calling my attention to this citation.) Cf. Leonardo Bruni, *Difesa contra i reprensori del popolo fiorentino nella impresa di Lucca*, ed. P. Guerra (Lucca, 1864), 27.

72. The literature on this subject is, of course, vast. In addition to H. W. Janson, *The Sculpture of Donatello* (Princeton, 1957), see G. Fasola, "La nuova spazialità," *Leonardo: Saggi e Richerche* (Rome, 1954), 293–311.

claimer might serve as a conclusion. First, the merchant diarist Giovanni di Paolo Morelli, looking back from the vantage point of the late Trecento upon the feuds of almost a century ago, observed that, instead of having recourse to the sword, the citizen now had recourse to the ballot.[73] This awareness of the rule of law deepened into Leonardo Bruni's self-conscious articulation of constitutionalism. His preference for popular regimes, which the Greeks called "democratic," was stated upon the conviction that only this type of government could safeguard "liberty and equality" before the law: "All our [Florentine] laws aim only for this, that the citizen may be equal because true liberty has its roots in equality."[74]

The citizen must live the *vita civile*, responding always to the imperatives of the collectivity. What more impressive tribute to the *paideia* of this new polis can be offered than the fresco of the Trinity painted in *circa* 1425 by Masaccio in the church of Santa Maria Novella. At the foot of this mural is the tomb of the Lenzi family. A Lenzi had recently been elected to the highest civil office in the republic *(Gonfaloniere di Giustizia)*; Masaccio probably commemorated him, clad in the red robes of this office, as the donor. Thus does the earthly city meet the heavenly city.[75]

While Masaccio portrayed Lenzi as an exemplar of the *vita civile*, and the sculptor Bernardo Rossellino placed a carving of Bruni's *History* of his beloved adopted city on the statesman's tomb, there would be some who, while acknowledging the triumph of law and equality, secretly grieved for a lost world of lawlessness and vitality. Not the least of these was Machiavelli, whose *History of Florence* set forth the following remarkable, and neglected, thesis that the triumph of equality and the rule of the magistrates began in the mid-Trecento. The price for the exaltation of civil authority was high: "And thus Florence lost the generosity of her character and her distinction in arms."[76]

---

73. *Ricordi cit.*, 131. In ancient times men used to build "torri alte and grosse" and wage war with crossbows: "e' s'usava allora di nimicarsi più colla spada in mano che colle fave, come si fa al dì d'oggi" (130–31).

74. E. Garin, "I cancellieri umanisti della repubblica fiorentina da Coluccio Salutati a Bartolomeo Scala," *Riv. Stor. Ital.* 71 (1959): 200.

75. E. Borsook, *The Mural Painters of Tuscany from Cimabue to Andrea del Sarto* (London, 1960): 143–44.

76. N. Machiavelli, *Istorie fiorentine*, 2:42. Quoted from Machiavelli, *History of Florence* (New York, 1960), 107. Cf. also 3:1; ibid., 111.

8

Heresy in Medieval and Renaissance Florence: A Comment

I should like to attempt to clarify a few points raised by John N. Stephens in his article "Heresy in Medieval and Renaissance Florence," in the February 1972 issue of *Past and Present*.

First, he has challenged the view that there is a relationship between the entry of minor guildsmen and "new men" into the government, on the one hand, and the breakdown of the privileges of the church and nobility, on the other. Dissenting from the view that these democratized governments did hinder the activities of the inquisition, thus permitting a wider diffusion of heresy, he contends that the "incidence of heresy seems to reflect no known trend in Florentine social history." He makes no reference to the time and circumstances of the initiation of measures against the Fraticelli. These do suggest a connection between working-class political self-consciousness and the diffusion of heresy. On 12 December 1382 a provision was presented to the communal councils directed against "certos fratres seu fraticellos."[1] It was rejected but introduced again on the following day; this time it passed against substantial opposition. In the Council of the Captain the vote was 179 to 81, while in that of the *Podestà*, 104 to 52. Since a two-thirds vote was required to enact a provision, we can see that it barely scraped through. So high a vote against any proposed legislation was most unusual. But the story does not stop here: three days later the councils met again, and this time a law was enacted reducing the representation of lower guildsmen in the government, as had been recommended by an

---

From *Past and Present* 62 (1974): 153–61. Reprinted by permission of Oxford University Press.

John N. Stephens, "Heresy in Medieval and Renaissance Florence," *Past and Present*, no. 54 (Feb. 1972): 25–60.

1. Libri Fabarum, vol. 44, c[arta] 77 (12 Dec. 1382). All documents cited are to be found in the Archivio di Stato in Florence.

"extraordinary commission."[2] This commission had been established earlier in that year when oligarchical reaction against the democratized regime of 1378–82 had led to severe repression of workers, their newly formed guilds, and their patrician adherents. In 1381 discussions had been held in the advisory councils to the signory on the subject of the Fraticelli. Opinions varied, but the important point remains: contradictory advice did little to encourage the government to take action against the Fraticelli or assist the inquisition in its efforts to rid the city of these noxious heretics. Now it may sound strange to sophisticated ears to stress the point that leading politicians in the democratized regime would speak before the signory contending that the chief magistrates of the state—the priors—ought to serve as spokesmen for the poor *(advocati pauperum)*. One speaker, so certain of the sacred responsibility of the priors, had proposed a little before what chroniclers described as the most astonishing piece of legislation to be introduced in a century of Florentine politics. This speaker had suggested the revolutionary step of cutting the interest rate of state bonds by two-thirds. What a web! Too complex to deny the existence of any socioeconomic dimension to religious life, or religious dimension to political life.[3]

In October of that same year, workers and artisans *(il popolo minuto)* had attempted to restore three of their own guilds. On the fifteenth the Executor of the Ordinances of Justice had condemned three citizens to death for conspiring against the state to establish illegal corporations. Four days later the signory was advised to break with the Ciompi and send communal magistrates "against the Ciompi *(contra ciompos)*" to

---

2. Provvisioni, vol. 71, fols. 175–176v (13 Dec. 1382). For the enactment of legislation lowering *minori* representation, see Provvisioni, vol. 71, fol. 187; Libri Fabarum, vol. 41, *c.* 80 (16 Dec. 1382).

3. The speaker in question was the armorer Simone di Blasio. Cf. Consulte e Pratiche, vol. 20, *c.* 84. For a discussion of the role played by this lesser guildsman, see N. Rodolico, *La democrazia fiorentina nel suo tramonto (1378–1382)* (Bologna, 1905), 277. Cf. also N. Rodolico, *I Ciompi* (Florence, 1945), 57–58, for the text of the debate over whether any action should be taken against the Fraticelli. The session noted by Rodolico occurred on 14 December 1381 and may well have been a reaction to workers' riots during the preceding month. Efforts to fix exact boundaries between religion and politics run the risk of committing a historical anachronism. During this period the priorate was referred to as the "savior of the world." Later, those who governed the Republic were seen as doing the work of God, while those failing to pay taxes were considered as having lost respect for God and the Florentine state.

confiscate their weapons. The proposals to take action against the Fraticelli made on 14 December 1381 may have been connected with the onset of worker unrest. The same inference may be drawn in the case of the proposal of 12 December 1382, enacted into law on the following day. Indeed, on 9 December the Captain of the People had sentenced two lesser people *(minuti)* to death because they had promoted a riot in October, hoping to compel the government to restore the same three guilds. Surely, proposals to act against the Fraticelli did have some link with socioeconomic conditions and worker unrest. Incidentally, in July 1383 a speaker before the signory called upon the government to deal with the Fraticelli; this was the first time since December of the preceding year that this issue had been raised, and it coincided with an unrest among wool carders who were attempting to reestablish the guild and coat of arms of the Ciompi.[4]

The first instance I have been able to find of prosecution of an alleged sympathizer of the Fraticelli by the Office of the Inquisition is recorded in the Atti del Podestà of 19–22 September 1383. The case dragged on and is recorded in several volumes.[5] The accused, along with others who had attacked officials of the inquisitor and *Podestà* while they were making the arrest, were placed on trial. The "secular arm" is praised in the documents for doing its duty "laudably *(laudabiliter)*," and the inquisitor is commended for his "fervour and vigour" in defence of the Catholic faith. Of great interest is the verdict designating the majority of the accused as artisans of minor guilds. Fines of two hundred and three hundred lire were to be paid by the "Syndics of the Blacksmiths' Guild of the City of Florence *(Sindici artis fabbrorum civitatis Florentie)*" who went surety for the minor guildsmen *(minori)* matriculated in their guild.

The law of 13 December 1382, later to be incorporated in the 1415

---

4. Consulte e Pratiche, vol. 20, *c.* 65 (19 Oct. 1381); Rodolico, *La democrazia fiorentina,* 475–79. For the sentence of the captain against the two *minuti,* see Rodolico, ibid., 479–81.

5. Cf. Atti del Podestà, vol. 3140, fols. 59–62, for the *inquisitionum* of 19–22 September 1383; ibid., vol. 3178, fols. 153–154v; G. Brucker, *The Society of Renaissance Florence* (New York, 1971), 252–53. I have been unable to locate earlier examples of cooperation between the bishop, inquisitor, and communal magistrates in the judicial records of 1380, 1381, or 1382. This does suggest that prosecution commenced with the installation of an oligarchical government. (I wish to thank Professor Reinhold Mueller for checking these references for me.)

statutes of the Republic, was enacted at a time when the popular impulse was waning in civic life. Its language was clear:

> With impious errors and machinations, these friars and Fraticelli in
> the city and its surrounding territory deceive many simple and ig-
> norant laymen, imbuing them with depraved and heretical opin-
> ions and diverting them from divine services, from the reception of
> the sacraments and from ecclesiastical burial.[6]

Contemporaries did believe a connection existed between the poor
and the Fraticelli. Subsequent volumes of the Consulte e Pratiche disclose
that the Fraticelli did not disappear, nor of course did the poor.[7] What
should be underscored is that no one spoke up on their behalf; instead,
the signory was encouraged to cooperate with the bishop and inquisitor
in bringing them to terrible justice. Prosecutions were initiated by the
state, and the Florentine courts were active in an effort to extirpate the
Fraticelli. That they failed is apparent from the minutes of the meetings
of the government in the years after 1382. The difference between these
sessions and earlier ones rests in the unanimity with which the signory
and its advisory councils favoured this vigorous policy of suppression.[8]

As to the content of the prophecies of the Fraticelli, surely they contain a mixture of social protest and political millenarianism. I do believe
a careful analysis will disclose that economic grievances and demands
for social justice were more in evidence before 1382. Dr. Stephens maintains that the teachings of the Fraticelli would not serve as an ideology
for the working class "since the poorer sort in the city wanted economic

---

6. Relevant sections of the document have been published in Brucker, op.
cit., 250–52.

7. For continued preoccupation with the Fraticelli, see Consulte e Pratiche,
vol. 22, c. 71v; ibid., vol. 23, c. 108; ibid., vol. 25, c. 56v; ibid., vol. 26, c. 182v. In
1388 speakers for the College of the Twelve urged communal magistrates to
obey the new law and cooperate with the bishop and inquisitor. In the following year the notorious execution of a leading Fraticello, Fra Michele da Calci,
took place. The narrative history of his trial and death stands as one of the great
vernacular accounts in all of medieval popular literature. The author (anonymous) and his audience lived in an environment of democratized sentiment.

8. Discussions in the Consulte e Pratiche disclose that the opinions of governmental advisors were unanimous on the question of aiding the inquisitor
against the Fraticelli. Cf. the references in the previous note.

equality not apostolic poverty." This logical statement ignores the historical context in which the poor derived intense spiritual satisfaction from regarding their lot as being sanctified and their person blessed by God. Further, their pleasure was heightened by the belief that rich merchants and prelates were damned. Finally, there was the promise of egalitarianism and social justice. In at least one instance we know that a scribe serving the cause of the workers was himself a heretic. Anyone examining the list of demands made by the Ciompi revolutionaries in the summer of 1378 will recognize the role played by educated, middling people in this movement. The first and most radical phase of the workers' revolution was over in the autumn of 1378; the signory was then controlled by a democratized but more conservative group. In that same autumn the advisory councils met and among the first proposals to be made was the necessity of punishing "those disseminators of rumours and prophecies *(isti seminatores scandalorum et divinationum)*."[9] *Divinationes* are of course prophecies, and the speaker's call for routing out the disseminators of these prophecies at a moment when the radical government had been ousted indicates a link between working-class unrest, on the one hand, and the prophetic movement, on the other. This at least appears to have been the opinion of the spokesman for the College of the Gonfalonieri. Furthermore, I have been unable to locate any comparable piece of advice in the earlier minutes of the advisory councils; it would seem that at precisely the moment of the fall of the Ciompi, such advice was forthcoming. Also, it should be noted that the inquisition had been rendered inoperative during the previous three years, so heretical prophets were freer than they had ever been.

These observations are not meant to imply that oligarchs had been sympathetic toward heretical ideas, but for a variety of reasons they had been reluctant to support certain activities of the inquisition. Anti-papal sentiment and hostility against attempts by the inquisitor to prosecute alleged usurers were but two of the many reasons for this stance.[10] For-

---

9. Consulte e Pratiche, vol. 16, *c.* 33 (13 Oct. 1378). Minutes of this session are cited by Rodolico in *I Ciompi,* 60. Cf. n. 20, for particulars on the scribe who served the Ciompi.

10. Another reason for blocking the inquisitor was the fact that hundreds of prominent Florentines had purchased church property confiscated by the state and were very anxious to protect their acquisitions. Cf. Consulte e Pratiche, vol. 20, *c.* 95 (4 Dec. 1382).

eign policy considerations always played a key role, and of course during the war with the papacy (1375–78) the inquisition was stymied. The problem, however, is much more complex than this, since the oligarchs were themselves compelled to twist and turn in order to adjust to the exigencies of the moment. Particularly critical were relations with Milan and the desire to observe the peace treaty with the Visconti, while not antagonizing the papacy. In any such discussion the vexing question of the role of the "new citizens" intrudes. Dr. Stephens quotes Anthony Molho's statistics on the enlargement of the lists of those eligible for public office. Indeed, based upon these one could prove that after 1382 there was a substantial democratization of the Florentine state. But unfortunately such an inference would be misleading: as early as the 1340s, old distraints were being removed so that additional Florentines might be declared eligible for office. The problem was not how many citizens were fully enfranchised nor even the extent to which the holding of office was democratized but, rather, how much power was exercised by the new citizens. By the late fourteenth century the state required the services of several thousand Florentines, and of this number only a very few held power. The difference between this interval and the years after 1343 lies in the degree of political impact exercised by new citizens and their patrician allies. It has been suggested that this coalition was responsible for the harshest legislation in communal history enacted against the inquisition and ecclesiastical courts. The two laws passed were initiated under unusual auspices: each was the consequence of a petition submitted by the captains of the twenty-one guilds—fourteen of which were *minori*. Leading spokesmen for these measures included both *minori* and new citizens.[11]

All population statistics, as well as quantitative assessments of economic mobility, support the view that the period between 1350 and 1380 was one of maximum increase. For example, the number of households listed in the tax records for the *estimo* of 1351 was 10,878, while in 1379 it was up to 13,372—an increase of over 25 percent. In 1404 it stood at only 13,551, and by 1427 it had fallen well below 10,000. Statistics on the ratio of those matriculating in guilds through hereditary right to all others substantiate this demographic profile. The preponderance of the former over the latter demonstrated so marked a rise that the mobility of

---

11. Provvisioni Duplicati, vol. 5, fol. 54 (2 Apr. 1345); ibid., vol. 6, fol. 35 (4 Apr. 1346); Libri Fabarum, vol. 24, *cc.* 39v–40; ibid., vol. 26, *cc.* 44v–45.

earlier times was almost completely reversed. Certainly, population figures and other indices do suggest that the entry of new men into guild and public life was prompted in large measure by demographic trends and economic factors more in evidence in the fourteenth than the fifteenth century.[12]

The question of how widespread heresy was is complex and a source of great confusion. Perhaps Dr. Stephens is correct: there may have been more heresy in the thirteenth century than in the fourteenth. But the question remains: what was the social, political, and economic content animating religious nonconformity? The principal supporters of the Cathars in thirteenth-century Florence were rich burghers and Ghibelline nobles. Among the chief adherents were magnates from the Cipriani, Nerli, Tribaldi, and Uberti clans; they and their religious beliefs were secure as long as Ghibelline magistrates held office. It was their close ties with the emperors that proved to be their undoing. In a word, they were destroyed because of their high contacts and rarefied political ideology. In the fourteenth century heretics originated from quite a different stratum of society. Perhaps the hypothesis that religious nonconformity in the cities was democratized has some merit. Dr. Stephens's difficulties in finding materials on the Fraticelli in mid-fourteenth-century Florence should not discourage us; the very lack of evidence of prosecutions or of receipts of the commune's third portion in the treasury records may prove significant. Two pieces of evidence suggest the active presence of Fraticelli: in the *Diplomatico* of Sta. Croce (5 August 1354) we have a record of a papal bull issued by Innocent VI, giving the general of the Franciscans authority to imprison, or place under restraint, apostates from his own order. At almost the same time, a book of prophecies written by a Florentine or Tuscan Fraticello was being dis-

---

12. Statistics presented by A. Doren in *Le arti fiorentine,* trans. G. Klein (Florence, 1940), 1:162, show that during the fifteenth century the ratio of those privileged to matriculate in the wool (*lana*) guild by hereditary right to all others had been completely reversed; in the Trecento the preponderance of new members were not enrolled through hereditary right. On population figures and demographic bibliography, see E. Fiumi, "Fioritura e decadenza dell'economia fiorentina," *Archivio Storico Italiano* 116 (1958): 468–70. Preliminary findings of David Herlihy suggest that mobility in fifteenth-century Florence was in fact downward; this demographic pattern supports the findings of Doren and others: cf. D. Herlihy, "Vieillir à Florence au Quattrocento," *Annales. E.S.C.* 24 (1969): 1,339ff.

seminated in the Arno city. This work, once believed to have been composed during that exceptional period 1377–78, is now dated earlier.[13]

It is clear from studies of the Cathars in Florence that poverty was played down and wealth seldom criticized. This was certainly not the case with the Fraticelli of the fourteenth century. In Florence perhaps as many as 15 percent of the population were paupers, and possibly another 30 or 35 percent barely subsisted. We must have a proper history of wages and prices before movements such as that of the Ciompi make sense. By the same token we must know who ministered to the needs of the city's *miserabili*. A final comment may well be that unrest among the city's poor was at its height during the second half of the fourteenth century because the corporate impulse for charity was ebbing, while the new communital impulse had not yet taken hold. It is striking that the origins of the new charity were to be in Tuscany and were to find their most eloquent partisans among the Observant Franciscans. Evidence from the Florentine *catasto* of 1427 discloses that the religious confraternities of the city held property valued at over three times that of the Republic's twenty-one guilds. Further, the charitable function of these confraternities increased considerably, as did the activities of hospitals. The general impression conveyed by this upsurge of philanthropy is that a more systematic program was initiated under state control to minister to the needs of the poor.[14] Accompanying these developments was an amplification of a sense of responsibility for the plight of the worker as revealed in the sermons and writings of leading Tuscan preachers—especially San Bernardino and Sant' Antonino.[15] Also, membership of *minori* in religious confraternities became a commonplace. If one compares

---

13. This new dating is noted by Dr. Stephens, who cites M. Reeves, *The Influence of Prophecy in the Later Middle Ages* (Oxford, 1969), 214–15, 412–13. A content analysis of Florentine prophecies might well suggest that those written around the Ciompi period were marked by egalitarian concerns and zeal for social justice. Cf. D. Weinstein's comments in "The Myth of Florence," in N. Rubinstein, ed., *Florentine Studies* (London, 1968), 33; and his notation of the appropriate manuscript source in n. 3 on same page, where "citizen battles (*le battaglie cittadinesche*)" of "the poor (*i poveri*)" against the rich and powerful are viewed as a struggle to make law prevail over the "most powerful (*più possenti*)" and the "nobles of lineage."

14. C. Canestrini, *La scienza e l'arte di stato* (Florence, 1862), 150.

15. R. de Roover, "Labour Conditions in Florence around 1400," in Rubinstein, *Florentine Studies*, 285–86.

sermons of the early fourteenth century with those of the mid-Quattrocento, one sees that much of the harsh tone against the lazy and shiftless *popolo minuto* has been dissipated.[16]

Dr. Stephens is quite correct in calling attention to the fact that much Fraticelli activity had its locus in Florence during the 1370s. It was at that time that the signory organized a debate between Fraticelli and orthodox clergy. At the insistence of the bishop the event was canceled. In a letter to the Vallambrosan hermit Giovanni dalle Celle, certain Fraticelli observed that "all the guild masters of Florence *(tutt' i maestri di Firenze)*" were at the appointed church waiting for the ideological skirmish to commence. Surely, however one translates *maestri,* many of them must have been artisans and shopkeepers.[17] The last piece of evidence we have for Fraticelli activity among the lower orders of Florence treats the trial and execution of Fra Michele da Calci in April 1389. After that the judicial records are silent on the subject of the diffusion of Fraticelli heresy among the lower orders. The results of Brucker's work as well as my own suggest that the era of most intense persecution did indeed occur between 1383 and 1389, just after the fall of popular government and with the inauguration of oligarchical rule.[18] One of the leading features of the new regime was of course fear of another workers' revolt, and, at a time when this anxiety was most intense, the oligarchical government cooperated effectively with the inquisitor to repress the Fraticelli heresy. Perhaps connections do exist between the increased state management of philanthropy and the desire to minimize worker unrest. Again, results from the *catasto* of 1427 lead us to suspect

---

16. Sant'Antonino realized that workers were at a disadvantage when bargaining with their employers, since they could not organize. De Roover notes that Sant'Antonino favored state intervention when necessary to see that employers were paying at least minimum wages, and to prevent workers from being defrauded. Rodolico, when analyzing evidence for the Trecento, contends that leading churchmen supported the interests of the wool manufacturers (*laniuoli*) enthusiastically: N. Rodolico, *Il popolo minuto (1343–1378)* (Bologna, 1899), 25ff.

17. G. Brucker, *Florentine Politics and Society, 1343–1378* (Princeton, 1962), 303.

18. M. B. Becker, "Florentine Politics and the Diffusion of Heresy in the Trecento: A Socioeconomic Inquiry," *Speculum* 34 (1959): 70–75. G. Brucker, in his *Renaissance Florence* (New York, 1969), 207, comments upon heresy's loss of "popular appeal" and the fact that it was confined chiefly to intellectual circles.

that the plight of the city's *miserabili* had improved in relation to the class immediately above them; this is suggested by David Herlihy's preliminary findings.[19]

It is always tempting to see such movements as the Ciompi as a simple reflex of upper-class politics. So, too, it is easy to regard the spirituality of *il popolo minuto* as the mirror image of the religion of their betters. Dr. Stephens is of course quite correct to suggest that proof of participation by known heretics in working-class movements is hard to come by. Yet there is one striking instance in late Trecento Florence: Guasparre del Ricco, though he wore the badge of the heretic for twenty-five years, continued to teach children to read at the Via Ghibellina. This heretic was also the scribe for Agnolo Latini, notary of the Ciompi.[20]

Finally, in Florence workers' unrest and millenarianism have not been viewed against the backdrop of an urban economy capable of generating enormous riches. The *catasto* of 1427 fixes the aggregate wealth of Florentines at ten million florins; after deductions the figure still totals more than seven million florins. Each household, then (the number was approximately ten thousand), would be worth an average of between seven hundred and one thousand florins. This is a very substantial sum, indicating that premodern, preindustrial cities such as Florence could produce great wealth. Therefore, it would be a mistake to see millenarianism and political prophecy as being utopian. Calls for equality and religious agitation between 1378 and 1382 were as much a response to economic realities as the defence of private property and guild hegemony so vigorously pursued by oligarchs after 1382.

---

19. Herlihy, op. cit.

20. M. Gukowski, "Chi fu a capo sommossa dei Ciompi?" *Studi in onore di Armando Sapori* (Milan, 1957), 1:713.

9

An Essay on the Quest for Identity
in the Early Italian Renaissance

Post-Enlightenment European romanticism and modern scholarship have lavished sympathy upon the nobility and northern European clergy of the later Middle Ages. Such tender concern has been amply justified by the many hard-won historical insights achieved over the last century and a half. Perhaps the best example of this solicitude has been evinced by Professor Gerhart Ladner in his recent study of alienation and order in the late medieval world.[1] Here the reader is made to experience many of the stresses and strains of a culture that would proclaim

From *Florilegium Historiale: Essays Presented to Wallace K. Ferguson*, ed. J. G. Rowe and W. H. Stockdale (Toronto, 1971), 294–312. Reprinted with permission.

This is a slightly expanded version of a paper given at the annual meeting of the American Historical Association held in Toronto, Canada, in December of 1967. The theme of this paper, the quest for identity in the Renaissance public world, is more fully explicated in a volume being prepared on Florentine cultural history in the trecento and quattrocento. No attempt will be made here to footnote this paper generously, since this task is more appropriate to the book. At present my purpose is to offer only an essay that might be useful for provoking further inquiry. The ego psychology employed here is highly simplistic and owes little to Eric Erickson; indeed, it is commonsensical. Without being irreverent, I should like to suggest that this holds true for Erickson's own historical writing and that Freudian theory is really seldom essential for making the crucial deductions.

1. "Homo Viator: Medieval Ideas on Alienation and Order," *Speculum* 42 (1967): 233–59, with extensive bibliography. Against the autumnal language regularly employed by historians to describe the ethos of the somber north in the fourteenth and fifteenth centuries are juxtaposed the imagery of spring, youth, and joy utilized to characterize the culture of Renaissance Italy. Such a vocabulary is misleading in the extreme, since it misrepresents the very documents upon which its metaphoric thesis is constructed. See A. Chastel, "Melancholia in the Sonnets of Lorenzo de' Medici," *Journal of the Warburg and Courtauld Institutes* 8 (1945): 61–67; E. Walser, *Gesammelte Studien zur Geistesgeschichte der Renaissance* (Bâle, 1932), 116ff.

an adherence to both the order of this world and the justice of the next. As Ladner and others have shown, the Dantean metaphor of the pilgrim lost in the dark forest has become a symbol of medieval estrangement. Jacques Le Goff reaches similar conclusions, although viewing medieval society from the colder vantage point of modern anthropology à la Claude Lévi-Straus. He sees late medieval culture as the locale for the assertion of spiritual doubt and Christian guilt at the expense of the hardy, less reflective values of an older military chivalry. This is particularly in evidence when reading late medieval romances where conflicting loyalties to God, the *patria*, and *la donna* created splits in personality and divisions in the psyche. Lately, Georges Duby has been studying the tensions in twelfth- and thirteenth-century society caused by familial aggression and the brutalization required to survive the hard career of knight errantry, while R. Nelli has indicated the explosive, often damaging, quality of medieval eroticism.[2] Arno Borst has contrasted the ideals of knighthood with its reality; for him the twelfth and thirteenth centuries witnessed a noble social stratum caught between lordship and service, living in a world of "Utopian exaggeration."[3] This world of lost or, at least, muted causes seldom fails to evoke an empathy; the language of historical narrative employed by modern scholars is replete with metaphors that would place this suffering world in the most affectionate light: sunset, twilight, and autumn are but a few.

If Ladner, Kantorowicz, and especially Oberman and Leff are correct in their assessments of the psychological tensions and intellectual ambiguities in late medieval culture, then more than empathy for northern Europeans is called for. Eugenio Garin and Charles Trinkaus have indicated the extent to which Italians were involved in the tense nominalist controversies of the early fourteenth century.[4] The awesome no-

---

2. Jacques Le Goff, *La Civilisation de l'occident médiéval* (Paris, 1964); Georges Duby, "Dans la France du Nord-Ouest; au XIIe siècle: les 'jeunes' dans la société aristocratique," *Annales Economies-Sociétés-Civilisations* 19 (1964): 835–46; R. Nelli, *Spiritualité de l'hérésie: le catharisme* (Toulouse, 1953); and esp. *L'érotique des troubadours* (Toulouse, 1963).

3. Arno Borst, "Das Rittertum im Hoch-Mittel-Alter-Idee und Wirklichkeit," *Saeculum* 10 (1959): 213–31.

4. E. H. Kantorowicz, "Mysteries of State: An Absolutist Concept and its Late Medieval Origins," *Harvard Theological Review* 48 (1955): 71ff., and *Selected Studies* (Locust Valley, N.Y., 1965); H. Oberman, "Some Notes on the Theology of Nominalism," *Harvard Theological Review* 53 (1960): 47–75; G. Leff, *Gregory of*

tion of the "absolute power of God" disturbed theologians and scientists alike. The hopeful expectation that an easy synthesis might be constructed between the promptings of faith and the teachings of reason was gravely disappointed. Doubt was soon cast on the possibility of maintaining a scientific base for theological inquiry. Criticism of prevailing epistemologies reflected the influence of the new and disconcerting insights of Duns Scotus and William of Ockham. Facile generalizations rendered by thirteenth-century Aristotelians convinced of man's educability came under criticism. Indeed, any sustained appreciation for the spiritual matrix of early Italian humanism would necessarily include a ready acknowledgment that Petrarch, Coluccio Salutati, Poggio Bracciolini, Marsiglio Ficino, and others responded to that philosophical and psychological dilemma characteristic of the autumnal northern Middle Ages. Like their contemporaries, they sought answers in Christian skepticism and fideism, and, while rejecting particular intellectual forms and even the language of discourse, they continued to harbor similar doubts.

Our purpose might reasonably be to consider the seemingly sturdy bourgeoisie of early Renaissance Italy with the same sympathy as is regularly extended to their northern confrères. Prey to the insecurities of late medieval culture, these sons of north Italy still struggled to uphold the structures and values of a public world. Should not their expenditure of energy in business and politics, against a background of religious anxiety, merit our deepest regard? A reading of the private correspondence of the fourteenth-century merchant Francesco Datini, or the sixteenth-century artist Michelangelo, reveals the spiritual and metaphysical travail of an Italian bourgeois attempting to effect a safe Christian passage through the menacing seas of this life.

During the thirteenth century northern Italy does differ from most of Europe in that the alternative of a civic culture is more readily available to a large segment of the population. Indeed, public education, the notarial arts, rhetorical training, and political careers are attractive possi-

---

Rimini, Tradition and Innovation in the Fourteenth Century (New York, 1961); C. Trinkaus, "The Problem of Free Will in the Renaissance and Reformation," *Journal of the History of Ideas* 10 (1949): 51–62, and "In Our Image and Likeness: Humanity and Divinity in Italian Thought" (Chicago: University of Chicago Press, 1970).

bilities for a people caught up in a commercial and urban revolution. In fact, newer scientific and scholastic developments do not immediately make the same inroads in the south as in the north. A forceful defense of the position that the triumph of civic education in Italy well antedated the coming of thirteenth-century northern philosophy could be advanced. It is a commonplace of intellectual history to suggest that scholastic thought did not flower so early in the south as in the north.[5]

What is striking in the city-state milieu of Italy has not been underscored sufficiently. At first blush it would appear that the north is more replete with tension and philosophical controversy. This generalization, if extended through the fourteenth century, appears still more convincing. The sense of tragedy north of the Alps is accompanied by a high degree of alienation. Most punishing of all to the traditional sense of identity of the intellectual were the anguished theological inquiries and interminable religious allegorizing. Endlessly, the unknowability of God was proclaimed and his arbitrary and capricious power celebrated by despairing prophets.

At the outset the Italian burgher seems so much less troubled, and yet he, too, was not without the ingredients for, in modern parlance, a first-rate identity crisis. By the thirteenth century so many of his traditional ego supports were in the process of deterioration. His landscape of socially defined roles was cluttered, while his schema of ceremonial identities was utterly confused. Chivalric codes were not likely to produce responsible leaders capable of performing the humdrum tasks of government. Extensive violence among magnates indicated that an education in courtesy seldom produced a minimal respect for burgher law. Messianic visions and erotic poetry contributed little to the maintenance of what contemporary documents euphemistically referred to as "the peaceful and tranquil condition of the *civitas*." Instead, they agitated the

---

5. Cf. P. O. Kristeller, *Eight Philosophers of the Italian Renaissance* (Stanford, 1964), as well as his many other studies, in which this problem is carefully analyzed. Indeed, the commonplace observation that north Italian culture in the late Middle Ages was essentially occupied with practical questions and political matters appears to be readily defensible. History, medicine, legal studies, and rhetoric dominated the culture, and seldom was there ample hospitality for sustained metaphysical and theological inquiry. For a negative evaluation of Latin literature, with its excessive interest in history and contemporary events, see A. Monteverdi, *Studi e saggi sulla letteratura italiana dei primi secoli* (Milan and Naples, 1954), 3–14.

public conscience and increased disaffection among the various orders of medieval society.[6] From two different vantage points the polis was seen as repressive and fatally compromised. Town law was as little sympathetic to the code of adultery as it was to the eschatology that fed the aspirations for justice of a working class. Yet the burghers themselves were torn: they too harbored deep sympathy for a society that would live in tune with the rule of love that prevailed when Christ and his apostles trod the earth.

The conscience of medieval townsmen of north Italy was beset by enervating conflict: On the one hand, they proclaimed the benefits of an open society with its insistence upon the nobility of deeds, while, on the other, they boasted pride of lineage. Similarly, they rhapsodized upon the topoi of work and thrift while despising the *gente nuova* who subscribed so wholeheartedly to these virtues. Their psyches were flushed with patriotic impulse, and yet they entertained monumental suspicions against aggrandizing and expansionist foreign policy: did not the people won in wars of conquest frequently carry the dread taint of treason in their blood? Although committed to doctrines of municipal expansion, the native-born citizen saw certain of the subject population damned simply because they were alleged to be the progeny of Roman conspirators and traitors. Moreover, while announcing the virtues of popular education and vernacular culture, this self-same citizenry continued to harbor abiding prejudice against the immigrant and his sons, whose successful acculturation in a new urban milieu was the highest tribute to be paid their polis.[7]

Their own society, measured against Christian perfection, was found corrupt and disordered. At work was a contest between a traditional hierarchical vision and a more horizontal view of social groupings. No cadre of their society appeared to be performing in accord with a vertical conception wherein *magnates et potentes* were animated by true civic concerns.[8] Indeed, the scale was sometimes in process of being overturned, for prudence and historical experience instructed burghers to look to the upper echelons of society for the names of those seeking to betray the polis. Seldom did kings, princes, and knights perform po-

---

6. M. Becker, *Florence in Transition* (Baltimore, 1967), 1:30–44.

7. M. Becker, "Florentine Popular Government (1343–1348)," *Proceedings of the American Philosophical Society* 106 (1962): 360–82.

8. Becker, *Florence in Transition,* 2:134–49.

litically in conformity with their proclaimed ideals. Burgher literature, which is after all our best source for these attitudes, expressed its deepest dismay when pope and prelate behaved at variance with sacred Christian principle. Soon this distress was converted to humor, thereby becoming bearable, as the novella thrived on the play of false religious identities. The reader stood forewarned always to keep in mind that those seeming to be most at home in the ceremonial orbit of the church were instead despicable strangers to the teachings of Christ. This was a prize sample of social wisdom; bourgeois literature from Boccaccio through Aretino prospered by reiterating the theme of social roles and ascribed rank.

This popular and colorful literature throbbed with a dominant message: those attempting to navigate the treacherous waters of the social world should remember that religious signs and group identities are always misleading, and, if they desire safe harbor, they would be wise to discount the religious world of appearances. Medieval poets constructed high tragedy from this spiritual disarray while still believing that *renovatio* (renewal) of temporal and spiritual realms was imminent. To be "cast down" in this world might be the beginnings of spiritual rebirth: did not Dante's pilgrim have to descend to the depths of hell before commencing his sacred ascent? The core of proverbial wisdom in the quattrocento emanated from a commitment to the literary observation that those without friends, political influence, or wealth were fated for destruction. Not a Poggio Bracciolini, Giovanni Cavalcanti, or Machiavelli expressed anything but absolute confidence in the irrevocable decline of the solitary voyager. And yet against this could be juxtaposed another abiding piety voiced by chroniclers, diarists, and letter writers who lavished further sympathy upon a beleaguered bourgeoisie. For a very different reason the world was ever menacing: those most dependent upon wealth or influence would soon be cast down by the wheel of *fortuna*. Conventional morality functioned in this way to augment tension and make passage through this life precarious.

The prevalent idea of how to confront these harsh realities was expressed by Boccaccio's celebration of wit, Sacchetti's apotheosis of niggardly prudence, and Machiavelli's hosannas to *virtù*.[9] There was also

---

9. Most valuable for Boccaccio studies is V. Branca's monograph, *Boccaccio medievale* (Florence, 1956); see also E. Li Gotti, *Franco Sacchetti, uomo "discolo e grosso"* (Florence, 1940), a particularly notable study. For an analysis of Machi-

that enormous civic legacy of the humanists—Salutati, Bruni, Poggio, and the rest—which stood as a stunning tribute to the need for repression of the citizen's own irrational proclivities in favor of the ordered polis circumscribed by law.[10] In any case this literature is characterized by an intense appreciation of the threat that the political, social, and economic world of the times posed to the always vulnerable individual. The motif of human frailty was elevated to a poetic ideal by Petrarch and a methodological construct by Machiavelli. For civic humanists such as Salutati and Bruni, all who ruled must acknowledge this fragility. By the early quattrocento, so sensitive had philosophy and literature become to the plight of the earth-bound voyager that they furnished him with a bifurcated code that recognized that the highest standards prevailing in the realm of personal ethics could not possibly be realized by the most virtuous of men in the public world. These secular counsels were constantly being advanced to men whose Christian anxieties were never quieted.

We also observe the weakening of confidence in those ritual bonds fixing loyalty and affection between men. Feudal ties of obligation had not been firm in north Italy for more than a century. Italy remained as the single great territory unable to produce a chivalric epic. Instead, she was to borrow from France a poetry epitomizing ideal courtly relationships. The indigenous vernacular poetry of very recent origin voicing trust in the social force of *amicitia* and *amore* was losing its élan by the early trecento. For Dante and his circle the secrets of the "gentle heart" could be understood only by a spiritual elite. *Amore* was directed toward the Virgin herself, while Christ became lord of courtesy; most of the contemporary world, however, was condemned to live without hope in an inferno.

Traditional concepts of loyalty and a high spiritualization of love did little to form the intimate world of men or tame antisocial behavior. Dante, Boccaccio, Sacchetti, and other literati saw the contemporary scene as the locale for aggression, seldom restricted by moral bonds or ties of friendship. Major chroniclers, from Matteo Villani and Stefani to Giovanni Cavalcanti, instructed their Florentine compatriots that tradi-

---

avelli's imagery, especially germane for this problem, see F. Chiappelli's *Studi sul linguaggio del Machiavelli* (Florence, 1962), 88ff.

10. Of Hans Baron's numerous works on the theme of civic humanism, see *The Crisis of the Early Italian Renaissance* (Princeton, 1955), 2 vols.

tional allegiances were valueless in troubled times; to rely upon the medieval staples of friendship and fidelity was to be a victim of *fortuna*. The motors of communal society were seen as naked self-interest and quest for power. New generalizations of historical interpretation were emerging, not the least of these being man's insatiable capacity to inflict harm on others without incurring divine wrath. The moral stance of the chronicler stood at variance with the cruel ethos he felt surrounding him. His historical metaphor was now drawn from the language of disease and pestilence. A century before Machiavelli images of bestiality and nature-run-rampant were historiographical coin.

In cultural historical terms what occurred was not that there was less *amicitia* and *amore* in society but, rather, that neither was to be celebrated programmatically, elevated to the level of an ideal or employed as a tool for understanding. The middle of the trecento witnessed the last of the great Tuscan poets of the "sweet new style"; the Petrarchan lyric soon took over, with its insistence upon the evanescence of friendship and love. Indeed, human emotions were characterized by this very impermanence, and ideals never served as a bridge to God. A sense of subjectivity was evidenced so that the poet observed his feelings about objects rather than the thing in itself.

Love was a disease for the Petrarchan, but, unlike the medieval man, he was condemned to seek no cure.[11] The chroniclers did discover pockets of isolated virtue inhabited by valorous men responsive to the

---

11. Likewise, *amore* did not serve as a civilizing force for Petrarch and his followers. Late medieval Italian poetry is characterized by substantial emphasis upon the socializing aspects of love and courtesy. Significant for the later history of the Renaissance is the fact that the *cri de coeur* of Petrarch is muted; the aristocratic repression of the cinquecento makes musicality and harmony the hallmarks of Petrarchism. Giorgio Santangello, in *Il Petrarchismo del Bembo e di altri poeti del '500* (Palermo, 1962), 23, speaks of the poet's "sentimento della caducità delle cose umana" as being coupled with his notion of style. This style, which Santangello considers to be "the most intimate and profound aspect *dell' anima del Rinascimento*," would seek a synthesis of "umanità e poesia." Such a synthesis will enable man to triumph over "la discordia delle cose" and gain "il mondo sereno della armonia." Petrarch's poetry, unlike that of his more scholastically minded forebears, did not present an abstract conception of human nature as fixed and immutable. As has been suggested by numerous commentators, the poet's own shifting emotions are accorded primacy; these are projected to the reader through the play of antithesis and assonance as well as the fabrication of technical difficulties.

promptings of *amicitia* and *amore,* but death, piteous and ineffectual, was generally their historical reward. By the second quarter of the quattrocento, Poggio and even Bruni voiced doubts concerning the modest possibility of sustaining the human community. The all-too-familiar literary motif of hypocrisy was firmly installed in humanistic political discourse. Renaissance prose writers had become staunch expositors of a comic view depicting men as bound together by their addiction to vice. Sometimes this view was extended to include a tragic dialectic between aristocratic ideals and burgher realities. Fantasy offered some release, with visions of women who combined the virtues of burgher fidelity with aristocratic passion, in a Renaissance counterpart of the unwieldy *Playboy* philosophy.[12]

More relevant, but less charming, is a stricter impulse detectable in public policy formulated over the second half of the trecento. Gone were so many of the hortatory frescoes adorning walls in the town council halls of north Italy.[13] Likewise, appeals by government to the good nature of the citizens were diminishing. Peace officials for making voluntary treaties among feuding families, communal-sponsored religious ceremonies staged to produce domestic accord, and even the ritual of exchanging the kiss of peace gave way before the onset of more coercive public policies. Judicial dispensation and remission of fines also dwindled. Artistic styles became more controlled and geometric, while rhetorical modes were standardized. The world of the polis was more commanding, and the classical revival added monumentality and durability to the milieu.[14]

---

12. See G. Preti's introduction to Castiglione's *Il libro del Cortegiano* (Turin, 1960), where he considers this and other relevant ambiguities. The writings of Leon Battista Alberti also reveal deep conflict on this score. See J. Gadol's review of a new edition of Alberti texts in *Renaissance Quarterly* 20 (1967): 484.

13. N. Rubinstein, "Political Ideas in Sienese Art: The Frescoes by Ambrogio Lorenzetti and Taddeo di Bartolo in the Palazzo Pubblico," *Journal of the Warburg and Courtauld Institutes* 21 (1958): 179–207.

14. For Brunelleschi and Alberti mathematics conferred a quality of indestructibility and eternity upon the world, while through geometric figures the divine mind spoke. G. Fasoli, "La nuova spazialità," *Leonardo: saggi e richerche* (Rome, 1954), 293–311; G. Argan, *Brunelleschi* (Milan, 1955). In mural painting we observe that Piero della Francesca, Domenico Veneziano, and Castagno lowered the horizon line in order to increase the monumentality of the figure. Cf. also L. Alberti's *On Painting,* trans. J. R. Spencer (London, 1956), 110. I wish to thank Professor Nancy Struever for allowing me to read her penetrating dissertation on Florentine rhetoric and politics.

As the individual in the novella stood isolated and less able to rely on traditional supports, there followed a withering away of comforting political ideology. That "demystification of politics" described by Ernst Kantorowicz was well in process.[15] Neither citizen nor polis could hope to take a sure reading of political longitude by siting on either of those twin stars in the medieval firmament—empire or papacy. The structure of north Italian chronicles illustrates the problems of attempting to subsume recent historical experience under traditional medieval schema.[16]

Classical historiographical style comes to the fore with its abiding sense of distance from the recent past. Imitation of Roman writers was accompanied by this feeling of disjunction from the historical universals of the late Middle Ages. History became the record of participation in a public world whose temporal bounds were set by presently shared political experience. Politics was viewed as a brutal struggle for office and advantage conducted by men to whom the principles of Ghibellinism and Guelfism were at best anachronisms and at worst pious frauds.[17] Old political nomenclature was disvalued; only when such terms could be translated into patriotic, civic rhetoric did they retain even a shade of their former meaning. The language of political discourse in the council halls of Florence displayed a remoteness from Christian metaphor and medieval political cosmology. Over the fourteenth century there was a decline in the messianic tradition and a lessening of confidence in the efficacy of Christian agencies for moral regeneration.

---

15. Cf. note 4 and also *The King's Two Bodies* (Princeton, 1957), 173–231. Further discussion is found in Michael Wilks, *The Problem of Sovereignty in the Later Middle Ages* (Cambridge, 1963); and Walter Ullmann, *Principles of Government and Politics in the Middle Ages* (London, 1961).

16. Becker, *Florence in Transition*, 2:43–49.

17. In the early quattrocento the influential Dominican, Giovanni Dominici, instructed his Florentine audience that "niuno partigiano va in paradiso . . . non essere guelfo ne ghibellino." Cf. *Regola del governo di cura familiare*, ed. Donato Salvi (Florence, 1860), 76. Even so staunch a champion of the *Parte Guelfa* as Lapo da Castiglionchio could only furnish bizarre etymology for the old political idiom. Writing in the early fifteenth century, the historian Gregorio Dati advised his readers that to many the origins of the terms *Guelf* and *Ghibelline* seem naught but "favole"; this is not to be marveled at, for many things have names for which one cannot assign reasons because they have insignificant and lowly beginnings. On Lapo, see R. Davidsohn, "Tre orazioni di Lapo da Castiglionchio," *Archivio storico Italiano* 20 (1897): 225–46. Cf. also Dati, *L'Istoria di Firenze dal 1380 al 1405*, ed. L. Pratesi (Norcia, 1904).

The erosion of the play of the sacred in the north Italian public world paralleled the decline of traditional ego supports for the individual. As the polis was loosened from the universal frame, the individual was likewise deprived of facets of his ascribed identity. The north Italian townsman was required to confront a society that had limited sympathy for the prevailing business ethic. Further, the solace a burgher might receive from membership in an extended family (*consorteria*) was on the wane. Even his security formerly gained from activities in the family business was being dissipated. Capitalism was becoming more impersonal; holding companies were being formed as the more intimate business structures of an older world receded. Wealth tended to be liquid so that estates were readily divisible and family fortunes not so durable. Patrimony and ancestral property were easily alienable; as a result, fewer clan holdings survived intact over the generations. Primogeniture was not so prevalent; more usually, all heirs shared equally in bequests. Common living quarters, joint ownership of property, clan fortifications, familial codes of honor, councils of the *consorteria*, all these were in decline in late medieval Florence.[18]

The burgher now stood in greater isolation than ever before. Separate households and the idea of privacy were displacing the heightened sociability of the extended family with its communal style of life. In Florence strict enforcement of law served to weaken the *consorteria*, while factious politics and the differential effects of economic trends militated against the old solidarity.[19] Once the medieval polis had been throbbing with expressions of that associative impulse characteristic of communal society. Guild, confraternity, tower society, Guelf and Ghibelline parties,

---

18. A general assessment of differences between developments in the north and south of Europe during the late Middle Ages might run thus: in the north, from the thirteenth century on, there was a marked tendency to replace the institutions of an individualistic feudal era, characterized by arrangements between vassal and lord, with corporate structures. Guilds, universities, leagues of clerics and nobles, parliaments, estates, and business partnership were of course on the rise. In the Italian cities, on the other hand, the flowering of corporatism was over by the late thirteenth century. The impulse had not been so strongly contested by powerful feudatories or checked by secular rulers. The southerner, then, lived in a society where neither corporate nor familial bonds were so supportive.

19. Especially useful for this essential, but neglected, question is R. Goldthwaite, *Four Florentine Families* (Princeton, 1969).

and other institutions acted to relieve individual isolation. Day-to-day cooperation in the councils of the *consorteria* and neighborhood militia prompted social cohesion. Lacking ample bureaucratic structure, the medieval polis relied upon grassroots political and social action. The effective associative structures of the late medieval world would bear out that quality in lifestyle aptly termed *Stufenkosmos* by the German historian Heinrich Miteis.[20]

The creative impulse toward cooperative forms in religious and secular life is certainly not the hallmark of the Renaissance. Instead, political systems became more unitary and bureaucracy more commanding; the effect was to dull corporate energies and enthusiasms. Voluntary societies of knights, foot soldiers, castle guards, and other similar groups were superseded by mercenaries. Guild courts and the tribunal of the merchants lost preeminence as state courts came to dominate. Procedures at law were formalized, while tax structures were regularized. The citizen could not easily draw strength and support from that myriad of quasi-public bodies once so effective in their operation.

There was also an accompanying decline of burgher confidence in the efficacy of collectivized concepts of honor, loyalty, and *carità*. These ideals tended to become personalized, and the early humanists, Petrarch, Boccaccio, and Salutati, minimized the possibility of their group implementation. Petrarch spoke to a broad audience when denying the existence of any overriding concern for the salvation of others. His neglect of the concept of *carità* was paralleled in the many bourgeois diaries and memorials whose emphasis was consistently upon the prudential.

When Petrarch entertained the traditional metaphor of "the ladder of virtues," it was only to affirm the reality of the lower two rungs (the political and purgatorial) for the men of this world. Even among the seemingly most ascetic of Christians the supreme virtues did not prevail. The weakening of abstract and generalized concepts of virtue led many in Petrarch's generation to posit secularized models and *exempla* from history; these would serve better to encourage the Christian to the good life. Indeed, one of the most prominent features of this new culture was to underscore the phenomenal and finite (that is, the historical) rather than the wisdom of the transcendent and philosophy of the infinite. This is merely a highblown way of stating that, at a time when ceremonial identity, ritual ties, and sacramental bonds were cast in doubt, early hu-

---

20. *Der Staat des hohen Mittelalters,* 2 ed. (Weimar 1944).

manism and Florentine burgher culture were colonizing the outer rim of the mind with a novel mode of historical consciousness.[21]

By the late trecento what was being celebrated in Florence was not the informal and abstract ties between men but "the chain of law." Whereas the individual had been separated from many associative and corporative imperatives, he was now liable to severe restraints. Free in one sense (with all the attendant anxieties), he now lived in a polis where public power became increasingly commanding. Here a dissent must be registered against the Burckhardtian view that the emergence of the individual was exclusively a process whereby north Italians were released from older restraints and ascetic norms to follow the impulses of an unbridled ego. This interpretation does not stress sufficiently the new pressures (social, political, and economic) to which the Renaissance citizen was liable. While it is true that the constraints of a corporate society were dissipated, the new repressive power of the Renaissance state was more than ample to shape and batter human egos. The law could be and was readily enforced against the *maiores et potentes* of Florence, beginning in the 1340s.[22] The strict containment of an obstreperous nobility and the domination of rural feudatories was no less significant. At the level of everyday citizen life the authority of the territorial state was still more telling. Conformity to the dictates of public law was no longer a fact to which a citizen might be persuaded; rather, it was the sine qua non of Florentine republican experience.

The citizen ego under novel compulsions, stripped of many ancient props, and separated from the comforting hierarchy of a medieval cosmos with its attendant sociability, proved highly adaptable. The emo-

---

21. See the special number of *Archivio di filosofia* (Padua, 1966) devoted to the problems of consciousness and demystification. On the desacralization of nature, see the monumental work of Pierre Duhem, *Le Système du monde de Platon à Copernic* (Paris, 1913–17). Here we observe a critique of traditional symbolism serving as a necessary prolegomenon to the rise of a new science: natural phenomena are considered not as God himself but, rather, as his creation. On emerging Renaissance historical consciousness, see E. Cassirer, *The Individual and the Cosmos in Renaissance Philosophy*, trans. M. Domandi (New York, 1964), 42ff.

22. M. Becker, "A Study in Political Failure: The Florentine Magnates, 1280–1343," *Mediaeval Studies* 27 (1965): 246–308. Coluccio Salutati extols the "legum catena" that bound the city together, existing over and above the ties of kinship, friendship, and even parentage. *Epistolario,* ed. F. Novati (Rome, 1891–1911), 1:21. Cf. also Salutati's "Invectiva," in *Prosatori latini del quattrocento,* ed. E. Garin (Milan, 1952), 32.

tional history of the early Florentine Renaissance was characterized by a quest for new ego supports. The principal thrust of the new humanism paralleled this emotional surge: from Petrarch through Salutati, Bruni, and Poggio, we observe a resolute and surprisingly consistent defense of the claims of the human ego. Gradually, customary contempt for the "active life" was challenged. Human desire for fame and renown was legitimized. Wealth and human industry were now regarded as both aids and tokens of virtue. This celebration of ambition and acquisitiveness was done in the name of religious and political ideals. As with Petrarch, sometimes the religious impulse verged upon the blasphemous: Scipio's elevation to the level of deity in the *Africa* is a case in point. Boccaccio's rendering of the Prometheus legend is so civic in tone that the author cannot imagine that the gods would have punished this mythic figure for bringing man the indispensable element for civilization.[23]

For the Florentine, structuring of ego could best be achieved through firm identification with the emerging Renaissance polis. This polis was beginning to assume an organic character in the minds of the citizenry by the late trecento. Its life and vitality were to be reckoned not in years but, rather, in centuries. Unconsciously, the grammar in the discussion of its nature changes; now "the commune" does thus and thus (*fa cosi*). Equally durable were the glory and rewards to be won in its service. The compensations of the public world were boldly proclaimed in the new civic art of the early quattrocento. Nor was it necessary to find moral justification for acts of conquest and the building of empire. In the medieval view wealth and armed aggression by the polis were sure to incur God's wrath. Now, the capture of Pisa or even the defeat of papal troops is taken as the harbinger of God's election of the Republic. Florentines writing in the vernacular in the late trecento enjoined *lo stato* to effect a *renovatio* of the Christian world; the narrow politics of the city-state had assumed a redemptive quality. *Lo stato* was sacrosanct, and the citizen, although emancipated from medieval collective notions and ascetic restraints, was expected to be a loyal if not subservient denizen of the polis.[24]

---

23. G. Boccaccio, *Genealogiae deorum gentilium libri,* ed. V. Romano (Bari, 1951), 4:4.

24. Gregorio Dati, after speaking of the well-ordered polis, says that the *concordia* is so great, and the melody that emanates so sweet, that the saints in heaven are moved to love the city and defend it from whomever would seek to

Identity was to be gained not by contesting imperatives of the public world, as in the time of Dante, but by conforming to them. In the late Middle Ages, when connections between things spiritual and political were firm, the individual dared withstand the injunctions of a civil order. Further, the public world did not yet have such extensive coercive authority. Again, while the individual was liberated, in the Burckhardtian sense, from certain constraints, the polis with its lures and power could better serve as an agency of repression and thereby structure citizen ego.

A survey of the abundant evidence from Florentine last wills and testaments shows a sizable increase in the number of civic bequests. Pious works, grants to hospitals, donations for support of orphans, dowries for poor girls, and even funds for construction of the first foundling home in Europe: these are the causes to which the civic-minded subscribed. The character of early Renaissance Christianity is imbued with a feeling for community; the ascetic, contemplative, and penitential are in recession as the values of an activist Christianity become more apparent. The content and form of sermons delivered by leading Tuscan clerics at this time are evidence of a response to this new lifestyle. Renowned figures like Fra Giovanni Dominici, San Bernardino of Siena, and San Antonino of Florence tirelessly emphasized citizen obligation toward their polis. San Antonino advised Florentines to bequeath their shares of government stock to the city; San Bernardino was eloquent in his defense of the active Christian life; Fra Giovanni denied the possibility of returning to the days of pristine purity when Christ and his apostles walked the earth. Instead of pursuing chimeras by seeking a return to "il primo stato della chiesa," men must follow "la più onesta usanza della patria."[25]

---

disturb its peaceful and tranquil condition. Cf. *L'Istoria di Firenze*, 171. Giovanni Cavalcanti addresses his fellow Florentines, praising them for subduing the obdurate nobility and conquering the foreigners resident in their land. The citizenry have unseated depraved tyrants, and each man can well be compared to Hercules. Indeed, this is the very essence of the commune—that multitude of brave men living under one law. Is it not so, then, that anyone rebelling against the "civile reggimento" or harming the commune in any way is like a husband who cuts off "i testicoli per dispetto alla moglie"? *I storie fiorentine* (Florence, 1839), 3:2. One of the telling differences between trecento chroniclers and their quattrocento counterparts stems from a general failure of the latter to create a base for individual dissent, and even opposition, to the imperatives of the state.

25. Giovanni Dominici, *Regola del governo*, 136: "Ora so bene posto che volesse di ridurre il primo stato della chiesa ne' tuoi nati, non potresti. Pure attendi,

Even the more ascetic of the Tuscan clergy will show intense sympathy with the perils confronting men of state embarking upon "an
earthly pilgrimage." The Vallombrosan, Giovanni dalle Celle, writing to
influential Florentine politicians and businessmen in the 1370s and
1380s, was to demonstrate deep appreciation of the plight of *veri Cristiani* dedicated to their polis.[26] The Augustinian Luigi Marsili, intellectual heir of Petrarch, was to proffer consolation to public men at a time
when the polis warred against the church. A programmatic difference
emerged wherein leading clerics sought to reconcile the public and private worlds of an activist citizenry. Interestingly enough, the ideal figure
portrayed by cleric and civic-minded artists is the Christian patriot. Cor-
respondent of both dalle Celle and Marsili, Guido del Palagio is as much
the symbol of his political generation as Donatello's statue of David is
of the next.[27] Religion and art combined to produce a new breed of men,
the civic prophets—the Joshuas and St. Georges who populated the
streets of Florence in the early quattrocento. Was Abraham less beloved
by God because he chose to follow the ways of this world? asks Coluccio Salutati. A younger contemporary, Bruni, also to become chancellor
of Florence, displayed particular compassion when describing the tribulations of public men and the difficulties of political decision. Rhetoric
and a new oratorical style assumed much of their character as a consequence of this new awareness. Part Christian, part patriot, the public
man will be depicted as reverent toward law and social usage; his character will be forged in daily confrontation with the thousand ills secular life is heir to. Heeding the Ciceronian maxim to stand in line and fight
resolutely, he presents a very different figure from the untamed egoist
constructed by Burckhardtians as typical of the Renaissance.[28]

---

seguitando la più onestà usanza della patria." On this and related themes, see
Christian Bec's valuable study, *Les Marchands écrivans à Florence, 1375–1434* (The
Hague, 1967). His treatment of San Antonino and San Bernardino begins on
page 255; his discussion of their views on civic duty is particularly illuminating.

26. F. Tocco, "I Fraticelli," *Archivio storico Italiano* 35 (1905): 348. *Lettere del
Beato Giovanni dalle Celle monaco Vallombrosano e d'altri,* ed. B. Sorio (Rome, 1845).

27. Becker, *Florence in Transition,* 2:60–62.

28. In the late quattrocento the Ciceronian ideal tends to become less mus-
cular and civic; *humanitas* is more frequently equated with that elegance and
refinement of culture, which allows the Florentine merchant to vie socially with
the chivalrous nobility of the north of Europe. Cf. K. Borinski, *Die Antike in Po-
etik und Kunsttheorie* (Leipzig, 1914), 1:108ff.

Humanists and clerics revealed a sympathy for the pious business-man-politician of the early quattrocento. Already, for at least a generation, a defense of the dignity of his world was seen in chronicles. It was the merchant, not the knight, who made the city great; wealth accumulated by the commercial class shall serve as "blood and sinew" of the Republic. There was also a stout defense for marriage and the family when Salutati contradicted Petrarch's views.[29] Pervasive throughout society was an elevation of the pleasures of life in the nuclear family. Again we can see this as a response to the loss of previous emotional supports. More intimate bonds of affection challenged courtly ideals, allegiance to *consorteria* and medieval, aristocratic eroticism. Like the civic world that conferred fame upon the individual, the nuclear family became a quintessential element of man's *humanitas*. The social phenomenon, brilliantly depicted by Philippe Ariès for the France of later times, had its beginnings in north Italy in the early Renaissance. The family was the focus of man's moral life, and women and children served to sustain and enrich the earthly pilgrimage.[30] Here lie the origins of new educational ideas, especially in the treatment of the young: children were to be kept at home; parents were to oversee their education; the cruelty of the medieval apprentice system was scorned. Wives were no longer idealized in chivalric fashion but were depicted as partner and helpmate. The frailty of children was to be the source of tenderness, while the wishes of daughters must not be ignored when selecting a spouse for them. Treatises on domestic management proliferated, while household concerns were raised to a science.

The individual emerged from the corporate and associative world of the late Middle Ages bereft of traditional supports. The prototype of the modern family would in part sustain him. Increased security provided by the Renaissance state made it easier for the individual to survive without depending upon the power of the extended family. With the breakup of the *consorteria* separate households were established and the idea of privacy challenged commitments to the wider sociability of

---

29. Not only did Salutati defend the institution of marriage from his beloved Petrarch's harsh judgments, but he repeatedly opted for the word *maritus* and not *uxorius*. His love for children became one of the most touching themes of his finest epistles. Cf. V. Rossi, *Il Quattrocento* (Milan, 1933), 131.

30. E. Panofsky, in his *Early Netherlandish Painting* (Cambridge, Mass., 1953), 22–23, discusses the numerous iconographic motifs of an intensely emotive domesticity originating in the northern Italian early Renaissance.

the declining medieval world. This stands as something of the price men must pay for alienation from the protracted sustaining values of an older society.

What is dominant is an exteriorization of perspective, whereby character and action are viewed from the vantage point of the public world. This angle of vision became more commanding as the extent of civic identification was amplified. There remained, however, deeper psychological needs not so easily satisfied. While some among the humanists assured the citizenry that a harmonious way was open to all who would love that larger human family, "il santo e buono Comune," the cost of repression was high. When Bruni decided to write a biography of Dante, he picked up Boccaccio's earlier work on the subject only to find the *Vita* full of sighs and bathed in the sweet elixer of love. Bruni preferred to stress the civic Dante, politician and warrior, whereas Boccaccio had portrayed the man of passion. Medieval strategies for gaining knowledge of the interior world grew apace during the late Middle Ages: scholastic psychology, introspective devices in chivalric literature, metaphysical poetry, and the rest all contributed. During the early quattrocento the pull of the public world was so intense, and humanists so anxious to proffer support to the beleaguered ego, that a gulf between the cultivated civic persona and the deepest recesses of interiority developed.

What was in process of being colonized in the human mind was the rim of consciousness visible to society and the psychic center ministered to by the ceremonial and liturgical. The culture was all too anxious to furnish justification for the civic persona as well as consolation to the unquiet center. The obligation to make viable connections between rim and core was not encouraged by early humanism. Petrarchism, so popular among north Italians, established mobility of ego as an operational principle. The human condition is, then, precisely defined by its failure to sustain ideals and commitments. Further, the psyche is depicted as being circumscribed by its own laws that render much of religious and ethical philosophy useless. The lyricism of the Renaissance became a noble stance in the face of inevitable loss. Renaissance poetry could be constructed from discouraging antitheses such as love and hate, youth and old age, thus demonstrating the evanescence of all things human. A depth psychology could not be readily formulated to connect these polarities of human experience. Italian prose employed a behavioristic psychology whereby character was revealed through actions and there was little temptation to delve into the recesses of the human mind.

Clearly, the comic view of antiquity becomes most entertaining and comfortable, for it alone described man's fate and charted his knowable personality. Significantly, the tragic mode was most alien to Renaissance dramatic art. Finally, in humanist historiography it is the phenomenological and limited that was championed against the transcendent and infinite. Renaissance historians rejected the grand quest for the noumenal more thoroughly than they did any other intellectual activity.

A new taste for the gaudy in religious ceremony accompanied the accentuation of styles and forms in civic life. What is suggested here is that the origins of the baroque can be found in the early Renaissance. In order to believe in the public world it was becoming necessary to exaggerate and aggrandize its qualities. Intellectuals were perhaps too tender and solicitous in their desire to provide justification for the newly acquired ego props. Moreover, their fideism and contempt for metaphysics and theology helped to encourage a separation between the deep center of irrational yearning and the rim of cultivated ego.

In the north of Europe neither public world nor civic Christianity served to structure personality. Moreover, the extended sociability and chivalric ethos of medieval times managed to sustain the individual ego. Metaphysics, theology, and pietism readily acknowledged mystical alternatives; hence guilt and expiation were at the level of consciousness. The northern intellectual may have suffered more, but he continued to maintain an awareness of evil and sin. His world witnessed the gradual recession of medieval magic (sacramental bonds, ritual ties, and ceremonial identities); therefore, the irrational was omnipresent, luring him to seek deeper understanding of its equivalent in himself. His sensibilities were becoming protestant: the colonization of the rim of the mind (the public world) would not be so extensive; his energies served to clear new pathways between the outer and inner worlds.

10

Individualism in the Early Italian Renaissance: Burden and Blessing

By way of prologue, I should like to underscore the impressionistic character of my historiographical and literary evidence.[1] This inquiry is a perspective upon other scholarly perspectives, a view of other views, and as such treats a few chronicles, some prose and poetry, and some celebrated art of late medieval and renaissance Italy. The particular works mentioned have been selected because they were in themselves crucial to leading scholarly interpretations of the culture of North and

---

From *Studies in the Renaissance* 19 (1972): 273–97. Reprinted with permission. This paper was presented at the Anglo-American Historical Conference in London in July 1970.

1. The present discussion does not consider the experiences of South Italy and Sicily. The exceptional nature of the culture of the South has been underscored by generations of scholars. In my particular case the materials consulted were chiefly prose, poetry, and chronicles; southern exemplars of these genres display notable differences from those of North and Central Italy. For instance, historical writing in Sicily lacks that high sensibility for "social fact" that characterized so many of the North Italian chronicles. See Gina Fasoli's *Cronache medievali di Sicilia* (Catania, 1950). Moreover, chroniclers focused upon the behavior of eminent personages from clergy and nobility, while *il popolo* played but a minor role. The emergence of the commoners serves to differentiate between the chronicles from South Italy and Sicily, on the one hand, and Lombardy and Tuscany, on the other. Of all the southern chroniclers only Michele da Piazza has an appreciation for social facts. Neither the histories of Saba Malaspina, the pseudo-Jamsilla, Bartolomeo di Neocastro, Nicola Speciale, nor Simone Lentini possess this sensibility. By the same token, literary developments displayed what one scholar has termed a "desolante agnosticismo politico." Cf. V. De Bartholomaeis' *Primordi della lirica d'arte in Italia* (Turin, 1943), 148. Another literary scholar, Folena, dwells upon the "anti-storico" bias of the aristocratic lay culture of Sicily. The vernacular poetry of the South was of prime importance for the development of North Italian culture. What this verse lacked, however, was a sense of lyrical development and a "true spiritual history." When compared with Tuscan or Bolognese poets (Guido d'Arezzo and Guinizzelli), the works of the Southerners seldom disclose a spiritual dialectic or have the intel-

Central Italy during this time.[2] Historical personages were chosen because their lives were also judged essential by scholars for an effective survey of this civilization.

A problem for any interpreter of late medieval or early renaissance Italy is the current imbalance in historical scholarship with its passion for economic and social history. Over the past years only modest interest has been displayed for the systematic increase of the small stock of psychological insights into the emotional characteristics of this period. For the most part, scholars have been satisfied to borrow psychological observations from a few historical classics when compelled to discuss emotional qualities of this age. This practice runs the serious risk of trivializing our understanding of the field. Hollow and mechanistic history is in prospect unless we are willing to advance new hypotheses and criticize the older sets of psychological generalizations.

My rather unventuresome assumption is that interpreters of the past must employ a psychology—no matter how informal or loosely held—when seeking for an appropriate context in which to place data. Few significant historical problems can be properly delineated without a full appreciation for the role of human emotion. A historian failing to register the contours of these emotions is liable to project past episodes onto

---

lectual movement of an internal history. Cf. Gianfranco Folena's chapter, "Cultura e poesia dei Siciliani," in *Storia della Letteratura Italiana*, ed. E. Cecchi and N. Sapegno (Milan, 1965), 273–316. Exceptions there are, of course: the canzone "Ben m'è venuto prima cordoglienza" by Iacopo da Lentini is the most notable. For additional bibliography on the theme of medieval Italian historiography, see O. Capitani, "Motivi e momenti di storiografia medioevale italiana," in *Nuove questioni di storia medioevale* (Milan, 1964), 729–800.

2. Certainly, a case can be made for dedicating historical studies to a variety of ends. One of these might well be the multiplication of alternate explanations, especially in the areas of human behavior where they are in short supply. In this type of endeavor we of course must recognize that the historian is concerned with the increase of possible explanations for past behavior and that his energies are devoted not "to narrating what really happened" but, rather, to multiplying the store of possible explanations. The historian's critical intelligence can be self-consciously directed toward rejection or acceptance of alternate explanations, the assumption being that the proper exercise of this faculty will bring him closer to that generalization capable of subsuming the largest quantity of data. If one, therefore, raises the question, can we ever know the thirteenth century? The answer would be, of course not, but we can know the reasons why we reject one explanation and accept another. In the area of psychological history the critical choice is too limited.

a sterile screen where they will be as lifeless as a nonevent in a Godard film or a Robbe-Grillet novel. Specialized studies of Italy are legion, but few are devoted to psychological problems. Burckhardt and Huizinga do yeoman service, and yet more ample options should be available to the scholar.[3]

When confronting Burckhardt's view of the Renaissance, his concept of individualism immediately engages our attention.[4] Without entering the scholarly debate over this perilously protean notion, we can observe the extent to which the Swiss historian was influenced by nineteenth-century conceptions of human volition and the strength of man's ego. Too influential were Schopenhauer's doctrines concerning primacy of the will and the capacity of an individual to impose form, however fleeting, on the swirl of life. Burckhardt referred to Schopenhauer, not Aristotle, as "master of those who know," viewing the assertion of brutal egoism as the hallmark of a renaissance civilization in which man's will had dispelled illusion and forestalled chaos.

Certainly, one need not read extensively into modern psychology to recognize that nineteenth-century confidence in the self-assertive and sustaining force of the ego is not altogether defensible. Even if we grant Burckhardt his impulse and assume the existence of a historical moment when late medieval culture declined and man stood free from the womb of illusion, still we must reserve judgment as to the extent to which the individual suffered from loss of supportive lifestyles and fantasies. What was the cost to the North Italian of the thirteenth century of the erosion of vital facets of his ceremonial identity? What was the price for the weakening of ritual-social ties in society or the slackening of sacramental bonds in politics? What public disorder and public grief ensued when the political landscape fell into disarray and the twin engines of salvation—empire and papacy—were seen to be in disrepair? Disappointment of messianic expectancies of course provoked frustration, while widespread diffusion of heterodox opinion threatened pious minds sustained by religious rite and hierarchy.[5] If we agree with Burck-

3. J. Burckhardt, *The Civilization of the Italian Renaissance* (New York, 1954); J. Huizinga, *The Waning of the Middle Ages* (Garden City, N.Y., 1954).

4. Bibliography on this theme is extensive, but see especially W. K. Ferguson, *The Renaissance in Historical Thought* (Cambridge, Mass., 1948), 179–94; and W. Kaegi, *Jacob Burckhardt* (Basel, 1956), vol. 3.

5. Writings on this subject are legion, but a few are of particular interest: see

hardt that a magic system did indeed begin to falter during the thirteenth century, then we must entertain the possibility that at that time certain traditional ego defenses proved less effective. Surely, our study of other cultures suggests that such changes can only produce anxiety. A world of deteriorating magic can be a most appropriate psychic setting for the beginnings of collective alienation. When Burckhardt's insights into the dissipation of illusion are placed in the context of twentieth-century psychology, we must confront the fact of psychic loss as well as of gain.

To illustrate we could construct a psychic balance sheet with two sets of entries: on the one side we would note the decline of the extended medieval clan with its *consorteria*, whereas on the other we could enter the emergence of the nuclear family of the Renaissance with its deepening affection for children and cherished domesticity. Chivalric worship of women recedes before the celebration of conjugal love.[6] The communal

---

R. Morghen, *Medioevo Cristiano* (Bari, 1953), 212–86; R. Manselli, *L'eresia del male* (Naples, 1963), and his and other contributions in the volume *Povertà e ricchezza nella spiritualità dei secoli XI e XII* (Todi, 1969).

6. From a methodological point of view the admonition of Federico Chabod is crucial: we must not confuse practical life with the life of the mind, or the day-to-day activities of man with his rational consciousness of these activities. Such a clear statement disposes of the naive disclaimer of the historian, who argues in the name of common sense that medieval practices differed not at all on the conscious level from those of the Renaissance. Our concern here is not with certain instinctual and fundamental passions but, rather, with their elevation to the status of a consciously articulated program of life. It is the programmatic that finds expression in the chronicle, the Tuscan lyric or fresco. To quote Chabod: "Ever since the world began men in their everyday life have always obeyed certain instinctive and fundamental passions; and love and ambition, sensuality and the need for amusement, the desire for riches and the yearning for political power are peculiar to men of all ages and countries. Hence, if we had to reconstruct history in the light of such considerations we should be obliged to regard as equal and alike in their significance all the things that have happened from the times of the Egyptians and the Babylonians down to the present day, and history would become a grey blur in which we could no longer distinguish one epoch from another. But this is not so; for when we speak of historical 'periods,' of the classical world and the medieval world, of the Renaissance, of the Age of Enlightenment, of Romanticism, to what are we referring if not to political, moral and cultural ideas and the institutions in which those ideas have found expression—ideas and institutions which characterize individual epochs?" See Chabod's *Machiavelli and the Renaissance* (New York, 1965), 162–64.

ethos that conferred corporate identity on the citizen diminished before the rise of impartial territorial states. This erosion of a more intimate medieval community was accompanied by a more secure public identity and the legitimization of the quest for citizen fame. Family partnerships, the guild, and the tower society were no longer so sustaining; against this, however, we find the renaissance impulse to elevate to a religious ritual the daily round of bourgeois activities.[7] Psychic debits and credits can be paired: communal living against greater privacy; clan loyalty against dedication to the state; a rational theology against fideism; metaphysical certainty as opposed to historical knowledge; and, finally, the intimacy of a medieval town compared to the grandeur of a renaissance city.

In discussing the theme of individualism it is tempting to sentimentalize the medieval experience while monumentalizing its renaissance counterpart. Despite apparent psychic benefits gained by the individual from participation in a more personal communal society, he was less secure politically than the citizen of the renaissance state. Renaissance bureaucracy afforded greater legal protection to the individual; civil war with its mass exiling was not chronic. But the price exacted for this stability was high: renaissance territorial states intruded alarmingly into private realms of feeling. Vigorous criticism of public policy so evident in the Middle Ages was converted into veneration for the state. The promptings of Christian morality were dulled as claims of the state were advanced against those of conscience.[8]

A telling correlation between Tuscan painting and literature is found in the sacralization of familial love and domesticity. Cf. E. Panofsky, *Early Netherlandish Painting* (Cambridge, Mass., 1953), 22–23; Francesco da Barberino, *Il trionfo d'amore*, ed. A. Zenatti (Catania, 1901), 36. Barberino is among the first of the European poets to lend spiritual validation to conjugal love. His forerunner in the area of prose may have been another North Italian, Albertano da Brescia, who also celebrated the sacred bond of familial love. Writing in the early thirteenth century, he suggested the image employed by Barberino a century later when husband and wife were depicted as a single figure with two heads. See Albertano da Brescia, *Dei trattati morali* (Bologna, 1873), 266. For an effective treatment of the theme of chivalric love, see the recent work of René Nelli, *L'erotique des troubadours* (Toulouse, 1963), 46, 175, 178, 250, 256, 264, 314.

7. For a general discussion of these topics, see Richard Goldthwaite's valuable study, *Private Wealth in Renaissance Florence* (Princeton, 1968).

8. See my review of Donald J. Wilcox's *The Development of Florentine Historiography in the Fifteenth Century*, in the *Journal of Historical Studies* 1 (Winter 1969–70): 297–302.

Another feature of altered sensibility to be entered on the psychic balance sheet concerned changes in the conception of history. The familiar thesis advanced by T. E. Mommsen and E. Panofsky contends that fourteenth-century Italy was the locus for a shift in historical consciousness culminating in a new awareness of self and place in the temporal continuum. Literati and early humanists were distanced from their immediate past by a radical feeling of discontinuity. Neither contemporary institutions nor princes and prelates were fit topics for dignified historical study—all they merited was satire. Personalities of the contemporary world lacked *gravitas,* and medieval accomplishments in metaphysics, logic, and science were ridiculed. Petrarch saw the thousand years since Rome's decline as a dark interval separating him from the world of pristine Christianity and classical Rome.[9] The church and empire of his day were equally removed, and the corrupt Latin language of his century poisoned discourse and literature.

A feeling of disjunction became a datum for the history of consciousness. Since literati felt themselves cut off from the recent past at a moment when conviction was mounting that a new age had begun, conceptions of culture and self were in process of redefinition. This new awareness played between perception and reality so that the world might be experienced with novel subjectivity, thus heightening the burden of self-consciousness. An instance of this was the poetry of Petrarch, so soon the vogue, describing the emotions nature evoked in the soul of

9. T. E. Mommsen, "Petrarch's Concept of the Dark Ages," *Speculum* 17 (1942): 226–42; E. Panofsky, "Renaissance or Renascences?" *Kenyon Review* 6 (1944): 225; and his *Renaissance and Renascences in Western Art* (Stockholm, 1965), 1, 108–13. For a discussion of distancing from the present, see Petrarch's introduction to his *De viris illustribus,* where he announces that contemporary princes furnish materials not (for) "historie sed satyre." For a discussion of this text, see N. S. Struever, *The Language of History in the Renaissance* (Princeton, 1970), 79–81. Important revisions have been made by Carlo Calcaterra and Guido Martellotti based upon the chronology of *De viris illustribus.* We can now appreciate the fragility of Petrarch's commitment to the "new concept of history." The profound effects of his spiritual crisis of 1342 dispelled the even tenor of his dedication to the ideals of a republican Rome. Subsequent versions of the *De viris illustribus* disclose his mounting concern with the consequences of the stain of Adam's fall on history. Petrarch's spiritual travail adds another dimension to the problem of alienation and history in fourteenth-century intellectual circles. Cf. Hans Baron's incisive discussion of the scholarship on this vital issue in *From Petrarch to Leonardo Bruni* (Chicago, 1968), 23–27.

a poet. This was a nature distanced from the poet, so that he could not depict it directly but only his reactions to it. So, too, renaissance history was narrated with an appreciation for the separation between the present and the immediate past; oratory and rhetoric also instructed men in the various forms for distancing themselves from audience and subject matter.[10] In the arts confidence diminished in the possibility that sacral time and space could be replicated; in its stead emerged single point, man-made perspective. The very doctrine of *imitatio* suggests an awareness of separation. Over the next century forms evolved describing this condition, while the content of painting, literature, and philosophy served to make it tolerable. If one takes the message of early humanism to heart, one sees that the new forms adopted by figures such as Petrarch and Salutati housed a philosophy of consolation.[11] These were but the first of the literary lay confessors who would minister to the beleaguered souls of North Italian townsmen. In the cities of this region problems of identity and the burden of individuality could not be subordinated so readily to traditional patterns of chivalry and courtly life or ascetic restraint and mystic flight. But Petrarch and the humanists came after several centuries of transition; the psychic ground had been prepared so that loss of sustaining ritual, ceremony, and hierarchy could be endured.

---

10. For bibliography on this and other matters, see N. Sapegno's chapter "Francesco Petrarca," in *Storia della Letteratura Italiana*, ed. E. Cecchi and N. Sapegno (Milan, 1965), 2:187–313, esp. 305–13.

11. Petrarch and Salutati are but two of the more talented exemplars of a trend toward the laicization of the priestly role. A recent assessment of Petrarch's intellectual commitment maintains that "the most persistent pattern in [his] long career as a writer is his urge towards the cure of souls through exhortation." Petrarch's interest is "in the 'cure of souls,' not their analysis: in the remedies for their ills, not their spiritual topography." Cf. C. Trinkaus, *In Our Image and Likeness* (Chicago, 1970), 1:11. Francesco Tateo, in *Dialogo interiore e polemica ideologica nel "Secretum" del Petrarca* (Florence, 1965), discloses that among the clerical precedents for his writings were Gregory the Great's *Regula pastoralis* and the *De gradibus humilitatis* of Bernard of Clairvaux. A reading of Salutati's letters indicates the vitality of his role as spiritual counselor and lay confessor. Two centuries before, such a function would have surely been performed by a cleric. The rise of lay culture in twelfth- and thirteenth-century Italy was marked especially by the enhancement of lay spiritual roles, and the theme of consolation was a persistent one. Indeed, the first serious Latin poem in late medieval Italy to gain a European audience was Enrico da Settimello's *De diversitate fortunae et philosophiae*. Cf. S. Battaglia, *La coscienza letteraria del medioevo* (Naples, 1965), 585–607.

Chabod's influential discussion of realism and individualism in the Middle Ages and Renaissance conceals a special difficulty crucial for interpretation.[12] Taking as exemplary of the medieval stance the chronicle of Acerbo Morena of Lodi, Chabod emphasizes only his tendency toward stock description of leading historical personages. Schematized and peopled by ideal types, this form of historical writing was realistic only in its particulars but never conceptually. Adherence to sensible reality remained emotional rather than intellectual, instinctual rather than premeditated: "The sensibility," says Chabod, "is human and mundane; but the spirit is nourished by an inner life whose centre lies outside the earthly city and carnal humanity." And yet it was exactly Acerbo's awareness at mid-twelfth century of the need for increasing the dramatis personae of his chronicle that proves revealing.[13] That Chabod ignores the fact that Acerbo was conscious of the need to go beyond the narrow bounds of medieval political typology in order to describe adequately the historical moment is telling. The chronicler was well aware that the traditional cast of historical characters was too limited for an effective narration of complex political life in the age of the Italian commune.

Earlier historical writings concerning the urban experience tended to be imagistic and iconic, with the individual readily subsumed under the rubric of an ideal type. Social and economic life was portrayed in a mosaic affirming exact subordination to hierarchy and ritual. Historical notation was paradigmatic with individual experience comfortably catalogued through a series of rhetorical topoi. Seldom were metaphors and similes taken from everyday experience; instead, chronicler and epic poet sought for an idiom allowing them to illuminate the twin polar surfaces of life—the celestial and the satanic. Although identity could be derived from an urban milieu, it lacked durable social dimension. Fusing abstraction about Roman patriotism with the symbolism of Christian hagiography, models of virtue were presented as senatorial apostles reproachless in their sanctity. Municipal pride prevented the easy diffusion of universalist historiography into North and Central

---

12. F. Chabod, *Machiavelli and the Renaissance*, 170.

13. *De rebus Laudensibus* in *Monumenta Germaniae Historica* (Scriptores), ed. P. Jaffe, vol. 18 (Hanover, 1863), 640–41. (I wish to thank my student Louis La Favia for directing my attention to many of the relevant passages in the Lombard and Genoese chronicles.)

Italy.[14] Nurtured by *amor patriae,* the author of the urban panegyric was able to relinquish his individuality by embracing a world in which the polar alternatives were martyrdom and salvation or betrayal and hell fire. Seldom was the existential or problematic character of urban life dramatized. The setting was achieved through employing a series of archaizing notations calculated to revitalize the sacred time and space of a paleo-Christian world.[15]

But by the eleventh and twelfth centuries these literary tactics were less effective. *Amor patriae* proved more costly for chronicler and citizen, and neither was able to realize that sublime moment of fusion of self with the perfect community. The investiture controversy presented harsh alternatives to clergy and laity, while the imperial-papal contest shattered the iconic surface of municipal life. Traditional ethical categories were less useful when recording the ambiguous role of prelates, nobles, and *il popolo.* Religious reformers and involved citizens challenged hierarchy and ritual in the name of lay piety. Municipal sacral prerogatives were affirmed against the Roman See; the Gregorian reforms were countered by increased devotion to local religious rites. For the chronicler a secure perspective was not easy; occasionally, events compelled him to switch allegiance in the middle of his work.

Italian urban chronicles do testify to the durability of *amor patriae.* Not since antiquity do we have evidence for so energetic a literary attempt to create ample civic space for the play of convulsive urban movements. The first of these historical commentators was the noble cleric

---

14. During the two centuries after the death of Charlemagne we observe a flowering of local history characterized by an intense municipal pride. Regional resistance to Carolingian reforms was tied to an abiding sense of urban identity. Even the Benedictine school at Monte Cassino remained extraneous from universalistic historical narrative (*ab origine mundi*). Cf. N. Cilento, "Le struttura del racconto nelle cronache benedettino—Cassinesi della Longobardia meridionale nei secoli IX e X," *Bullettino del Istituto Storico Italiano per il Medio Evo* 73 (1962): 85–112. The development of universalist historical conceptualization came quite late to medieval Italy. Romualdo di Salerno's history, written late in the twelfth century, was the first narrative in this genre. Also, historical philosophizing was not so fashionable in Italy as across the Alps.

15. See Otto Demus's "A Renaissance of Early Christian Art in Thirteenth-Century Venice," in *Late Classical and Medieval Studies in Honor of Albert Mathias Friend Jr.* (Princeton, 1955), 348ff. Cf. also G. Martini's useful review essay, "Lo spirito cittadino e le origini della storiografia comunale lombarda," *Nuova Rivista Storica* 54 (1970): 1–22.

Arnolfo, who began his *Gesta episcoporum mediolanensium* in the conventional mode.[16] Intended as a diocesan chronicle, the traditional form broke when the author reached his own times. This cracking of the historical mold was a commonplace in the urban chronicle after the eleventh century. The pattern of court history, the monastic annal, and the universal chronicle could not easily contain the experience of urban life. Contemporary events in the towns were not readily subsumed within literary genres thriving elsewhere in medieval Europe. Arnolfo's descriptions pulsated with the vitality of "a populace always avid for novelty and displaying excessive zeal against clergy." These spontaneous civic movements, coupled with the energies of misguided Gregorian reformers, altered the secure moral landscape of an older municipal world. The chronicler was prey to increasing tension as the navigation of treacherous urban tides became more difficult. Confronted with harsh personal choices, the chronicler's sense of political identity required a more problematic articulation. Arnolfo defended the ancient liberties of Milan and the right of the people to elect their bishop. He stood for the time-honored customs of the clergy of Lombardy and the Ambrosian liturgy. He desired to dismiss the obstreperous *patarini* from his historical narrative, but no familiar rhetorical tactic sufficed; the usual etymological analysis of the term *patarini* was insufficient to dispose of this hardy clique of reformers. He also sought to disvalue the historical significance of the laity but was unable to displace these "idiotae" and their "base-born" leaders. Inadvertently, the diocesan chronicle was being converted into an urban record. The present stood in marked contrast to a time of lost innocence, but this idyllic past was recent and possessed political dimension—no lost Eden, this, but the historical duchy of Lombard rulers.

Devotion to *patria* induced him to assert the rights of Milan over papacy, empire, and neighbor. Opposed to papal reformers, he allied with the concubinary clergy, simoniacs, and civic and religious idealists. Proud of a united Milan of rustics and knights doing battle confidently behind the city's standard, he was yet vulnerable to other exacting claims. His hostility to Rome was economic and political, but now citizen disparagement of ecclesiastical hierarchy called the redemptive power of the church into question. It was difficult to invoke traditional

---

16. *Gesta Archiepiscoporum Mediolanensium* in *Monumenta Germaniae Historica,* ed. L. Bethmann and W. Wattenbach 8 (Hanover, 1848), 1–31.

religious formulas to assuage anxiety; vexing political choices placed his soul in jeopardy. At first he searched for a social explanation for the onset of corruption, but his release from tension came with a rush when he experienced a conversion very like that of Saint Paul and Saint Augustine. Although he went over to the papal party, he did not renounce his municipal allegiance.

The components of individuality were exposed in Arnolfo as he consciously experienced conflicting sources of his own identity. Moreover, he was unable to subordinate his personality to class affiliation or clerical status or lose it in any extratemporal vision. The two Landolfi, continuators of this Milanese narrative, experienced the civic struggle with even greater immediacy. More secure in their civic identity, they were more personal in their appeal to history. The older Landolfo viewed the clergy as highly dependent upon the polis, preferring death to the safety of exile.[17] The chronicler was not immune to the love of glory and was fired by *caritas* for his *patria*. Candidly, he acknowledged the claims of community and lent them an appropriate religious dimension. To this familiar stance novel elements were added: first, the prerogative of the faithful to utilize all means for advancing the coming of the Kingdom of God; and, second, justification of the political role of *il popolo*. For the first time in any Italian chronicle *il popolo* joined prelates and lords in advancing Milan's cause. Involvement of *il popolo* in civic life had a spiritual dimension, and both Landolfi affirmed the imperatives of lay piety.

The response of these chroniclers testified to the democratization of historical writing. New orders in medieval society were surfacing, and their political as well as their religious aspirations were not scorned. The younger Landolfo regularly quoted the everyday speech of *milites* and *populares*.[18] He experienced the urban world deeply and without theological reserve; unlike his predecessors he never quoted Scripture. The chronicler could not easily distance himself from tensions he was describing by resorting to ordinary theological formulas. Narrators found themselves becoming implicated in history through their own partisanship.

The earliest of the medieval chronicles to be composed by a layman

---

17. Landulfus Senior, *Mediolanensis Historiae Libri Quatuor,* op. cit., 32–100.
18. Landulfus Junior, *Historia Mediolanensis* in *Monumenta Germaniae Historica,* ed. L. Bethmann and P. Jaffe (Hanover, 1868), 20:17–49.

was Caffaro's *Genoese Annals.*[19] Here, for the first time, was disclosed a communal sensibility linking the honor and fortune of a mercantile order with civic well-being. Appreciating the economic and social bonds of society, the chronicler portrayed his Genoese burgher contemporaries of the twelfth century in the act of shaping their own history. Men sought to satisfy natural human desires, and power and glory were rewards for success. Caffaro described the expansion of territory and increase of governmental authority as the overwhelming preoccupation of the ruling cadre. He had often served with the consuls and tells us that at first they worked "for the honor of the city of Genoa." Later in the chronicle they are seen as striving "for the increase of the domains of the Genoese republic."

Caffaro desired to validate the juridical personality of the collectivity so that grants from popes and emperors as well as privileges gained through conquest and crusade were amply recorded. Still, he traversed a world where allegiance to pope and emperor might provoke ruinous conflict, while treaties with feudatories seldom permitted a firm purchase on the future. Sharp commercial rivalries and citizen factionalism were rarely assuaged by bland proclamations of civic ideals.

Like other later chroniclers, Caffaro's effort to validate the commune in a world of hierarchy and conflicting allegiances caused him to rely upon legal formulas. He and his collaborator were the first to employ the notarial style in composing historical narrative. Continuators of this chronicle recorded investment of burgher time and patrimony in a civil milieu so that merchants became increasingly dependent upon the durability of communal institutions. Caffaro himself closed his narrative with melancholy hints of civic disruption. The continuators lived with the chronic threat of civil war and loss of patrimony and status.

The greater the psychic involvement and patrimonial investment, the more the fear of loss. Poets and chroniclers consecrated the history of the commune by cataloguing innumerable triumphs and newly won privileges. Indeed, the sole contribution of Italy to Latin literature of the

---

19. *Annali Genovesi di Caffaro e de' suoi continuatori,* ed. L. T. Belgranno (Rome, 1890). Shortly before 1152 it is probable that Caffaro commenced to dictate his chronicle to the notary Columba, so great was the concern for giving this history a juridical validity. Cf. G. Arnaldi, "Il notaio-cronista e le cronache cittadine in Italia," in *La storia del diritto nel quadro delle scienze storiche* (Florence, 1966), 293–309.

twelfth century was the communal epic that did so much to aggrandize the communal ego.[20] The struggles of Bergamo, Brescia, Como, Milan, and Pisa were seen as transcending municipal limits. By associating local contests with the investiture controversy, the Crusades, and the imperial papal struggle, poets could equate communal imperatives with divine mandate. *Il popolo* were portrayed as performing the work of God, with *pedites et milites* drawing inspiration from both the poetry of Vergil and the words of Christ. Classical and Christian Rome lent assurance that to defeat enemies of the commune was to win glory and achieve immortality. But citizens did suffer and the pathos of the poet was real; carnage and death made the chronicler melancholy even during moments of triumph.

Dramatic celebration of the *Gesta* of the community in a world under threat of alien domination was dependent upon the persistence of the ideal of social stratification. Only when the community was durable and the individual could be readily accommodated within the hierarchy could this epic genre flourish. If hierarchy were menaced, then the poet could neither be confident about the durability of community nor fix the destiny of the individual to the collectivity with certainty. In so notable a communal epic as the *Liber Maiolichinus,* describing the splendid victories of Pisa over the Saracens (1114–15), we observe an exact accommodation between individual and hierarchy.[21] Also, we see a perfect blend of Christian zeal and civic patriotism. Pisan citizenry and clerics were cited with a frequency directly proportional to their position in the social structure. The poet was not required to increase the number of personality types; traditional models served quite well, since all the characters were playing familiar parts. Status was sufficiently secure to allow for the use of customary epithets to delineate ideal types. Again, the historical surface was abstract and iconic; the community

---

20. A. Monteverdi observes that Latin literature in Italy from 1000 to 1200 was not of superior quality. But for some rhymes and odes of Alfano da Salerno we have a tiresome abundance of prose and poetry treating contemporary events; historical and legal writing dominates the literary scene. Cf. Monteverdi's *Studi e saggi sulla letteratura italiana dei primi secoli* (Milan and Naples, 1954), 3–14.

21. *Liber Maiolichinus,* ed. C. Calisse (Rome, 1904). See C. Fisher, "The Pisan Clergy and an Awakening of Historical Interest in a Medieval Commune," *Studies in Medieval and Renaissance History* 3 (1966): 143–219, particularly the last few pages.

lacked that amount of social ambiguity required to produce more individualized forms of historical notation.

By the late twelfth century, however, the literary impulse to link the
destiny of the individual with the collectivity was dissipated. Giuseppe
Chiari, modern literary historian, argues persuasively that all the finest
examples of the communal epic antedate the 1180s.[22] Simultaneously,
the urban panegyric was losing its effectiveness. Here, too, Italy had led
the way; from the eighth century until the late twelfth, her contributions
to this genre were abundant. This form of civic poetry proclaiming the
durability of the public world was Italian in origin. As we have observed, it was infused with the energies of *il popolo* in the eleventh and
twelfth centuries when its stately hexameters were opened to civic passion and the politics of a merchant patriciate.

To turn to the Florentine Giovanni Villani or the Paduan Giovanni
da Nono is to confront marked change in literary perception of experience. Writing in the early fourteenth century, Da Nono attempted to
compose an urban panegyric obeying the precepts of civic hagiography.[23] Unlike his twelfth-century forebears, he was unable to balance
the equations between ancestry and power or wealth and status. His urban genealogy was in startling disarray as he inadvertently revealed the
gross proportions of the body politic. Villani's proud description of Florentine wealth was followed by a disconsolate account of the republic's
corrupt politics and "insane expenditures."[24] The last books of his
chronicle revealed the failure of each of the Florentine orders: neither
nobles nor *haute bourgeoisie* nor newcomers had the talents to give society an ethical direction. At this juncture we might follow an easy line of
explanation and contend that this dramatic alteration in social perspective was largely a consequence of the discrepancy between traditional

---

22. *La poesia epico-storica latina dell'Italia medioevale* (Modena, 1939). Cf. also
his *L'epica medioevale latina e la Chanson de Roland* (Genoa, 1936).

23. J. K. Hyde, "Medieval Descriptions of Cities" *Bulletin of the John Rylands
Library* 48 (1966): 308–40. For further discussion of Da Nono, also see Hyde,
Padua in the Age of Dante (Manchester, 1966), 63–90, 260–61. On the theme of ur-
ban patriots writing chronicles in other Italian cities, see A. Buck, "Zür
Geschichte des italienischen Selbstvertstandnisses im Mittelalter," *Medium Ae-
vum Romanicum* (Munich, 1963), 63–77.

24. For a translation of Villani *Laudatio urbis*, see R. Lopez and I. Raymond,
Medieval Trade in the Mediterranean World (New York, 1954), 71–74. Cf. also Villani's *Cronica*, ed. F. Dragomanni (Florence, 1844–45), 6:69; 11:88; 11:94.

conceptions of hierarchy and changing realities of socioeconomic life. Certainly, the increased amplitude of consciousness of civic space can be attributed in part to this separation. Chroniclers and poets stretched their social and political sensibilities by attempting to conserve traditional conceptions of stratification and legitimacy while at the same time acknowledging the social variations from these norms. This explanation, however, does not treat the question of why these authors were so attracted to the ambiguous details of everyday life. Could they not have dismissed them as petty matters and taken refuge in a bitter dualism that would underscore the perennial contest between the forces of good and evil? After all, this had been a popular Augustinian solution throughout the Middle Ages.

Before the twelfth century urban literature had expressed trust in firm bonds between past and present. An unconscious archaism was postulated upon the spiritual vitality of Christian martyrs and Roman patriots whose lineal descendants thrived in the late medieval world. This comforting belief in historical continuity was little disturbed by a sense of anachronism; instead, the sensibility that sacred time and space could be readily replicated was strong. Such celebrated documents as the *Honorantiae Civitatis Papiae* contained full descriptions of economic and social activity but were informed by a spirit of retrospective fantasy.[25] Over the next centuries such narratives were to contain increased detail on the life of the city. In the twelfth century writers tended to respond with greater intimacy to the physical city, and, for the first time, we have descriptions that are personal and do not conform so exactly to rhetorical doctrine. In the next century we observe an intensification of involvement between the urban panegyrist and the "social city." From Moses of Bergamo to Bonvicino of Milan we note a heightening of consciousness concerning lifestyle. Materials are provided on occupation, attire, the consumption of food and wine, the size of dowries, numbers of teachers, flour mills, and even the cost of maintaining the communal lion.[26]

---

25. For a translation of appropriate portions of this text, see Lopez and Raymond, op. cit., 56–60. The document is also published by A. Hofmeister in *Monumenta Germaniae Historica* (Scriptores) 30, pt. 2, 1450–57. Cf. also A. Solmi, *L'amministrazione finanziaria del Regno Italico* (Pavia, 1932), 21–24.

26. Giuseppe Martini in his recent article, "Lo spirito cittadino," op. cit., 10–12, speaks persuasively about Moses of Bergamo, who composed his civic verse (*Liber Pergamimus*) around 1120 (just before the younger Landolfo of Milan

This enumeration of society and the public world disclosed startling discrepancies; poet and chronicler initiated this enterprise with a
sense of urban pride, but soon unhappy social perceptions intruded. By
comparing the lifestyles of the past with those of the present the writer
became painfully aware that he was living in a new and dissolute age.[27]
Whereas his forebears had prospered under a modest regimen, and
glory was the preserve of an ancient nobility, now it was evident that
simple customs were being subverted. The city was being corrupted by
the practice of usury and avarice. Social climbing and luxury poisoned
the wellsprings of citizen morality. Here we can observe a telling paradox: on the one hand the author would extol the wealth and grandeur
of his city, while on the other he must despise the very mechanisms promoting it.

From Riccobaldo of Ferrara to Rolandino and Mussato of Padua,
and, finally, Dante and Giovanni Villani, the idea that wealth ineluctably
caused decadence heightened a sense of alienation from the recent
past.[28] Few chroniclers failed to praise past achievements and lament
present decadence. This was no simple posing of a contemporary world
grown vice ridden against a lost Arcadia; the virtue of the past and the

---

wrote his chronicle), as possessing an "incipient lay conscience." Setting aside
the first adjective, one can only agree that Martini's emphasis upon the poet's
conception of the city was liberated from the world of ecclesiastical tutelage.
This reflects the decline of episcopal authority and the rise of the first aristocratic
citizen commune. Title for the city's nobility was no longer sought in its apostolic foundation or its holy martyrs, though these references are not forgotten;
instead, its "lay and profane" origins were sedulously explicated. Cf. also G.
Cremaschi, *Mose del Brolo e la cultura a Bergamo nei secoli XI e XII* (Bergamo, 1946).
Bonvicino, writing in 1288, furnished a secular explanation for Milan's historical situation. He posed the question, What was the cause of the city's problems?
Was it her pride that prompted the Lord to make an example of her? The reply
was no. Had not Milan fought valiantly against the German emperors on the
side of the church? The first explanation was the prevalence of civic discord,
while the second focused upon the lack of a port for the great city. For selections
from this panegyricist, see Lopez and Raymond, op. cit., 66–70. The text, *De mag-
nalibus urbis Mediolani,* has been edited by F. Novati (Rome, 1898).

27. Charles Davis, "Il buon tempo antico," *Florentine Studies,* ed. N. Rubinstein (London, 1968), 45–69 is a valuable analysis.

28. F. Chabod, "La 'concezione del mondo' di Giovanni Villani," *Nuova Rivista Storica* 13 (1929): 334–37; J. Hyde, "Italian Social Chronicles in the Middle
Ages," *Bulletin of the John Rylands Library* 48 (1966): 107–32.

evil of the present had durable social qualities. The reasons for the decline were political and economic; analysis of change was secularized,
and, although explanations might prove historically satisfying, they remained morally disconcerting. The locus of failure was at first internal-
ized with the individual incurring blame: avaricious and luxury loving,
citizens were judged derelict in performing civic duties and were responsible for municipal decline and the rise of tyranny. Soon the blame
was generalized, and writers raged puritanically against corruption induced by those breaking the hierarchical bonds of society. In the Quattrocento one of the major attractions of classical history was its capacity
to offer a view of the past both less punishing and more consoling.
Wealth, expansion, and even class antagonisms could be justified by
renaissance historians on grounds that they all redounded to the advantage of the polis.[29]

By the late thirteenth century poets consciously employed an ar-
chaic language to distinguish a virtuous ancestry from its vile progeny.
A feeling for differences between generations and even taste in art and
style became pronounced.[30] Artists were increasingly aware of this separation from the past; they sought to imitate a sacred pictorial vocabulary. In North Italy a chivalric literary culture, enclosed entirely in the
anonymous play of courtly love, did not thrive. Such indifference before
reality presupposed the aristocratic security of a moral conservative.
This stance was repudiated in literature as poetry and prose were infused with political fervor and civic concern. The aristocratic isolation
of the tragic style broke when moral abstraction lost its appeal to a popular audience. Where traditional ritual and ceremony were celebrated
the sentiments were frequently undermined by a satirical style. Delight
in chivalry became an exaltation of decorations and trappings until feudal ceremony was converted into burgher spectacle. Consciousness of
loss heightened awareness of historical anachronism; the very doctrine

---

29. M. Becker, *Florence in Transition* (Baltimore, 1968), 2:228–50.

30. E. Sestan, "Dante e Firenze," *Archivio Storico Italiano* 123 (1965): 105. Sestan refers to the leading scholars of Dante's language: Castellani, Migliorini, Par-
odi, Segré, Schiaffini, and Zingarelli. In the writing of poetry we observe a shift
toward a language increasingly self-conscious of its liturgical and hagiograph-
ical usages. Cf. M. Corti, *Studi sulla sintassi della lingua poetica avanti lo stilnovo*
(Florence, 1961); *Vita di San Petronio,* ed. M. Corti (Bologna, 1962). For further
discussion of the theme of conscious archaism, see G. Bertoni, *Il duecento* (Milan, 1951), 160ff.; *Poeti giocosi del tempo di Dante,* ed. M. Marti (Milan, 1956).

of *imitatio* popularized by Petrarch depended upon realization of this separation from the past.

Italian historiography of the thirteenth and fourteenth centuries elevated the themes of political mutability and social change to the level of methodological principle. Chroniclers appropriated bits of Aristotelian philosophy and medieval science to confirm this methodology.[31] Correlation was sought between the prevalence of social vice and the origins of municipal decline; periodization was couched in moral terms with violation of communal liberty by despots boldly connected with the corruption of citizen character through usury and avarice.[32] The social dimension of sin was acknowledged, and the individual became increasingly vulnerable to the passage of time and the verdict of history. Meanwhile, rigorous application of the communal ethic condemned acts of political individualism as grievous crimes against a just God.

Although the civic role of the individual was affirmed and his social identity established, yet he was expected to comport himself in the commune with a humility befitting a monk. Chroniclers enriched the language of narrative in order to highlight the unique and idiosyncratic; new historical types exercised a fatal fascination upon literati, but no easy ethical warrant was in prospect for these characters. We can appreciate something of the burden placed upon the citizen ego when we consider the strong commitment by literati to the corporate ethic. The slightest deviation from communal norms merited strict historical censure.[33] The minutes of the Florentine signory of the late thirteenth century disclose that hostility toward the promptings of political individualism was not confined to a few literati. The process of governmental policy making was itself corporate rather than individualistic. Only a

---

31. N. Rubinstein, "Some Ideas on Municipal Progress and Decline in the Italy of the Commune," in *Fritz Saxl 1890–1948* (London, 1957), 165–81; B. Nardi, *Saggi sull' Aristotelismo padovano dal secolo XIV–XVI* (Florence, 1958), 1–74. It is notable that the first group of medieval chroniclers to be committed to certain methodological premises derived from Aristotelianism were Paduans whose city was the center for such philosophical activity.

32. See G. Arnaldi's masterful analysis of this theme in Paduan historiography in *Studi sui cronisti della Marca Trevigiana nell'età di Lizzelino da Romano* (Rome, 1963).

33. Cf. G. Villani, *Cronica*, 8:8. For additional bibliography on this theme, see M. Becker, "Towards a Renaissance Historiography in Florence," *Renaissance Studies in Honor of Hans Baron*, ed. A. Molho and J. Tedeschi (Dekalb, Ill., 1971), 143–71.

century later did this system of guild politics recede before the direct
and sustained participation of single prominent citizens. A neglected aspect of Quattrocento humanist historiography was the successful effort
of Bruni and others to furnish moral justification for the new style of political leadership.[34] But in the thirteenth and early fourteenth centuries
documentary evidence reveals that the communal ethic was quite effective in stifling individualistic political opinion. Chroniclers scorning
Giano della Bella for his failure to obey communal norms were simultaneously intrigued by his commanding personality. Beneath their dep-
recation of his egoistic political style they recognized his capacity for
leadership.[35] Again we are at an emotional crossroad: how to affirm the
corporate ethic while at the same time acknowledging the commune's
desperate need for civic leadership? How could those virtues required
for leadership be nurtured when chroniclers, poets, and artists were so
zealous in exposing the base motives of false heroes? How could individuals capable of assuming civil command prosper when art, literature, and theology proclaimed the menace of the sin of pride? While the
force of ego was recognized, still it was denied ethical endorsement.

Similar ambiguities were suggested in the poetry and prose championing the nobility of deed over lineage. Opting for an open society
and democratization, literati yet continued to disvalue social ambition
and economic enterprise. Advocates of the popularization of knowledge and education for social mobility, these literati sought to preserve
hierarchy. Sponsors of a popular culture without elitist warrant, they
still despised the very parvenus and *rudes* they were attempting to civ-
ilize (*digrossare*).[36] Fervent spokesmen for lay piety, they remained anx-

---

34. Bruni's *Historiarum Florentini populi libri XII* deserves to be studied not
only for its treatment of constitutionalism and *libertas* but also because of its
sponsorship of Florentine imperialism. The themes of territorial expansion and
defense of the polis usher in a sensibility that more dynamic styles of civic leadership will be required.

35. Cf. n. 33; and D. Compagni, *Cronica*, ed. I. del Lungo (Florence, 1889), 1,
12–14.

36. M. Becker, *Florence in Transition* (Baltimore, 1967), 1, 39–43. Significant in
this context is the recognition accorded social determinants in interpretations
of the past. In describing the civic heroism of Cicero, literati such as Dante, Latini, and Villani commented upon this Roman's parvenu status. His triumphs
were all the more remarkable, since he was a "cittadino di Roma, nuovo e di
grande altezza." Cf. C. T. Davis, "Brunetto Latini and Dante," *Studi medievali*,
ser. 3, 8 (1967): 424.

ious to conserve ecclesiastical structure and ritual. Critical of St. Augustine's doctrine of the sinful origin of the state, they stressed instead its positive beginnings and moral ends. Against this optimistic prognosis, however, they posited the certain onset of ethical decay and communal decline. Agreeing that reason, not force, was at the base of Roman expansion, they severely condemned the population growth and imperialism of their native towns. Sympathetic to the noble impulses of the citizenry of antiquity, whose quest for glory promoted the public good, they were reluctant to transfer this attitude to their own contemporaries.

Whereas a citizen's identity became increasingly public, it remained without firm moral sanction. Even the allegedly durable merchant ego was easy prey to sudden qualms and paralyzing guilt; such psychic devastation was the stuff of the urban novel and notarial cartulary.[37] The very conception of the "common good" implied a challenge to citizen identity anchored in allegiance to clan or social order. This lofty expression of the communal ethic would substitute dedication to a more abstract community for the tangible and immediate benefits of kinship. Primary loyalty to *consorteria*, guild, or *parte* was countered by a vigorous propaganda, the most aesthetic expression of which was to be found in the frescoes and poetic inscriptions adorning the walls of Tuscan council halls. Previously, conceptions of citizen identity had been less exacting so that easier accommodation was possible between conflicting claims. But by the late thirteenth century contests between affection for commune, dynasty, papacy, and empire induced a deep political foreboding into the public world. Now, citizen literature suggested the difficulties of navigating through a polis whose civic dimensions were exquisitely moral. Economic and political actions had spiritual consequences for the soul of both merchant and noble. The former found it increasingly hard to justify his acquisitiveness, while the latter, no longer so secure within the frame of ritual and ceremony, was

37. We observe that in urban chronicles of the early thirteenth century wealth and power are seen as expressions of God's love for man. In the latter half of the century an interesting reversal occurs with obsessive concern being expressed by chroniclers for the sin of usury. This deepening of moral conscience coincides with the diffusion of lay piety and the onset of large-scale restitution of usury. Cf. G. Arnaldi, *Studi sui cronisti*, 44ff.; J. K. Hyde, *Padua in the Age of Dante*, 113–17, 177–234; E. Fiumi, *Storia economica e sociale di San Gimignano* (Florence, 1961), 86–87.

denied the satisfaction of blood feud and vendetta. Preachers provoked the merchant to self-doubt and introspection, while poets and chroniclers insisted that the *milites* find an ethical mandate for their behavior. Communal legislation kept pace by regulating business excesses and the many forms of honorific violence.

If strong tensions existed between the demands of the corporate ethic and citizen ego, supports were also in prospect. Juridical ties firmed the identification of citizen with polis. Legal studies, rhetoric, and a deepened interest in contemporary history were hallmarks of this public culture. How different it was from the civilizations of other leading intellectual centers in Europe![38] Here, in North Italy, metaphysics, theology, and the study of pure science were of less consequence, and scholasticism was to bloom only much later. The practical and immediate were treasured, with artists and literati ministering to the anxieties of secular pilgrims traversing a menacing terrain. Knowledge of the perilous odyssey of merchant pilgrims carried with it remedies for consolation. The destiny of the *viator* was secularized and his character revealed by literati at the moment when he confronted the extremes of *fortuna* or *amore*. The measure of the man was in his ability to survive the buffets of fortune and win the trophies of love.[39]

But understanding and sage counsel could do little to relieve the individual of burdens of selfhood or order the cluttered landscape of community. Dante had sought to project his private sufferings onto a screen of universal history; in this way personal tragedy could assume general meaning. Yet he and other literati were unable to subsume their own immediate history under any ideal schema. A feeling of selfhood was ineradicable, and the finest prose and painting of the period were

---

38. P. O. Kristeller, *Eight Philosophers of the Italian Renaissance* (Stanford, 1964), 73–74; also his *Studies in Renaissance Thought and Letters* (Rome, 1956), 569ff.

39. See V. Branca's persuasive remarks in *Boccaccio medievale* (Florence, 1957), 68–73: carnal passion obtains its highest consecration and tragedy in those spiritual moments of love and death. Thus, in the lyrical and subjective we discern a solemn and heroic tension. In this interior climate we have the echoes of this tension, always solemn and heroic, standing as the highest exemplars of tragic passion.

In his *De viris illustribus* Petrarch argues that the historian must deal with the truly illustrious deed rather than the merely fortuitous. Earned nobility cannot be discerned in the chance event or lucky action. Cf. N. S. Struever, *Language of History*, 78.

characterized by a belief that man's earthly character was the outward expression of his spiritual destiny. While iconic depiction of personality persisted, new techniques were being developed in poetry and painting to generate the artistic illusion of individuality. In the Cimabue *Crucifix* we note the portrayal of intense conflict between the iconic and historical Christ; perhaps in this single painting soon to be imitated throughout North Italy we possess a most revealing emblem of this time of transition.[40] The artist's technique allowed him to disclose the human Christ at the very moment when He struggled to be free from the icon: image was receding before the onslaught of personality.

The history of the individual was no longer so readily structured by hierarchy and *consorteria;* his public world was not given lasting meaning by crusading enthusiasms, visions of an age of ultimate justice, or decisive victories by angelic popes or messianic emperors. The cherished principles of Guelfism and Ghibellinism were now fit topics for bizarre etymologies.[41] As millenarian and eschatological impulses proved less vital, a sense of selfhood became more probable. Moreover, ideals of collective *renovatio* declined in favor of more personal notions of salvation. Confidence in the rejuvenation of a faltering world through the activities of newly founded religious orders was absent in contemporary urban literature. Church and empire no longer served in the familiar dual role of worldly institution and intermediary between human and divine history. The polis was no longer exempt from decay because it had contracted sacred alliances with either church or empire.[42]

Profound economic change in process during the first part of the fourteenth century increased the isolation of the individual. Again we shall observe that literature and art ministered to the beleaguered citizen ego. Legislation in Tuscany began to reflect the multiplication of procedures among clans for alienating patrimony and disposing of shares.[43] Property could be held more readily by individuals so that the

40. For much of the discussion that follows, I am much indebted to my colleague, Professor Bruce Cole of the Department of Fine Arts, University of Rochester.

41. To cite only one of many examples, see the eccentric definition presented by that Florentine arch-Guelf Lapo de Castiglionchio in R. Davidsohn, "Tre orazioni di Lapo da Castiglionchio," *Archivio Storico Italiano* 20 (1897): 225–46.

42. L. Green, "Historical Interpretation in Fourteenth-Century Florentine Chronicles," *Journal of the History of Ideas* 28 (1967): 161–78.

43. I wish to thank Professor Richard Goldthwaite of Johns Hopkins Uni-

possibilities of private investment were greater. Written agreements for the purpose of holding patrimony in common were rare in Florence; guild regulations permitting new types of nonfamilial relationships between partners were a response to the decline of traditional forms of clan enterprise. Meanwhile, merchant courts tended to recognize the distinct personalities of business firms. These new forms of merchant enterprise increased the risks of the citizen entrepreneur.

As the strong bonds of extended association were weakened in the world of business, so, too, they were attenuated by the rude intrusion of the state into clan life. If I suggest that principal developments in early renaissance culture were intimately connected with these social, economic, and political changes, which in turn increased the sense of personal isolation, then the concept of Burckhardtian individualism takes on its burdensome and negative dimension. At a considerable psychic price the citizen was released from a world of ritual, ceremony, and the supportive associative impulse. At this moment the arts came to his side. We note the emergence of a positive valuation of burgher life, consecrating new ideals of domesticity that were to give meaning and structure to a world become more solitary.

If we compare the panels of two nativity scenes done by Nicola and his son Giovanni Pisano, we observe the beginnings of this transition in Tuscan sculpture. In the Baptistry of Pisa, on a pulpit completed in 1260, Nicola portrayed the Virgin Mother as austere, monumental, and detached. A Roman goddess, she paid no attention to her child but reclined like a queen, accepting her destiny while receiving the formal embassy of the shepherd. In the pulpit completed in 1301 at St. Andrea in Pisa, Giovanni's Mary Annunciate retreats in fear and awe as she learns the dread message from an overwrought angel. Altogether, the scene is intimate and filled with human concern and tenderness. A striking difference between the two portrayals involves the bathing of the Christ Child. For Nicola the washing was a ritual, whereas for Giovanni it was a warm domestic act.[44] Now, for the first time in the history of European painting, iconographic motifs representing intensely emotional domesticity appeared in early Trecento Tuscany. Sacred events were viewed in their most tender and intimate moments, with Christ's apostles com-

---

versity for allowing me to read his manuscript: "The Florentine Palace as Domestic Architecture." *American Historical Review* 77 (1972): 977–1012.

44. A. Bertram, *Florentine Sculpture* (London, 1969), 13.

porting themselves like virtuous citizens. Sanctity was not so much a consequence of celestial grace as a matter of effort and honest social conduct. In the twenty-eight scenes of the *Life of St. Francis* in the church of San Francesco at Assisi, the sacred subject was "set boldly in the context of ordinary existence and lively human feeling."[45]

Florentine depictions of the Annunciation, the Nativity, the Christ Child, the Man of the Sorrows, the Meeting of Joachim and Anna, and scenes of the Virgin's childhood all stressed possibilities for effective spiritual contact between husband and wife, mother and child, and father and son.[46] The incarnate Christ became "nostro fratello" and the Madonna was portrayed only slightly enlarged, so that the difference between the mother of God and the viewer rested solely in her virtuous mien. Art explored the deepening contours of familial bonds, with affection being lavished on women and children and paternity finding favor in the sight of God. But all was not smooth in the burgher odyssey: narratives of human isolation, while not rivaling this extensive affirmation of spiritual ties in burgher life, remained as pictorial testimony to man's capacity for suffering. *The Expulsion from the Temple*, the *Lamentation of Christ*, and the *Story of Job* were popular reminders.[47]

We can observe the difference between the art of the age of Giotto and the earlier Italo-Byzantine school in the convergence of the sacred and profane. This vision was committed to the notion that sacred events could be treated as historical episodes possessing a temporal dimension that would render them objectively real, that is, having their locus in time and space as humanly conceived. Such a view was in itself destructive of eschatological speculation and the millenarian tradition of schematization. Cimabue's conviction that *virtus* coincided with *mediocritas* weakened allegory and symbolism, substituting in their stead a prosaic concreteness. The ecstatic was being displaced by the prudential, and in the process literary and artistic conventions were formulated to depict laic personalities. The religious space of Tuscan art was opened to burgher emotion. The viewer became a spectator, even a participant,

---

45. E. Carli, José Gudiol, and G. Souchal, *Gothic Painting* (London, 1965), 16–17.

46. E. Panofsky, *Early Netherlandish Painting* (Cambridge, Mass., 1953), 22–23.

47. M. Meiss, *Painting in Florence and Siena after the Black Death* (Princeton, 1951), 27–30.

in a sacred moment whose location was in a space and time not very different from that which he traversed.

Prudential burgher culture had numerous spokesmen for *mediocritas;* virtues were in process of being secularized as the doctrine of the mean challenged the ecstatic and the overwrought.[48] North and Central Italy were the first to confront the decline of medieval culture and its millenarianism because individuals possessed a public world. The price, however, for this civic identity was high. Detached from a world of traditional ritual they were burdened with the knowledge of ceaseless change.

The psychological setting for leading elements of renaissance culture was well in prospect by the early Trecento. The urge to validate and enhance burgher emotions appeared to stem from the need to assuage anxiety and overcome feelings of isolation. In the novella exemplars of commercial virtue were ensconced beside heroes of chivalry.[49] The literary topoi of early humanism focused upon the legitimacy of the acquisitive impulse, the desire for secular glory, and dignity of the contemporary world. Defense of the status of women, approval of matrimony, dedication to the education of children, as well as an abiding concern for the virtues of household management, were paramount literary preoccupations. That humanists continued to disagree over the possibilities of combining high spirituality with worldly elegance or true piety with service to the state indicates that literature gravitated around these perennial problems, although no unequivocal solutions were forthcoming. The greater portion of these questions concerned the role of the citizen in the public world: human individuality was detached from the cosmic order only to be hostage to *fortuna*, dependent upon *virtù* and *ingenio*, or at the mercy of history.

Huizinga, though not central to this discussion, does of course merit notice. Surely he was quite correct to observe that North and Central Italy were not sealed off from the decaying world of medieval chivalry or to the emotions of an over-elaborated Gothic. Even in such advanced centers as Quattrocento Florence, Gentile da Fabriano and Lorenzo Monaco were the popular painters, while the Flemish masters

---

48. E. Battisti, *Cimabue* (Milan, 1963), 18–80; A. Della Chiesa, *Pittura lombarda del Quattrocento* (Bergamo, 1961), 12–13.

49. V. Branca, *Boccaccio medievale,* 18ff.; M. Becker, *Florence in Transition,* 1, 11–64.

would soon find a ready audience.[50] The iconic was not displaced by the illusionistic: Pietro di Miniato, Mariotto di Nardo, and Bicci di Lorenzo rivaled Brunelleschi, Donatello, and Masaccio in burgher taste. Attachment to the international style ran deep and the triumph of the classical impulse was much more evident in civic monuments than in private art. Indeed, this might suggest that such a separation between private and public emotion was a commanding cultural trait of the period. Yet, even here there is a distinction to be made: although attachment to the courtly, the iconic, the allegorical, and the international mode was powerful, the perspective toward them all was being modified. In fact, it was quite as possible to achieve historical distance from the world of the courtly as from antiquity. Painters and literary men moving in the chivalric tradition could be as alienated from this world as humanists were from theirs. It was a self-consciousness that informed the paintings of the Life of St. Martin at Assisi: a nostalgic reminiscence for a lost way of life suffused this work of Simone Martini. A century later Gentile da Fabriano and Pisanello continued to pay dreamy homage to these lost ideals.

We could observe comparable distancing of the artist from the political icon in Martini's *St. Louis of Toulouse Crowning Robert of Anjou* (1317) or from the religious image in Ambrogio Lorenzetti's solemn and enigmatic Madonna in the church of Vico l'Abate near Florence (1319). Full separation of the artist, orator, and chronicler from a sacral universe enabled him to view a world of magic in retrospect. This was an essential condition for the onset of the Renaissance. Only when we observe the detachment of Martini, and see that he still displayed a fascination for the picturesque, can we take pleasure in this fact of loss (*Investiture of St. Martin as a Knight*). By the early Quattrocento, Pisanello was placing medieval personalities, sublimely indifferent, in a nightmarish world on the eve of the Apocalypse. A sense of melancholy was the response to the recession of aristocratic ideals of harmony. Mantegna painted with a nostalgia for the lost world of heroes; such a self-consciousness concerning ideals and artistic conventions of past civilizations was a hallmark of renaissance culture. If a feeling of alienation con-

---

50. This is not to suggest that courtly style was without lively and progressive qualities. Classical influences and advanced techniques were readily accommodated within this genre from the time of Pisanello through to Veronese. Cf. E. Sindona's *Pisanello,* trans. J. Ross (New York, 1961).

tributed to this sense of historical detachment, then countervailing re-
sponses served to describe the restorative possibilities open to the individual. The young Donatello presented model figures combining piety
and civic dedication, while Ghiberti's sculptures blended worldly elegance and high spirituality. But perhaps those renditions closest to the
burgher world of Quattrocento Florence were done by the aged Donatello and the youthful Masaccio. How demanding were the secular
odysseys of Mary Magdalen and Saint John! How used up and exhausted they were! How little comfort the world seemed to offer the
moral pioneers in Masaccio's Brancacci Chapel frescoes! But, although
there was no surcease, these rugged figures would endure.

11

Aspects of Lay Piety in
Early Renaissance Florence

*In the long run, utility is simply a figment of our imagination and
may well be the fatal stupidity by which we shall one day perish.*
—Friedrich Nietzsche

Anyone examining the *provvisioni* of the Florentine signory will be
struck by the numerous enactments of successive governments dealing
with religious confraternities, pious foundations, and public charities.
After a reading of these provisions, a very unsurprising hypothesis
emerges: during the course of the fourteenth and fifteenth centuries
management and control of activities of these bodies came increasingly
under the purview of the signory. The documents indicate particular
reasons for this development; numerous requests were made by religious organizations for governmental funding in time of crisis. When
the communal councils voted subventions, a measure of government
supervision was almost certain to follow. The first amply documented
crisis was the Black Death, and the year 1348 marked a historical moment at which governmental regulation was initiated on a large scale.
Medical and health problems were so colossal that traditional philanthropic institutions were in need of subsidies. In the wake of the Black
Death private benefactions and testamentary gifts increased astronom-
ically, and for the following two decades the government acted to guard
the swollen patrimony of the confraternities and pious foundations,
while at the same time exercising stronger control over public charity.
The problem of accountability and proper dispensation of resources was
a matter of mounting civic concern. This trend toward regulation, so noticeable during the second half of the fourteenth century, was not
confined to confraternities and pious foundations but extended to a va-

From *The Pursuit of Holiness*, ed. C. Trinkaus and H. Oberman (Leiden, 1974),
177–99. Reprinted by permission of Brill Academic Publishers.

riety of other quasi-public and ecclesiastical organizations as the authority of the state grew.[1] A consequence of augmented state power was the signory's repeated efforts to stamp out seditious behavior and politicking by the religious confraternities. The signory was especially anxious to curtail religious demonstrations because they might provoke unrest among the populace. Fear of secret brotherhoods of workers was also intense, and the Ciompi revolution of 1378 did little to allay these anxieties. Also, there was apprehension over the activities of *fratellanze* in the *contado;* these associations were viewed as undermining Florentine hegemony over Tuscany. These brotherhoods might well become centers for instruction in heresy. Less political but more influential was heightened public interest in problems of sanitation and hygiene. Those confraternities most directly involved in the administration of health care and the distribution of foodstuffs came to work in closer collaboration with communal officials. The signory legislated on these vital matters and also appointed captains, treasurers, and notaries to oversee their activities. Governmental intervention was frequently aimed at preventing the frivolous, even fraudulent, waste of charitable endowments. There is reason to believe that public supervision found favor in the eyes of would-be benefactors, who often preferred to have lay rather than ecclesiastical control exercised over their bequests.[2]

---

1. The present study is part of a more general inquiry into the validation of laic roles in the early Italian Renaissance. For a description of the boundaries of this problem, see my article "An Essay on the Quest for Identity in the Early Italian Renaissance," in *Florilegium Historiale,* ed. J. Rowe and W. Stockdale (Toronto, 1971), 295–312. It is essential to recall that the clericalized church of the late Middle Ages did not possess a highly articulated theology pertaining to the role and place of laity in the church. Cf. L. Landini, *The Causes of the Clericalization of the Order of Friars Minor, 1209–1260, in the Light of Early Franciscan Sources* (Chicago, 1968). On the subject of charity, it should be understood that no presumption exists that lay philanthropies reduced the incidence of poverty in Renaissance Florence, Venice, or any other Italian urban center. On the trend toward Florentine regulation of pious foundations, confraternities, guilds, the Parte Guelfa, and other quasi-public bodies, see *Camera del Comune, Entrata,* beginning with vol. 32 for the years immediately preceding the Black Death and *Provvisioni* starting with vol. 36. (All documents mentioned in this article are to be found in the Archivio di Stato at Florence.)

2. See the advice of Ser Lapo Mazzei to Francesco Datini: "Oft have I had it in mind to say to you, if you add not some words to the Will you have made, the Bishop of Pistoia is like to get your whole fortune—and will squander it to

During the fourteenth century responsibility for care of the indigent, infirm, aged, orphaned, starving, dying, and dead devolved upon the Republic. Hospitals, foundling homes, centers for poor relief—in fact, all charities—grew more and more dependent upon government. Many times a petition would be presented to the signory by a citizen or corporate group raising questions as to the integrity or efficiency of particular executors of charitable foundations. After an inquiry the need for establishing principles of accountability would become apparent. Also, disputes between patrons and heirs on the one side and communal officials on the other were endemic. The terms under which the original benefaction was inaugurated were ambiguous, and the signory became a court of last resort. The tendency over the second half of the fourteenth century was to displace the original patron or religious order in favor of administration by a public body. Moreover, the intention of the patron was reassessed in terms of civic needs. These developments were accelerated when confraternities and pious foundations petitioned for tax exemptions, subsidies, and even protection from ecclesiastical exactions. By early Quattrocento the state came to serve as regulator and benefactor of philanthropic institutions.[3]

When the signory assumed the role of supervisor of charity, it availed itself of the services of the Republic's numerous guilds and fraternal organizations. These associations of laymen were regularly charged with administering pious works and philanthropies. The communal councils confirmed these functions so that they might manage endowments and benefactions more efficiently. Frequently, this involved displacing clerical executors in the name of eradicating abuses, real or imagined. The impulse was clearly to make more income available for maintenance of hospitals, infirmaries, orphanages, houses for the aged, and centers for alms giving. Artisan and merchant corpora-

---

free himself from debt, and in horses and banquets." Mazzei concluded by advising Datini to add a codicil to his will stating that the Commune of Prato or its consuls or men appointed by Prato or Florence should nominate the poor people to whom his fortune was bequeathed. Cf. Iris Origo's sensitive study *The Merchant of Prato* (New York, 1957), 366–67. For a discussion of control over workers by the Florentine government, see N. Rodolico, *Il Popolo Minuto* (Bologna, 1899); and *I Ciompi* (Florence, 1945); G. Brucker, "The Ciompi Revolution," *Florentine Studies*, ed. N. Rubinstein (London, 1968), 314–56.

3. For a sampling of this type of governmental enactment, see *Provvisioni*, 67, f. 241r; ibid., 78, f. 221r; ibid., 109, f. 76v; ibid., 160, f. 212r.

tions as well as the religious confraternities were entrusted with the sacred obligation of ministering effectively to Christ's poor. It is well to remember that the poor man in his misery was a replication of Our Lord Christ. Unlike earlier philanthropies directly sponsored by corporate bodies exclusively for their own membership, these new trusts involved a concern for the well-being of the community as a whole.[4]

When the signory assumed these prerogatives, it contended that it was only serving the original philanthropic intentions of the benefactor. Such claims were made most frequently during times of crisis when, as we have seen, the needs of the sick and poor were great and the pious foundations themselves required large infusions of communal money. Since certain of these foundations became public institutions for medical assistance and poor relief, they were of course the first to be regulated in the interests of public sanitation. Leading communal magistracies, such as the Eight, intervened in the management of philanthropies in order to improve hygienic conditions in the city.

In late medieval Florence decisive political roles were played by a host of corporate bodies. In spiritual matters they were ideologically committed either to the pope or the emperor and, therefore, intensely partisan. In the case of leading confraternities they played a military role in combating heresy during the middle years of the thirteenth century. At the same time, the guilds were being organized into a militia for defense of the Republic against its internal enemies. Indeed, if one were to catalogue the political world of the thirteenth century, one of its most prominent features would be the numerous *societates* and *fraternitates* performing limited and sometimes contradictory functions. It might be well to recall that these associations, while quasi-public, were often pitted against one another (the Guelf party versus Ghibelline). Not surprisingly, these associations practiced a philanthropy designed to insure its restricted membership against the many risks of quotidian life. This corporate sense of charity also can be viewed in the activities of the extended family, where the individual was protected by his kinsmen. Not

---

4. B. Pullan, in his book *Rich and Poor in Renaissance Venice* (Cambridge, Mass., 1971), 133ff., finds a comparable impulse at work in that city. He also suggests that this broader sense of community had its origins in Tuscany. The present inquiry indicates that this is the case, with the Tuscan beginnings antedating Venetian developments by perhaps half a century. It should not be assumed, however, either in the instance of Venice or Florence, that the new philanthropy actually reduced the percentage of indigent.

only was the *consorteria* physically supportive, but guild and confraternity supplied spiritual reassurance and charitable benevolence. By mid-fourteenth century, however, this corporate world was losing much of its vitality. While the confraternities and guilds remained at the center of philanthropic life, the part they played was largely administrative. Further, the signory acted to curb the activities of those quasi-public bodies, which had been so divisive in past Florentine politics.[5] The state became the guarantor (ideally) for maintenance of civic order, and the once politically partisan corporate units took on a benign and charitable face when engaging in the construction of an extended Christian community.

The great benefactions of late Trecento and early Quattrocento were made by men who preferred having state officials as executors rather than ecclesiastics. In this transition a variety of precedents were established: the right to alienate property under governmental supervision; the right to sell shares of communal stock when part of the original benefaction; and, finally, the right to liquidate unprofitable investments. The Republic acted to protect the captains and syndics of pious foundations and confraternities from civil litigation by disgruntled heirs. In the Quattrocento these officers were empowered to loan money to the government at rates of interest varying from 5 to 15 percent. This they did in the "name of charity" and for "love of country." Very large bequests were now being made with sizable blocks of public bonds. Confidence in the state as a trustworthy executor of pious benefactions was a benchmark of lay spirituality by early Quattrocento.[6]

I

While the politics of those centuries of communal revolution have been carefully investigated, the religious dimensions of these movements

---

5. G. Brucker, *The Society of Renaissance Florence* (New York, 1971), 83–84; U. Morini, *Documenti inediti o poco noti per la storia della Misericordia di Firenze (1240–1525),* (Florence, 1950), doc. 2, 10, 12; L. Passerini, *Storia dei stabilimenti di beneficienza e d'istruzione gratuita della cillà di Firenze* (Florence, 1853), 419–24.

6. *Provvisioni*, 190, fols. 43v–44r; ibid., 191, f. 121v. L. Passerini, op. cit., 355–56, quotes the comments of the Florentine chronicler Giovanni Cambi, who described the office of Cistercian overseer of the accounts of Santa Maria Nuova "chome, d'un bancho di merchante," lending to the commune, motivated by "la carita e amore."

have been neglected. Central to these struggles throughout north and central Italy over the late Middle Ages was the quest of a laity for spiritual authentication. Italian townsmen in the twelfth and thirteenth centuries were as anxious to gain an ample share of the spiritualities of the late medieval world as they were of winning political office. Civil contests were linked to intense struggles by an urban laity to achieve spiritual influence and representation in the church. The consequences were an increase in the membership of middling families in the cathedral chapters, the councils of the bishop, and organizations supervising church construction. The right to build private chapels, bury one's dead close to the altar of the cathedral, and place one's children in one of the prestigious monasteries of the city was quintessential to an urban laity. At the heart of these impulses was the aspiration to have greater clerical empathy and religious support for the trying earthly pilgrimage of townsmen seeking to satisfy spiritual and secular demands. Being businessman, husband, soldier, father, patriot, politician—and, above all, Christian—induced tensions to mount as roles multiplied.[7] In earlier centuries the laity had secured a place in Christian society simply by imitating monks and clerics; now the goal involved an attempt by secular men to find models of piety in order to validate these assorted, and often conflicting, roles. The thrust was away from a culture whose principal remedies had been asceticism and withdrawal toward a religious program dramatizing that problematic world where lay virtues would find both their justification and limit.

Of course, the force of lay piety was general throughout Europe, but citizens of Italian communes had a greater opportunity to reach their spiritual objectives: first, they possessed the necessary political power; second, because of the *retardataire* character of Italian culture, the claims of an urban laity were honored more readily.[8] The culture lacked many of the formal ingredients of an aristocratic, scholastic, and curial civilization. The absence of courts, dynasties, and monastic centers of classical studies allowed lay culture to surface more easily since competing forces were weaker. The failure to establish those literary genres connected with the medieval civilizations of the North permitted Italian let-

---

7. M. Becker, "Individualism in the Early Renaissance: Burden and Blessing," *Studies in the Renaissance* 19 (1972): 273–97.

8. M. Becker, "Towards a Renaissance Historiography," *Renaissance Studies in Honor of Hans Baron*, ed. A. Molho and J. Tedeschi (Dekalb, Ill., 1971), 151–53.

ters to be more vulnerable to the aspirations of an urban laity contending for spiritual and psychological acknowledgment of its problems. It
was not that the Italian townsman was so different from his French
counterpart but, rather, that political and cultural conditions lent him
the opportunity to dramatize his religious hopes.

Florence was a great center for the expression of laic piety, and before attempting to analyze leading aspects of this movement we might
note certain features of its society and economy. Most striking was the
phenomenal growth of the city: its population increased by 300 percent
within a century. As of 1278 it stood at 73,000 inhabitants. It is not, however, with the fact of number that we should be concerned but, rather,
with the curious character of the attendant social change. This was a
startlingly nouveau society, and the greater share of its leading families
were, as the chroniclers put it, "men of recent origins." Equally relevant
to our inquiry is the gradual undermining of the feudal nobility. At approximately that time almost half of the urban nobles were scions of
wealthy businessmen. Meanwhile, the seventy-four *consorterie* of the
contado were substantially reduced in prestige and power. Our concern
is not with the pursuit of social data but, rather, to attempt to assess the
cultural consequences of this burgeoning and oddly mixed society. First,
we must consider briefly the implications of this democratization for
spiritual life. If there is any single generalization concerning upper-class
bourgeois behavior in the thirteenth century, it would treat the alacrity
with which the *popolani grassi* sought to participate in religious life. Over
a third of the churches in the city were in the hands of laity; the populace had already joined the clergy in ousting the simoniacs. Now Florence became the first Italian town where the companions of Saint Francis were to preach. In 1218 they were given a fixed establishment under
the protection of Cardinal Ugolino (the hospital of San Gallo); three
years later the convent of the Clares was founded at Monticelli. Florence
was the first center for lay monasticism with the establishment of the
Third Order of the Franciscans. It should also be noted that the greatest
number by far of manuscripts of the *Fioretti* survives to this day in Florence.[9] In 1221 the chapter of the Cathedral gave the Dominicans the
church of Santa Maria Novella; only seven years later the Franciscans
were to receive Santa Croce. In the decade of the forties the *Laudesi* of

---

9. G. Petrocchi, "Inchiesta sulla tradizione manoscritti dei 'Fioretti di San
Francesco,'" *Filologia Romanza* 3 (1957): 311–25.

Santa Maria Novella were formed to sing hymns in Latin and the vernacular composed by clerics and laymen. This *compagnia* had no paral-
lel in Western Europe, and every night it assembled to sing these *laudi*.
Also of interest is the fact that most of the surviving manuscripts in the
volgare are in the Tuscan tongue.

For the next century and a half democratization of spiritual life proceeded with an intensity difficult to match in any part of Europe. No single explanation will cover this multifaceted phenomenon, but surely the
fact that the city had no proper nobility to monopolize the spiritualities
was a prime factor. A visit to Santa Croce reveals the high rate of religious investment that Florentine burghers made when given an unri-
valed opportunity to enter the sacred portals and bury their dead. This
of course was new: before the thirteenth century lay burials inside
churches were rare, with the privilege usually reserved for royalty. Now
the new aristocracy of the Bardi, Castellani, Peruzzi, Rucellai, Strozzi,
and others entered the holy precincts *en force*. The commune entrusted
construction and maintenance of those buildings most closely identified
with the soul of the city (the Baptistry, Duomo, San Miniato) to the *arti*
of those self-same merchants and bankers. The artistic revolution initiated by Cimabue and Giotto opened the sacred world of Christ and his
apostles to a burgher audience no longer distanced from the holy personages. In fact, the highest moments of the Christian drama were to occur in a historical milieu not so different from the ordinary world of a
burgher patriciate.

The burgher conscience was informed by the popularizings of Dominicans and Franciscans and nurtured by a socioeconomic milieu in
which they could continue to participate in the benefits of a religious
community. The absence of a *true* nobility allowed for the quickening of
lay spirituality. In Trecento art and religion we can observe the elevation
of the values of domesticity and the round of family life to the status of
a cultural ideal. Lay piety provided support for this program with the
citizenry participating in numerous religious confraternities. By the late
thirteenth century these organizations had proliferated in Florence so
that the Arno city stood first among all the towns of Tuscany. In fact, surviving documentation suggests that it outstripped virtually all urban
centers in the founding of these pious bodies.[10] Moreover, changes in

---

10. At the end of the fourteenth century Florence had at least forty-two confraternities, while in all of central Italy they numbered seventy and in north Italy

the structure of the confraternities paralleled those already noted in the field of communal administration. Over the fourteenth century the tendency was toward greater secular control of both confraternities and the disposition of charity. Within the sodalities the shift was in the direction of giving the laity a stronger voice, and this was replicated by governmental intervention and control. The fourteenth century was the locus for further democratization of the spiritualities as laity came to play roles once the exclusive preserve of monks and clerics. Burghers were anxious to imitate Christ and his apostles—especially those acts of charity and mercy that were at the heart of the ministry of the Redeemer and his disciples. An industrial city such as Florence, where a third of the population depended upon the prosperity of wool manufacturing, provided ample opportunity for such benevolence. Further, economic changes were weakening traditional corporate structures that had previously been so supportive. Indeed, as the individual's isolation increased and he lost guild and *consorteria* support, he might be aided by the many charitable institutions founded between the mid-fourteenth and mid-fifteenth centuries.

II

Preachers, humanists, even sculptors, affirmed that the paths of the Florentine patriot and Christian pilgrim did in fact converge in the City of Man; no necessary contradiction existed between one's duty to God and obligation to his fellows.[11] Though the burgher odyssey might be wearing, still, the quest for salvation had a persistent social and political dimension. The art of early Quattrocento Florence proclaimed a new ideal: a Christian community located in a more ample social space generated by broader human concerns could be realized in historical time. Love of God could be reconciled with love of country, and citizen interest could transcend the constricted and narrow allegiances of the world of the *con-*

---

about forty. Cf. G. Monti, *Le confraternite medievali dell'alta e media Italia* (Venice, 1927), 1:147–93; 2:23; I. Hijmans-Tromp, *Vita e opere di Agnolo Torini* (Leiden, 1957), 20.

11. M. Becker, *Florence in Transition* (Baltimore, 1968), 2:55–68. G. Brucker, in *Renaissance Florence,* detects a marked shift in Florentine behavior as citizen resources were being increasingly devoted to civic and social problems; see pp. 209–10. See also Ser Lapo Mazzei, *Lettere di un notaro a un mercante,* ed. C. Guasti (Florence, 1880), 2:313–16, 319, 324.

sorteria and medieval corporation. The message of leading humanists such as Coluccio Salutati underscored this notion of extended sociability.[12] The idea of *caritas* was transvalued into a generalized conception of philanthropy. An enduring monument to this new concern were the frescoes of the Brancacci Chapel, where the young Masaccio depicted a radically new sense of Christian community. The apostles were ordinary men performing simple acts of charity in city streets and in a countryside identical to a Tuscan ambience. Further, these pious gestures served to create a network of interpersonal relationships that was at the center of this sacral community. The anguish of Adam and Eve was more deeply felt because their alienation was juxtaposed against that world of good works constituting the ideal Christian community.[13]

The writings of chroniclers also serve to highlight the transition from a conception of sanctity as being the special preserve of orders and individuals, to one in which holiness is viewed as a function of the collected good works of a community. Recent scholarship has stressed the fact that the Florentine Quattrocento was a time of increased civic benefactions. Indeed, the traditional historical interpretation accenting the onset of secularization as a hallmark of the Florentine Renaissance is not helpful in this regard. Economic indicators suggest that in representative zones of the Florentine *contado* there was a sizable augmentation of gifts to ecclesiastical foundations. The ownership of land by hospitals and other charitable institutions almost doubled between 1427 and 1498. This amazing growth was matched by the endowments of foun-

---

12. This facet of Salutati's thought has not been sufficiently featured by scholars. Separation of civic life from the ethos of *caritas* was not prominent in writings of most humanists of the early Quattrocento. Moreover, affirmation of citizen obligations and the social nature of the *true* citizen prompted Salutati and others to define *caritas* as that virtue that alone can "foster the family, enlarge the city, and guard the kingdom." Against this position his opponents argued that as far as sociability was concerned, bees and ants must be rated more highly than men; "Who does not know of the great prudence that exists in the forms of society of bees and ants and similar insects? Both justice and compassion are much more developed among certain animals than among certain men." Cf. E. Garin, *Italian Humanism*, trans. Peter Munz (Oxford, 1965). Of course, Salutati promised to write *De vita associabili*, unfortunately never written or lost, and throughout his life he remained eminently concerned with the theme of social responsibility.

13. F. Hartt, *History of Italian Renaissance Art: Painting, Sculpture and Architecture* (Englewood Cliffs, N.J., 1969), 158–64.

dations in San Gimignano. In 1315 the ecclesiastical corporations of the city and district owned 12 percent of all taxable wealth. In 1475 this figure rose to 28.8 percent, with the patrimony of hospitals far outstripping those of monasteries and convents. Similar patterns have been noted for the town of Pistoia, where the number of hospitals increased almost threefold during those years. Of course the most celebrated of these benefactions was the Ceppo of Francesco Datini, whose original bequest was the enormous sum of 70,000 florins.[14]

Recently, scholars have described this upsurge of civic charity as a "new direction in Christian piety," and nowhere was this impulse more prominent than in Tuscany. Leadership was assumed by Siena and Florence, and in both centers pious foundations were consolidated with tighter administration of trust income. The Observant Franciscans brought a new awareness to problems of philanthropy as they sponsored the assimilation of small charities into larger, more efficient, organizations. The formation of great foundling hospitals like the Innocenti in Florence became a model for all of Europe, even winning praise from Martin Luther. San Bernardino, who as a young man cared for the sick, served on the board of yet another model hospital, Santa Maria della Scala in Siena, popularizing the conception of extended responsibility of citizens for the poor, the infirm, and the aged. The keystone of his faith was *caritas,* and he proclaimed that all men were the body of Christ. Ultimately, all goods should be held in common, and no one should have a surplus when others stood in need: "While in his true fatherland in heaven, man may be destined to lead a contemplative life, it is his calling in this world to act and to love. Even the keys of wisdom are in the hands of love." He and Sant'Antonino, prior of the Dominican friary of San Marco and later archbishop of Florence, were spokesmen for a philanthropy responding to the breakdown of corporate exclusiveness. Both were economic thinkers whose ideas pertaining to labor and the responsibility of the rich toward the proletariat marked them as the leading theorists of their century. In addition to subtle analy-

---

14. E. Fiumi, *Storia economica e sociale di San Gimignano* (Florence, 1961), 216–23; E. Conti, *La formazione della struttura agraria moderna nel contado fiorentino* (Rome, 1965), 3, pt. 2; D. Herlihy, *Medieval and Renaissance Pistoia* (New Haven, 1967), 245–49. B. Pullan, op. cit., 133ff. discusses the debate over this question in recent scholarship as it pertains to Italian other than Tuscany. See also G. Brucker, op. cit., 209–11.

ses of wage theory and the needs of workers, Sant'Antonino formed the
first religious confraternity dedicated to the assistance of those "worthy
poor" who were too "shamefaced" to seek welfare.[15]

The Catasto of 1427 permits us to indicate particular areas of change
in philanthropy. Most notable is the size of the patrimony of religious
confraternities in relation to the guilds. The former held three times
more real property than the latter. While the guilds remained as ad-
ministrators, it was the confraternities that moved to the fore in the field
of philanthropic activities. It is probable that by the early Quattrocento
virtually all Florentines above the poverty level were enrolled in one or
more of the city's numerous confraternities. These laic associations were
among the principal beneficiaries of more than 100,000 florins in alms
and legacies for the year 1427. One example of spectacular gains was the
hospital endowed by Bonifazio Lupi: in 1362 he donated 300 florins to
purchase land and construct a building for the care of the "infirm poor."
The hospital received sizable testamentary grants, and by the 1430s the
value of its buildings was 24,000 florins, and the income from its properties stood at 700 florins. Santa Maria Nuova was founded about 1288
by Folco Portinari, the father of Dante's Beatrice, to care for the sick;
originally, it had but twelve beds, and if we place four in a bed, as was
the medieval practice, it accommodated forty-eight. Over the next century care was provided for three hundred patients annually, and the income of the hospital from communal subsidies and legacies rose astro-
nomically. The foundling hospital of the Innocenti was of course a
favorite of the Florentines, and by mid-fifteenth century it was furnish-
ing care for orphans at the rate of approximately fifty new children each
year. In most instances poor relief and health care were the responsibility of the membership of the confraternities. In fact, without their energy and funds these pious institutions could not have survived. The
Misericordia, the Bigallo, and scores of others were the sinews of these
holy enterprises.[16]

---

15. Works on the social theories of these two saints are legion; especially
valuable is R. de Roover's *San Bernardino of Siena and Sant'Antonino of Florence:
The Two Great Economic Thinkers of the Middle Ages* (Boston, 1967).

16. Figures presented from the Florentine Catasto of 1427 are taken from C.
Canestrini's *La scienza e l'arte di stato* (Florence, 1962), 150–52; they have been
corrected in D. Herlihy's printout, which he has kindly made available to me.
The totals presented in my paper, however, remain approximations, since it will
be necessary to investigate the patrimony of charitable foundations as well as

In 1427 the total for alms and legacies by Florentine citizens was approximately 108,000 florins; this figure represented about one-sixth of the sum of all income enjoyed by citizens. If we add to this the yearly revenues of churches and pious foundations, then another 130,000 florins must be entered. The aggregate income for spiritual purposes reached 238,000 florins, and this figure was around 35 percent of the income of the citizenry. Such a sum was probably more than that realized by all landed investments. It should also be noted that ecclesiastical holdings in Florentine territories were well in excess of 1,500,000 florins.

The Quattrocento state became increasingly concerned with the administration of public assistance. In a city where at least 16 percent of the population were at the poverty level, and another 30 percent barely subsisted, welfare was to be a pressing matter.[17] The years between the 1340s and 1380s had been a time of worker unrest, with the Ciompi revolution of 1378 and the *minori* government (1378–82) serving to frighten the oligarchs. In the decades immediately thereafter we note the founding of hospitals, hospices, and orphanages in greater numbers than ever before. At this time, too, the signory grew intensely interested in increasing the income of pious trusts and preventing mismanagement of ecclesiastical foundations. The government repeatedly intruded into the philanthropic activities of the confraternities to maximize efficiency. The

---

bequests of donors. The problem of exaggeration of pious bequests remains; also, the amounts actually distributed to the poor are still unknown. Herlihy corrects Canestrini's population figures as well as the total given for Florentine households. For the patrimony of the Bigallo and Misericordia, see H. Saalman, *The Bigallo* (New York, 1969), doc. 19. According to the Catasto, the Bigallo-Misericordia Compagnia listed assets of over 18,000 florins, and ten hospices were under its jurisdiction. For Santa Maria Nuova, see L. Passerini, op. cit., 301–45. For the hospital of Bonifazio Lupi, see G. Brucker, op. cit., 210–93; L. Passerini, op. cit., 216–27.

17. It is of interest to note that poverty statistics for Florence do not differ appreciably from those of other European cities in the fourteenth and fifteenth centuries. Despite the acceleration of civic philanthropy in such wealthy centers as Venice and Florence, we do not know what percentage of the poor were actually ministered to by the confraternities. In the case of Venice the figures presented in Brian Pullan's recent study indicate that only 8 percent of the city's poor were beneficiaries of the charity of the Scuole Grandi. (I wish to thank Professor Reinhold Mueller of Hobart College for this information.) For a discussion of poverty levels in other European centers, see M. Mollat, "La notion de la pauvreté au Moyen Age," *Revue d'Histoire de l'Église de France* 52 (1966): 14–19.

high incidence of worker and artisan unrest had been prompted in part
by the dismantling of *minori* and *minuti* organization; under the stress
of competition and economic individualism, many traditional corporate
supports eroded. The conception of philanthropy became more generalized as the state assumed responsibilities once the preserve of a multitude of quasi-public associations. Expressive of this new ethos was the
selection of the officials over the funded public debt to serve as
guardians of the patrimony of widows and orphans. Also illustrative of
this trend were a series of enactments establishing a state insurance system for provision of dowries for girls.[18]

III

This movement toward an extended sense of civic responsibility was encouraged both by political exigencies and the desire of a large segment
of the laity to participate directly in that round of acts of charity that
would make them worthy in the sight of God. Quattrocento ritual and
ceremony firmly placed the laity in sacral space as they literally acted
out the *imitatio Cristi;* the confraternities were centers in which this
burgher drama was to unfold. A close connection obtained between laic
spirituality and Florentine humanism; confraternities were the locale for
delivery of sermons and orations by leading humanists. Laic interest in
questions of salvation and immortality were preeminent in the writings
of these literati throughout the Quattrocento. Ficino and others were the
focus for groups of pious laymen seeking spiritual illumination in philosophical and theological discussion. That the men of the confraternities
could assemble to consider problems of doctrine was itself a dramatic
manifestation of intellectual democratization. Further, the humanists
themselves had democratized the role of priest and stood in relationship
to their disciples as cleric to parishioner. Since the time of Petrarch
literati assumed the part of lay confessor; now this role was generalized
in the confraternities.[19]

---

18. For a discussion of the *Monte delle doti,* see M. Becker, op. cit., 71–72, 152,
236–37. Nunneries regularly petitioned the signory for the right to collect
dowries of those girls who had entered convents. (I wish to thank Professor Anthony Molho for this information.)

19. On this theme, see C. Trinkaus, *In Our Image and Likeness* (Chicago, 1970),
I, especially chapters 1 and 2 on Petrarch and Salutati, 1–102; P. O. Kristeller,

The political ideas of eminent humanists like Coluccio Salutati have been well explicated, but occasionally they have been separated from their religious matrix. The Florentine chancellor's appreciation of the associative life was rooted in his ample definition of charity. Always empathetic to the spiritual strivings of a laity, he proclaimed the primacy of faith existentially understood as well as the overarching need for *caritas* if the human community was to flourish. Without the history of the charitable and civic-minded actions of our forebears, even Holy Scripture would lose its appeal and fail to inspire men with compassion and love. What is evident in the writings of Salutati is his conception of a Christian community capable of realization through the civic and philanthropic actions of ordinary men not so different from those who followed Our Lord during his ministry on earth.[20]

Humanists of the next generation challenged the ideal of voluntary poverty. In its stead they opted for justification of wealth in terms of its social and political benefits. Again, Bruni, Poggio, and others were responding to the dissolution of traditional forms of communal life. A reading of their histories of Florence discloses that they had almost no comprehension of older corporate structures. The crisis they confronted during the first part of the Quattrocento induced an understanding for the role of wealth in sustaining civic life. The broader community could no longer be supported by the restricted allegiances of the past; institutions of the commune such as the guilds and *Parte Guelfa* were too parochial. Feeling for one's city and fellows required contempt for those

---

"Lay Religious Traditions and Florentine Platonism," *Studies in Renaissance Thought and Letters* (Rome, 1956), 99–122. For the names of leading humanists delivering sermons before the prestigious confraternity of the Magi, see R. Hatfield, "The Compagnia de' Magi," *Journal of the Warburg and Courtauld Institutes* 33 (1970): 125–134; among those noted were Girolamo Benivieni, Donato Acciaiuoli, Cristoforo Landino, Pier Filippo Pandolfíni, and Alamanno Rinuccini. For Marsilio Ficino's connections with the confraternity movement, see Kristeller, op. cit.

20. Quintessential to this conception of community was Salutati's elevation of the *mercatores et artifices* to an equal status with the *milites* of the city. Democratization at the upper levels of society was a growing theme in vernacular and humanistic literature during Salutati's lifetime. Cf. E. Garin, "I cancellieri umanisti della repubblica fiorentina da Coluccio Salutati a Bartolomeo Scala," *Rivista Storica Italiana* 71 (1959): 185–208. For an assessment of the status of the merchant at an earlier time, see A. Sapori, *Le marchand italien au Moyen Age* (Paris, 1952), xxiv–xxvi.

hypocritical friars preaching the doctrine of voluntary poverty. Underlying humanist polemics against monasticism was the implicit rejection of any claims that the clergy held a monopoly over God's sacred manna. Neither Poggio nor Lorenzo Valla denied the value of monastic institutions, but they did attack any denigration of the spiritual prerogatives of laity. Firm endorsement of the dignity of the secular odyssey sometimes encouraged an invidious, ironic comparison between monk and layman. The former, it would seem, took the easier path toward salvation living under vows, while the latter selected the hard road when remaining in the world of temptation. Monks appeared to care more for salvation of their own souls than for the spiritual well-being of others. In securing the spiritual dignity of the laic role, Bruni, Poggio, and Valla also contended that contempt for honest work and praise of mendicity destroyed the very fabric of civilization. Indeed, those lofty eras in world history had frequently been times of great civic wealth. The intention of many humanist polemics against monastic targets was to enhance the possibility of realizing a "true" Christian community where affluent citizens would be fully cognizant of their social responsibilities. In the interests of such a community humanists authenticated laic emotions and drives.[21]

The centrality of the confraternity occurred at a historical moment when older forms of sociability were in decline. The claims of spirituality advanced by the nobility and higher clergy were not to be displaced. Throughout the Quattrocento Tuscan artists and literati were able to portray life styles rooted in the world of traditional hierarchy. For example, we find the painter Piero della Francesca depicting the heraldic aspirations of Sigismondo Malatesta while at the same time demonstrating an acute sensitivity toward the burgherlich world of the confraternity, with its simple values of a humanity dependent upon divine mercy and protection. Sir Kenneth Clark describes one Piero brilliant at making the illusion of heraldic fantasy convincing and another equally capable of confirming "the illusion of reality and depth" for his bourgeois patrons.[22] The members of the company of the Madonna

---

21. C. Trinkaus, op. cit., 103–70; E. Garin, *Italian Humanism*, 43–56; F. di Zenzo, *Saggi su l'umanesimo* (Naples, 1968), 99–120.

22. K. Clark, *Piero della Francesca* (London, 1968), 22–32. Of interest is the fact that Piero was first mentioned in a Florentine document in which Domenico Veneziano (7 September 1439) received payment for frescoes in the choir of S. Egidio, the chapel of S. Maria Nuova.

della Misericordia, who gave him his first commission, were depicted as kneeling within the "cave of the Virgin's cloak." The space they occupy and the air they breathe has all the properties of an everyday world—"only a little finer and more luminous." The burgher world of spirituality had achieved parity with that of curia and court. Artists and literati could dramatize just as effectively the merchant viator as the knight.

The confraternities relinquished their political role, assuming in its stead extensive cultural and social responsibility. Their popularity was assured, and by the Quattrocento they included in their ranks virtually all the citizens of Florence. Youth confraternities multiplied, as did charitable foundations for dowring girls.[23] Hospices for the aged, orphanages, and hospitals were among the principal charges of these lay companies. There is a paradox in this: at a time when Florentine society was more atomized than ever, the idea of a Christian community took hold. So persuasive was this ideal that humanists were to argue that the bonds of spiritual community could not even be severed by sin. Again, the Brancacci Chapel is illustrative of this ideal. Masaccio's frescoes show Adam and Eve being expelled from Eden. The scriptural message is clear: as punishment, man falls into the world of suffering and death, process and mutability. But for Masaccio loss of the Edenic state is only a preliminary to the re-creation of another more durable community marked by man's exquisite concern for his fellows.[24]

The backdrop for this new vision was an urban society of heightened competition, decline of the corporate ethic, and erosion of the supports of family business and *consorteria*. The confraternities were agencies for social and spiritual insurance at a moment when contemporary sensibilities dwelled upon economic risks. Evidence from the Florentine *catasti* of the fifteenth century discloses that the upper classes were beginning to feel the adverse effects of downward mobility; they appear to have been reproducing themselves at a rate greater than the capacity of the economy to absorb them. Of great interest is the fact that Sant'Antonino and others were proclaiming that religious confraterni-

23. R. Trexler, "Ritual in Florence: Adolescence and Salvation in the Renaissance," in *The Pursuit of Holiness*, ed. C. Trinkaus and H. Oberman (Leiden, 1974).

24. A. W. Skarstrom, "'Fortunate Senex': The Old Man, A Study of the Figure, His Function and His Setting," chap. 4. (Ph.D. diss., Yale University, 1971). U. Procacci, *All the Paintings of Masaccio*, trans. P. Colacicchi (New York, 1968).

ties must now assume responsibility for the fallen rich ("the shame-faced") in addition to their usual sacred charges.[25]

The idea of charity was presented as a collective enterprise. In humanist writings, as well as in religious ritual and civic pageant, the City of God was understood to be the Christian community of those having charity in their hearts rather than self-love. Demarcations between the lives of the clergy and laity would diminish as Florence found favor in the sight of God. The apotheosis of a secular city was regularly dramatized by writers of distinction such as Gregorio Dati, Matteo Palmieri, Gianozzo Manetti, and others. Again, the role of the confraternity was vital. Within these companies laymen could reenact the sacred drama of Christ, take common meals, join in hymn singing and prayer, confess, and listen to sermons composed by their own members—all this under secular auspices. Pledged "to observe the laws of God" and rules of civic comportment, the brothers were charged in their statutes to "see if there is anyone among you who trusts himself to be Christ and will govern you according to the precepts of Christ."[26] The official envisioned was in fact the *governor* who was a type of lay abbot. On Holy Thursday it was decreed that "the governor will wash the feet of the brethren and will offer a simple meal to commemorate this day on which Christ washed the feet of his disciples and then shared a meal with them." The confreres were then reminded that their chief mission was charity, and they were ordered to distribute bread and wine to the poor of the city and countryside whom the orderlies were to identify. "And each [brother] who takes these alms [to distribute] must indicate the name of the pauper to whom he is giving them before he leaves . . . so that each one knows who has been visited and who has not, to avoid a double distribution to one, and nothing to another."

Philanthropy was being converted into a way of life rather than a series of isolated gestures. Charity lost much of its dramatic and episodic character as it was transvalued into a systematized sequence of interrelated acts. The shift was from the corporate to the communital,

---

25. Vespasiano, *Renaissance Princes, Popes and Prelates,* trans. W. George and E. Waters, intro. M. Gilmore (New York, 1963), 157–63, W. Gaughan, *Social Theories of Saint Antoninus from His Summa Theologica* (Washington, 1950), 45–47. See n. 16.

26. R. Hatfield, "The Compagnia de' Magi," op. cit., 124–25; G. Brucker, op. cit., 206–8.

with confidence placed in the *virtù attiva* of ordinary citizens now judged capable of fulfilling their civic obligations and performing the daily round of "sante operazioni." How different was the assessment of Dati from such Trecento chroniclers as Stefani, who repeatedly reminded his readers that it had been "the good people" who had called for the crucifixion of Christ. In the eyes of leading commentators of the first part of the Quattrocento, it was the concord of the city nurtured by citizen dedication to charity and civic good works that gained for Florence the mercy and love of God. So sweet was the melody orchestrated by this harmony that it ascended to heaven, moving the saints to defend the city from its enemies and advance it above all others in Italy.[27]

The culture resonating from the confraternities was part of a network of ideals serving as a bridge to a larger society, with religion and civic veneration interlaced. The thrust toward democratization of the spiritualities had culminated with secure placement of the laity within the frame of a sacred community. The confraternities took responsibility for numerous public festivals in which the political allegory of the Holy City was explicated in gaudy detail. The Magi, most famous of these companies, enrolling some seven hundred members, performed a "sacred representation" on Epiphany in which Florence was transformed into the "image of Jerusalem." The beginnings of the *sacre rappresentazioni* were in the *laudi* composed to be sung by the religious guilds. Among writers of *laudi* in the fifteenth century were leading humanists as well as the mother of Lorenzo de' Medici, while authors of sacred representations included Lorenzo himself and his kinsman Lorenzo Pierfrancesco. The origins of secular drama were also in the companies: Politian's *Orfeo*, which marked its beginnings, was patterned after the *sacre rappresentazioni*. The correspondence between the Platonic Academy and the companies has already been noted, as has the fact that members of the Academy also composed sermons to be delivered to the confraternities. The observation that these lay congregations, not the universities, were to serve as sponsors of the "new culture" of the sixteenth century is of course apposite.[28]

---

27. G. Dati, *L'Istoria di Firenze dal 1380 al 1405*, ed. L. Pratesi (Norcia, 1904), 140, 171; Marchionne di Coppo Stefani, *Cronica fiorentina*, ed. N. Rodolico in *Rerum Italicarum Scriptores*, new ed. 30 (Città di Castello, 1903–55), rub. 564.

28. P. O. Kristeller, "Lay Religious Traditions and Florentine Platonism," op. cit., 100–112; P. Toschi, *Sacre rappresentazioni Toscane dei sccoli XV e XVI* (Florence,

At first glance much of the art and literature of Quattrocento Florence seems without roots in the social world. Unlike the culture of the Dugento and Trecento, which was nourished by the world of hierarchy, corporatism. and commune, this new civilization appears to be abstract and lacking in social dimension. Main currents in Florentine thought after the 1430s have been described as formalistic and evasive—a flight from the political and economic issues of the day. A vast literature had emerged focusing on themes of *caritas, amore, humanitas,* and purification of the *anima.*[29] Solicitude of men of letters toward the spiritual problems of the laity had deepened. The priestly role of humanists was accented as poets and philosophers sought to describe the possibilities of spiritual communion among men. God was a necessary partner in the reconstitution of a Christian community. The quest for unity and religious peace was to be realized when men, secure in the value of their own humanity, formed societies animated by a mutuality of spiritual concerns. Much underlying these new ideals was a continuation of older literary themes; from its inception Florentine humanism had addressed itself to the problem of the loss of a sense of community. Civic humanism sought to present alternatives to a citizenry confronted by an erosion of corporate ties. Efforts were made to authenticate new social values and formulate codes of behavior more relevant for individuals living in greater isolation. To modern scholars the stress on charity and love might indeed look evasive until one realizes that they surfaced with compelling social force. These virtues alone could foster the family, guard the city, and even enlarge a Florentine empire. Men were regarded as God's creatures charged with the solemn obligation to care for one another; man's dignity did not reside in solitary experience or in strategic personal relationships. Neither pride of caste nor cultivation of autonomous feelings of selfhood were sufficient to endorse this *dignitas;* instead, man's consciousness of his solidarity with all men was quintessential.[30]

1960); E. Garin, *Science and Civic Life in the Italian Renaissance,* trans. P. Munz (New York, 1969), 90–91.

29. For bibliography and a discussion of the literature on these topics, see M. Schiavone's introduction to his edition of Ficino's *Teologia Platonica* (Bologna, 1965), 1:3–71. Cf. also Schiavone's *Problemi filosofici in Marsilio Ficino* (Milan, 1957).

30. E. Garin, "Problemi di religione e filosofia," *Bibliothèque d'Humaisme* 14 (1952): 70–82: Trinkaus, op. cit., 2:459–592.

Such a view represented the deepening of the sentiments of lay piety as the claims of an extended sociability found a treasure-trove of religious metaphors. This response to the falling away of traditional social and political supports represented an attempt to discover effective principles for constituting a society. The model for community was lodged in the world of the confraternities and academies. These associations were crucial to the thought of a Ficino or a Pico, for there men demonstrated the talent for mutuality and love. Ficino's *Commentary on the Symposium* could be enacted as a *love feast*, with its ready analogue in the *prandium caritatis* of the sodalities.[31] The seven works of temporal mercy were no longer seasonal gestures or occasions for special ceremonies. Love was the key to Ficino's theology as well as to his epistemology, but also on a more mundane level it was the lifeblood of a Christian community and nurture of the brotherhoods. Finally, Neoplatonic philosophers and poets depicted the movement of the human soul from love of God to love of *humanitas* as evidenced through acts of civic piety. For Manetti and others the life of Socrates became a model for laic sanctity: an ordinary citizen gained immortality by conquering his self-love when sacrificing his life for an ideal spiritual community.[32]

IV

Emblematic of this new conception of *caritas* was the greatest single philanthropic monument to be constructed in Florence in the first half of the fifteenth century—the Ospedale degli Innocenti.[33] Begun in 1419 by Filippo Brunelleschi, it was located at the end of a recently opened street (via dei Servi), which runs from Santissima Annunziata to the Duomo. The Foundling Hospital and its piazza provided Florentines

---

31. R. Sears Jayne, *M. Ficino's Commentary on Plato's Symposium*, in *University of Missouri Studies* 14 (1944); *Commentaire sur le Banquet de Platon*, text and translation by R. Marcel (Paris, 1955); L. Tonelli, *L'amore nella poesia e nel pensiero del Rinascimento* (Florence, 1933).

32. E. Garin, *La cultura filosofica del Rinascimento italiano, Ricerche e Documenti* (Florence, 1961), 102–82. On Manetti, see Garin's *Italian Humanism,* 56–60; for Matteo Palmieri and the "Transition to Platonism," see ibid., 66–69. Cf. also Trinkaus, op. cit., 683–721.

33. Hartt, op. cit., 115–19; P. Hendy, *Piero della Francesca and the Early Renaissance* (New York, 1968), 17–25; E. Luporini, *Brunelleschi: Forma e Ragione* (Milan, 1964), 79ff.

with a radically different stage for noble action. On each side of the square a great loggia was planned with a short flight of steps leading up to it. Never before had so large and rational a space been constructed to express man's humaneness. In the first of the great buildings completed in 1424 in the new style (the Foundling Hospital), we note its "airy plan" and many courtyards expressing exactly this "rational humaneness." The poetry of the open-arcaded loggia on the ground floor fronting on the Piazza dell'Annunziata was an invitation to all men to initiate a new era of peace and trust. Here amid the beauties of proportion and ornament, exactly measured to sacred scale, Florentines could carry on "sacred conversations." Deeds of mercy and acts of charity were placed in a civic setting of harmony and concord.

That this new world was visionary is indisputable. But the "imaginative increments" of this idealized polis arose from close connections with social and political change. First, democratization of the spiritualities converted the physical city into a model of the New Jerusalem; in fact, the façade of Santissima Annunziata did resemble Quattrocento imaginings of the Holy Sepulchre. In Florence burghers could readily translate private piety into a public tableau. Just as pictorial space was opened to the merchant pilgrim who joined the holy personages, so too civic space came to include the ordinary citizen. Not checked by a true aristocracy, a court, or a curia, spirituality took on public dimension as it was refracted through the prism of merchant life and action. The energies released elevated the polis to a community of lay monks, and the confraternity became a paradigm for this new society. Ideas of *caritas* and *amore* became programmatic, and in the century after the 1340s, when communal politics lost so much of its cohesion, the signory sought to institutionalize the public expression of these qualities. Government by corporate interest groups and juridically defined cadres was in crisis. A more impersonal and individualized politics was emerging, and this in turn was predicated upon the increased atomization of society. These changes left the individual more isolated while at the same time permitting philanthropic impulses to break the customary bounds of limited familial allegiances and restricted corporate obligations. The drive to extend these concerns was an amplification of lay piety guided by a century of governmental control.

At the heart of the Quattrocento dilemma induced by economic change was the failure of a battery of collective ideals. These values had their locus in kinship groups, juridically defined social cadres, consortiums of nobles and commoners, and a plethora of self-regulating corporate bodies. All of these contributed to a belief in an organic, noncompetitive society in which men subordinated egoistic impulses to *il bene comune*. Of course the efficacy of such doctrines was in serious dispute, but their verity was rarely challenged. That men could not always satisfy the claims of "distributive justice" did not invalidate this commanding concept. In the hundred years after 1340 corporate and associative energies, once so vital, atrophied and were ritualized. The best thinkers in Florence, from Bruni to Machiavelli and Guicciardini, recognized this failure and sought to discover new principles that might animate civic life. What few men could face was the clear emergence of self-interest and competition as predominating over traditional Christian and communal values. Lay piety, always strong in Florence, projected a comprehensive vision of a new ideal of community—that of Christian brotherhood—acted out by humble citizens in the ordinary round of civic life. This vision was elevated to an enduring art form by the generation of Brunelleschi and Masaccio when the frontiers between philanthropy and sanctity were opening to merchant pilgrims.[34]

---

34. Since writing this paper, I have learned from Professor Richard Goldthwaite that pious foundations sold annuities to finance their building programs. And, of course, Santa Maria Nuova served as a bank. See n. 6.

Afterword

The editors of this volume, my former graduate students Carol Lansing and James Banker, have generously asked me to provide a bit of information concerning my early experiences with medieval and Renaissance Italian history and offer a few comments about the direction taken in these fields of study.

My entry into these areas was a consequence of a curious mix of accidents. My two professors at the University of Pennsylvania were the medievalist John LaMonte and the classicist William McDermott: my major interests were in ancient and medieval history. LaMonte was a historian of the Crusades, and he approved my dissertation on a failed crusader, Walter of Brienne, whose family had claims on the Duchy of Athens, set up as a consequence of Frankish crusading zeal. I soon lost interest in Walter's many-sided career in France, South Italy, and elsewhere and began to focus on his two trips to Florence: first, as a surrogate for his lord, Charles Duke of Calabria and then, more important, as despot in his own right over Florence in 1342. It was this latter experience that truly evoked my curiosity. The city of Florence had remained singular among Italian city-states in its persistent dedication to republican government. The question that captured me was why despotism was not to succeed in Florence, and Walter's tenure opened a window into this vexing matter. Parenthetically, I might mention that I received no training in Italian Renaissance history, since back in the 1940s it was an undeveloped, underpopulated discipline in the United States. My own teacher, LaMonte, had been a student of Charles Homer Haskins, who was a champion of the twelfth-century Renaissance, regarding the Italian Renaissance of the fifteenth and sixteenth centuries as little short of counterfeit. Therefore, my approach to Italian history in general and Florentine history in particular was highly charged by gleanings from medieval scholarship. I was interested in guilds, immigrants to the city (*novi cives*), feudal immunities and privileges, as well as fiscal policy and relations between commune and church.

It was only later that I came into contact with the writings of the refugee scholars Hans Baron and Erwin Panofsky, among others. Italian scholarship in the fascist period had neglected the Renaissance in favor of the study of Roman antiquity and medieval corporate and associative life. Thus, when first coming to Italy in 1953 to work in the Florentine archives, I found few young Italian scholars concerned with Renaissance history; there was, however, considerable interest in the medieval period. The archivist, Guido Pampaloni, was particularly helpful to me in locating a volume of treasury records for Brienne's tenure; this, in turn, led to an enormous cache of communal fiscal records numbering into the thousands, covering the second half of the fourteenth century and much of the fifteenth century. Among these documents were four sturdy volumes of the first Florentine *Monte* (funded communal debt), discovered, literally, strewn about on the top floor of the Uffizi. From the *Monte* and treasury records it was now possible to formulate hypotheses concerning the transition of the medieval commune into a territorial state. Certainly, the need to raise revenue in order to wage war was a crucial factor in this transformation. The growing power and assertiveness of the territorial state was in substantial part, then, the result of indebtedness incurred in financing these wars.

At this time I became familiar with the work of Millard Meiss's *Painting in Florence and Siena after the Black Death* and found it inspirational. I decided that if I were to write a history of the transformation of the commune into the territorial state, it should attempt to integrate the culture with the politics and economics: literature, the fine arts, and philosophy should be spoken for. I found Meiss to be of particular value because he commenced his study with a thoughtful treatment of the major economic and political forces at work. Only after this did he engage in an analysis of stylistic change in painting before and after the Black Death. With Hans Baron I was equally inspired, but cautious, about his overarching thesis dealing with Florentine republicanism and the emergence of civic humanism. But both Meiss and Baron, beginning from different vantage points, aimed at an integrated view of society and culture. Their ambition was in fact contagious; the one moved from economics to art and literature, whereas the other traveled from politics to political philosophy and civic art. My quest was also encouraged by the work of scholars such as Erwin Panofsky, Ernst Cassirer, and the philosopher Eugenio Garin.

In addition to being guided by the high aspirations of a Meiss, a

Baron, or a Panofsky, I was deeply attracted to scholarship on classical Greece. At one time I had hoped to do a comparison between the humanistic rhetoric of Florence and the discourse of Periclean Athens. In this I did not succeed, but the very idea of *paideia*—both gentle and stern—which was to inform my work, came from a reading of German monographs on Athenian culture. I still believe that such a comparison would be fruitful, perhaps generating new views on the relationship between social change and styles of philosophical and political discourse.

Specific problems of interpretation had confronted students of Florentine history. At the turn of the nineteenth century the formidable historian Gaetano Salvemini advanced a "soft" Marxist view of the material causes of the conflict between the *magnati* and *popolani grassi* in Tuscany. This account of "class struggle" was grounded in an analysis of economic interests. Salvemini's interpretation represented an advance over the results of earlier historical inquiries, often predicated on racial theories on the difference between Germanic Teutons and Italianate Romans. His judgment remained largely unchallenged until Niccola Ottokar's deft analysis of communal politics some three decades later. In displacing Salvemini's class interpretation, Ottokar presented a contest between political rivals having little basis in class or economic interests. His version successfully refuted Salvemini's rigid division between feudal nobility and a burgeoning bourgeois guild society of merchants, bankers, and wool manufacturers. Ottokar's deficiency rested in his portrayal of a political world virtually immobile: the civic struggles transpired in a closed atmosphere isolated from dynamic historical imperatives. Dissatisfied with this static view, I sought to delineate the forces of change. My conclusions can be summed up by turning Jacob Burckhardt's epigram "The state as a work of art" into the harsher tag, "The state as a work of communal finance." The change was prompted, as has been noted, by the need to raise revenue to underwrite public credit to finance the many wars dominating the politics of Tuscany over the next century and a half. The requirement to support a mounting public debt compelled the signory to curtail medieval privileges, ecclesiastical liberties, and feudal immunities while tightening the regimen over the *contado* and subject cities. Closer regulation of many aspects of citizen life followed in a sustained effort to meet the spiraling expenses of a sometimes aggressive and sometimes defensive foreign policy.

Of course, other forces were in play, not the least of which was the fuller participation of the *novi cives* in public life. Indeed, medieval Florentine history was characterized by massive emigration from country-side to city; obviously, this left a mark on civic culture. Perhaps a division could be made between the century and a half after 1200, in which the socialization of the immigrant was a dominant feature of the civic experience, and the subsequent two centuries, in which population declined precipitously. The cultural imperatives and civic prospects of this later epoch played out in a very different environment, being less preoccupied with socialization of the immigrant and directed more toward refinement of taste, self-control, and self-cultivation.

Unsolved problems were abundant, not the least of which was Florence's relationship with its *contado* and subject cities. Was it exploitative or symbiotic? On balance my inclination is toward the latter rather than the former. A final question—one of so many—and perhaps the most engaging for me, might be stated thus: What is essentially Florentine about Florentine history? Many historians are not drawn to this question and can work with great profit in the Arno city or, indeed, any other city. For myself it was vital to attempt to understand what set Florence apart. Insofar as an answer is possible, it might involve understanding the singular circumstances in which Florentine culture developed: not the locale for a major university, feudal court, or powerhouse ecclesiastical institution of learning, Florence was required to invent itself. Moreover, having no proper nobility, it was very difficult for affluent Florentines to gain a secure sense of where they belonged in the pecking order. The absence of an a priori sense of hierarchy provoked personal needs, not easily satisfied by generally available norms and cultural models.

I tend to believe that there is *reality* behind the so-called myth of Florence or the myth of Venice or the myth of you name your city. . . . One of the weaknesses of social science methodology is that it levels the historical field by reducing complex experience to ready-made categories. Of course, one would not do without the scholarly benefits of its application, but at a certain point it is necessary to draw back and ask, what else is there? These and other vexing problems beguiled me over forty years and still do. Working in the Florentine archives, however, did induce a case of schizophrenia: how to fulfill the general expectations of undergraduates (altogether legitimate) about what constituted the Italian Renaissance while at the same time conveying the fruits and uncertainties of minute archival research? As in many other fields of study, the two demands are not easily met.

Here I must express my thanks to the many graduate students it has been my delight to teach and know as friends. They allowed me to convey—sometimes in rough terms—the tentative findings drawn from my explorations. They gave as good as they got. I feel rather like Chaucer's Clerk, who aptly summed up a splendid experience with the line, "And gladly wolde he lerne, and gladly teche."